Oakeshott on History

British Idealist Studies Series 1: Oakeshott

www.imprint-academic.com/idealists

Oakeshott on History

Luke O'Sullivan

ia

IMPRINT ACADEMIC

Published in the UK by Imprint Academic
PO Box 200, Exeter EX5 5YX, UK

Published in the USA by Imprint Academic
Philosophy Documentation Center
PO Box 7147, Charlottesville, VA 22906-7147, USA

ISBN 0 907845 290

A CIP catalogue record for this book is available from the
British Library and US Library of Congress

For my parents, friends and teachers

Contents

Abbreviations. viii

Preface ix

Introduction 1

Chapter 1   History, Religion and Politics, 1901–1939

From School to University 29

The Idea of Character. 34

Philosophy, Poetry and Politics 39

Religion. 50

Contemporary European Politics 54

Chapter 2   The Philosophy of History, 1925–1939

The Philosophy of History in the Nineteenth Century 67

Unpublished Writings on History from the 1920s. 72

Philosophy, Experience and Modality 82

Practical Experience. 90

Scientific Experience 92

Historical Experience 96

History and the Social Sciences. 107

Oakeshott's Philosophy of History Before 1939 110

Chapter 3   The History of Character, 1945–1958

Peace with Germany. 115

Rationalism and the Peculiarities of the English 118

Rehabilitating Hobbes. 124

Faith and Scepticism. 135

The History of Character 141

Chapter 4 The Philosophy of History, 1947–1975

History and Other Modes. 151
History and Contingency 163
History as a Language. 167
History and Morality 172
History as an Aesthetic Fiction? 178

Chapter 5 Modern European Politics, 1958–1975

The Origins of Modern Politics. 183
Societas and *Universitas* 189
The State as a *Societas* 195
The State as a *Universitas* 200
Philosophers of *Societas* 208
Philosophers of *Universitas* 213

Chapter 6 The Philosophy of History, 1975–1983

Human Conduct and History 219
Past 222
Occurrences and Situations. 233
Relating Events. 236
Change 243
The History of Thought and the History of Political Thought . 247

Conclusion 259
Bibliography 273
Index 289

Abbreviations

Abbreviations of titles of works by Oakeshott used in the text

CA	*Hobbes on Civil Association*
EM	*Experience and its Modes*
HC	*On Human Conduct*
LSE	*London School of Economics Archival Material*
ML	*Religion, Politics and the Moral Life*
MP	*Morality and Politics in Modern Europe*
OH	*On History and Other Essays*
PF	*The Politics of Faith and the Politics of Scepticism*
RP	*Rationalism in Politics and Other Essays*
SP	*The Social and Political Doctrines of Contemporary Europe*
VL	*The Voice of Liberal Learning*

Preface

A large part of the initial appeal to me, in 1992, of a study of Oakeshott's ideas on history was that they had received little attention: Oakeshott was best known as a political thinker. The thesis on which this book is based was completed in 1996, but, ten years after I initially began work on the subject, it remains, to my knowledge, the only full-length study of his ideas on history, which are at least as important as anything he had to say on the philosophy of politics. There have, however, been significant changes in what seems, at the beginning of the twenty-first century, to be fast becoming a subject in its own right: 'Oakeshott studies'. The formation of the Michael Oakeshott Association, thanks to the efforts of Leslie Marsh, who also organised the first conference exclusively devoted to Oakeshott's work at the London School of Economics in 2001, was a welcome development, but perhaps the most important was the acquisition in 1997 by the LSE of Oakeshott's papers. This collection, discussed in more detail in the Introduction, was only thoroughly catalogued in 2001 by Anna Towlson, who deserves the thanks of Oakeshott scholars everywhere for her efforts. In referring to papers in the Oakeshott archive, this book follows the reference numbers used in the arrangement she devised unless otherwise stated. It will be some years before the archive is fully explored, but as much use as possible has been made of it here.

Oakeshott has the distinction of having authored not one but two of the handful of ground-breaking investigations into the critical philosophy of history that the twentieth century produced. The story of how his ideas changed in the fifty years separating *Experience and its Modes* and *On History* occupies half of the present study, the organization of which reflects the fact that 'history', the word, is a homonym. 'History', that is, can refer both to events in the past and to a form of enquiry peculiarly concerned with such events. It would hardly be too much to say that all Oakeshott's writings on the philosophy of history were devoted to working out the implications of this for the nature of historical understanding. Yet it seemed impossible to ignore what Oakeshott had to say on the other sense of history, history as events rather than as a form of enquiry. The other half of this book, therefore, addresses Oakeshott's work on the history of political thought, an almost equally neglected subject.

It proved easiest to work through the material in chronological order, holding these two main strands apart and letting them unfold in tandem, making connections where possible. So, chapters one, three, and five deal with Oakeshott on the historical past. Beginning with his pre-World War Two career at Cambridge, first as a student, and then as a lecturer in history, they cover his writings on Hobbes and the quasi-historical figure of the Rationalist, culminating with his understanding of the moral and political experiences of post-Renaissance Europe as the product of a tension between two conflicting ideas of the state.

Chapters two, four, and six discuss Oakeshott's contemporaneous writings on the nature of historical enquiry. Initially, he had to overcome scepticism about the possibility of historical knowledge: his later writings distinguished history from other 'modes' of experience such as philosophy and natural science by specifying the postulates characteristic of historical enquiry such as agency and contingency. An integral part of this process was a fundamental shift in Oakeshott's conception of the relation of philosophy to other forms of thought, from a conception of it as 'queen of the sciences', exempt from the 'arrests' suffered by the other modes, and offering an undistorted vision of things as they really are, to a more modest view of it as one 'voice' amongst others. History thus ceased to be seen as an unsatisfactory mode of enquiry from the philosophical perspective, becoming simply, like philosophy itself, a conditional form of theorising.

Somewhat ironically, given that Oakeshott himself maintained that there was no necessary connection between his ideas on the philosophy of history and any particular view of historical events, it turned out that there were few such connections, at any rate of any very direct sort, to be made. There were certain views of historical events which Oakeshott's philosophy of history appeared to characterise as unhistorical, or which at best were placed in the category of speculative philosophies of history, such as the Marxist view, but even such negative prescriptions concerning permissible delineations of the past usually have to be inferred from what he wrote, rather than being explicit.

This book argues for two conclusions which should lead to a permanent revision of our understanding of Oakeshott's intellectual legacy. Firstly, that Oakeshott's writings on historical events gradually led him to a novel account of the history of liberalism understood first and foremost as a commitment to the rule of law (as distinct from, for example, a commitment to free markets). Secondly, that his writings on the philosophy of history over the same period established historical study as an autonomous form of enquiry. Two articles on Oakeshott which appeared in between the completion of the thesis and the appearance of the book do not modify these broad conclusions in any way, but the work done for them led to some corrections in matters of detail, for example, in the discussion of Oakeshott's relationship to Gierke.

I will always be grateful to the Australian government and people, and to the Australian National University, for their generosity in funding several happy years in Canberra as an Overseas Postgraduate Research Scholar. I was lucky enough to meet a fellow Oakeshott scholar there, Dr Glenn Worthington, with whom I had countless useful and enjoyable conversations. Professor K. Haakonssen supervised my work there with good humour and invariably supplied constructive criticism. His continuing encouragement has been especially valuable. The late Professor P. Bourke, Professor F.B. Smith, Dr J. Shearmur, and Dr A. Vincent were all kind enough to read my work.

While at ANU I profited from conversations about Oakeshott with Professors K. Minogue, Q. Skinner, W.H. Greenleaf and C.N.L. Brooke, Dr Arthur Witherall, and Mrs J. Plaat. Without the gracious permission of the late Mrs S. Letwin and Professor W. Letwin, then literary executors of Oakeshott's estate, much of the unpublished material used in the book would then have been unavailable to me. Mr L. Davidson and Professor N.K. O'Sullivan were good enough to furnish me with the remainder. I would also like to thank the librarians of the ANU, Cambridge University library, Gonville and Caius College library, and the LSE archives, as well as Mrs P. Weatherly, archivist and historian of St. George's School, Kent. Last but certainly not least, the extraordinary secretarial staff of the History Program in the Research School of Social Sciences — Beverly Gallina, Janice Aldridge, Helen Macnab and Anthea Bundock — consistently went far beyond the call of duty in assisting with everything from technology to travel.

When the thesis was completed, I found myself unusually fortunate in my three external examiners: Professor David Boucher, then the only author to have shown any sustained interest in the areas of Oakeshott's thought which this book discusses, and a major force in the restoration of interest in British Idealist philosophy; Professor Conal Condren, who had studied with Oakeshott at the LSE, and a formidable scholar of the history of political thought in his own right; and Professor Reba Soffer, who made Oakeshott part of her investigations into the history of British political thought, and has since been kind enough to buy me the odd dinner or two. It is largely thanks to their positive reception of the thesis, and the constructive criticism of Professor Terry Nardin, himself the author of an authoritative study of Oakeshott's philosophy, that I was persuaded to revise it for publication. None of the above, however, should be made to bear any responsibility for its shortcomings. Since the subject of Oakeshott's ideas on history continues to be relatively unfamiliar, forgiveness is asked for more exposition and quotation than might have otherwise been necessary.

Introduction

As soon as Michael Oakeshott succeeded Harold Laski as Professor of Political Science at the London School of Economics in 1951, he made it clear that he did not share his predecessor's views. He criticised 'ideological' politics, including socialism or Marxism of every hue, and rejected as an 'illusion' the idea 'that in politics there is anywhere a safe harbour, a destination to be reached or even a discernible strand of progress.'[1] The reception the Labour MP Richard Crossman, a former Oxford philosophy tutor and later editor of the *New Statesman*, accorded this inaugural lecture set the tone for the 'generally unsympathetic press'[2] Oakeshott received throughout his seventeen years at the LSE. Crossman described Oakeshott as a 'cavalier iconoclast' who was determined to destroy the 'School dedicated by the Webbs to the scientific study of the improvement of human society.' He was a 'Conservative' whose views led ultimately to 'relativism'.

Oakeshott, as Crossman understood him, left us with no standard 'by which [British Parliamentary government] can be said to be better than [the German militarist tradition]'. He had even unwittingly emulated the Marxist ideas he attacked; like Marx, he wanted 'to heap contempt and ridicule on Utopians and sentimentalists who believe that the individual can transcend his tradition and that principles are worth fighting for.'[3] Oakeshott clearly felt he had been misconstrued. He dismissed Crossman as a 'professional idealist' convinced of his own 'monopoly of sincerity'. Rather than trying to

---

[1] See Oakeshott's inaugural lecture on 'Political Education', reprinted in *Rationalism in Politics and Other Essays*, 2nd edn., ed. T. Fuller, Liberty Press, Indianopolis, 1991, p. 66. This edition of *Rationalism in Politics* is the one cited throughout this work.

[2] G. Feaver, 'Michael Oakeshott and Political Education', *Studies in Comparative Communism*, vol. 2, 1969, p. 162.

[3] R.H.S. Crossman, Review of 'Political Education', *New Statesman and Nation*, vol. 42, 1951, pp. 60–1.

establish a 'seminary for training political hedge-preachers in some dim orthodoxy', he retorted, he was trying to maintain 'the deservedly high reputation' of the LSE for teaching 'undergraduates . . . how to think for themselves.'[4] These categorical denials did not prevent Crossman's charges being echoed by Bernard Crick, to whom Oakeshott was a 'sceptical, polemical, paradoxical, gay and bitter spirit', unmistakably a Tory as well as a 'lonely nihilist'.[5]

After Oakeshott assented to Irving Kristol's request for a collection of his essays,[6] published as *Rationalism in Politics* in 1962, he received further public attention, again mainly hostile. Oakeshott, however, almost never replied to his critics.[7] Those who wished to describe him as a Conservative thinker could do so with little fear of his contradicting them. They could point not only to his inaugural lecture but also to the polemical essays and articles he had written shortly after World War Two ended. These essays attacked 'Contemporary British Politics' as the advance of despotism with the Labour Party in the vanguard. Oakeshott had outlined 'Stalin's Four Weak Points' in the *Evening Standard* (under the headline *Man Who Took Laski's Job Attacks The Communists*).[8] Yet he never explicitly proclaimed himself a Conservative — his essay 'On Being Conservative' was an examination of the conservative 'disposition' rather than a statement of allegiance to a Conservative political party, and nowhere did the author state that the essay was a self-portrait.[9]

On Oakeshott's death in 1990, *The Times* suggested that he 'influenced many generations of students and readers who became supporters of Mrs Thatcher', and that, though he had no direct influence on the then Prime Minister, he 'more than anybody else . . . articulated the real philosophical foundations' of her policies.[10] This view remained current even at the beginning of the twenty-first century; the wild claim that Oakeshott's ideas 'hold the key to reviving a

---

[4]   Oakeshott, Letter to the Editor, *New Statesman and Nation*, vol. 42, 1951, p. 100.

[5]   B. Crick, 'The World of Michael Oakeshott or the Lonely Nihilist', *Encounter*, vol. 20, 1963, p. 65.

[6]   See the letters from I. Kristol, then senior editor at Basic Books, to Oakeshott dated 26 April and 14 September 1960 at LSE 11/4.

[7]   D.D. Raphael was the only reviewer of *Rationalism in Politics* to draw a public response from Oakeshott. See Oakeshott, 'Rationalism in Politics: a Reply to Professor Raphael', *Political Studies*, vol. 13, 1965, pp. 88–92.

[8]   Oakeshott, 'Stalin's Four Weak Points', *Evening Standard*, 20 November 1950, p. 9.

[9]   *RP*, p. 407.

[10]   *The Times*, Editorial, 22 November 1990, p. 11.

beleaguered Tory Party' received an airing in the usually sober *Times Higher Educational Supplement* in 2002.[11]

The fortunes of Oakeshott's reputation, however, had begun changing some years before. Although some still dismissed him as a devotee of a Burkean 'romantic historiosophical [sic] communalism' who 'damned egalitarian and welfare do-gooding',[12] others increasingly praised him as a political philosopher of the first rank. His *On Human Conduct*,[13] published in 1975 after his retirement, was to be spoken of in the same breath as Hobbes's *Leviathan* or Hegel's *Philosophy of Right*.[14] In the 1970s and 1980s he began to acquire a following; at provincial English universities like Hull and Durham, 'people . . . subscribe[d] . . . to the philosophical ideas of Oakeshott', including his ideas about politics.[15] And doubts were being aired as to whether he really was best regarded as a Tory propagandist. The confusion was reflected in the coverage given to him in 1984 by the French magazine *Le Figaro*. On the one hand, Oakeshott was 'le gourou qui inspire encore toutes les grandes décisions de Margaret Thatcher'; on the other hand, 'au moins n'est-elle [Thatcher] pas socialiste et a-t-elle renoncé à intervener dans l'economie, mais selon Oakeshott, elle fait preuve d'une certaine brutalité dans ses manières, étrangère á l'esprit conservateur'.[16] Oakeshott publicly disclaimed all pretensions to guru status,[17] and it is not at all clear that 'conservative' is the best label for his philosophy, at least not without considerable qualification.

In 1985, Coats argued that Oakeshott's political philosophy aimed at 'a restatement or reformulation of liberalism'.[18] Significantly, when Oakeshott was sent the article containing this description of him, he paid it a handsome compliment, writing to a friend that it 'makes better sense of . . . what I have written than I managed to

[11]   D. Walker, 'A Traditionalist with the Eye', *Times Higher Educational Supplement*, 18 January 2002, pp. 20–21.

[12]   E. Gellner, Review of R. Dahrendorf, *LSE:A History of the London School of Economics and Political Science*, *Times Literary Supplement*, 9 June 1995, p. 3.

[13]   Oakeshott, *On Human Conduct*, Oxford University Press, Oxford, 1975.

[14]   K. Minogue, 'Oakeshott and the Idea of Freedom', *Quadrant*, vol. 19, 1975, p. 83.

[15]   D. Boucher, *Texts in Context: Revisionist Methods for Studying the History of Ideas*, Martinus Nijhoff, Dordrecht, 1985, pp. 258–9.

[16]   G. Sorman, 'C'est le maitre a penser des conservateurs britanniques', *Le Figaro*, 27 October 1984, pp. 110–12.

[17]   Oakeshott, Festschrift Speech, LSE 1/3.

[18]   W. Coats Jr., 'Michael Oakeshott as Liberal Theorist', *Canadian Journal of Political Science*, vol. 18, 1985, p. 411. Cp. the article with an identical title by P. Franco in *Political Theory*, vol. 18, 1990, pp. 411–36.

make myself.'[19] Since Oakeshott rarely gave such an enthusiastic reception to his critics, it is worth explaining what Coats thought Oakeshott's liberalism involved. The dangers of anachronism in positing a 'liberal tradition' extending back to the seventeenth century (or even further) are well known.[20] Nevertheless, students of history and politics have rarely been deterred from speaking in these terms by the possible pitfalls involved. For Coats, one may 'use "liberal" . . . to indicate a view of the state as subordinate to, and arising from, the freedom of individual conscience — or sometimes individual appetite — regardless of whether or not the claim is grounded in some "natural right"', which J.S. Mill's "liberalism", for example, was not.' This allows that liberalism is at any rate 'modern', for 'ancient writers like Plato and Aristotle . . . saw political association as a means for habituating nonphilosophic citizens to moral virtues, regardless of individual judgement and choice.'[21]

The 'fundamental assumption of liberalism', which Coats argued Oakeshott shared, is that 'value is individual'. For the liberal, 'All judgements of good, bad and worth must be made and judged for individuals as individuals, not parts of wholes.' In liberal political thought, then, 'the state may functionally comprehend the individual in some respects, but is good or bad for individuals considered as such . . . rather than . . . as contributors to . . . some sort of whole . . . political, social, natural, cosmic and so forth'. This assumption, 'explicit or otherwise', Coats argues, is shared by 'accounts ranging from the Hobbesian and Lockean states of nature to modern defences of economic freedom', and indeed, Oakeshott himself described liberalism as 'one of the most notable idioms of European political experience and reflection'.[22] Coats's argument also has obvious implications for those who see Oakeshott as an 'organic' conservative bent on submerging the individual in a romantic communalism.[23]

Despite these changes in reputation since the 1960s, discussion was for a long time largely restricted to Oakeshott's writings on political philosophy. For example, if we examine books not exclusively devoted to him, but in which he is treated as a major figure, it is almost invariably in the context of political theory that he makes

[19]   Oakeshott, Letter to N.K. O'Sullivan, 8 February 1986, private collection.

[20]   See, for example, the contributors to *Traditions of Liberalism*, ed. K. Haakonssen, Centre for Independent Studies, St Leonard's (Australia), 1988.

[21]   Coats, 'Oakeshott as Liberal Theorist', pp. 773–4.

[22]   Oakeshott, Reader's report on F.A. Hayek, *The Constitution of Liberty*, LSE 1/2/3.

[23]   Coats, 'Oakeshott as Liberal Theorist', pp. 774–5.

his appearance.[24] Authors grouped him with Strauss, Hayek, and Schmitt as a member of the 'intransigent right';[25] they 'revisited' his critique of 'Rationalism'; they have discussed his response to 'post-modernism'; and so on.[26] Similarly, Greenleaf's *Oakeshott's Philosophical Politics*,[27] the first study entirely given over to Oakeshott, concentrated, as the title suggests, mainly on Oakeshott's political thought. For over twenty years, this remained the only introductory volume available. The title of a longer work by Franco, *The Political Philosophy of Michael Oakeshott*,[28] published in 1990, reveals the same focus. Even Gerencser's *The Skeptic's Oakeshott*, published ten years later, though it rightly identified scepticism as a permanent theme in Oakeshott's work, mainly examines its implications for his political philosophy.[29]

By the mid-1990s, though, Oakeshott was beginning be regarded as one of the most significant thinkers to emerge from Cambridge in the century.[30] Grant's *Oakeshott*, the first comprehensive introductory study, described Oakeshott as 'probably the greatest living political philosopher in the Anglo-Saxon tradition'.[31] The increased acclaim was accompanied by a recognition that Oakeshott's frame of reference had little to do with recent incarnations of the English conservative party. Coats's *Oakeshott and his Contemporaries*, for example, argues that Oakeshott's thought is best understood in relation to

---

[24] Covell linked Oakeshott with 'contemporary Conservatism' in *The Redefinition of Conservatism: Politics and Doctrine*, Macmillan, London, 1985. Devigne's *Recasting Conservatism: Oakeshott, Strauss and the Response to Postmodernism*, Yale UP, New Haven, 1994, offered a comparison of his political ideas with those of Strauss. Even feminist theorists have discovered Oakeshott's political philosophy, as witnessed by Mouffe's *The Return of the Political*, Verso, London, 1993. The literature in periodicals and learned journals reveals the same concern with political thought. H. Wells's examination of the *Social Sciences Citation Index* and the *Arts and Humanities Citation Index* demonstrated that in the early 1990s *Rationalism in Politics* was cited more than twice as often as *On Human Conduct* between 1975 and 1990: see 'The Philosophical Michael Oakeshott', *Journal of the History of Ideas*, vol. 55, 1994, p. 130.

[25] P. Anderson, 'The Intransigent Right at the End of the Century', *London Review of Books*, 24 September 1992, pp. 7–11.

[26] P. Franco, 'Oakeshott's Critique of Rationalism Revisited', *Political Science Reviewer*, vol. 21, 1992, pp. 15–43.

[27] W.H. Greenleaf, *Oakeshott's Philosophical Politics*, Longmans, London, 1966.

[28] P. Franco, *The Political Philosophy of Michael Oakeshott*, Yale UP, New Haven, 1990.

[29] S.A. Gerencser, *The Skeptic's Oakeshott*, St Martin's Press, New York, 2000.

[30] R. Grant, 'Michael Oakeshott' in *Cambridge Minds*, ed. R. Mason, Cambridge UP, 1994, where Oakeshott rubs shoulders with the likes of Frazer, Russell, Wittgenstein, and Leavis.

[31] R. Grant, *Oakeshott*, Claridge Press, London, 1990, p. 9.

the ideas of those thinkers who had the greatest impact upon him, including St Augustine, Montaigne, and Hegel.[32]

One might expect that every aspect of the writings of a man belonging in such eminent company would have been thoroughly explored. Yet of all the books on Oakeshott's philosophy, only one has given significant space to his writings on history, Nardin's *The Philosophy of Michael Oakeshott*.[33] Nardin rightly locates Oakeshott's philosophy of historical understanding within a broader debate on the nature of understanding in the human sciences that can be traced back to the first half of the nineteenth century. Nevertheless, the historical context of Oakeshott's ideas on history and the history of their development was something he deliberately eschewed, organizing his discussion thematically 'rather than treat Oakeshott's writings individually and chronologically'. As he acknowledges, his approach carries a certain cost 'from the standpoint of the intellectual historian'.[34] The approach taken here is precisely the one he decided to eschew, and is intended to complement his.

Oakeshott began his scholarly career with the study of history. He went up to Gonville and Caius College, Cambridge, in 1920, to study history, and he remained at Cambridge, employed as an historian, for over two decades thereafter. Indeed, the historian of his College and of the University[35] has portrayed him as one of the leading figures in history in Cambridge in the 1940s. He even became Director of Studies in history at Caius for a brief period after he returned from military service in 1945. A historian by profession before he became known as a political thinker, he combined interests in history and politics at Cambridge from the start. Throughout his career, he worked to formulate a comprehensive vision of European political history that has never been thoroughly explored.

The speculative temperament Oakeshott displayed from a very young age ensured he was not only interested in Europe's political past. He was also fascinated by the status of our knowledge about that past. The question of what it is that we know (or even whether we can really be said to know anything) when we claim to know about historical events had already been posed, but he did as much

---

[32] W.J. Coats, *Oakeshott and his Contemporaries*, Susquehanna UP, Pennslyvania, 2000.

[33] T. Nardin, *The Philosophy of Michael Oakeshott*, Pennsylvania State UP, Pennsylvania, 2001. This work is now the starting point for those seeking a detailed critical overview of Oakeshott's ideas.

[34] *op. cit.*, p. viii.

[35] C.N.L. Brooke, *A History of the University of Cambridge*, vol. 4, Cambridge UP, Cambridge, 1993, p. 327.

as anyone in the twentieth century to supply an answer. His writings on the philosophy of history are addressed not only to the sceptic who denies that historical knowledge is possible, but to the problem of what makes history a distinctive form of thought. And his estimation of the importance of history in his own life and thought is put beyond doubt by his declaration that 'I am more grateful for having been brought up to read history than for almost anything else'.[36]

Oakeshott's writings on these two distinct senses of 'history', 'events' and 'enquiry', have not been entirely ignored, although critics have usually engaged with what he had to say about history as *disciplina* rather than as *res gestae*. The historians and philosophers who have discussed Oakeshott's philosophy of history in passing include Postan, Cobban, Forbes, Elton, Pocock,[37] Collingwood, Mandelbaum, Dray and Walsh. There are also a few pieces devoted directly to Oakeshott's philosophy of history. Himmelfarb has an essay on the subject in her book *The New History and the Old*.[38] Boucher has published instructive articles examining the influence of the later nineteenth century British Idealists on Oakeshott's philosophy of history, and comparing it with Collingwood's views. He has also briefly addressed Oakeshott's treatment of the history of political thought.[39] Nevertheless, the discussion of Oakeshott's ideas on history in both these senses has been brief, and only a handful of books and scholarly articles have treated 'Oakeshott on history' as a subject in its own right. There is no full length study of the topic, but there is reason for thinking that the time is now ripe.

In recent years, as one reviewer observed, it has become possible to speak of an 'Oakeshott industry'.[40] As well as the proliferation of secondary literature, we must mention the appearance of much rare or previously unpublished material. In 1989 there came a collection of essays on education, *The Voice of Liberal Learning*, followed by an

---

[36] Oakeshott, address to the LSE history society, LSE 1/3.

[37] All of whom have been associated with history at Cambridge.

[38] G. Himmelfarb, 'Does History Talk Sense?' in *The New History and the Old*, Harvard UP, Cambridge Mass., 1987.

[39] D. Boucher, 'Overlap and Autonomy: The Different Worlds of Collingwood and Oakeshott', *Storia, Antropologia e Scienze del Linguaggio*, vol. 4, 1989, pp. 68–89; 'The Creation of the Past: British Idealism and Michael Oakeshott's Philosophy of History', *History and Theory*, vol. 23, 1984, pp. 193–214; 'Politics in a Different Mode: An Appreciation of Michael Oakeshott, 1901–90', *History of Political Thought*, vol. 12, 1991, pp. 717–28.

[40] R. Grant, Review of Oakeshott, *Religion, Politics and the Moral Life* and *Morality and Politics in Modern Europe*, *Times Literary Supplement*, 15 April 1994, p. 31.

expanded edition of *Rationalism in Politics* in 1991.[41] Almost immediately after Oakeshott's death, two more volumes went to press. *Religion, Politics and the Moral Life* assembled many of Oakeshott's early
theological writings and some previously unpublished pieces on
political philosophy:[42] *Morality and Politics in Modern Europe* contained lectures on the history of political thought that Oakeshott
gave as a visiting lecturer to Harvard in 1958.[43] In 1996, another posthumous work (which appears to date from the 1950s), *The Politics of
Faith and the Politics of Scepticism*, appeared.[44] In it, Oakeshott argued,
as he had at Harvard, that modern European political history was
the product of the interaction of two contrasting political styles, a
position which he had first arrived at the end of the 1930s and would
continue to refine and develop for the rest of his career.

The most recent development is the establishment of an Oakeshott
archive at the LSE, which contains a significant amount of unpublished manuscript material, some of which provides the sources for
the publications just alluded to. While this collection may not revo-
lutionise our knowledge, it definitely enlarges it considerably, not
only respecting Oakeshott's life, but also his intellectual development, and his place in the history of ideas. The series of twenty-one
numbered notebooks stretching from 1922 to 1981, in which he
recorded his reading and jotted down his thoughts, would do so by
themselves.[45] However, the archive also contains over fifty boxes of
papers, including manuscripts, correspondence, photographs, press
cuttings, and even military records, all of which will no doubt be
invaluable to future biographers.

General impressions are that Oakeshott appears to have worked
harder and more methodically than perhaps he would have liked to
let on, and that he knew more people than the image of him as a retir-
ing philosopher insistent on the gulf between theory and practice
would suggest. One area in which he was undeniably conservative
in his published works was the use of footnotes, so it is now far easier
to trace not only what he called the 'rambling path' of his footprints
in life but also the course of the intellectual 'conversations' he was

[41] Oakeshott, *The Voice of Liberal Learning: Michael Oakeshott on Education*, ed. T.
      Fuller, Yale UP, New Haven and London, 1989.
[42] Oakeshott, *Religion, Politics and the Moral Life*, ed. T. Fuller, Yale UP, New Haven
      and London, 1993.
[43] Oakeshott, *Morality and Politics in Modern Europe*, ed. S. Letwin, Yale UP, New
      Haven and London, 1993.
[44] Oakeshott, *The Politics of Faith and the Politics of Scepticism*, ed. T. Fuller, Yale UP,
      New Haven and London, 1996.
[45] Oakeshott, Notebooks, LSE 2/1/1–21.

involved in. These mostly turn out to have begun early and ranged widely. Some of the additions to the existing picture were hardly unsuspected. Written proof of a distinct interest in Epicureanism, and repeated perusals of Nietzsche, will surprise few,[46] though it is nice to know he read some of Foucault's *Histoire de la Sexualité* (aged 80 or so),[47] and the rumoured notes on Heidegger's *Being and Time* have finally surfaced.[48] Other items provide more circumstantial evidence. Oakeshott's reading of Hobbes can now be traced reliably back to 1921, when he declared (in what was actually a commonplace of the time) that 'the seventeenth Century is the key to the whole history of England.'[49]

There are genuinely important items; for instance, without the previously unknown long essay from 1943 on the principles that ought to govern a settlement with Germany,[50] there might be no evidence that the war that brought a temporary stop to his academic career had not stopped Oakeshott from writing altogether between 1940 and 1946. This essay bridges the pre- and post-war eras, and shows clearly the philosophical and historiographical importance the dramatic idea of character was taking on for him. Oakeshott was one of the few English thinkers who took the unfashionably 'Victorian' idea of character seriously, though it might be said to have undergone a minor revival since.[51] Other items in the collection are just hilarious material for a life lived to the full. What price could one put on the correspondence with Roper and Roper, solicitors, regarding a charge of indecent exposure after Oakeshott was seen bathing naked in Dorset in 1955, accompanied by his own account of the incident (complete with map), and an enthusiastic letter of support from a committed Canadian nudist who sent him ten shillings towards his legal expenses?[52] No such escapades marred the life of Kant, although Oakeshott was one of his philosophical descendants.

Sadly, the nude bathing incident does not figure in the present book, though its contents are undeniably affected by this opening of the archives. For example, there are four papers on the philosophy of

---

[46] See Notebook 11, LSE 2/1, and the Notebook at LSE 2/4/4 for Epicureanism; Notebooks 2, 6, 8, 10, and 12, LSE 2/1, for Nietzsche.

[47] Oakeshott, Notebook 21, LSE 2/1.

[48] Oakeshott, Notes on Heidegger, LSE 3/5.

[49] Oakeshott, 'Thomas Wentworth first Lord Strafford', LSE 1/1/1.

[50] Oakeshott, 'Peace with Germany', LSE 1/1/11.

[51] See, for example, John Casey, *Pagan Virtue An Essay in Ethics*, Clarendon Press, Oxford, 1990, esp. chapter one, 'Persons'.

[52] Oakeshott, Correspondence, LSE 11/3.

history from the 1920s and 1930s, the existence of which was hitherto
unsuspected. They allow us to trace the development of Oakeshott's
philosophy of history up to the time of the publication of *Experience
and its Modes* — as, of course, does the existence of the manuscript of
the book itself,[53] and the correspondence relating to it.[54] There is also
a complete set of the last lectures he gave at the LSE on the history of
political thought, familiar only to those who heard them.[55] This is not
to mention a substantial amount of correspondence which includes
other major twentieth-century thinkers such as Popper and Hayek.

It is the ideal time, therefore, to set Oakeshott's work on political
philosophy to one side, and focus on his work on the philosophy of
history and the history of political thought. Before we begin, however, we must state yet again that these writings fall into two entirely
different categories. It cannot be emphasised enough in all that follows that Oakeshott's writings on 'history' addressed two distinct
meanings of the word. His writings on the philosophy of history
were philosophical, not historical. They discuss 'history' as a form of
enquiry and examine what is sometimes called 'the problem of historical knowledge' — how we can know, if indeed we can know,
'what actually happened' in the past. By contrast, his writings on the
history of political thought are *not* philosophical. They purport to
represent knowledge of 'what actually happened' rather than to
enquire into the form and status of such knowledge.

Let us take Oakeshott's work on the history of political thought
first. The very category 'the history of political thought' has provoked much debate. Some of the leading scholars of Oakeshott's
generation, such as Strauss, Voegelin and Arendt, have been criticised for fostering 'the myth of the tradition', the idea that a 'conventional chronology of classic works including at least those of Plato,
Aristotle, St Augustine, St Aquinas, Machiavelli, Hobbes, Locke,
Rousseau and Marx' was an 'actual historical tradition' rather than a
pedagogical convenience no older than the expansion of higher education in the later nineteenth century.[56] Oakeshott, however, did not
subscribe to this 'myth'. Ancient, medieval and modern political

---

[53]   Oakeshott, Experience and its Modes (MS version), LSE 1/1/9.

[54]   Oakeshott, Correspondence, LSE 4/4/1.

[55]   In a course that covered the entire academic year, Oakeshott would give ten
       lectures on Greece, five each on Roman and medieval politics, and ten on the
       modern period. Two sets of these lectures are preserved at LSE 1/1/21, with
       slight variations. The present work treats them as a single series of thirty
       lectures, listed individually in the bibliography.

[56]   J.G. Gunnell, *Political Theory: Tradition and Interpretation*, Winthrop Publishers,
       Cambridge Mass., 1979, p. xx.

thought, on his view, did not constitute a single tradition of enquiry. Moreover, the study of the history of political thought as he conceived it was not confined to the great texts. He treated 'political theory' and 'political thought' as categories which included policy statements and manifestos as well as abstract philosophical works. Finally, he believed that the study of political thought must also involve the study of political actions and events.

By an extension of Coats's interpretation, the unifying theme in Oakeshott's work on the history of modern political thought can be described as a concern with the history of 'liberal' thought and practice. This was a common element in his writings on such seemingly disparate topics as twentieth century ideologies, Thomas Hobbes, and the development of the modern European state. Throughout his career, he produced numerous overviews of the course of European political history, encompassing the medieval and classical eras, in which the emergence of the modern state, and of the kind of person most suited to it, were amongst the chief events. In doing so, he was deliberately challenging other influential large-scale views of the historical process. For example, one reason the Marxist scheme of successive feudal, bourgeois, and capitalistic stages of production was unsatisfactory was because it over-emphasised the economic aspect of modern individualism. C.B. MacPherson's interpretation of Hobbes's philosophy as a justification of the new 'possessive individualism', for instance, neglected Hobbes's emphasis on law, obligation and authority in making him the advocate of a new capitalist society.[57]

Turning now to the philosophy of history, Boucher has argued that throughout his career Oakeshott was concerned to show that historical enquiry is 'an activity built on postulates and capable of generating conclusions appropriate to itself.'[58] In the vocabulary of *Experience and its Modes*, historical enquiry is an 'autonomous mode of experience'. Because Oakeshott's writings on the nature of historical knowledge are not directly related to those on the history of political thought, there would be no contradiction in holding his views on one of these subjects while holding quite different ideas on the other. Yet there are similarities of a kind. As Boucher has pointed out, the emphasis on individuality in Oakeshott's work on political philosophy and the history of political thought is reflected at the epistemological level in his views on historical enquiry.[59] For exam-

---

[57]   See chapters three and five, below.

[58]   Boucher, 'The Creation of the Past', p. 213.

[59]   *op. cit.*, p. 212.

ple, Oakeshott regarded the objects of historical study as individual
and therefore unique. In contrast to scientific enquiry, which he
believed dealt only with the generic aspect of events, historical study
was concerned with 'concrete universals', as his Idealist predecessor
F.H. Bradley called the objects of historical knowledge — uniquely
individual mixtures of particularity and genericity.

Oakeshott's contrast of history with science locates him within a
broader debate, for the philosophy of history in the twentieth century has been dominated, numerically at least, by supporters of the
view that history is or at any rate ought to be like a natural science.
The positivistic view of thinkers such as Ayer that all genuine propositions were either analytic or empirical was made to include historical enquiry.[60] Ayer himself had not wanted to deny significance to
propositions about the past, making an historical statement a kind of
empirical proposition so that 'some possible sense experience
should be relevant in the determination of its truth or falsehood' in a
manner analogous to the propositions of natural science.[61]
Oakeshott's rejection of the positivistic conception of historical
enquiry made him a dissenting voice and lent his writings on this
subject a high degree of continuity as he sought again and again to
find arguments that would establish an alternative position.

The relatively unfamiliar nature of Oakeshott's work on both the
philosophy of history and the history of political thought, and the
availability of much unknown and unfamiliar material, provide
powerful justifications for approaching the history of the development of his ideas on these subjects through the close study of the
texts he produced; these constitute the 'events' in a history of his
thought. Of course, we shall not ignore contextual considerations.
To do so would be particularly inappropriate given Oakeshott's
belief in the 'conversational' character of knowledge,[62] the more so
because in the last quarter of the twentieth century, historical and
contextual understanding became almost synonymous. Thanks not
least to the efforts of a later generation of Cambridge historians,
there has been a heightened awareness of the need to enquire into
the intellectual background of a text as well as the intentions of the
author. As Haakonssen argues, however, neither context nor

[60] Oakeshott's rejection of the positivistic account of history does not mean that he
      was hostile to positivism in all areas of thought. In many ways his own account
      of the philosophy of science is analogous to positivistic views current in the
      1930s. What he objected to was the extension of this positivistic account into
      inappropriate areas.
[61] A.J. Ayer, *Language, Truth and* Logic, 2nd edn., Victor Gollancz, London, 1948,
      pp. 31, 37, 39.
[62] Cp. Oakeshott, 'The Voice of Poetry in the Conversation of Mankind', in *RP*.

authorial intention suffices for the historian of ideas, who must seek 'an understanding of the logical possibilities in a theory'. We must recognise that 'the historian has to understand . . . ideas, not just as mental, social and linguistic events, but as intellectual phenomena with their own logic'[63] and, to expose this logic, close attention to the words in which their authors expressed their ideas is necessary, though no doubt not sufficient, in any attempt at intellectual history.

Another difficulty stems from the inescapable element of reflexivity in writing an historical essay on the ideas of a sometime historian and philosopher of historical enquiry. It seemed best to preserve the distinction, by no means unique to Oakeshott, between the two senses of history, alternating chapter by chapter between his discussions of the history of political thought and the philosophy of history. Some coming and going between the different senses of 'history' is necessary in each of these chapters, but if done too rapidly it produces confusion. Keeping them as separate as possible has the additional virtue of reflecting the fact that they represented two quite different subjects in Oakeshott's own mind. He insisted that his philosophy of history did not provide any method for historians to use; it did not represent the 'theory' behind his writings on the other sense of 'history' with which he was concerned, the events and ideas in the history of political thought. Unlike Hegel or Marx, Oakeshott did not see the philosophy of history as concerned with identifying the hidden, 'inner' dynamic to events which would give overall meaning to the past.

The assertion that there is no connection between Oakeshott's views on the two distinct senses of 'history' must immediately be qualified in several respects.[64] Oakeshott's view of historical enquiry did not, he believed, enjoin any particular views on historical events, or particular methods of studying them, or ways of writing about them. At the most, he seems to have thought he could provide a method of identifying certain *kinds* of statements about the past (such as the Marxists') as non-historical — but not therefore necessarily meaningless or worthless on those grounds alone. Furthermore, Oakeshott's philosophy of history argued that the assumption of agency, or 'human conduct' as he came to call it, was integral to historical understanding, and that the idea of 'character' had a crucial part to play in the understanding of action. As well as investigating the presuppositions of the ideas of character and agency in his

---

[63] *Traditions of Liberalism*, p. xv.

[64] We have already remarked on the fact that individuality is a theme common to both.

philosophy of history, he made use of them in his writings on historical events, constituting a formal link between his philosophy of history and his view of the past.

We shall see the early importance of the idea of character in
Oakeshott's thought in chapter one. Three little-known essays written during the 1920s on Thomas Wentworth, Lord Acton, and 'Shylock the Jew' employed the vocabulary of 'character', a common
feature of Victorian-Edwardian thought.[65] This was quite self-conscious on Oakeshott's part; his early essay on Lord Strafford
approaches seventeenth-century English history as a conflict
between various character types. Another group of three unpublished manuscripts provides some useful insight into his early ideas
on the history of political thought, and on the nature of history and
philosophy more generally.

The first is 'An Essay on the Relations of Philosophy, Poetry and
Reality'.[66] This establishes the early influence of Spinoza in the context of a discussion of two contrasting paths to knowledge of Reality,
at this time conceived of very much in the upper case. In it,
Oakeshott outlined a conception of philosophy which in some
respects was overshadowed by the importance he attached to 'poetry', which at this time was his term for both artistic and even religious experience at large, but is nevertheless recognisable in
important respects as unchanged into the 1930s. The second is
Oakeshott's generally dissatisfied response to the political science
papers he had sat for the Cambridge History Tripos.[67] The third is 'A
Discussion of Some Matters Preliminary to the Study of Political Philosophy'. Long enough to be considered in effect Oakeshott's first
book, it attempted to provide the positive conception of political philosophy he felt the political science papers in the Tripos had lacked.[68]

The broader context of the two latter essays was Oakeshott's belief
that the nineteenth century had witnessed the reduction of society to
a confrontation between a mass of individuals, on the one hand, and
the state, on the other. Hence he was sympathetic to those of his contemporaries with 'pluralist' ideas, particularly the Cambridge historian F.W. Maitland, but also some more surprising names, such as
Durkheim and Laski (in his pre-Marxist days), all of whom could be

---

[65] See S. Collini, 'The Idea of "Character" in Victorian Political Thought',
Transactions of the Royal Historical Society, vol. 35, 1985, pp. 29–50.

[66] Oakeshott, 'An Essay on the Relations of Philosophy, Poetry, and Reality', LSE
1/1/33.

[67] Oakeshott, 'The Cambridge School of Political Science', LSE 1/1/2.

[68] Oakeshott, 'A Discussion of Some Matters Preliminary to the Study of Political
Philosophy', LSE 1/1/3.

said to fear 'state omnipotence'.[69] He also leaned heavily on the work of British Idealists such as Bosanquet in his efforts to show that, far from being antagonistic, 'the state' and 'the self' implied one another. In Platonic fashion, he saw the *persona* of the individual as a reflection in miniature of the nature of the state,[70] a connection he would later explore in historical terms. At this stage, however, he contrasted historical knowledge quite unfavourably with philosophy.

Oakeshott's writings on religion are relevant to a study of his ideas on history because he inherited the nineteenth century debate about the relationship of historical scholarship to Christian belief. The question was whether Christianity could be preserved in the face of increasingly detailed historical study. In the later 1920s, Oakeshott, this time following F.H. Bradley, tried to separate Christian belief from a historical knowledge of Christianity and the life of Christ. Both senses of history are important here; on the one hand, he addressed the respective limits of religious faith and of historical knowledge; on the other hand, he was concerned with the history of the church and of types of Christian personality.

In the 1920s, Oakeshott had been something of an optimist, hoping despite the recent war for a moral and religious transformation of society. In the 1930s this mood faded rapidly, mirroring the changes in Britain and Europe at large. He believed that he was witnessing the end of a particular kind of liberal thought and practice, a prospect he viewed with mixed feelings. Nineteenth-century liberalism had plainly been a failure; the war had shown that. The attempt to revive and transform it into a more genuinely popular phenomenon that would integrate what E.H. Carr called, in the title of a work Oakeshott later reviewed, the 'New Society', also seemed to be failing by the early 1930s.[71] In Germany and Italy, it seemed to have failed conclusively. Essays on Locke and Bentham, part of an ongoing attempt to grasp the situation, identified these thinkers as having contributed to a liberal orthodoxy which the radical doctrines of communism, fascism and national socialism were now challenging.

Oakeshott was, however, unhappy with his explanation of these doctrines in terms of phenomena such as secularisation and nation-

---

[69] D. Nicholls, *The Pluralist State: The Political Ideas of J.N. Figgis and his Contemporaries*, 2nd edn., MacMillan, London, 1994, p. 55.

[70] Cp. *Republic*, Bk. VIII. 544 d–e.

[71] Oakeshott, Review of E.H. Carr, *The New Society*, LSE 1/2/1.

alism, and complained, much as he had in 1925, that he did not really feel he had got to the bottom of the matter. A hint of the idea that was to result in a fundamental change of direction can be found in the documentary reader he edited on *The Social and Political Doctrines of Contemporary Europe*, published in 1939. In a note, he claimed that all modern European political ideas and practices fell into one of two categories. On the one hand, there were those who favoured the 'total' planning of society by the state, so that the individual was absorbed into the collectivity. On the other hand, there were those who preferred the state to provide a framework of law within which individuals and groups retained as much discretion as possible in the handling of their own affairs.[72] Although Oakeshott came to think only the latter sort properly deserved the name, he contended that the term 'liberal' had been applied to thinkers of both kinds, and even to thinkers with a foot in both camps at once. Historic liberalism, he always maintained, was an ambiguous doctrine with a complex history.

The history of this tension between the planned and the unplanned society interested Oakeshott in one form or another for the rest of his career, but his approach to it was always marked by the use of the same large-scale, relatively short analysis. The longest essay he ever published on the subject, 'On the Character of a Modern European State', was less than a hundred and fifty pages. Given that his philosophy of history identified the use of evidence as a condition of critical historical enquiry, including the concept of evidence, it seems almost a paradox that Oakeshott appears to have done very little historical research himself, in the sense that he appears to have spent little time consulting archives and the like. We have noticed his claim that his philosophical theories about the nature of historical enquiry implied no 'method'. Yet the way he wrote about the past did imply a certain method, or lack thereof. He eschewed the critical apparatus of footnotes and bibliography that few modern professional historians would dare omit, in favour of reading various texts in the history of political thought and the works of historians, then producing a synthesis, a 'grand narrative', dealing with several centuries at a time.

We cannot escape the question of whether Oakeshott's writings on the past were in fact 'history' at all. An unequivocal answer is not offered here, but any answer must depend on the criteria of judge-

---

[72]   *The Social and Political Doctrines of Contemporary Europe*, rev. edn, ed. Oakeshott,
        Cambridge UP, New York 1950 (1939), pp. xxii–xxiii.

ment employed. It must be said in Oakeshott's defence that his own thought often supplies us with the means of criticising them. We shall argue that *when judged by his own standards*, his essays on past events more than once violated the conditions of historical enquiry, and do not really deserve to be considered 'historical' in genre, certainly not exclusively. Chapters four and five, for example, show that Oakeshott sometimes viewed the past from an aesthetic perspective which he himself had identified philosophically as non-historical. Of course, that recognition has not deprived his ideas on European political history of all interest. Historians such as Black have acknowledged Oakeshott's work when conducting their own long-term surveys of the European past.[73]

Whereas chapter one is predominantly concerned with Oakeshott's early ideas on historical events, chapter two is devoted to the first formation of his philosophy of history. The philosophical debates over the nature of historical enquiry in the nineteenth and twentieth centuries are vital for understanding the problems he tried to face at this time. A clear distinction had barely yet emerged between 'philosophy of history', in the sense of attempts by thinkers such as Kant, Hegel, Marx, and Spengler to discern an overall pattern in past events, and 'philosophy of history' which investigated the assumptions of a type of enquiry exclusively devoted to the study of past events. The story is partly of how Oakeshott came to make it part of his mission to establish this distinction on a firmer footing.

Those who did make a philosophical study of historical enquiry can be divided for our purposes into three groups. Some, such as Buckle in England, believed that history was the study of a realm of law-governed causality, and that it should resemble a natural science as closely as possible. Others believed that history could not be scientific in this sense, and that it was therefore insignificant, such as Schopenhauer in Germany. Finally, others still believed that historical study implied a form of knowledge quite different from that found in natural science, and that the task of the philosopher of history was to give an account of the peculiar conditions it entailed. Dilthey and Bradley in the later nineteenth century, and Croce and Collingwood in the early twentieth, all took this view.

That Oakeshott could be quite disparaging about the value of historical enquiry for the study of politics as compared to philosophy

---

[73]   A. Black, *Guilds and Civil Society in European Political Thought from the Twelfth Century to the Present*, Methuen and Co., London, 1984, p. xiv.

did not mean that he was not interested in the logic of historical enquiry in its own right. There are three papers written in the later 1920s which indicate this decisively. Drawing on Bradley and Croce, Oakeshott advanced a view of history as an independent form of enquiry, neither an art like poetry nor a science like physics. However, he also struggled unsuccessfully to overcome scepticism about the possibility of historical knowledge. He could find no way of bridging the gap between the knowing subject and the object of knowledge, between the historian and an ever receding set of past events.

Seen in this context, *Experience and its Modes*, at one time the point of departure for the study of Oakeshott's philosophy of history, now appears to have involved significant alterations to his earlier ideas. His presentation of history as an autonomous form of experience was an implicit rejection of his own earlier scepticism about the possibility of historical knowledge as such. Nevertheless, readers of the book have often been confused by the fact that, thanks to lingering traces of philosophical rationalism, Oakeshott still tended to contrast history (and all other forms of experience) unfavourably with philosophy. For example, Himmelfarb and Meiland have both been misled by Oakeshott's description of history as a defective mode of experience from the point of view of the philosopher. Both misinterpreted this as a claim that historical knowledge was unsatisfactory simply as such.

An integral part of Oakeshott's approach to the philosophy of history was to ask how history was related to other forms of human activity. In addition to philosophy, *Experience and its Modes* identified 'practical' and 'scientific' attitudes to experience. We will pay close attention to the discussion of both of these 'modes', as he called them, for an understanding of Oakeshott's philosophy of history must grasp what that philosophy was intended to exclude, as well as what it included.

In 'practical' experience the world was the object of will and desire; the organising principle of this 'mode' was the tension between the real and the ideal, the present and the future, the world as it is and the world as it ought to be. Practical experience also entailed a different relation to the past to that found in historical experience. It was characteristic of the practical past, Oakeshott argued, that it was useful. The past was used as a source of religious, moral or political instruction for the present and the future. The distinction between practical and historical views of the past is not unique to Oakeshott (it can be found in Schweitzer's *Quest of the His-*

torical Jesus,[74] which he admired,) but he was the first to develop it in detail.

'Scientific' experience meant the world as understood by the natural sciences. Although this was Oakeshott's longest discussion of the philosophy of science, he dealt with it mainly to sharpen the contrast with history. For the dominant school of logical positivism, science was an extension of ordinary 'common sense' thought. Ayer's *Language, Truth and Logic,* published three years after *Experience and its Modes,*[75] expressed this view. Oakeshott, though, regarded ordinary and scientific thought as exclusive of one another, and historical thought as exclusive of both. The scientific model of experience understood the world *sub specie quantitatis,* under the category of quantity. This gave a unique view of experience. It was not, however, to be taken as a model for other modes to emulate. This view placed Oakeshott at odds with philosophers of history such as Mandelbaum who endorsed the view that history was analogous to a natural science.

Oakeshott's philosophy of history proper discussed the postulates which he believed differentiated history from other modes of experience. We have already noticed one of these postulates, a distinctively historical conception of a 'useless' past free from didactic, moral considerations. Other postulates included distinctively historical conceptions of 'fact', 'truth', and 'reality'. This enumeration of the conditions of the possibility of historical knowledge, however, was still frequently confused by Oakeshott with arguments about the relative inferiority of history to philosophy.

By the mid- to late 1930s, there are signs that Oakeshott had begun to unravel this confusion. He ceased to make such large claims for philosophy and became less interested in trying to establish that history was an inferior means of access to reality. In a 1936 debate with a fellow Cambridge historian, M.M. Postan, over the relation between 'History and the Social Sciences', Oakeshott did not even raise the relation between history and philosophy.[76] This impression is confirmed by a 1938 piece on 'The Concept of a Philosophical Jurisprudence' in which he discussed the relationship of historical and legal studies.[77] Furthermore, ideas usually associated with his

---

[74] A. Schweitzer, *The Quest of the Historical Jesus,* tr. W. Montgomery, Adam and Charles Black, London, 1910.

[75] Oakeshott, *Experience and its Modes,* Cambridge UP, Cambridge, 1933.

[76] Oakeshott, 'History and the Social Sciences', in *The Social Sciences,* Le Play House Press, London, 1936, pp. 71–81.

[77] Oakeshott, 'The Concept of a Philosophical Jurisprudence', *Politica,* 3, 1938, pp. 203–22, 345–60.

post-World War Two work, such as 'tradition', were beginning to appear.

Chapter three returns to the history of political thought. It begins with another unpublished essay, Oakeshott's wartime consideration of the conditions of a peace settlement with Germany. This revolved around an analysis of the German character, and involved another vehement condemnation of National Socialism. It would be interesting to know how far his experience of the war was responsible for stimulating his interest in Hobbes, which first became noticeable in the 1930s. Under the influence of Leo Strauss and what he called a 'revolution' in Hobbes studies,[78] Oakeshott conceived an admiration for Hobbes which marked a departure from his early Idealist and pluralist sympathies. Oakeshott wrote more on Hobbes than on any other author, but his essays on the seventeenth century philosopher have not generally been integrated with his other writings on the history of political thought.[79] We shall see, however, that it was Oakeshott's work on Hobbes that led him back to the history of morals.

Oakeshott read Hobbes as attempting to recast the Christian myth of the Fall to reflect a new conception of human individuality, presaged in the medieval period by theological changes in the understanding of personality. Hobbes was presented as the first modern philosopher to examine the 'morality of individuality' which first appeared with the Italian Renaissance. Oakeshott claimed that in *Leviathan* itself, Hobbes had been concerned with the character who expressed this morality. The type of the 'just' or 'proud' man, he believed, was one of the means by which Hobbes sought to solve the problem of obligation. He went further — Hobbes's philosophy of the state as an association in terms of civil, 'positive' law made him, in effect, a liberal before liberalism. His interpretation of Hobbes had begun to affect his view of the history of political thought at large. It also had certain methodological implications for the history of ideas, relying as it did on the controversial view that Hobbes had both an esoteric and an exoteric doctrine.

Oakeshott's contemporaneous writings on Rationalism and the figure of the Rationalist attracted far more attention than his writings on Hobbes. We saw above that during the immediate post-war years, Oakeshott entered the debate on national reconstruction with

[78]   Oakeshott, 'Thomas Hobbes', *Scrutiny*, vol. 4, 1935, p. 269.

[79]   An important exception is the essay by I. Tregenza, 'The Life of Hobbes in the Writings of Michael Oakeshott', *History of Political Thought*, vol. 18, 1997, pp. 531–57.

polemical attacks on creeping collectivism in 'Contemporary British Politics'.[80] His essay on 'Rationalism in Politics' has much the same polemical flavour. Indeed, M.M. Postan dismissed the character of the Rationalist as a 'straw man',[81] a peg on which Oakeshott could hang all that he disliked about the modern world. There is some truth in this. Oakeshott's 'history' of Rationalism bore several of the hallmarks that he had described as characteristic of the practical attitude to the past. For example, his description of how early modern theories of knowledge had led to a Rationalist conception of politics and the role of the state was as much a diagnosis of present ills as an explanation of seventeenth century epistemology. Like Hayek and Popper, though for different reasons, he feared peace-time totalitarianism.

Although Oakeshott's writings on Rationalism are among his best-known works, they have not usually been read in conjunction with his writings on Hobbes. When we place them together we can see that both were concerned with the tension he had identified before World War Two between the planned and the unplanned society. Hobbes, on Oakeshott's reading of him, saw the function of the state as the maintenance of an authoritative framework within which citizens could pursue their affairs. The Rationalist, by contrast, was a believer in planning, insisting on using 'social engineering' to render everything conformable to a predetermined notion of the good life. Behind Oakeshott's attacks on Rationalism there lay a version of English history in which Rationalism was an alien, continental European phenomenon which had already got a pernicious hold on English life.

As the 1950s wore on, however, Oakeshott's work was no longer dominated by the two figures of Hobbes and the Rationalist. He became more interested in how the contrary dispositions they represented fitted into the history of morals in medieval and modern Europe. Just as each had represented a certain manner of governing, so each represented a corresponding character type. Hobbes and the Rationalist blended into a story of the disappearance of a morality of 'communal ties'[82] in which people knew themselves primarily as members of a group and the rise of a morality which valued the self-determined individual above all else. Hobbes's character of the just man typified the new morality; the Rationalist, many of whose

[80] Oakeshott, 'Contemporary British Politics', *Cambridge Journal*, 1, 1947–8, pp. 474–90.
[81] M.M. Postan, 'The Revulsion from Thought', *Cambridge Journal*, vol. 1, 1947, p. 153.
[82] *RP*, p. 365.

features would shortly be incorporated into the new characters of the 'mass man' and 'anti-individual', was contemporary with a reaction against it.

Chapter four deals with the philosophy of history between 1945 and the publication of *On Human Conduct* in 1975. Oakeshott's concern with the relation of history to other forms of knowledge was as keen in this period as it had been when he wrote *Experience and its Modes*. In fact, despite the abandonment of some of his earlier terminology, certain of his opinions on the subject had changed little. For example, he still considered science and history as mutually irrelevant forms of explanation. In other respects, however, there were significant changes. The most important was the shift to a more modest view of philosophy. In essays such as 'The Voice of Poetry in the Conversation of Mankind' and 'Work and Play', he modified the intellectual map put forward in his earlier work. Philosophy was now simply one voice amongst others. Consequently, history was no longer described as defective by comparison.

Between 1947, when Oakeshott reviewed Collingwood's work on *The Idea of History*,[83] and 1975, when he published *On Human Conduct*, the philosophy of history continued to be dominated by the view that history shared the logic of the natural sciences. Philosophers like Hempel defended this thesis; historians like A.J. Cobban agreed with them, believing that if they could not describe their work as a search for causes then all hope of finding an intelligible relationship between events was lost. Oakeshott became increasingly interested in finding a relationship between historical events which was not causal but which allowed them to remain significant. He believed he had found it in the idea of 'contingency', which appears to owe more than a little to the Machiavellian notion of *fortuna*.

In *Experience and its Modes*, Oakeshott had criticised Bury's conception of contingency in historical explanation as meaning nothing more than 'chance' or 'accident'. By 1975, however, 'contingency' had moved to the forefront of his philosophy of history. It is one of the most difficult parts of his work to grasp, and the present study cannot claim to have explained it fully. We may safely say, however, that he thought it was a relationship employed not only in history but in fiction and in daily life. He called it a kind of event-making, in which one event is explained by an immediate relationship to other

[83]   Oakeshott, Review of R. G. Collingwood, *The Idea of History*, *English Historical Review*, 62, 1947, pp. 84–6.

events.[84] This view has similarities with the 'narrativist' philosophies of history of Danto and Gallie. Oakeshott used it to challenge
the view that history was like a natural science, emphasising instead
that historical explanation and analysis relied on something similar
to the relationships found in stories.

The 1960s saw a period of widespread scepticism in the humanities and historical studies were no exception. J.H. Plumb, another
Cambridge historian, claimed that historical study had been the discipline most deeply affected by a general 'crisis of the humanities'
and had 'lost all faith in itself as a guide to the actions of men'.[85]
Given Oakeshott's belief in the impractical nature of historical
enquiry, it is unsurprising that he did not share this concern. He
remained outside the circles affected by the 'ordinary language' philosophy of the 1950s which had done much to precipitate the 'crisis'
by emphasising the importance of 'separating . . . factual from
merely normative or metaphysical assertions'.[86] 'Normative assertions' were precisely what Plumb hoped historical study might provide. Nevertheless, we may still detect something of a 'linguistic
turn' in Oakeshott's work that reflected changes about him. There
were even certain similarities with those of the new generation of
historians such as Skinner — both emphasised the contextual nature
of historical knowledge.

Alongside new, linguistic concerns, older debates, over such
issues as the place of moral judgement in historical study, continued
to flourish. Oakeshott's view that moral judgement (as distinct from
the recognition and explanation of moral conduct) had no place in
history led Cobban to accuse him of maintaining a distinction
between 'fact' and 'value' which produced paralysis of the moral
faculties. The traditional view was that historians ought to be judges
of character.[87] Oakeshott had originally argued against this on the
grounds that moral judgements of the past belonged to the practical
mode and were therefore non-historical. He maintained this position, but altered his reasoning somewhat. He now claimed that the
inadequacy of moral judgements about the past as *historical*

---

[84] History was distinguished by insisting that the historical understanding of an
    event be exclusively in terms of its relationship with antecedent events; in
    fiction and daily life no such postulate is required.

[85] *The Crisis in the Humanities*, ed. J.H. Plumb, Penguin, London, 1964, p. 8.

[86] *The Return of Grand Theory in the Human Sciences*, ed. Q. Skinner, Cambridge UP,
    Cambridge, 1985, p. 4.

[87] T.H. Green remarked in his *Lectures on the Principles of Political Obligation*, intro.
    A.D. Lindsay, Longmans, London, 1960, p. 199, that historians 'would have
    fewer readers if they confined themselves to the analysis of situations . . . and
    omitted judgments on the morality of individuals.'

explanations[88] was due to the fact that describing past doings as right or wrong says little or nothing about why they occurred. This, for Oakeshott, was the real focus of historical understanding.

Oakeshott also introduced a new 'mode' or 'voice', which he took to include all forms of aesthetic activity and enjoyment. This too had to be distinguished from historical knowledge. In particular, Oakeshott suggested that although the relationship of historians to their characters was analogous to the relationship novelists had to theirs, there were still categorial differences between an historical novel and a work of history.

Chapter five is our final chapter on the history of political thought. Oakeshott's later writings on that subject covered a vast area and wove political events and political ideas very closely together. For analytic purposes, we will separate his treatment of political events and political ideas. We will begin with a discussion of the significance he believed that earlier periods of political history had for the modern era. Here we will be basing ourselves mainly on his LSE lectures, as these are the only place in which he gave extended discussion of Greek, Roman and medieval politics. The attitude a thinker adopts to such earlier periods can be very revealing. For example, Oakeshott admired the Greeks as the inventors of politics, but he was even more impressed by the achievements of the ancient Romans in legal practice. This distinguishes him from Leo Strauss, for example, who was far more of a Hellenist, believing that modern politics needed to recover the tradition of active citizenship he found in the ancient *polis*.

As Oakeshott's interest in Rationalism declined, he concentrated more and more on linking his history of morality to the history of the modern state. These themes permeated his later writings on the past, from the lectures he gave at Harvard in 1958 to the essay 'On the Character of a Modern European State' in *On Human Conduct*. They were also recognisably continuous with his earlier efforts. 'Civil association' was the name he now gave to the liberal understanding of the state; the character-type of the 'individual' was his latest version of the liberal *persona* most suited to civil association. We should not allow this continuity to be obscured by several changes in vocabulary. In the later 1950s, Oakeshott drew a contrast between 'individualist' and 'collectivist' styles of governing. In the 1960s he used

---

[88]   There was, of course, no suggestion that such judgements were illegitimate in themselves. Indeed, Oakeshott recognised that in some circumstances (a criminal trial, for example), a judgement of guilt or innocence was exactly what was required.

'*telocracy*' and '*nomocracy*' and in the 1970s he employed two Latin terms, *societas* and *universitas*.

All these terms, however, referred to the same distinction. On the one hand, the state had been thought of as a purposive, 'goal-directed' association whose members were united in the pursuit of a certain enterprise, be it the pursuit of salvation or of wealth. On the other hand, the state had been understood as an association in terms of non-instrumental law, the business of which was to maintain a framework of legal rules leaving members of the association free to pursue their own ends, individually or in groups. This was clearly a more precise restatement of the tension in modern European politics which Oakeshott had identified before 1939, between the belief in 'planned' and 'unplanned' societies.

Such a dualistic structure for the history of modern European politics was not novel. Black has remarked that Hegel, Gierke, Tönnies, and Durkheim all suggested binary oppositions which together made up European political life. All of these thinkers assumed that 'medieval man until at least the thirteenth century ... identified himself with the norms of his community, whereas modern ... "European" man is an individualist'.[89] All opposed a tradition of community to a tradition of individualism. Gierke, for example, contrasted the medieval Germanic folk-community which he tried to revive in the modern world with the liberal, contractarian, individualistic view of society that had increasingly dominated the West since the Reformation. In turn, Oakeshott, like Gierke, argued that both the medieval and the modern world were characterised by a dualistic tension between two classes of beliefs about the nature of the state and the place of the individual within it.

It is for this reason that Oakeshott wanted to use the concepts of *societas* and *universitas* in combination. Each entailed a different notion of the *persona* appropriate to the new form of government they were intended to describe, the modern state. In a *societas*, the 'individualistic' associates wished only to be ruled; in a *universitas*, 'anti-individuals' expected guidance and management from the state. Neither concept, however, gave an adequate understanding of the modern state by itself. Although Oakeshott's preference for 'civil' over 'enterprise' association was quite clear, he believed that the historic states of modern Europe had always been a balance of both. The terminology may be unusual, but it should not distract us from realising Oakeshott was discussing a well-established theme in

[89] A. Black, 'Society and the Individual from the Middle Ages to Rousseau', *History of Political Thought*, vol. 1, 1980, pp. 145–66.

the history of political thought, and one which survived his death. A later generation of scholars has made *The Individual in Political Theory and Practice* one of the main factors contributing to 'The Origins of the Modern State in Europe' between the thirteenth and eighteenth centuries.[90]

We then turn to Oakeshott's discussions of particular thinkers according to whether they had favoured the analogy of *societas* or that of *universitas* for understanding the modern state. These must also be seen in the context of his own earlier work. For example, most of those whom he had regarded before World War Two as theorists of 'representative democracy' in the liberal tradition now reappeared as philosophers of the state as a *societas*. There was also considerable overlap between Oakeshott's selections and the choices of other scholars such as Plamenatz when compiling a list of 'canonical' liberal thinkers. Nevertheless, some of Oakeshott's connections were unusual and surprising. For example, he made Hobbes and Hegel stand together as theorists of 'civil association'.

Chapter six is devoted to Oakeshott's final work on the philosophy of history, in particular the three essays which make up the bulk of his last book, *On History*, published in 1983.[91] The essays it contains had been developed in the seminar he held at the LSE after 1964, meaning that much of *On History* was being prepared at the same time as *On Human Conduct*. However, the two books have rarely, if ever, been considered together as complementary elements of a single enterprise. This chapter begins, therefore, by considering the relationship between *On Human Conduct* and *On History*. The former devoted more attention to the status of history in relation to philosophical, scientific and practical activity. The latter gave more detailed attention to the postulates of historical enquiry itself, chiefly to the ideas of 'Past', 'Events', and 'Change'. Each of these postulates was the subject of a separate essay in *On History*, and since that work has yet to receive any lengthy discussion, it is appropriate to attempt a detailed examination of Oakeshott's handling of them.

The essay on 'Past'[92] took up once again the argument that there is more than one kind of past and the historical past was a kind of past

---

[90] See *The Individual in Political Theory and Practice*, ed. J. Coleman, Clarendon Press, Oxford, 1996. This volume is the sixth of seven in a series dedicated to the theme of 'The Origins of the Modern State in Europe'.

[91] Oakeshott, *On History and Other Essays*, Blackwell, Oxford, 1983.

[92] Late in his career, Oakeshott tended to drop the definite article and speak simply of 'past' rather than 'the past', presumably to underline his argument that 'the' past was never understood in an unqualified way but was always seen from an historical or practical or fictional perspective.

distinct from all others. The new twist Oakeshott gave to this argument was that historical enquiry postulated a distinctive relationship to the present as well as to the past. The argument that the historian could never escape the present now posed no obstacle to historical understanding. What was important was how objects encountered in the present were regarded — the same item could be understood as historical evidence of a vanished past or in some other, non-historical fashion, perhaps with regard to its utility. In his attempt to establish this point, Oakeshott confronted the pragmatic view, which he associated with Heidegger, that the adoption of an historical attitude in the present was in fact impossible.

Oakeshott's argument that the historical past exists only in historical writing as the conclusion of evidential reasoning also implied a certain view of historical events. In the essay on 'Historical Events', he tried to provide an ideal model of the levels of complexity through which historical reason passes, from static situations of the sort he believed Namier and Braudel had constructed to dynamic, changing events. He then developed the argument of *On Human Conduct* that the relation between these events was a contingent one, returning for the final time to the debate with 'scientific' philosophers of history such as Hempel.

The essay on 'Historical Change' attempted to distinguish a distinctively historical mode of change from other conceptions of change such as the teleological and the organic, with which, Oakeshott claimed, it had often been confused. By his own account, his arguments were inspired by the account of change and continuity in Aristotle's *Physics*. Aristotle's discussion, he claimed, had helped him to the conclusion that in historical understanding, a changing individual, be it a person or an institution, maintains an identity exclusively through continuity.

The essays in *On History* discuss only some of the problems in the philosophy of history that Oakeshott was considering between the late 1960s and early 1980s, and we will conclude by placing them in the broader context of his thought at the time. We can do so by examining two unpublished papers from this period, on 'The Emergence of the History of Thought', and 'Political Thought as a Subject of Historical Enquiry'.[93] Why Oakeshott did not work these two essays up for inclusion in *On History* when it was published in 1983 is something of a mystery, but they provide useful insight into his own

---

[93] Oakeshott, 'The Emergence of the History of Thought', LSE 1/1/23, and 'Political Thought as a Subject of Historical Enquiry', LSE 1/1/27.

understanding of the significance of his final book. It is time now, however, to turn back to the beginning of the century, and look at the young Oakeshott.

Chapter One

History, Religion and Politics, 1901–1939

From School to University[1]

Michael Joseph Oakeshott was born in Kent in 1901, eight months after the death of Queen Victoria, 'to parents of the unaffluent but educated and public-spirited middle class.'[2] One remarkable fact about the Oakeshott family was the intellectual and literary society they enjoyed. Michael's father, Joseph Oakeshott, a civil servant in the Inland Revenue, was a senior Fabian, counting George Bernard Shaw as a friend.[3] Michael's angry response to Crossman's accusations[4] should perhaps be seen in light of the fact that in 1894 his father had been one of a handful of those consulted by Sidney Webb over the proposal 'to found a London School of Economics and Polit-

---

[1] Oakeshott still awaits his biographer. These details are taken partly from Grant's *Oakeshott*, and his article 'Inside the Hedge: Oakeshott's Early Life and Work', *Cambridge Review*, vol. 112, 1991, pp. 106–9, as well as N. Johnson's obituary in *Proceedings of the British Academy*, vol. 80, 1993, pp. 403–23. *The Achievement of Michael Oakeshott*, ed. J. Norman, Duckworth, London, 1993, p. 148, contains some amusing anecdotal material and republished obituaries.

[2] Grant, *Oakeshott*, p. 11.

[3] According to A.M. McBriar, *Fabian Socialism and English Politics, 1884–1918*, Cambridge UP, Cambridge, 1966, pp. 176–7, 351–2, J.F. Oakeshott was the author, in whole or in part, of Fabian tracts 14, 39, and 54. He was also apparently involved, together with G. Wallas, S. Webb and G.B. Shaw, in delivering Fabian lectures to the community at large; in 1891, for example, he had addressed the West Ham Secular Society on 'Everyday Ethics', and the Popular Co-op society on 'The Middle Class and Social Reform'.

[4] See the 'Introduction', above.

ical Science', and had continued to sit on library and administrative committees for some years after the School was founded.[5]

From 1912 to 1920 Oakeshott's parents sent him to St. George's school in Kent, where he received 'a fairly conventional academic education', including the classics.[6] He was a sporting and an academic success, becoming Captain both of the school and of the rugby team in his final year.[7] The headmaster, the Rev. Cecil Grant, became a friend, and Oakeshott continued his association with the school for the rest of his life. As an old man, he reflected privately that 'I was lucky: my schooldays were filled with wonder.'[8] The school evidently helped kindle his interest in two of the subjects which would engross him throughout his scholarly career, history and politics, to judge from several short pieces he published in the school magazine in 1919.

An essay on 'An Experiment in the Teaching of History' defended the view that 'it is only by understanding contemporary History that we can gain a right view of the past.'[9] Oakeshott eventually changed his mind about this completely, arguing that the historical past must be understood in terms of its own past rather than our present. Nevertheless, it appears that the problems associated with understanding the past had begun to capture his imagination at an early stage. So had the problems of politics. 'Socialism as it Is!' was a reply to a fellow pupil who had argued that 'true socialism' was an 'evolutionary' rather than a 'revolutionary' doctrine.[10] Oakeshott suggested that 'socialism' encompassed both evolutionary and revolutionary creeds, from Fabianism to anarchism. He agreed with his socialist interlocutor that 'liberty is, under the present system, conditioned by the capitalist.' He also appeared to believe that in 1919 this state of affairs was coming to an end. 'Now . . . Capitalism can push no further . . . Socialism carries it on.'

Nevertheless, the socialist aim of 'the nationalisation of land and capital for public use and benefit' would in time also 'serve its purpose and move into the past.' At 17, Oakeshott believed in a kind of socialism broader than this transient historic doctrine of nationalisa-

[5]   S. Caine, *The History of the Foundation of the London School of Economics and Political Science*, G. Bell and Sons, London, 1963, pp. 23, 35, 68, 70.
[6]   Johnson, *op. cit.*, p. 403.
[7]   See the letter of reference from Cecil Grant in response to an application by Oakeshott for a school teaching post, dated by Oakeshott 17 June 1924, LSE 5/1.
[8]   Oakeshott, Notebook 21, LSE 2/1/21, p. 28.
[9]   Oakeshott, 'An Experiment in the Teaching of History', *Georgian*, vol. 14, 1919, p. 6.
[10] Oakeshott, 'Socialism as it Is!' *Georgian*, vol. 14, 1919, pp. 39–40.

tion. As he saw it, any searcher for truth or servant of the public good was a 'socialist', and in this sense, he wrote, there had been socialists throughout history. By altering the meaning of socialism so that it was not the exclusive province of the contemporary 'left', he was able to accommodate himself to it.

Oakeshott's schooldays ended in 1919. After narrowly failing to win an Exhibition to read history at Selwyn College, Cambridge, he was awarded a Scholarship at Gonville and Caius to read for the History Tripos. He went up in 1920 and became the only student there to obtain first class marks in either part of the History Tripos in 1922–23: he gained a lower first (a now defunct degree class) in both parts I and II.[11] The reading he undertook for his degree demonstrates the continuity between the historical scholarship of the nineteenth century and the early part of the twentieth. His 'basic grounding' in history after World War One involved reading Maitland, Stubbs, Dicey, Acton and Ranke, to name a few.[12] Maitland's work in particular had an enduring impact; he became Oakeshott's 'model historian'.[13]

At Cambridge, compulsory undergraduate study of English constitutional history reflected Maitland's legacy.[14] The medieval period in which Maitland had worked, and which later became crucial to Oakeshott's own understanding of the history of modern political thought, was taught to him by Coulton and Brooke. Coulton was a fellow of St John's College; in the 1920s he was at work on *Five Centuries of Religion* and *The Medieval Village*. He was 'an Actonian in his belief in the importance of moral judgments in history, scorning the quest for impartiality.' Oakeshott came to think that exactly the reverse approach to moral judgement was characteristic of historical writing, but that did not prevent him from later describing Coulton as one of his 'great teachers'.[15]

Brooke, a 'true scholar'[16] to whom Oakeshott dedicated his collected essays on *Hobbes and Civil Association* ('Z.N.B.'), had brought

---

[11] Oakeshott's final examination marks are recorded in the *Cambridge University Reporter* (*CUR* hereafter), 17 June 1922 and 16 June 1923. A measure of Oakeshott's achievement is suggested by the fact that only one upper first in history was awarded throughout the university (to G.J. Yorke of Trinity) to candidates in either part of the Tripos in 1922–23.

[12] Details of Oakeshott's undergraduate reading are based on the entries he made in the Caius College library borrowing register for 1920–23.

[13] Oakeshott, untitled address to the Maitland Society at Downing College, LSE 1/3. The LSE notepaper suggests this address was written after 1951.

[14] Brooke, *The History of Cambridge University*, p. 326

[15] *VL*, p. 124.

[16] Oakeshott, Festschrift speech, LSE 1/3.

Bury's *Cambridge Medieval History* to completion. He was the first historian to be elected to a Fellowship at Caius since Sir John Seeley's death in 1895. As Director of Studies at the College he presided over the growth of history there, favouring a 'scientific history with its roots deep in the German scholarship of the nineteenth and early twentieth centuries.' Oakeshott himself held Brooke's position a few years after World War Two, and it may be that Brooke's belief that 'a teaching fellow should try to teach the whole of history' was one of the things that inspired his attempts at overviews of long periods in the history of political thought.[17]

Neither Brooke nor Coulton had much of a philosophical bent. As an undergraduate, Oakeshott gained his introduction to philosophy from McTaggart. McTaggart, whom he later hailed as another of his 'great teachers',[18] was one of the last great exponents of Idealism. Russell, G.E. Moore, and the Tractarian Wittgenstein had initiated a 'wholly opposed'[19] style of philosophical thought, sometimes known as Cambridge Realism. Realism, and the logical positivism of A.J. Ayer, would dominate British philosophy in the 1930s. Oakeshott preferred McTaggart's approach. As an undergraduate he attended the lectures McTaggart regularly gave on Friday evenings during term at Trinity.[20] In these lectures, McTaggart presented the object of philosophy as the 'systematic study of the ultimate nature of reality'. Philosophy differed from other ways of knowing the world, such as 'Theology' and 'Science,' not on account of its systematic character but because it enquires into the premises which these other studies assumed as ultimate — the existence of God or matter.[21]

Oakeshott later attempted a similar map of the different forms of intellectual endeavour, and he retained a lifelong sympathy for the conception of philosophy as the criticism of presuppositions held by McTaggart. Although McTaggart himself never applied this conception of philosophy to historical enquiry, the History Tripos gave the young Oakeshott ample opportunity to do so; in the essay paper

---

[17] These descriptions of the study of history at Caius are taken from T.E.B. Howarth, *Cambridge Between Two Wars*, Collins, London, 1978, pp. 68, 107–8, and C.N.L. Brooke, *A History of Gonville and Caius College*, Boydell Press, Woodbridge, 1985, pp. 246, 261, 282.

[18] *VL*, p. 124.

[19] A.N. Quinton, 'Absolute Idealism', *Proceedings of the British Academy*, vol. 58, 1971, p. 304.

[20] Oakeshott's attendance at these lectures is recorded by Grant, *Oakeshott*, p. 13 and Johnson, *op. cit.*, p. 405

[21] J.McT.E. McTaggart, *Philosophical Studies*, ed. and intro. S.V. Keeling, Edward Arnold, London, 1934, p. 183.

which all candidates had to attempt, such speculative propositions as 'The study of the past is futile unless it helps us to explain the present' were common fare.[22]

The History Tripos catered for an interest in politics as well as an interest in philosophy, and Oakeshott was sufficiently interested to take the Political Science papers in both parts of the Tripos. Here he was emulating Maitland, who had combined work on medieval English legal history with forays into political science in the introduction he wrote for *Political Theories of the Middle Age*, his translation of a portion of Gierke's massive *Das Deutsche Genossenschaftsrecht*. Ernest Barker, who became the first Professor of Political Science at Cambridge in 1927, and later published his own translation of some of the subsequent sections of Gierke's work, commented in 1915 that 'Under the influence of the great jurist Gierke, Maitland was led to embrace the doctrine of the "real personality" of the group.'

Gierke, employing a speculative, Hegelian, philosophy of history, saw European, and especially German, history, as a continual struggle for dominance between two contrasting types of association. The first was communal, consensual, and protective of its members, and was typified in the medieval era by the guild. The second was ruthlessly individualistic and absolutist, and was favoured in particular by rulers seeking to remove all challenges to their authority. It had culminated in the modern State, which was highly suspicious of any groups which stood between it and the host of disaggregated individuals who made up its subjects.[23]

Via Maitland, Barker noted, Gierke's theory was 'pressed into service both by defenders of Trade Unionism and by those High Churchmen who argue for the independence of ecclesiastical societ-

---

[22] The sample question is quoted in R. Soffer, *Discipline and Power: The University, History and the Making of an English Elite, 1870–1930*, Stanford UP, California, 1994, p. 166.

[23] Gierke's main concern in defending group life against state incursions was to establish the 'real personality' of the group as the basis of entitlement to legal recognition, thus assuring to groups such as guilds and corporations an existence that did not depend on the will of the ruler. Black observes that for Gierke 'the real personality of voluntarily formed associations was implicit in the social forms . . . and political evolution actually found throughout German history, for example in the medieval towns and guilds . . . Such bodies behaved as if their members believed they could decide and act as collective entities': see *Guilds and Civil Society*, p. xv. Black also argues that Gierke was simply wrong to believe that real personality was essential to the legal acquisition of corporate status and security of freedom of association. A helpful contemporary discussion of the philosophical problems posed by the idea of the real personality of groups can be found in A. Vincent, 'Can Groups be Persons?', *Review of Metaphysics*, vol. 42, 1989, pp. 687–715.

ies.'[24] In *Englishness and the Study of Politics*, Stapleton observed that political Pluralism 'developed in the first decade of the twentieth century, mainly in response to the seemingly high-handed treatment of voluntary associations in the Taff Vale (1901) and Free Church of Scotland (1900-4) cases. It acquired further momentum ... against the background of the militancy of labour, the suffragettes, and the Irish Unionists.'[25] 'Pluralist' writers like Maitland and Gierke 'believed that a permanent association ... manifests a unity which enables us to treat it in certain respects as a "person".'[26]

Legal recognition of the real personalities of the plurality of groups composing society, the pluralists hoped, might end the Spencerian contest of 'the man versus the state'. For example, Maitland's pupil J.N. Figgis believed that membership of groups ensured individuals had freedom to develop their personality. 'The theory of liberty', he wrote, 'is always concerned at bottom with human character.'[27] Other sources — for instance Bosanquet's *Philosophical Theory of the State* — also acquainted Oakeshott with the idea that the nature of the state was inextricably linked to the nature of the self.[28] Nineteenth-century interpretations of classical authors reinforced this lesson. For example, W.L. Newman's commentary on Aristotle, with which he was familiar, noted that in the Politics 'the good citizen was a different being in an oligarchy, a democracy and an aristocracy.'[29] No reader of Plato's *Republic* can help noticing his identification of the form of the just *polis* as the soul of the just man writ large.

The Idea of Character

As an undergraduate at Caius, Oakeshott became editor of the College magazine, the *Caian*.[30] Three of the essays he published in it, on

[24]　E. Barker, *Political Thought in England, 1848–1914*, Thornton Butterworth, London, 1915, pp. 15, 175.

[25]　J. Stapleton, *Englishness and the Study of Politics. The Social and Political Thought of Ernest Barker*, Cambridge, Cambridge UP, 1994, pp. 68–9.

[26]　Nicholls, *The Pluralist State*, p. 14.

[27]　J.N. Figgis quoted in Nicholls, *op. cit.*, p. 21.

[28]　'The relation of a given mind to the mind of society is comparable to the relation between our apprehension of a single object and our view of nature as a whole. The former term, in each case, we cannot but suppose to be an individualised case of the latter'. Bosanquet, *The Philosophical Theory of the State*, 2nd edn., Macmillan, London, 1910, p. 297.

[29]　W.L. Newman quoted in C.H. McIlwain, *The Growth of Political Thought in the West*, MacMillan, London, 1932, p. 79.

[30]　See the letter of reference from the Dean of the College at LSE 6/1, dated 13 June 1923.

Shakespeare's Shylock, Lord Acton, and Lord Strafford, show how prominent this vocabulary of character was in his early work.[31] It is appropriate that between them these essays discuss a fictional character, a man still very much within living memory, and a historical person, as it was later a cardinal point of Oakeshott's philosophy of history that the assumptions entailed in understanding fictional, practical, and historical persons were identical in many important respects. And indeed, it is arguably the idea of character that eventually allowed him to reach this conclusion. The early essays we are to examine here, however, are undeniably pieces of juvenilia. The prose, by modern standards, has a tendency to become somewhat purple, exhibiting a youthful penchant for melodrama, and the style as well as the content is notably Carlylean.

The essay on Shylock,[32] subtitled 'A study in villainy', argued that Shylock was a dramatic success for Shakespeare because, although a villain, he was a character with a 'positive purpose inherent in itself.' A character he defined as essentially 'a person who in the event of necessity can stand alone.'[33] In true Carlylean fashion, Oakeshott saw Shylock as representing one of two opposing principles involved in the working out of a drama on a cosmic scale. In Act IV, Scene 1, the court scene, in which Shylock demands his pound of flesh from Antonio, 'the forces of good and evil are met face to face'. The play itself was a success because Shakespeare had effected a dramatic resolution in which 'the spirit [of the law] is victorious by means of the letter.'

Oakeshott saw in Shylock's defeat the reconciliation of a higher justice with the positive law of Shakespearean Venice. In the court scene, 'the cards in the players' hands change from their apparent value to their real and spiritual worth.'[34] This equation of the real with the spiritual, also notable in the other essay Oakeshott published in the *Caian* as an undergraduate, 'Lord Acton', was a familiar element of Romantic and Idealist rhetoric. The upper case, so typical of nineteenth century Idealism, was freely employed by Oakeshott, who argued the predilection of the late Regius Professor for contemplating 'the Ideal, the Infinite, the Eternal' explained his slender

---

[31]   Oakeshott, 'Shylock the Jew', *Caian*, vol. 30, 1921, pp. 61–7; 'Lord Acton', *Caian*, vol. 31, 1922, pp. 14–23; 'Thomas Wentworth first Lord Strafford', LSE 1/1/1.

[32]   Shylock seems to have been a favourite character with Idealist philosophers. Cp. G.W.F. Hegel, *Philosophy of Right*, 2nd edn., trans. T.M. Knox, Clarendon Press, Oxford, 1949, p. 19.

[33]   Oakeshott, 'Shylock', pp. 63, 66, 61.

[34]   *op. cit.*, p. 67.

oeuvre.[35] Just as Shakespeare was a playwright trying to express the inexpressible, so Acton was an historian whose 'powers of production were paralysed ... by nothing less than what has been called the nostalgia of the infinite', by a failure to reconcile the real and the spiritual.[36]

Nevertheless, Acton was presented as a character in a truly heroic mould, a man of creative genius and as 'great' as one could wish. To underline the 'penetrating and exalted' nature of Acton's idea of history, Oakeshott repeated Bryce's recollection of hearing Acton explain his 'project for a History of Liberty' for the first time: 'the whole landscape of history had been suddenly lit up by a burst of sunlight'. He also thought it a favourable comparison to place this work on the same footing as Diderot's *Encyclopédie*, that definitive Enlightenment undertaking. *The Cambridge Modern History*, completed in 1904, was to Oakeshott a product of this spirit.[37] By the 1930s, Oakeshott's enthusiasm for Diderot's project had waned considerably; Bentham, whom he saw as having embraced it, was criticised for his 'hydroptic thirst for information' and belief in the possibility of 'encyclopaedic knowledge'.[38] In 1922, however, it was to the 'encyclopaedic spirit' that he attributed Diderot's and Acton's willingness 'to grasp at and embrace the whole'.

Even in 1922, Oakeshott was not wholly uncritical of the Actonian pursuit of perfection. Acton's preference for the Ideal, a life in which thought alone is real and action a mere distraction, was admirable as long as it remained directed at the advancement of learning. Yet this disposition was not appropriate in all areas of life. Acton's protest against those in politics who 'sacrificed the ideal to the expedient ... failed, as it must.' That did not mean, however, that Oakeshott thought an ideal politics (whatever that might be) was inherently unachievable. 'Not until all possess that vision of the larger, infinite world, of the Perfect man ... can all live by it', he wrote, making no claim that such a vision could not possibly be possessed by all.[39]

Whatever Acton's political shortcomings, Oakeshott emphasised, he was not to be thought of as a failure simply because there were few visible results of his labours. Oakeshott laid down the general maxim that 'Success does not lie in some culminating act, but in the

---

[35] 'Lord Acton', p. 19.

[36] Oakeshott, 'Shylock', p. 62. Cp. Oakeshott, 'Lord Acton', p. 17.

[37] 'Lord Acton', pp. 19, 21.

[38] *RP*, p. 138.

[39] 'Lord Acton', p. 23.

continuance of the effort itself',[40] a declaration of principle which he would develop in his discussions of religion. This principle also figures, in a slightly different way, in his essay on Wentworth, who, like Shylock, was a figure in a cosmic drama. Oakeshott's sympathy for Wentworth, the ally of the hated Laud in the policy of "thorough", is certainly remarkable. The 'characteristics of the essential Wentworth' were 'ardent loyalty to the King, distrust and dislike of his ministers because of their self-interestedness and incompetence, and a mature sense of duty to England, cost what it might.'[41]

Wentworth's acceptance of office after making his name in opposition to the Crown led many to stigmatise his lack of principle, and Parliament eventually forced Charles I to submit to his execution, but Oakeshott defended him staunchly. Wentworth was, Oakeshott declared (in a repetition of his verdict on Acton), 'a genuine great man', not as creative perhaps, but notable for his 'independence of thought and action, rather than … any striking originality'.[42] That Oakeshott chose to write on Wentworth reflected his belief in the fundamental importance of the seventeenth century for English history. This was, of course, another commonplace; even in the mid-nineteenth century Cambridge historians such as Stubbs and Freeman felt 'the seventeenth century was too close to them' to be happy about teaching it to undergraduates.[43] They were not worried about the passions it would provoke amongst students so much as the rifts it might open amongst colleagues.

The last echoes of this old sensitivity towards the period are heard in Oakeshott's discovery of a 'very real universal aspect' in its events. This search for universal meaning was something he later came to see as characteristic of speculative philosophy of history, rather than the kind of historical writing he was seeking the assumptions of. However, the way in which he regarded people as at once 'unique personalities' and 'types' was also the germ of his later philosophy of character in the 1950s. In the early 1920s, the universal meaning Oakeshott believed he had found in the seventeenth century bore on the kind of co-operation his essay on Lord Acton had hinted was necessary in order to realize an ideal politics.

The seventeenth century revealed that although 'Co-operation and competition are taken to be opposites . . . in truth the former is

---

[40] *loc. cit.*

[41] Oakeshott, 'Thomas Wentworth', p. 21.

[42] *op. cit.,* p. 45.

[43] J.W. Burrow, *A Liberal Descent: Victorian Historians and the English Past*, Cambridge, Cambridge UP, 1981, p. 100.

the outcome of the latter'. Conflict between two apparently completely opposing sides, each with irreproachable motives, produced
a resolution embodying 'some of the fundamental principles of
both'. Of course, this is an idealised and unhistorical view of the seventeenth century, but the interest for us lies with the ideas underpin-
ning Oakeshott's position. These turn out to have been as much
artistic as philosophical. Oakeshott accompanied his arguments
with liberal use of poetic quotation, and drew on Browning's
account of Wentworth's life without comment as an unproblematic
source. 'O virtuous fight! When right with right wars, who shall be
most right', he exclaimed, quoting *Troilus and Cressida*.[44] The
description of the period as 'tragic' would seem to Oakeshott twenty
years later to be an inappropriate application of an artistic genre to
past events. Here, however, he argued the source of the tragedy was
'the conflict of reforming energy with actual men and institutions',
played out by these conflicting energies expressing themselves
through particular individuals.

As for Wentworth's death, it came only when his usefulness to the
larger historical process had passed. 'England must press on, and he
stood in the way'. Wentworth's fate, like Acton's, illustrated Ranke's
principle of 'the absolute independence of success and of the world's
judgment'. It did not affect his status as 'one of the greatest, doubtless the sternest, but also the most deeply human and most wholly
patriotic, educators of English Liberty'.[45] As with Shylock, whether
Wentworth was a bad man did not matter: Oakeshott quoted
Creighton's remark that 'The first lesson of history is the good of
evil'. In *Experience and its Modes*, the claim that generalisations of this
sort could be derived from historical study was something he would
explicitly criticise Lord Acton for, but in 1921 he agreed unhesitat-
ingly with Acton's remark that 'There are conditions in which it is
scarcely an hyperbole to say that slavery itself is a stage on the road
to freedom.'

Thus, Shylock's, Acton's, and Wentworth's deeds were all made
meaningful for Oakeshott in terms of their dispositions, that is, their
character. Such an explanation of action (or inaction, in the case of
Acton) is significant not least for what it excludes. Shylock's villainy
and Acton's inability to produce the great works his contemporaries
expected of him are not explained in terms of physical, psychological, social or economic forces but in terms of their individual characters. Shylock, for example, does not act as he does in Oakeshott's

[44]   Oakeshott, 'Thomas Wentworth', p. 13.

[45]   *op. cit.,* pp. 46–7.

eyes simply because he is a Jew, or a member of a mercantile class. For this interpretation, Oakeshott may have been indebted to the literary criticism of A.C. Bradley, who had argued in *Shakespearean Tragedy* that 'the main source of deeds is character'.[46] Oakeshott's originality lay in detaching the substance of the idea of character from the Victorian moralism with which it was entangled, allowing him to explore its historical and philosophical implications. This, of course, is not to say he detached the idea of character from morality; it is doubtful whether it can be so detached, and he certainly did not try. His critics might say he did not even detach it altogether successfully from moralism, as we shall see later on.

Philosophy, Poetry, and Politics

When Oakeshott completed his degree in 1923, he was awarded a studentship at Caius which allowed him to visit Germany that summer. This proved to be the first of several visits to Germany which he made in the years up to 1931. A Senior Tutor at Caius, E. K. Bennet, had introduced him to German literature, and while he was abroad in 1923 he combined reading Nietzsche, Hölderlin, and Burckhardt with studies in theology at the universities of Marburg and Tübingen. He may have heard Heidegger, then preparing *Sein und Zeit*, lecture at Marburg, and he definitely made notes on the book after it appeared in 1927.[47] At 22, however, Oakeshott was at least as interested in 'tramping off with the Wandervögel, an informal student movement' dedicated to nature-worship, camping out and (according to D.H. Lawrence, of whom Oakeshott then thought highly) 'free love', as he was in history, philosophy or theology. It is wise to note that 'Whilst [Oakeshott's] thinking undoubtedly reveals debts to the world of German thought and sensibility, apart from his acknowledgement of Hegel Oakeshott was never very explicit about what he owed to that source'.[48]

'An Essay on the Relations of Philosophy, Poetry and Reality' is the first of another group of three essays that are best dealt with together, as they all date from the period immediately after Oakeshott's graduation. He may have written it for his MA, which he was formally awarded in January 1927.[49] The essay, which is

---

[46] A.C. Bradley quoted in Collini, 'The Idea of Character in Victorian Political Thought', p. 33.

[47] Three distinct sets of notes by Oakeshott on *Sein und Zeit* are at LSE 3/5, all undated.

[48] These details of the years 1923–5 are taken from Grant and also from Johnson, whose caution is well taken. Cp. Johnson, *op. cit.*, p. 405.

[49] Oakeshott's MA certificate is at LSE 6/1.

around seventy pages long, developed a conception of philosophy also employed in the two others we are about to examine: his criticism of the Political Science papers he had studied for the Tripos, 'The Cambridge School of Political Science', and his consequent attempt to create a more satisfactory approach to political philosophy in what seems to have been a dissertation for a studentship he held prior to undertaking the MA, 'A Discussion of Some Matters Preliminary to the Study of Political Philosophy'.

The much shorter essay on poetry is nevertheless an important piece in its own right for at least two reasons. Firstly, it demonstrates that Oakeshott's concern with different forms of experience dates right back to the beginning of his intellectual career; he was wrestling with the problems involved in classifying and relating the different regions of human thought and activity from his early twenties. Secondly, it establishes that Oakeshott took the concept of modality from his reading of Spinoza. Many of the alterations he made to the concept can be traced to other sources, some are unique to Oakeshott himself, but the most important source for his ideas about modality was the *Ethics*. The essay is introduced by a quotation of Spinoza's definition of 'Reality (*substantia*) [as] that which is in itself and is conceived through itself: I mean that, the conception of which does not depend on the conception of another thing from which it must be formed'.[50]

From this definition Oakeshott eventually developed the idea that any form of understanding, such as science or history, must have its own unique self-standing conditions. The 'autonomous' modes of *Experience and its Modes* clearly developed out of the epistemological pluralism found in this essay, which led Oakeshott to insist 'men are limited if they persist in confining themselves to the use of one faculty, or seek to merge into one all their faculties of knowing'. In *Experience and its Modes*, history, philosophy, science, and practical experience would all find their proper places.

In 1923, though, Oakeshott was interested less in the conditions of each mode than in whether philosophy or poetry offered the more complete conception of reality. The proposition he wished to defend was that there were two main approaches to the investigation of reality, 'the approach of the Intellect, recorded in the history of Philosophy; the other, the approach of Intuition, set down for the most part in the history of Mysticism.'[51] Hegel and Rousseau supplied his contrasting examples of the two tendencies, though he acknowl-

---

[50]   Oakeshott, 'Philosophy, Poetry, and Reality', p. 1.

[51]   *op. cit.,* p. 3.

edged that both tendencies were visible in each. We will meet this idea of a tension in human nature again, much later on, in Oakeshott's mature work on the history of political thought. Here he was more concerned with the mutually exclusive claims of intellection and intuition to 'KNOW' reality. Modern civilized man tended to reject the claims of intuition in favour of the intellect, but this was a mistake, he argued. 'Reason, as the word is commonly used, does not cover the whole range of man's powers of knowing.'[52]

The religious thrust, and Kantian background, of this argument is made explicit in the conclusion where Oakeshott declares: 'Our knowledge of God, as Kant clearly says, is the product of the moral consciousness, and not of science or metaphysics. It is not reason but feeling which determines our idea of God. This is why religion and poetry, on this point, outweigh philosophy.'[53] Oakeshott in his youth was much impressed with Bergson, and made use of his view that 'intellect is but a tool evolved expressly to deal with situations in which man is placed in the material world' in his attempt to circumscribe the claims of reason. He would come to think that it was not necessary to take such a pragmatic view in order to make room for the extra-rational facets of human life. It was over precisely this point that he came to differ with Heidegger in *On History*, for example.

A concern with correct definition is a common feature of all three of the manuscripts we are interested in here, and it is important to notice which features of it survived in Oakeshott's later work and which did not. In one sense, all his subsequent efforts to lay bare the conditions of historical understanding (and of all the other forms of experience) can still be seen as a search for definitions; but he became much clearer that 'the word is not the thing'. At this early stage he was ready to claim that 'if an object or aspect of an object does not correspond to this general description it will be rejected as unreal'. While the 'English Hegelians' (represented by Sir Henry Jones) argued that a thing simply is its attributes, Oakeshott adopted what he thought of as the Platonic position, that thinghood involves an underlying substance apart from anything it may do or qualities it may possess.

At stake, Oakeshott thought, was the notion of personality, which, of course, was synonymous in his mind with the idea of character. Even if we 'strip a man of his activities, strip him of his qualities,' we

---

[52] *op. cit.*, p. 10.

[53] *op. cit.*, pp. 64–5.

still 'love him for himself, for what he is.'[54] Oakeshott later changed
his mind about this completely, embracing the position he identified
with Jones. The persons who figured in historical narratives in *Experience and its Modes*, for example, were certainly possessed of continuity (bounded by birth and death), but they had no 'core which [the
historian] supposes to have remained untouched by outward circumstances'.[55] History, as a relation of change, had no room for the
concept of permanent essences.

Even in 1923, Oakeshott saw 'those basic principles of general
method which are common to all philosophy' as themselves the outcome of a process of continual refinement in which philosophy had
become distinguished from natural science and history (though
there was no suggestion of necessity in this progressive development).[56] Another Spinozistic borrowing, the description of philosophy as a view of the world *sub specie aeternitatis* (literally, 'under the
aspect of eternity') familiar from *Experience and its Modes*, seems to
have been introduced here for the first time. What perhaps changed
least in the decade intervening between this essay and the publication of *Experience and its Modes* was the ambitious nature of
Oakeshott's early view of philosophy.

Here, it is described as the attempt 'to formulate a "*theoria*" of the
whole universe . . . a systematic enquiry into the ultimate nature of
Reality'; this is very similar to Oakeshott's presentation of it as the
only possible way of achieving a completely satisfactory view of
experience. What did change, of course, was his view of the place of
the poetic-mystical-religious-intuitive form of experience which he
was contrasting with it. His more restricted view of the latter was to
lead, if anything, to an even more unrestrained view of the power of
philosophy in 1933 than in 1923. Although he would stand by his
claim in this essay that 'Philosophy cannot, without betraying itself,
run into a field, pluck a flower and treasure it as a word of God',[57] he
would no longer have accepted the idea that understanding a flower
as the word of God represented unconditional Reality.

The idea that philosophy seeks the underlying rationale of other
forms of experience, including history, is clearly already present,
though not pursued. Philosophy aims to reduce 'the innumerable
facts of Science and History to a grammar of life'; it seeks 'in these

---

[54] *op. cit.,* p. 8.

[55] *EM*, p. 121.

[56] Oakeshott, 'Philosophy, Poetry, and Reality', pp. 14, 64.

[57] *op. cit.,* p. 27.

principles . . . the one master principle'.[58] His description of philosophy as 'the enemy of life' was still applicable in his later work, in the
sense that he regarded philosophy as destructive of the ideas of practical life. The Spinozistic insistence that 'the natural working of our
intellect is in the mode of geometry'[59] however was later quietly
dropped, but the essentially analytical and classificatory conception
of the philosopher's task, the idea that he simply restates in other
terms what we already know, remained.

The section of this essay on 'Poetry' is Oakeshott's most substantial known statement on aesthetics in the pre-war era. Those interested in this aspect of his thought have previously had to draw
almost entirely on his 1959 essay 'The Voice of Poetry in the Conversation of Mankind'. These youthful reflections provide previously
unavailable insight into how his ideas developed. We have seen that
Oakeshott wished to contrast two ways of understanding reality, the
intellectual and the intuitive. 'Poetry' here is made to stand, as in his
later writings, for all aesthetic experience, because he regarded it as
typical of artistic work at large. But, in contrast with the later essay, it
is also made to embrace much more — not only the usual activities
grouped under the head of artistic endeavour, such as painting,
music, and sculpture, but also, as hinted above, religious and mystical experience, and in fact, 'intuitive' experience generally.

This 'poetic' knowledge, then, does not simply aim at pleasure,
nor does it 'represent' anything. 'The true poet presents us with no
problems, art and propaganda are eternally separated . . . Poetry
does not propagate ideas, but an immediate feeling and intuition or
spirit.'[60] It is an encounter with the essence of reality, which is why
Oakeshott regarded it as ultimately indistinguishable from religion.
The cumulative progress of philosophy through the gradual elimi-
nation of error is foreign to it: reality is apprehended directly and at
once. Oakeshott writes as if there were a world of 'things in themselves' normally hidden to us to which the poet has privileged
access. Poetic 'inspiration comes not from the world as we see it, but
from another world of which ours is but a shadow, to which ours is
but a chaos.'[61] Oakeshott tended to push his claims too far in this
essay. The assertion that 'The poet fails when he does not literally
become what he contemplates' is, when taken at face value, absurd.
Nor is it the only hyperbolic proposition in the essay: the poet takes

[58]   *op. cit.*, p. 18.
[59]   *op. cit.*, p. 19.
[60]   *op. cit.*, p. 31.
[61]   *op. cit.*, p. 33.

on what are explicitly said to be 'priestly' qualities when described as 'a messenger from the realms of gold sent to guide us to our Rest . . . the *point d'appui* between the temporal and the eternal, the finite and the infinite.'[62] Distinctions between various ways of conceiving time were later to become very important in Oakeshott's discussion of the various modes. For example, in historical understanding, the past was liable to change, because it was the outcome of designation and inference, but the practical view of the past tended to see it as fixed and finished.

We should also notice Oakeshott's use of Spinoza's concept of the intellect to limit the powers of rational enquiry. He quoted proposition XXX of the *Ethics* ('Intellect, finite or infinite, in actuality, must comprehend the attributes of God and the modifications of God and nothing else',) to support his argument that philosophy is not capable of unconditional access to Reality. There is of course a real difference between knowing certain facts, such as the height of the Eiffel tower and the date of its construction, for example, and experiencing the view of Paris it provides. Although he was stretching this analogy too far in asking it to support his view of poetry as unconditional knowledge, it may have provided the germ of the distinction he would later make between taking part in an activity and enquiring into its conditions.

The importance of understanding the kind of intellectual task on which one had embarked also loomed large in Oakeshott's essay suggesting how the Political Science papers he had sat for the Historical Tripos might be improved. He had 'looked forward with some eagerness' to the lectures on political science', because he 'desired to know what . . . to think about our life as human beings in society', but in place of 'some guidance in the maze of the *Contrat Social*' by 'the much abused Rousseau', he was 'put off with the difference of the internal organization between the states of the South and those of the Middle West of the U.S.A., and some statistics about Proportional Representation.'[63]

Instead of learning about Spinoza, Berkeley, and St Paul (regarded by Oakeshott at this time as 'perhaps the greatest political philosopher'), he complained, he had been subjected to a disappointing mixture of the comparative study of governmental institutions, anthropology ('the social organization of the Hottentots and Melanesians',) and 'the glories of the historical method'. He seems to have meant by the latter the attempt to create a 'purely inductive sci-

[62]   *op. cit.*, pp. 36, 42.

[63]   Oakeshott, 'Cambridge School', p. 5.

ence' of politics based on a view of history as 'simply a mass of facts,' which J.R. Seeley had championed at Cambridge.[64] The results of this method certainly entailed little sensitivity to anachronism, if Oakeshott was not exaggerating when he claimed to have been told that Plato was a Whig and a Puritan.

The lack of a clear conception of what kind of a 'science' political science was supposed to be reflected competing conceptions of the subject within the University itself. Ideas like Seeley's had been firmly rejected by F.W. Maitland in *The Body Politic*, and Oakeshott explicitly followed him. He rejected the idea of history as 'simply a mass of facts out of which a science of political facts arises'[65] which he claimed was implied by inductive political science. He also rejected the applicability of the methods of the 'exact' or natural sciences in political science; if it were to be described as a science at all, it was a moral science, dealing in meanings, not facts. When Oakeshott rejected the applicability of the methods of natural science to historical enquiry in *Experience and its Modes*, then, the distinction between the moral and the natural sciences had already been available to him for around a decade.

Political science as taught at Cambridge also left key terms, such as 'politics' and 'state', totally lacking in definition. An obsession with the outward forms of institutions had led to an unthinking identification of the state with the government. Until the all-embracing character of the problem of the state was recognised as permeating every area of the life of man, as 'the study of the nature and meaning of human association and the principles that underlie it',[66] any meaningful criticism of the most satisfactory theory of the state, namely the Idealist theory, was impossible.

What was needed was a political philosophy which could identify a concept of 'the State' which remained 'in essence entirely unchanged amid the metamorphoses of form and outward appearance'.[67] Such ideal models, Oakeshott later decided, were restricted to philosophy; they had no place in history, where change was a fundamental postulate. This change was due, at least in part, to his conception of philosophy containing the means of self-criticism. His understanding of philosophy as 'the critical examination of conceptions' which searches out their 'logical necessity' and 'coherence'[68]

---

[64] *op. cit.,* p. 8.

[65] *op. cit.,* p. 8.

[66] *op. cit.,* p. 26.

[67] *op. cit.,* p. 16.

[68] *op. cit.,* p. 21.

had the potential to be turned back on his own ideas. Even at this stage Oakeshott firmly distinguished philosophy from both the moral and historical sciences. Quoting Lord Balfour, he insisted on the difference between the search for the logical grounds of an idea and its causes, physical or historical.[69] To neglect this difference inevitably resulted in confusion, another point we will see emphasised over and over again in *Experience and its Modes*.

Oakeshott's essay on the reform of the Tripos included a brief outline of 'the History of Political Science — the history of man's struggle to think rightly about his relation to his fellow creatures'.[70] According to this, there had been three major periods in the history of political thought. The first, the era of Socrates, Plato, and Aristotle, ended with the ancient world. The second began with the 'rebirth' of 'true reflective thought' at the Renaissance, in the work of thinkers such as Machiavelli, Hobbes, and Spinoza. The third and final 'great epoch of political theorizing' was 'that engendered by Rousseau, the tide of whose thought has not yet spent itself'. The way in which this history was to be taught was also important. To ignore the times in which these thinkers lived was as a mistake, but here too, it was important to deal with context in the right way, not simply as a set of isolated facts about an age, but as 'an account of facts in relation to one another'. History, Oakeshott declared, 'cannot be intelligibly narrated except with an ever recurring reference to those elements of thought and action which, running through the whole length and breadth of it, bind it together.'[71]

There are obvious similarities here with the argument Oakeshott later put forward that the historian 'accounts for change by means of a full account of change.'[72] However, there are also some important differences. Because Oakeshott distinguished at this early period between the contexts or conventions of life, including language itself, and the thoughts of which such conventions were merely expressions, the historian's task became one of penetrating through appearances to the reality. The argument that 'History must pluck aside conventions, value them truly and not abuse them, for its concern is with the story, not of forms, but of "real things"' was one he would later reject. There was, he would come to think, no 'golden chain of "real things" binding together all thought and life', no great chain of being waiting to be uncovered.

---

[69] *op. cit.*, p. 22.

[70] *op. cit.*, p. 17.

[71] *op. cit.*, p. 29.

[72] *EM*, p. 143.

It is not so clear whether Oakeshott changed his mind on another of the suggestions he made, that the Political Science papers should help to satisfy the desire of the undergraduate for 'sound guidance about that aspect of life which is common to all — life as the citizen of a state, as a man among men'. On the face of it, his assertion that 'we are citizens of a country, members of a community, and there can be no study so intimately connected with our life as this we call Political Philosophy' seems to directly contradict his later insistence that political philosophy (as well as history) was incapable of generating practical policy. However, Oakeshott also stated that 'from history, on the whole, we can infer only what has been, and not what will be'; in fact, what he had in mind was that 'education of personality . . . alone will avail to guide aright that continuing effort we call social reform.'[73] This could be said to be a belief he never lost; study of 'liberal arts' such as philosophy and history benefited society in indirect ways, through enlarging the imagination and understanding. The aim of creating 'a wiser generation of citizens and leaders' through education is a far cry from a political or historical science that is to guide social engineering.

'A Discussion of Some Matters Preliminary to the Study of Political Philosophy' built on the conception of philosophy as the search for definitions of the real essences of things developed in the essay on philosophy and poetry, and on the demand for such a definition of 'The State' expressed in his essay on political science at Cambridge. The essay displays a continued fondness for Spinozistic rationalism, common in Romantics and Idealists generally in the nineteenth century. This even permeated Oakeshott's theological writings — 'God is the life of Reason', he wrote elsewhere in the same year.[74] This Spinozism, fused with Hegelianism and Platonism, lay behind his quest for a set of definitions which could provide the starting point for 'systematic thought' about politics. A quotation from the *Phaedrus*, that 'those who would deliberate well . . . must know what the thing is on which they are deliberating' was placed at the head of the opening page.[75]

The problem Oakeshott confronted, against the background of a society indelibly marked by the experience of total warfare, was how to reconcile the apparently contradictory claims of 'the state' and 'the self'. In typical Idealist fashion, he attempted to do so by arguing

[73]   Oakeshott, 'Cambridge School', pp. 33–4.
[74]   Oakeshott, *Religion, Politics and the Moral Life*, ed. T. Fuller, Yale UP, New Haven, p. 60
[75]   Oakeshott, 'Political Philosophy', pp. 1, 3, 11.

that the two may be understood as different aspects of a single
whole. The whole discussion was couched in terms of reconciling
the individual with the general will. Hegel, Rousseau, and
Bosanquet, Oakeshott believed, had all dealt with this problem. The
resolution, he claimed, was to be found in the 'real will' of the self
that is truly individual, the hallmark of which is that it 'wills the universal' — this 'universal', of course, being identified with the state.[76]

Virtually all of the 'couple of hundred pretending explanations
and definitions of the State' which Oakeshott had collected confused
'the real and essential quality of statehood with a particular manifestation'. Burke, Bosanquet, Hegel and de Stael were practically the
only thinkers who had managed to approximate Oakeshott's own
notion of an ideal definition of the state. They were to be praised for
their recognition that the essence of the state is its spiritual unity.[77]
Two of the most prominent targets of criticism were Laski and
L.T. Hobhouse, the first Professor of Sociology in Britain (at the LSE)
from 1907 until his death in 1929. Oakeshott was unimpressed by
their attempts to use the new discipline of sociology in place of his
own metaphysical approach to politics. Laski, in Oakeshott's opinion, fell into the trap of 'using a criterion suitable for testing a practical program in order to prove a theoretic position'. As for 'Mr
Hobhouse', Oakeshott wrote, 'he thinks he has put forward a real
objection to the Hegelian theory of the State' simply by saying that 'it
turned the edge of the principle of freedom, by identifying freedom
with law.'[78] The opposition of liberty and law put forward here by
the 'New Liberal' Hobhouse became a central concern of
Oakeshott's writings on the history of political thought. He came to
believe the reverse, that Hegel's identification of them was the most
important element in the history of 'liberal' thought.

At the same time, Oakeshott had considerable sympathy for the
political pluralism the pre-Marxist Laski represented. In a striking
passage which recalls his schoolboy belief in the end of capitalism,
he talked of a 'new movement'. In the course of arguing that 'law
and statute must no longer be considered as mere arbitrary commands . . . but as subordinate to the State — society — to serve its
needs', Oakeshott described Laski, together with Durkheim, Pound
and Duguit, as pioneers of a 'sociological interpretation of law'. The
'new movement' which lay behind this sociological interpretation,

---

[76] Cp. Bosanquet's chapters on 'The Conception of a "Real Will"' and 'The
Analysis of a Modern State: Hegel's *Philosophy of Right*', in *The Philosophical
Theory of the State*, and LSE 1/1/3, pp. 137–8.
[77] Oakeshott, 'Political Philosophy', pp. 93–4, 183.
[78] *op. cit.*, pp. 185–6, 188.

he predicted, 'will succeed (while attempting to put a too-exalted so-called "state" in its place) in saying to government and the petty political faiths and interests of modern Europe, "Give place", and relegating it to its proper position, will allow the true "state" to take its place as sovereign.'[79]

Oakeshott's outburst against a false or perverted conception of the state which had come to dominate in modern Europe and his hope of an imminent radical transformation of this situation indicates a youthful character quite different to that of the older man. In letters he wrote late in life, Oakeshott recalled being a patriotic boy, who tried to run away and join the navy at age twelve and cycled round England to swim in all her rivers.[80] World War One, which filled the later years of Oakeshott's adolescence, does not seem to have shaken this patriotism, although older boys from his school lost their lives overseas.

In 1925, Oakeshott could still write that 'We cannot refuse to acknowledge something real in the impulsive love of country and countryside which plays so great a part in the life of most of us', and go on to quote Coleridge. In his first treatise on politics he argued that 'In times of crisis . . . the degree of statehood possessed by an association will be abnormally great'. He claimed that on these grounds 'England in 1914 was more of a state than she was during the great industrial strikes of 1911-12'.[81] Oakeshott's love of the Eng-lish countryside and of the outdoor life survived into the 1930s and beyond, but his belief that wartime was the time at which a state was most fully like itself did not. In 1931 he praised the way in which a novelist had captured 'the atmosphere of England' in 1914, now understanding those days as a time of 'growing barbarousness' with 'the smell of blood in the air'.[82]

Oakeshott's hope for an Actualisation of the Real, Ideal State could be attributed to the same optimism which led him to hope for a 'religious revival' in the later 1920s. But at a deeper level, his ambig-uous combination of an insistence that a philosophical theory of the state must remain solely within the ideal realm of reason with the hope of an ideal transformation of practical politics might be thought to reflect a deeper ambiguity within the Idealist tradition itself. Green and Bosanquet, for example, had not kept their own

[79]   *op. cit.,* pp. 168–9.

[80]   Oakeshott, Letter to N.K. O'Sullivan, 9 February 1987, private collection.

[81]   *ML,* p. 61, and Oakeshott, 'Political Philosophy', p. 78.

[82]   Oakeshott, Review of L. Britton, *Love and Hunger, Cambridge Review,* vol. 52, 1931, p. 351.

political philosophies separate from their practical reforming activities.[83] Barker recognised Green as heir to the utilitarianism of
Bentham and J.S. Mill, not least because of his belief that the one
thing necessary was for 'The State [to] liberate [the] energies [of the
good will] by removing obstacles to action'.[84] Perhaps because of
this tension, Oakeshott concluded his 1925 work unsatisfied. 'I have .
. . failed,' he declared, 'to get a clearer view of the real nature of political philosophy.' He was perhaps unduly self-critical when he
claimed that the entire piece lacked 'any real unity of treatment,' but
we may agree that it was 'by no means free from internal contradiction'.[85]

Religion

Oakeshott was a practicing Christian as a young man, and had been
Chapel clerk as an undergraduate at Caius.[86] In the latter part of the
1920s, he began reviewing for *The Journal of Theological Studies* and
The Modern Churchman, and helped J. Needham to edit a collection of
essays debating the relations of *Science, Religion and Reality*. He
became a member of the 'D' Society, which still survives as a society
for undergraduate theological discussion at Cambridge, and later
described the participants as 'theological modernists'. Another
member of the society, J.S. Boys Smith, a theologian at Cambridge
and a friend of Oakeshott's, recalled that the aim of the society in
those days was to study the 'Doctrine of the Church of England in
the light of knowledge acquired since its formularies were
compiled.'[87]

The nature of Oakeshott's 'Theological modernism' must be
understood in the light of the nineteenth century attack on the 'historical basis of Christian belief' by 'Hegelian-inspired Biblical critics
of the so-called Tübingen school, particularly Baur and David
Strauss.'[88] Oakeshott's response to what has been called 'The Victorian obsession with the historical Jesus'[89] was to separate Christian-

---

[83] For the ways in which the philosophy of Green and Bosanquet affected political
and social practice see A. Vincent and R. Plant, *Philosophy, Politics and
Citizenship: The Life and Thought of the British Idealists*, Blackwell, Oxford, 1984.

[84] Barker, *op. cit.*, pp. 10–11, 59–60, 32.

[85] Oakeshott, 'Political Philosophy', pp. 192–4.

[86] Letter of reference from the Dean, LSE 6/1.

[87] For Oakeshott's membership of the 'D' Society in the 1920s see T. Fuller,
'Introduction' to *ML*, p. 4.

[88] Vincent and Plant, *Philosophy, Politics and Citizenship*, p. 7.

[89] M. Cowling, *Religion and Public Doctrine in Modern England*, vol. 1, Cambridge
UP, Cambridge, 1980, p. 265.

ity and history in the hope of preserving both. In the nineteenth century, he wrote, 'all intellectual effort had a tendency to run to history, and the reading of history became itself a means of grace and even a religion', as he believed it had for Troeltsch and Schweitzer. There had arisen a faith in history, in 'an ideal of *wie es eigentlich gewesen*', which was 'little better than an illusion'. This was not an attack, of course, on that ideal in historical scholarship, but on a thoroughly 'practical' ideal which believed in 'history' as a redemptive process.[90]

Thus, Oakeshott's essays on religion introduced several themes which permeate his later writings on both senses of 'history'. With regard to history in the sense of 'enquiry', 'Religion and the Moral Life' (read to the 'D' Society in October 1927 and subsequently published as a pamphlet) developed the idea of religion as a form of 'practical' activity, which Oakeshott would distinguish (in *Experience and its Modes*) from the activity of historical enquiry. 'The Historical Element in Christianity' also dealt with this relation of practical Christian belief to the past of historical enquiry. As for 'events', 'Religion and the World' introduced the characters of the religious and the worldly man, significant precursors of the characters of the individual and the anti-individual in Oakeshott's later writings on the history of politics and morals.

'Religion and the Moral Life' addressed the question of whether Christianity and the morality of what Oakeshott called 'our civilisation' (leaving open whether it was English, British, European or Western civilisation which was meant) were compatible or not. As in 1923, he drew heavily on F.H. Bradley's view of 'religion as the completion of morality'. By itself, he argued, 'morality is self-contradictory and so . . . abstract'. The self-contradiction stemmed from the fact that 'out of every moral success the further 'ought' springs up to condemn you once more: it is a series without an end.' Religion, by contrast, demands that the ideal shall not lie always ahead, but that it should be realised in the present. 'What in morality was a mere "should be" in religion becomes an "is".' Rather than there being a 'gulf . . . fixed between what we call civilisation and Christian morality', Oakeshott concluded, 'our civilisation' is largely the product of Christianity, as is 'our changing morality'.[91] This conception of a world of practical needs, of which religion was a part, distinct from philosophy, science, and, Oakeshott would conclude, history, displays a shift from Oakeshott's 1923 essay on philosophy and poetry.

[90] *ML., p. 69.*

[91] *ML*, pp. 41–2, 45.

It is much closer to the description in *Experience and its Modes* of the practical mode of experience.

Another essay of importance for understanding Oakeshott's later writings on historical enquiry is 'The Historical Element in Christianity'. Oakeshott set out to criticise the idea that 'a belief in the necessity of that which is *prima facie* historical', that is, in the atonement, was essential to Christianity. He argued that 'Christianity has been identified with either the whole original Christianity, which is held to include this particular belief [in the atonement]; or with a central core, of which this particular belief is a part, which has remained unchanged throughout the history of our religion'. He regarded both views as mistaken.[92] For Oakeshott, the belief in the necessity of an event or events in time was itself historical, part of the Hebraic inheritance of Christianity. Such a belief was justified insofar as it helped to satisfy the 'felt need for an almost sensible perception of the object of belief' which was a foundation of the religious impulse. It was of no value in itself. Oakeshott claimed that there was no 'essential core' to the Christian religion, arguing that belief in the necessity of events in past time drew 'an arbitrary line . . . across the change and variety of the process of history, and identity is denied merely at the point at which some little education is required to recognise it.'[93]

In this fashion, Oakeshott introduced an explanation of historical identity and change that was of great importance in his philosophy of historical understanding. Historical identity, he argued, consisted in 'a kind of qualitative sameness', so that 'identity, so far from excluding differences, is meaningless in their absence.' The identity of Christianity, for example, lies 'first, in the avoidance of any absolute break in [its] existence, and, beyond that and governing that, in some qualitative element to be discovered only by reference to its character', that unquantifiable concept. This argument pointed to a radical conclusion — that 'the characteristic of being Christian may properly be claimed by any doctrine, idea or practice which, no matter whence it came, has been or can be drawn into the general body of the Christian tradition without altogether disturbing its unity or breaking down its consistency'. Oakeshott did not hesitate to grasp the nettle and embrace this very catholic conception of Christianity. The ability of Christianity to 'give actuality to the believed', he concluded, need by no means rely on history.[94]

---

[92]   *ML*, p. 64.

[93]   *op. cit.*, pp. 65, 71.

[94]   *op. cit.*, p. 67.

Christianity's relationship to personality was as problematic for Oakeshott as its relationship to history. For example, he criticised William James's pragmatist identification of the self with the body, arguing that selfhood was not a quality of discrete physical units. Rather, the self depended on other selves. 'A self not only requires its society, but in its fullest sense, is its society'. Similarly, a 'state' was more than a collection of selves in close physical proximity. Associates in a state, he agreed with Aristotle, were joined by a tie of friendship. This view that personal identity involved participation in a larger whole was presented as part of a metaphysical thesis, in which the self was said to be a mirror in miniature of the universe itself. Finite actual selves presupposed such a higher unity, he argued.

Stripped of these metaphysical beliefs, this view of the self would form part of a contextual attitude to historical understanding in which individuals are seen in relation to their own time and place. Moreover, it allowed a dynamic conception of selfhood, which now replaced Oakeshott's earlier view of the self as a permanent substance. He quoted Bradley's remark in *Appearance and Reality* that 'the ego which pretends to be anything either before or beyond its concrete filling is a gross fiction' in support of this point.[95]

Oakeshott was as concerned to give content to the religious self as he was to specify its form. In 'Religion and the World,' he embodied the various dispositions he considered virtuous in the character of the religious man. On this occasion he was interpreting James i.27, 'pure religion is to keep unspotted from the world',[96] and rejected, in effect, 'the Calvinistic conception of the world as a veil between man and God and between the religious and the moral life.'[97] As Fuller has noted, 'Oakeshott marks the tendency in Christianity from the beginning to dichotomise the world.'[98] The character of the religious man was intended to resolve this dualism.

This character is an ancestor of Oakeshott's 'individual', with whose emergence he believed the history of the modern world began. The place of the religious man in history, like that of the individual, is in the modern period. He is defined in part by a contrast with his opposite, the worldly man, a character who subscribes to an 'external standard of value ... what is prized is success, meaning the achievement of some external result', a criterion of value already

---

[95] Oakeshott, 'Political Philosophy', pp. 111, 127, 129, 131, 133 n. 1.

[96] *ML*, p. 27.

[97] Cowling, *op. cit.*, p. 264.

[98] Fuller, 'Introduction' to *ML*.

rejected by Oakeshott in his essay on Acton. This worldling is in the grip both of the 'withering hand' of the future, 'the Moloch to which the present is sacrificed' and of the past — he is a slave to 'history and tradition' on the one hand and a 'career' on the other. The 'religious man' will have nothing to do with all this. He desires an 'extemporary life' and he amply fulfils the criterion of character which Oakeshott had put forth in his essay on Shylock. That is to say, in the event of necessity he can stand alone.[99]

To realise the character of the religious man would require a 'religious revival' that would have a transforming effect. It would mean 'an end to the vulgar mass called "work" . . . "things done" would cease to have any value in their result, but only insofar as they could prove themselves of worth as elements in the present experience of the most permanent and stable thing in life — our selves'[100] There is some justification for seeing in this dislike of the 'middle-class passion for safety' the attitude of a 'bohemian' or 'lily of the field'. Yet it is right to recognise also that this was a 'serious-natured' essay.[101] As in his early writings on politics, Oakeshott expressed a strong preference for non-instrumental values in delineating the (moral) character of which he approved. If we are not to 'make humanity a Sisyphus and its life the pointless trundling of a useless stone', we must appreciate that life is lived in the present, and that 'the most important thing is to preserve, at all costs, our integrity of character'.[102]

Contemporary European Politics

From 1928, Oakeshott assumed a more active role in the teaching of history at Cambridge. As a young lecturer, he was apparently 'something of a dandy,' known for appearing before his audience 'in a yellow velvet jacket with a red rose pinned to the lapel'.[103] The charismatic powers of oratory which were so well attested to during his days at the LSE, where Oakeshott indulged his penchant for drama by finding 'a mysterious back entrance that enabled him to appear through the curtain behind the lectern, greeted each time by

---

[99] *ML*, pp. 35–7.

[100] *Ibid.*, pp. 31–2.

[101] Grant, *TLS* Review, p. 31.

[102] *ML*, p. 34.

[103] J.L. Auspitz in Norman, *op. cit.*, p. 3.

a storm of applause', had obviously been honed earlier on.[104] His raffish image acquired a new dimension when he followed the publication of *Experience and its Modes* with a work called *A Guide to the Classics*, which had nothing to say about Greeks and Romans. Subtitled *How to Pick the Derby Winner*, it was a betting manual that he co-authored with another Cambridge don, Guy Griffith.

Whether or not his dress sense and love of the turf had anything to do with it, Oakeshott's lectures became famous at Cambridge. One who heard them recalled that Oakeshott 'had a deep influence in Cambridge . . . through his lectures, which sparkled and glittered and lit up the patterns of the past.' This listener even ventured to suggest that 'together with M.M. Postan and H. Butterfield', Oakeshott was to the generation of the 1940s what such prominent figures as 'J.H. Plumb, Geoffrey Elton and Owen Chadwick were to the 1950s and 1960s'.[105] Herbert Butterfield, for instance, made Oakeshott's acquaintance in the 1920s as a housemate and fellow graduate student. Both were members of the Cambridge Junior Historians Society, which, like the 'D' society, still survives. The society was an initiative of J.H. Clapham, who was too old to be a member himself. In 1929, Oakeshott and Butterfield both resigned, apparently 'in protest at the refusal of the seniors to withdraw', but by 1931, the exclusion of those over 40 having been secured, both had returned to the fold.[106] They also shared an interest in religion, and it is even said that Oakeshott deferred to Butterfield's knowledge of theology in the 1920s.[107]

For the first two years Oakeshott lectured only in the Lent term, offering a twice weekly course on 'The Philosophical Approach to Politics'; now in the LSE archives, they are similar in approach to 'A Discussion of Some Matters Preliminary to the Study of Political Philosophy'.[108] Reviews Oakeshott wrote in this period also suggest that he was still attached to an Idealist political philosophy based on the idea of an 'ethical or metaphysical' General Will.[109] Between 1930 and 1932 Oakeshott offered courses on 'The Philosophical Back-

---

[104] For Oakeshott's LSE lectures see N.K. O'Sullivan, 'Obituary', *The Independent*, 22 December 1990.

[105] Oakeshott's Cambridge lectures are described in Brooke, *History of the University of Cambridge*, p. 327.

[106] For Oakeshott's membership of the Junior Historians Society see Brooke, *op. cit.*, p. 236.

[107] Professor Skinner (another Caian) in conversation.

[108] For this lecture course see LSE 1/1/7.

[109] Oakeshott, Review of J.S. MacKenzie, *Fundamental Problems of Life*, *Journal of Philosophical Studies*, vol. 4, 1929, p. 265.

ground of Political Thought in the Nineteenth Century', 'Idealist Political Thought', and 'The Philosophical Background of Utilitarian Political Thought'. In October 1931, his appointment was announced as a probationary Faculty Lecturer, listed below the appointment of one L. Wittgenstein (PhD, Trinity) to the Moral Sciences Faculty.[110]

Oakeshott was obviously not the only person to have been dissatisfied with the teaching of politics at Cambridge, because when Barker became Professor he had reformed the course in very much the manner Oakeshott had suggested, introducing papers on 'The Theory of the Modern State' and 'The History of Political Thought'. Having complained about the way the course was taught, Oakeshott now had to teach it himself, which he did between 1932 and 1948-9, the last year he spent at Cambridge. In particular, we may regret the apparent loss of the lectures he gave on 'Hegel and Marx' in Lent 1934, on 'The Political Theory of Karl Marx' in 1937-8, and 'Some Currents in Medieval and Modern Political Theory' in 1945-6.[111]

A 1932 essay on 'John Locke' written for the tercentenary of his birth contrasted Locke's 'moderate individualism' and 'steady love of liberty' with a Montaigne-like 'radical individualism'. It was 'the Locke who was in at the birth of the Whig party and who provided liberalism with its gospel and creed' who attracted Oakeshott's attention. Although Locke was not to be credited with the invention of liberalism, he was the 'filter by means of which Puritanism was drained of its immoderation and "enthusiasm" and was converted into what the eighteenth century knew as Whiggism and the nineteenth century as liberalism.' More important for our purposes than the historical truth of this view is Oakeshott's opinion that Lockean liberalism in the 1930s was 'dead', and that he appeared to welcome its demise.

Locke, to Oakeshott, had been 'the apostle of the liberalism which is more conservative than conservatism itself . . . which has a horror of extremes, which lays its paralysing hand of respectability upon whatever is dangerous or revolutionary.'[112] The chance to transform this liberalism 'under the stimulus of the romantic movement . . . into something less boring and upholstered' had been missed, and in 1932 'Democracy, parliamentary government, progress, discussion and "the plausible ethics of productivity"' were 'not merely absurd and exploded' but 'uninteresting'. This dismissal of 'parliamentary

---

[110] *CUR*, 2 October 1931.

[111] Lecture lists published in *CUR*, 1928–48.

[112] Oakeshott, 'John Locke', *Cambridge Review*, vol. 54, 1932, pp. 72–3.

government' must, of course, be viewed in the light of the fact that
Oakeshott knew from Maitland if nowhere else that parliaments, or
at any rate English parliaments, were older than Puritanism. Moreover, he was entirely typical in pronouncing the death of liberalism
in the 1930s. A mood of disillusion, even despair, had followed the
disappointment of hopes for a more peaceful world and a better society after 1918.[113] The depression, the collapse of the post-war democratic regimes and the rise of Fascism, National Socialism and
Communism, all contributed to what Oakeshott saw as a widespread revolt against the legacy of Locke and 'so-called Victorian-
ism'.

We should not, then, accept Oakeshott's criticisms entirely at face
value. He summarised the 'message of Locke's philosophy' as 'the
view that it is equally unwarrantable either to doubt everything or to
make extravagant claims on behalf of the human mind.' One might
be forgiven, on reading *Experience and its Modes*, for forming the
impression that this was also the message of Oakeshott's own philosophy. His description of Locke as attempting to determine 'the
limits of human understanding' might equally apply to the
post-Kantian enterprise he himself was engaged in. Indeed, despite
the 'dangerous mixture [of] common-sense and philosophy' which
Oakeshott found in Locke, whose 'colloquial use of the word "experience" resulted in an ambiguity which rends his philosophy from
end to end', he was far from wholly dismissive. He acknowledged
Locke as 'a genuine, perhaps a great, philosopher', on account of his
modesty and independence of mind.

In the same year, Oakeshott wrote a review essay for the centenary
of the death of Jeremy Bentham, defending J.S. Mill's verdict that
Bentham's significance lay in his influence on the Victorian reformers of English law against the new view that Bentham had also made
an important but neglected contribution to philosophy. Bentham's
utilitarianism was conventionally regarded at this time as a lineal
descendent of Lockean ideas,[114] so it is not surprising that Oakeshott
treated him as a major figure in the history of the kind of 'liberalism'
he believed was currently under attack. However, he also
emphasised Bentham's connections with the French Enlightenment.
Bentham was a 'creature of the eighteenth century . . . the companion
in thought of Helvetius, Diderot, Voltaire and D'Alembert', the

[113] J. Stevenson, *British Society 1914–45*, Penguin, London, 1984, p. 414.

[114] According to W.L. Davidson in 1915, 'Utilitarianism . . . accepted the English
    tradition, going back to Locke' and including 'Hume, Bentham, the Mills, Bain':
    see W.L. Davidson, *Political Thought in England: The Utilitarians from Bentham to
    Mill*, Thornton-Butterworth, London, 1915, pp. 15–26.

same French *philosophes* for whom Lockean epistemology had held
such an attraction. As a *philosophe* (Oakeshott blended Bentham
together with this new character so that the two gradually became
indistinguishable) Bentham was credulous. He 'begins with a whole
miscellany of presuppositions which he has neither the time, nor the
inclination, nor the ability to examine'. In fact, he is a rationalist
(Oakeshott's Rationalist of the post-war years owes more than a little
to the *philosophe*) 'in the restricted sense that he believes that what is
made is better than what merely grows'. It was not that this disposition was not admirable, but, like the Christian belief in the necessity
of historical events, it was justified only by the 'sense of life' which it
engendered in those who possessed it.[115]

Somewhat ironically, given that he had portrayed Bentham as an
exemplification of a type, Oakeshott commented in a 1934 review of
Barker's translation of Gierke, *Natural Law and the Theory of Society*
that 'The difficulty and the danger in composing a history of political
ideas lies in the fact that it is almost impossible not to de-individual-
ise the writers who come under review,' as 'each tends to be represented as an example (with, of course, certain peculiar traits) of a
general idea or theory'. Though he found *Das deutsche
Genossenschaftsrecht* 'impressive', he thought Gierke had fallen into
this trap. Gierke rightly argued that Hobbes or Rousseau, for example, could not be understood apart from 'the background of Natural
Law theorists in which they appear to take their place', but
Oakeshott emphasised that 'while a writer like Hobbes may reach
conclusions which place him along with others in a "school," his reasons and conclusions may be so unlike those of other writers that to
think of him as a member of a "school" may be seriously misleading.' He reiterated the caution he had made in discussing Bentham,
that 'when we come to consider what a man actually thought, it is
not [his] bare ideas which are important, but the grounds and reasons for them . . . the *ratio decidendi*'. It was the reasoning Hobbes
used to support his conclusions that set him apart from his contemporaries. We must be aware, Oakeshott insisted, that '"Schools" of
thought are classifications of beliefs, and these, when they cut across
a classification of reasons for belief, must present us with an imperfect view.'[116]

In his introduction to Gierke's work, Barker had outlined his own
view of the relation between 'Society and the State'. Barker, like

---

[115] *RP*, pp. 137–9.

[116] Oakeshott, Review of O. Gierke, *Natural Law and the Theory of Society*, *Cambridge
Review*, vol. 56, 1934, pp. 11–12.

Gierke an admirer of Hegel, attempted to qualify the organic unity of the state on which Gierke placed so much weight. Gierke, following members of the nineteenth century German school of Historical Law such as Savigny, tended to see 'law as the historic product of the folk-mind', and had promoted this view in areas which went far beyond scholarship. In Germany, Gierke had 'plunged into the busy war of ideas which attended the construction of the German civil code' in order, in his own words, 'to penetrate [it] with a German spirit'. Barker saw Gierke's tendency to exalt the real personality of the Germanic Fellowship as part of a tradition which extended back to the Romanticism of the late eighteenth century and which 'had risen to a *fluctus decumanus* in this year of grace 1933' with the rise of Hitler to power.[117]

Oakeshott was not happy with the answers either Barker or Gierke had proposed to the problem of the relation between the individual, society or the group, and the state. He thought Gierke's attempt to replace 'the individualistic foundation upon which the whole Natural Law theory of Society was constructed' with a doctrine of the real personality of groups lacked 'the power of a fully thought out theory'. But he was just as dissatisfied by Barker's efforts. He criticised Barker's view of State and Society as two separate entities, the former supervening on the latter without eliminating it, on the grounds that it simply reproduced 'the seventeenth century notion that when man entered political society he surrendered, not the whole, but a part of his natural rights.'

This was a mistake Oakeshott associated with a 'Lockean' strain of individualism, and it is significant that as early as 1934 he had declared that 'it is a notion from which Hobbes might have rescued us if we had listened to him.' Despite his conclusion that 'Our political theory ... is still under the domination ... of the categories of seventeenth century thinkers ... which nobody has yet shown us how to replace', it was to the author of *Leviathan* that he was beginning to look for ideas.[118] Stapleton justly observes that the differences between Oakeshott and Barker are 'well reflected in their choice of early modern heroes; while Barker followed Locke's route to the limited state, Oakeshott took the more unconventional path of Hobbes'.[119]

---

[117] See the 'Introduction' to O. Gierke, *Natural Law and the Theory of Society*, ed. E. Barker, Cambridge UP, Cambridge, 1950, pp. xviii, liii–liv.

[118] Oakeshott, Review of Gierke, *loc. cit.*

[119] Stapleton, *Englishness and the Study of Politics*, p. 145.

Oakeshott did agree with Barker that Hitler's rise to power in 1933 had to be explained in the light of German history. In a lecture on 'National Socialism', he remarked that 'No other nation has produced anything quite like the literature of self-assertion and self-admiration as Germany. From Fichte onwards it has been pouring from the German printing presses. *Mein Kampf* . . . easily sinks into its [context]'. More recent events, such as the rise of a middle class, 'the average of humanity when it has escaped the tyranny of need . . . ruled mainly by . . . fear of sinking back into the proletariat and hope . . . of rising' had also played a part. When middle class savings were lost in the inflation experienced under the Weimar Republic, National Socialism 'could provide what a fearful and leaderless German middle class could understand'. But 'the crisis did not produce the leaders and their doctrine', for Hitler had formulated much of his program as early as 1920. Rather, 'the leaders and the doctrine appointed themselves beforehand and when the crisis came they . . . made themselves indispensable.'[120]

Hitler's Germany provided Oakeshott with an example of a government which was not engaged in maintaining a 'system of private law' composed of 'reciprocal rights between individuals' (the characteristic of 'liberal democratic' government) but in establishing duties 'between individuals and the state' by command. National Socialism had replaced law by will. Hitler's anti-Semitic racial doctrines (Oakeshott was lecturing after the passage of the Nuremberg race laws) and the insistence on 'pure German blood' were to be understood in this light. 'Here, if anywhere, is in the making what Nietzsche called the barbarian of the twentieth century', he told his audience.[121]

In a lecture series accompanying the documentary reader Oakeshott edited on *The Social and Political Doctrines of Contemporary Europe*, he argued that there had been three trends at work in post-Renaissance Europe. These were secularism, the rise of the nation-state, and the breakdown of rationalism 'and the substitution for it of a philosophy of relativism of one sort or another.'[122] National Socialism pushed them all to extremes. Nationalism, for example, became the doctrine of race. What National Socialism had introduced, Oakeshott argued, was not the spirit of spontaneous associa-

---

[120] Oakeshott, 'National Socialism (I)', unpublished lecture, c. 1936, private collection, p. 3.

[121] Oakeshott, 'National Socialism (II)', unpublished lecture, c. 1936, private collection, p. 3.

[122] Oakeshott, introductory lecture on 'The Social and Political Doctrines of Contemporary Europe', LSE 1/1/10.

tion Gierke had desired in which the group, 'the people', took on a life of its own but a new tribalism, 'with its ban on marriage outside and ban on any sort of communication with what is outside the tribe'.

National Socialism also pushed the modern tendency towards secularism to its limits. There was a sense in which National Socialism did not seem to be a wholly secular doctrine, for 'as in syndicalism and Fascism,' there is an attempt to provide something more 'heroic' than the merely material, 'commercial' ideals which it attributed to democracy and socialism. This, however, was not the whole of the matter for Oakeshott. Previously 'a criticism and a modification of the religious outlook which considered man to have a known destiny beyond this world; Secularism in National Socialism has become, what it was fast becoming elsewhere, a religion in itself. The destiny of the individual is considered not in terms of his immortal life, or of his earthly life, but of the life of the race to which he belongs.' Nazism was destructive of individuality precisely because it shared in the 'empty and foolish' modern 'ideal [of] the domination and rule of this world for its own sake.' We need hardly point out the influence Oakeshott's earlier writings on religion had on his criticisms of National Socialism.[123]

The third tendency at work in modern Europe, scepticism or relativism, had reached 'the apotheosis of irrationality' in Germany. Whereas 'reason is integral in liberal democratic belief' and even Marx believed 'in the use of intelligence in settling the idea of a society', National Socialism and Fascism constituted 'an absolute repudiation of reason in all the forms known to Western European civilisation'. Hitler and his followers did not care that their doctrines were 'in direct contradiction of what is known to be the [historical and scientific] truth'. Truth, in fact, had been 'made subordinate to force'. 'Nothing is valid against the dictates of national and racial prejudice.' To the Nazi, indeed, 'reason is merely a liberal-democratic perversion of nature.'

Oakeshott rejected the economic interpretation of the historical genesis of National Socialism and Fascism, which he ascribed in particular to Communism. Their rise to power was not to be understood as 'Economic Imperialism [or] capitalism playing its last card.' While Oakeshott believed the Communists were right in thinking that 'big industrial interests' had backed Hitler in the early years of his regime, he argued that 'from their own point of view, the industrial capitalists backed the wrong horse.' There has been endless

[123] Oakeshott, 'National Socialism (II)'.

debate ever since 1933 over the extent to which big business did in fact aid Hitler's bid for power, but we are not called on to decide that here. Our interest is in Oakeshott's reasons for rejecting the Communist interpretation of history.

The 'ordinary Capitalist-Communist categories' were inadequate to explain events in Germany or Italy. Marxist categories led only to a distorted understanding of the situation. 'The Communist is apt to apply the simple test — to whom do the means of production belong? But the answer is not — "In Russia they belong to the people and in Germany they belong to private owners" '. What was important was that 'In Russia and Germany the means of production are almost entirely in the control of the government'. National Socialism and Fascism had adopted a method of 'national planning' which recalled seventeenth century mercantilism. 'Ownership is not significant, what matters is control, and this control of the government is absolute.'[124]

Anyone wishing to dispute the Communist interpretation would have had ample opportunities to do so in Cambridge in the 1930s. In the History Faculty itself, 'Marxist apologetics were largely confined to a group of brilliant undergraduates', including E. Hobsbawm and H.J. Habbukuk; G.M. Trevelyan had become Regius Professor in 1927 and a 'faculty in which Peckthorn, Temperly, Kitson Clark, Winstanley, Simpson and Lapsley were still prominent figures was not easily given over to fashionable radicalism.' In the University at large, however, there was a 'leftward movement . . . in the thirties' in which 'many intellectually gifted people acquired what can only be described as a salvationist belief in Stalin's Russia and consistently preached pacifism and disarmament, while at the same time urging armed resistance to Fascism.' Oakeshott sided with the History Faculty rather than the university, but other Caians, such as J. Needham, did not. Needham received the Webbs' *Soviet Communism* in 1936 'with an enthusiasm bordering on rapture.' 'This magnificent work . . . difficult to find sufficiently sober words', and so on.[125]

In a review of a collection of Marxist essays including several contributions by Cambridge dons, Oakeshott again adopted a highly critical stance. In Marxism he found himself confronted with an 'official philosophy', something which clashed sharply with his own insistence in *Experience and its Modes* that there were no 'authorities' in philosophy.[126] The reader, he complained, was 'left with the

[124] *op. cit.*

[125] Howarth, *op. cit.*, pp. 198–9, 209.

[126] *EM*, p. 8.

impression that Marx is the only thinker who has ever handled this philosophy; the rest are humble servants of the . . . oracle . . . Dialectical materialism is like a theology turned into a gospel, and a gospel turned into a dogma.' It was 'esoteric' as well as 'official'. 'It is difficult . . . not to become conscious of the existence of some hidden source of knowledge or inspiration which, if only [we] were privileged to share it, might make plain much that must otherwise remain obscure'. A commitment to the cause was essential in order to attain this esoteric knowledge. Unless we are 'actively participating in the class struggle today,' we will 'certainly fail to understand.'

Aspects of Dialectical Materialism provided Oakeshott with an illustration of 'both the importance of [historical] generalisations to [Marx's] philosophy and the extreme danger of such an alliance between philosophy and history.' The Marxist belief that 'every philosophy is conditioned by the general social and economic circumstances in which it is conceived and elaborated' and that 'a "true" philosophy is that which is most closely tied and tied most consciously to the circumstances of its generation . . . naturally lead those who hold them to issue statements about the course of history.' Consequently, he argued, Dialectical Materialism must stand or fall 'with [the] truth or falsehood of these judgments.'[127]

Oakeshott believed he had found an example of the kind of historical statement on which Marxists relied in the proposition that since 'the Renaissance, European humanity . . . has had forced upon it for its special task for humanity the solution of the problem of economic production.' The consequence allegedly derivable from this proposition was that 'materialism' was 'the proper starting place for philosophy under modern conditions'. He did not accept either the premise or the conclusion. The Marxist historian had the same faults as Gierke, only more so — 'The analysis of an idea is substituted for the patient and detailed exploration of a period, and history in any true sense disappears.' In a rather weary tone, he conceded that 'It is possible, of course, to analyse any considerable historical change into the three steps which the Dialectic presupposes, and perhaps it is also possible to find Quantity turning into Quality, and the Negative being Negated', but he followed this with the declaration that 'if you think in such an analysis you are providing a history . . . of this change, you must be more than ordinarily foolish.'

The Marxist's business, Oakeshott claimed, was 'merely to illustrate his general theory by finding it everywhere exemplified in the

---

[127] Oakeshott, Review of H. Levy and others, *Aspects of Dialectical Materialism*, *Cambridge Review*, vol. 56, 1934, pp. 108–9.

world, and in that he can hardly fail,' just as those who seek "proofs" of Christianity can hardly fail to find evidence of miracles. 'The best that can be said [for] what Marx and Lenin wrote', he concluded, 're-mains yet unsaid.'[128] His criticisms of the Hegelian-inspired Marxist philosophy of history raise issues that are dealt with at length in the next chapter.

For all his disagreements with it, Oakeshott did not deny the importance of Communism in the politics of inter-war Europe. Like National Socialism and Fascism, he included it in *The Social and Polit-ical Doctrines of Contemporary Europe*. All three ideologies, he believed, could be seen as part of a European-wide revolt against the 'liberalism' Locke, Bentham, and the philosophes had helped to cre-ate. Both National Socialism and Communism were rooted in dissat-isfaction with the persona of the liberal individual understood as a rational calculator of self-interest. Hitler criticised 'liberal democ-racy' because it was based on an individualism which understood society as a 'collection of self-interested individuals' participating in a market. So did Communism, which presupposed 'a new type of man' as essential to the overthrow of the liberal order.

Of the five doctrines Oakeshott included in his 1939 cross-section of political thought in modern Europe, Roman Catholicism was the odd man out. Its inclusion was due to the ambiguity of the European political heritage. 'No greater . . . contrast could exist,' he wrote, 'than that between the Liberal Democratic conception of govern-ment . . . and the Catholic doctrine . . . yet both of these views belong to our civilization.' Oakeshott singled out Catholicism not only on account of its greater age ('it appears in the modern world to some extent as a stranger') but also because it was 'the only contemporary representative of a genuine Natural Law theory.' For that reason, it served to remind us of 'an inheritance we have neglected.' Catholic political doctrine, he wrote, 'at least has the help of a profound philo-sophical thinker, St. Thomas Aquinas, and is not dependent . . . on some vague leaning towards a half-understood and wholly con-fused pragmatism', unlike the 'remarkably unsatisfactory' excur-sions into philosophy by followers of all the more modern doctrines. Catholicism 'at least does not suffer from the peculiar deadness of last year's fashion. Catholic . . . doctrine might (by the ignorant) be considered a harmless museum piece, but the corpse of liberty . . . stinks'.[129]

[128] *Ibid.*

[129] *SP*, pp. xv–xvi, xix.

'Conservatism', like Catholicism, Oakeshott considered an 'authoritarian' doctrine in the strict sense that it took heed of legitimacy. Yet any detailed discussion of it is conspicuously absent from his catalogue of contemporary doctrines. Whether this was because Oakeshott did not consider it a 'doctrine' or because he thought there was simply very little Conservatism about in the 1930s is unclear. He did remark that 'many of the principles which belong to the historic doctrine of Conservatism are to be found in . . . Catholic doctrine,' but he did not say what these were.[130] Elsewhere, he appeared happy with a description of Conservatism as an 'historical phenomenon', with no essential core (a description which recalls his own view of Christianity) and concerned with 'a belief in quality, inequality (as a fact to be faced) energy and permanence'. At the same time, he recognised 'genuinely conservative defects' such as an 'undue satisfaction with what has already been accomplished in the way of establishing equality of opportunity' and 'a belief that "the founders of Conservatism" were better than their successors.' Nevertheless, Conservatism was not a subject on which he spilt much ink before World War Two; allusions to it are few and far between.[131]

Oakeshott ended the 1930s pessimistic and dissatisfied, though the abandonment of his youthful hopes for the future altered rather than erased his Romantic disposition. Romanticism, after all, is quite as compatible with pessimism as with optimism, and Oakeshott's pessimism had by no means plumbed its depths by 1939. His unquestionable dissatisfaction, to a greater or lesser extent, with all the political ideas that he saw before him, unmistakably took a different tone from that in which he had raised the possibility of a 'religious revival' in the 1920s. 'The social and political doctrines of contemporary Europe', he concluded, 'are striking mainly in virtue of their defects as doctrines and their remarkable success in subjugating whole communities.' Moreover, as in 1925, Oakeshott did not feel his own understanding of modern European political thought was satisfactory. There was, he told his students, 'so much incongruous matter' in his published collection that 'it has been strongly bound; otherwise it might disintegrate from spontaneous combustion.'[132]

The position Oakeshott had reached by 1939, that European political ideas were to be explained in terms of varying degrees of diver-

[130] *op. cit.,* p. xx.

[131] Oakeshott, Review of K. Feiling, *What is Conservatism, Cambridge Review,* vol. 51, 1930, p. 512.

[132] Oakeshott, introductory lecture on 'The Social and Political Doctrines of Contemporary Europe', p. 9.

gence from a liberal-democratic norm under the pressure of trends such as secularism and nationalism, was unsatisfactory. Yet a hint of the very different direction that his thought would take after the war lay concealed in a footnote in which he observed that the difference between 'left' and 'right' was far less important than the 'fundamental cleavage' between those who would 'plan and impose a way of life upon a society' and those who 'not only refuse to hand over the destiny of a society to any set of officials but also consider the whole notion of planning the destiny of a society to be both stupid and immoral.' Fascist, Communist, and National Socialist societies were all prepared to 'hand over to the arbitrary will of a society's self-appointed leaders the planning of its entire life.' This division was the basis not only of Oakeshott's post-war attacks on Rationalism but also of his later contrast between the corporate enterprise state and the state as an association in terms of non-instrumental law.

The two different kinds of 'liberalism' Oakeshott had identified in his comments on Locke could also be seen in these terms. On the one hand, there was the 'crude and negative' kind of individualism which Hitler and Stalin alike attacked. This kind of 'liberalism', however, had more in common with such ideologies than their respective supporters would have cared to admit. All were 'materialistic' and all were based on 'the plausible ethics of productivity'. In this sense, Oakeshott still believed, as he had at school, that liberty and capital were linked in the modern world. Yet he had come to see (liberal) capitalism and socialism as having more in common with one another than either had with the kind of liberalism which opposed the 'planned' society.

On the other hand, there was a doctrine of 'Representative Democracy' of which this sort of 'liberalism' was 'but an incomplete expression'. Precisely because historically it had been bound up with the 'narrow' kind of individualism, liberalism needed 'a radical restatement which has yet to be provided', and in 1939 Oakeshott was clearer about what it excluded than about how it might be described in positive terms. 'Anyone anxious to extract the true metal of the liberal doctrine from the base ore from which it has never yet been successfully separated' would at least know where not to look once the war was over.[133]

---

[133] *SP*, p. xxiii.

Chapter Two

The Philosophy of History, 1925–1939

The Philosophy of History in the Nineteenth Century

Only in the mid-nineteenth century, and then largely only in Germany, did philosophers begin to give sustained attention to history as a form of enquiry. Prior to that, 'the philosophy of history' usually meant attempting a 'universal' view of history, discerning the overall meaning of the past. Both Kant and Hegel had a 'philosophy of history' in this latter sense. To Hegel, for example, 'speculative' or 'philosophical' history meant applying to the past the already established conviction that 'the history of the world . . . presents us with a rational process', the self-revelation of the Idea.[1] Only after Hegel's philosophy declined in popularity, and the cry of 'Back to Kant' went up, did 'the philosophy of history' as we know it today appear. And it is significant that it did so in this context of German neo-Kantianism.[2] Kant himself had very little to say about history as a form of enquiry. However, he did believe that 'History is concerned with giving an account of the will's manifestations in the world of phenomena.' Moreover, the human actions studied by historians are 'determined in accordance with natural laws, as is every other natural event.'[3] The three basic positions adopted by those who turned

---

[1] G.W.F. Hegel, *The Philosophy of History*, trans. J. Sibree, Dover Publications, New York, pp. 9–10.

[2] T.E. Willey, *Back to Kant: The Revival of Kantianism in German Social and Historical Thought, 1860–1914*, Wayne State UP, Detroit, 1978, p. 22.

[3] I. Kant, 'Idea for a Universal History with a Cosmopolitan Purpose', in *Political Writings*, 2nd edn., ed. H. Reiss, Cambridge UP, Cambridge, 1991, p. 41.

their philosophical attention to history in Germany may all be seen in the light of these suggestions.

The first involves arguing, as Kant had, that historical enquiry is concerned with the phenomenal realm, but that this does not deny 'the free exercise of the human will'. A pupil of Hegel's, J.G. Droysen, who had been inspired by von Humboldt as well as Kant, explored this position in his *Grundriss der Historik* (1857). Droysen argued that history was concerned with a distinct class of phenomena within the empirical realm, namely those, which display 'growth' and 'advance' as well as 'repetition'. He set up 'Nature' and 'History' as two distinct orders of understanding, 'the widest conceptions under which the human mind apprehends the world of phenomena.'[4] As Droysen put it, 'man's nature is at once sensuous and spiritual', and the meaning of historical events seems to lie, not in their sensuous phenomenal content, but in the 'inner', spiritual realm. He argued that it is the inner or noumenal realm which is the source of meaning in historical enquiry.

The second possibility is to argue that historical understanding deals exclusively with the phenomenal realm in which objects and events are causally related by mechanical laws. In England, H.T. Buckle, writing, like Droysen, in the 1850s, invoked Kant in his attempt to apply the methods of the natural sciences to historical enquiry. He believed that in order for history to become a science, it must become, like natural science, a realm of necessity. Buckle's 'treat[ment of] Will in general . . . as a term of a sequence like any other . . . scandalised the "high priori" philosopher and the preacher'.[5] His work received a sardonic review from Droysen, who congratulated Buckle on discovering that 'Kant's teaching is precisely the reverse of what has hitherto been supposed'.[6] Nevertheless, there have been supporters of the view that history should adopt or at least approximate the assumptions and methods of the natural sciences ever since.

The third possibility is that history deals neither with a peculiar class of phenomenal objects deriving rationality from an 'inner' or 'noumenal' existence nor with phenomenal objects determined solely by physical laws but with the accidental and the irrational. Schopenhauer, who may be regarded as a neo-Kantian of a sort, put

---

[4]   J.G. Droysen, *Outline of the Principles of History*, trans. E.B. Andrews, Ginn and Co., Boston, 1875.
[5]   J.M. Robertson, *Buckle and his Critics*, Swan Sonnenschein, London, 1895, pp.10–11.
[6]   Droysen, *op. cit.*, pp. 66–7.

forward this view in his chapter 'On History' in *The World as Will and Idea*,[7] but understandably it held little appeal for later neo-Kantian philosophers such as Windelband, Rickert, Simmel, and Dilthey who were trying to place history on as firm a footing as they believed Kant's critical philosophy had placed the natural sciences.[8] Such a view dismisses rather than explains historical understanding.

In England during the same period, debate over the philosophy of history was more or less confined to the older sense of the term. The 'Germano-Coleridgean' Liberal Anglicans, for example, were interested in the relation between sacred and profane conceptions of past time and 'the problem of progress' rather than the nature of historical enquiry as such.[9] George Eliot's translation of Strauss's *Life of Jesus* (1846) further fuelled the debate over the relation between secular and religious ideas of the past. (When critics claimed Strauss's work was an attempt to render the life of Christ mythical rather than historical, they did not mean that Christ's life had previously been thought to be the result of an historical enquiry; the life of Jesus was revealed history). Nevertheless, these debates led at least one thinker to fix on the notion of historical enquiry itself, for it was in response to them that F.H. Bradley composed his pamphlet 'On the Presuppositions of Critical History' (1874).

Bradley, unlike Buckle, did not understand history on the analogy of a natural science. Unlike scientific results, he argued, historical conclusions 'never transcend the region of practical certainty. The result is never theoretically [i.e. inductively] proved.' Yet although Bradley distinguished historical thought from scientific reasoning, by equating history with the production of practical or 'moral' certainties he seems to deny history the autonomy which in other respects he contends that it has.

Oakeshott quite correctly described Bradley's essay as 'one of the earliest discussions in English of the logical and epistemological questions connected with history.'[10] Such discussions remained comparatively rare even into the Edwardian period. With the qualification that 'the theories of the earlier British Idealists implied an historical point of view,' historians have generally endorsed

[7]   A. Schopenhauer, *The World as Will and Representation*, vol. 2, tr. E.F.J. Payne, Dover Publications, New York, 1966, pp. 439–46.

[8]   Willey, *op. cit.*, p.137.

[9]   D. Forbes, *The Liberal Anglican Idea of History*, Cambridge UP, Cambridge, 1952, pp. viii, 1.

[10] Oakeshott, Review of F.H. Bradley, *Collected Essays*, *Philosophy*, vol. 11, 1936, p.115.

Collingwood's remark that 'the nineteenth century Idealists in England were not ... historically minded.'[11] Bradley's attempt to present
history as a 'critical' form of enquiry with distinct 'presuppositions'
of its own, thereby securing for religion a sphere quite 'beyond [the]
realm' of history, found no immediate continuators.

Meanwhile, in Germany, Dilthey had begun working on the difference between the human and the natural sciences in the 1860s.[12]
He initially separated them by assigning matter to the natural sciences and mind to the human sciences, but the psychological basis
for the human sciences that resulted ultimately proved unsatisfactory as a means of expanding Kant's critique of the categories of the
understanding to include, *inter alia*, history.[13] In his later, 'hermen-
eutic', period, he distinguished, as Nardin puts it, 'the study of mental processes, which can be explained in terms of general laws, from
the study of mental content — beliefs, desires, arguments, and ideas
— which must be understood in terms of their individual characteristics.'[14] The later Dilthey suggested that there was an 'I-world' relation or 'life-nexus', which was 'the ... basis for the human sciences'.[15]
The categories of purpose, value and meaning, which, he believed,
gave order to the life-world we ordinarily inhabit, were all
employed in historical understanding.

Like Bradley, Dilthey had separated history from natural science.
Neither, however, separated it decisively from 'practice'. In
Dilthey's case, having argued that the life-world is through and
through temporal, a temporality reflected in the language of human
beings and the memories which constitute them continuing identi-
ties, he reached the conclusion that historical enquiry was historical
thought of exactly the same kind as was found in 'practical' thought.
This view is easily compatible with reductionist pragmatism.
Heidegger, for example, regarded himself as a continuator of
Dilthey's, and he endorsed Nietzsche's conclusion that history is jus-

---

[11] R.G. Collingwood, Letter to de Ruggiero, January 1931, quoted in Boucher, 'The
Creation of the Past', p 184. The qualification is made by Boucher and also by
Collini, who writes that the 'theoretical and substantive problems of history'
suffered from 'comparative neglect' at the hands of the British Idealists: see
'Sociology and Idealism in Britain 1888–1920', *Archives Européenes de Sociologie*,
vol. 19, 1978, p. 31.

[12] J. Owensby, *Dilthey and the Narrative of History*, Cornell UP, New York, 1994, esp.
chapter one, 'Revising the Transcendental Project'.

[13] W. Dilthey, *Introduction to the Human Sciences*, ed. A. Makkreel and F. Rodi,
Princeton UP, Princeton, 1989, pp. 448, 489.

[14] Nardin, *op. cit.*, p. 105.

[15] Makkreel and Rodi, 'Introduction' to Dilthey, *op. cit.*, p. 22.

tified only in the service of life.[16] The past which historians study, on Dilthey's view, is our past, the past of the life-world that we presently inhabit.

Turning to the early twentieth century, we find a similarly pragmatic streak in the work of the Italian philosopher Croce. Croce's *History: Theory and Practice*, written shortly before World War One, was the only work on the philosophy of history apart from Bradley's with which Oakeshott appears to have been familiar in the 1920s. Collingwood was an admirer of Croce's, and his argument that historians 're-enact' the past in their own minds owed much to Croce's view that 'the deed of which the history is told must vibrate in the soul of the historian.'[17] Croce, like Bradley, defended the autonomy of history, taking 'Buckle and the many tiresome sociologists and positivists' to task for their attempts to 'reduce history to a natural science.'[18]

Croce nevertheless maintained the pragmatist view that 'true historical interest . . . sheds light upon an order of facts answering to a practical and ethical want.' An historical problem was 'related to my being in the same way as a love affair . . . or . . . a danger which threatens me.' For Croce, present practical interests governed all historical writing and historical works only became histories 'when I have thought or shall think them, re-elaborating them according to my spiritual needs.'[19] Oakeshott came to take a much less 'practical' view of historical enquiry.

Furthermore, Croce argued for the 'identity of philosophy with history', for 'when . . . history has been raised to the knowledge of the eternal present, it reveals itself as at one with philosophy, which . . . is . . . the thought of the eternal present.'[20] Here again, Oakeshott would not follow him. Though he initially thought of philosophy as absolutely present experience, he never accepted that history could become wholly present in the manner Croce described. By definition, history had some relation to the past, or it became an absurdity.

Croce's attempt to establish historical enquiry as autonomous had reached a position which might be described as the very reverse of Schopenhauer's. History, instead of being denigrated, is exalted. Collingwood displayed a similar tendency to assert the historical

---

[16] M. Heidegger, *Being and Time*, trans. J. Macquarrie and E. Robinson, Blackwell, Oxford, 1992, pp. 448–9.

[17] B. Croce, *History: Theory and Practice*, trans. D. Ainslie, Russell and Russell, New York, 1960, p. 22.

[18] *op. cit.*, p. 46.

[19] *op. cit.*, pp. 13, 29.

[20] *op. cit.*, p. 61.

nature of all thought, declaring that 'all metaphysical propositions are historical propositions.'[21] It would appear that the attempt to establish the autonomy of historical knowledge had foundered once again. For if there is really no distinction between history and philosophy, then history cannot be an autonomous form of enquiry.

We have now gone past the point at which Oakeshott entered the debates over the nature of historical enquiry, for Collingwood made the claim just mentioned in 1940. We must retreat to the early 1920s. But we will do so in the knowledge that, by then, questions about the nature of history and its relations to science, religion, philosophy and the practical world had all been raised. Nor will we be unduly alarmed by Oakeshott's philosophical vocabulary. His 'modes' of experience, the scientific, the historical and the practical, were simply his names for the familiar terms within which debates were already being carried on.

Unpublished Writings on History from the 1920s

In his 1925 'Discussion of Some Matters Preliminary to the Study of Political Philosophy', Oakeshott had distinguished history from philosophy only to brand it a less adequate form of understanding. 'History cut[s] away the mere forms of thought until . . . we come to understand exactly what were the experiences of the past . . . Philosophy . . . test[s] and interrogate[s] these experiences, discover[s] their coherence and logical justification [and] show[s] how they must be changed to make them coherent.'[22]

This sounds somewhat Hegelian, an impression strengthened by Oakeshott's note in his copy of Hegel's *Phenomenology of Spirit*, purchased in 1926. 'The *Phenomenology* is the classification of the various, adequate and inadequate, manifestations of spirit; while the Philosophy of History is the genealogical table of these manifestations in time. The former shows them as necessary, the latter as actual.' For example, the facts of political life may be studied either philosophically or historically. However, 'History does not concern itself with the meaning of events, except their proximate meaning as expressed in other events.'

In other words, history studied only the 'outer', inessential aspect of events. It was 'necessary' but 'sad' to have to look 'at the feeble manifestations [of the 'will to live the "good life"'] in history'. History, unlike political philosophy, could not produce definitions of the state — 'it is an error . . . to suppose that a definition is contained

---

[21] R.G. Collingwood, *An Essay on Metaphysics*, Oxford UP, Oxford, 1940, p. 49.

[22] Oakeshott, 'Political Philosophy', p. 9.

in an historical account of the construction or growth of a thing',
because 'the meaning of the genus' is not to be found 'in the contingent peculiarities of the individual example.'[23] Oakeshott later came
to think understanding 'contingent peculiarities' the essence of the
historian's task, but at this stage, he was only interested in establishing that to the philosopher, the writings of Aristotle, or any other
author, were of interest only insofar as he had 'discover[ed] something . . . above the influences of [a] particular time and place.'
Oakeshott, we saw, was powerfully attracted in the 1920s to the view
that there was a 'best and truest' or 'final and real' meaning to be had
in philosophy. Philosophical definition could penetrate to the timeless 'actual meanings,' the 'conceptions themselves' which 'lie
behind words'.[24]

In 1925, then, Oakeshott thought of political philosophy as the
definition of universal terms such as 'the State'. History was unsatisfactory precisely because it could not provide such definitions. He
also thought that historical enquiry involved understanding events
in terms of their subsequents, perhaps because history revealed
manifestations of 'will' which had to be understood in terms of their
effects. Again, he later reversed this view entirely, insisting that historical events must be understood in terms of their antecedents, the
preceding events that led up to them, and not what came after.
Oakeshott also assumed a single independently existing past, which
formed a common point of reference for historians and philosophers
alike. This 'realism' was quite consistent with other views he held at
the time. For example, the distinction between 'real things' and their
'partial verbal equivalents' parallels the distinction of a really extant
past and our knowledge of it. Both, however, were distinctions he
would later abandon.[25]

The beginnings of this process can be traced through two unpublished papers written during these years. The first, which is untitled
— we shall call it 'History is a Fable' after the quotation from Napoleon which appears at the head of the first page — appears to have
been written in 1923.[26] The second, entitled 'The Philosophy of History', was probably composed in 1927, to judge from a letter from
W.W. Buckland, another Cambridge historian to whom Oakeshott

[23] *op. cit.,* pp. 79, 24.

[24] *op. cit.,* pp. 32–3, 8.

[25] *op. cit.,* p. 31.

[26] The essay, at LSE 1/1/50, is undated, but it is accompanied by an envelope
      stamped 'BOW S.O.E / 12.15 pm 6 OC 23' and addressed to 'Michael Oakeshott,
      Caius College, Cambridge'. On the front of it Oakeshott wrote '"History is a
      fable men agree to believe" Napoleon'.

had sent it for comment.[27] Both papers exhibit familiarity with the philosophies of history of Bradley and Croce, and reflect their attempts to establish history as an independent form of knowledge.

In the first, Oakeshott set out to distinguish 'the historic method' from 'science' and 'art', suggesting that he was doing 'historiography'. This was 'a branch of study . . . which makes it its business . . . to deduce some general principles about the writing of history.' His declaration that this was 'not without some use'[28] to historians marks another significant difference between his earlier and later views; that the philosophy of history was of no direct help to historians was a fiercely held conviction in his later work. In the second paper, Oakeshott employed the term 'the philosophy of history' for the first time. Perhaps recognising that he had not in fact been offering advice to historians on how to go about their business but investigating the assumptions of historical writing, he now stated that the philosopher sees history as 'one among a number of attitudes which the mind is capable of adopting towards the objective world; and the philosophy of history . . . consists in reflexion about the way in which the historian approaches his object.'[29] If we ignore the reference to an 'objective world', this sentence could be from *Experience and its Modes*, which continued the attempt to display history as 'a kind of thinking, different alike from science and philosophy.'[30]

Both papers prefigured the concern of *Experience and its Modes* with a '*confusion des genres*', aiming in particular to prevent the assimilation of history to natural science. In the first, Oakeshott criticised the *Introduction to the Study of History* by the French historians Langlois and Seignobos. In France, Marc Bloch and Lucien Febvre were already leading a reaction against the work of these two scholars, founding the *Annales d'histoire economique et sociale* in 1929. However, Bloch and Febvre were reacting as much against their subject-matter (political history) as against their theories of history; Oakeshott concentrated exclusively on the latter. He quoted a passage in which Langlois and Seignobos looked forward to a 'day . . . when, thanks to the organisation of labour, all existing documents will have been discovered, arranged, and all the facts established of which traces have not been destroyed.' This dream of an historical workshop or factory survived the redirection of attention in terms of

[27]	Oakeshott, 'The Philosophy of History', LSE 1/1/5. The letter from W.W. Buckland preserved with the essay is dated 24 April 1927.

[28]	Oakeshott, 'History is a Fable', p. 1.

[29]	*EM*, p. 5.

[30]	*EM*, p. 30.

subject matter that the Annales School gradually effected, and has since been espoused by members of the Annales themselves, such as F. Furet. Oakeshott, however, never ceased to be critical of the positivistic divorce between the 'reception' and 'construction' of historical facts which he believed Langlois' and Seignobos' views implied.[31]

Spengler's *Decline of the West* was another example of a 'pseudo-scientific' conception of history. Spengler's search for 'a general law of [the] birth, growth and decay' of nations using a 'systematic technique of analogy', or the comparative method, was to be based on 'the facts' which had been settled by the ordinary historian.[32] However, there was no such 'general and permanent' set of 'facts'. The subject-matter of history was 'both individual and past' and hence fulfilled neither criterion. Spengler's belief that Western civilisation was now passing through the same 'necessary phase of its existence' as late Greco-Roman civilisation experienced in its 'period of imperialism and great material prosperity'[33] was based on an erroneous belief that 'history is a science in the same sense that physics is a science.'

Interestingly, however, Oakeshott was prepared to accept Schlegel's lectures on the philosophy of history (1828) as historical. Schlegel's attempt to trace 'in reference to the whole human race the progress of the restoration in man of the lost image of God'[34] had not assumed that 'the facts of history are known and settled' or attempted 'to construct general laws' or denied 'the uniqueness of historical events'. Unlike Spengler's 'morphology of history'[35] which allowed the reader to see 'the path which must be followed by all civilisations' to the year 2200 and beyond, Schlegel's 'plan' or 'plot' made no claim to predict future developments. In attempting to see history as 'a single coherent whole',[36] he had been doing 'plain history'. By the 1930s, however, Oakeshott had become far less sympathetic to such 'speculative' philosophies of history.

Both papers drew heavily on Bradley. Bradley's attempt to describe the relation of historical knowledge to Christian belief had thrown Oakeshott an important lead by distinguishing firmly between two meanings of 'history'. '*Geschichte*' or written history,

---

[31] Langlois and Seignobos quoted in Oakeshott, 'History is a Fable', p. 6. Cp. F. Furet, *Dans l'atelier de l'histoire.*

[32] Oakeshott, 'History is a Fable', p. 8.

[33] *op. cit.,* p. 6.

[34] *op. cit.,* p.13.

[35] *op. cit.,* pp. 3–4.

[36] *op. cit.,* p. 16.

Bradley argued, was not equivalent to '*Was geschieht*', past events. Written history did not simply reproduce past events. History must be 'critical'; historians must judge and select from evidence in order to compose an account at all.[37] Oakeshott eventually placed Bradley's essay with the rest of his work on philosophical psychology. As a later member of the same 'school as Bentham and James Mill', Bradley had treated the philosophy of history as a psychological problem,[38] resolving history into two elements, 'events in time', and their 'recollection in the mind of the historian'.

Nevertheless, Oakeshott initially adopted Bradley's 'psychological' approach, dividing history into 'two main elements — (i) events in time, and (ii) the recollection of events in the mind', or an object of knowledge (past events) and a subjective element (the mind of the historian). The result, at least in the first paper, was an unwelcome scepticism. Despite Bradley's belief that history must be critical, he had assumed that 'history apart from the historian does exist.'[39] Sharing this assumption, Oakeshott found it impossible to explain how historians could give an objective account of past events, for they necessarily 'observe facts differently from one another' according to their different temporal positions in relation to the events in question.

Historians were trapped, so to say, within the horizon of their own perspective. We can only come to know 'new fact,' Oakeshott argued, by 'interpreting it [according] to our own experience', for 'Everything we read or observe depends for its meaning upon the present state of our knowledge, as much as upon the thing itself.'[40] Consequently, the historian must 'labour under a point of view which is probably antagonistic to those of his sources.' Historical knowledge was 'but the reaction of the records of history upon a different personal experience . . . and is not more likely to correspond with the fact than any other, previous or to come.'[41] Until he abandoned the idea that there was an independently existing past that the knowing subject inevitably distorted, he had to give up hope 'of ever arriving at the absolute truth of the event which took place'.[42]

---

[37]   F.H. Bradley, 'The Presuppositions of Critical History', in *Collected Essays*, vol. 1, Oxford UP, Oxford, 1935, p. 3.

[38]   Oakeshott, Review of F.H. Bradley, *loc. cit.*.

[39]   Oakeshott, 'History is a Fable', p. 4.

[40]   *op. cit.*, pp. 8–10a.

[41]   *op. cit.*, pp. 18a, 20a.

[42]   *op. cit.*, p. 28.

Small wonder, then, that Oakeshott concluded 'In the place of what [history] regarded as a witness it finds a writer of fiction.'[43]

In the second paper, by contrast, he inclined towards the view that 'what we call 'the past' has no final and absolute existence' independent of the present. This was an essential precondition of *Experience and its Modes*, which rejected the idea of a 'correspondence' between historical writing and the past in favour of the idea that historians 'construct' an account of the past, the truth of which was dependent on the internal 'coherence' of the inferences they had made from evidence.

In the later 1920s, however, Oakeshott had not overcome his scepticism entirely. He remained convinced that we cannot get an 'accurate' view of the past because of the time that has subsequently intervened, or, in other words, because 'the future influences the past.'[44] This suggests that he still believed that historical understanding makes sense of events in terms of their subsequents, the events that followed them. The past studied by historians was still our past, the past which has led up to us; there was as yet no firm contrast between practical and historical kinds of past in Oakeshott's mind. The objects the historian studied were distinguished merely in virtue of being in the past, and not by their belonging to a particular kind of past.

The absence of this distinction, so important in *Experience and its Modes*, is well illustrated by Oakeshott's remark that 'the fashion at the present time is to reverse the judgements of past writers apparently from no other motive than that of mere contradiction.' This 'fashion' had resulted, according to Oakeshott, in such judgements as 'Marcus Aurelius was a bad man' and 'Pitt was an incompetent scoundrel'. Yet there was no suggestion that such judgements of moral character were historically illegitimate as such on the grounds that they belonged to a practical world of value distinct from the world of historical experience.[45]

---

[43] *op. cit.,* p. 29.

[44] Oakeshott, 'The Philosophy of History', p. 10.

[45] *op. cit.,* p. 34. R. Soffer, *Discipline and Power: The University, History and the Making of an English Elite, 1870–1930,* Stanford UP, California, 1994, p. 173, brings out quite clearly the fact that English historians in the nineteenth century simply did not make any distinction between 'practical' and 'historical' views of the past. They commonly assumed that the past to be studied was 'our' (national) past which led up to an (improving) present. At Cambridge, Soffer argues, it was only after World War One that young historians began to question the view that the purpose of historical enquiry was to provide a moral lesson for the present; Oakeshott, like Butterfield, would appear to have been part of this trend.

We can only speculate about how Oakeshott arrived at the distinction between practical and historical attitudes to the past. He may have drawn on works not directly concerned with the nature of historical enquiry. For example, he could have found inspiration in Schweitzer's *Quest of the Historical Jesus*, which he borrowed repeatedly in the 1920s and at the end of his life still considered 'a matchless critical review of a century and a half of engagements . . . to infer an historical situation from what has survived in record.'[46] Schweitzer criticised the 'wholly unhistorical' eighteenth-century 'rationalism' which sought 'not the past, but itself in the past. For it, the problem of the life of Jesus is solved in the moment it succeeds in bringing Jesus near to its own time . . . and showing that His teaching is identical with the intellectual truth which rationalism deifies.'[47] Here we have a ready-made distinction between an historical attitude to the past and a 'rationalist' practical attitude that treats the past as present for its own ends.

A third unpublished essay on the philosophy of history, 'What do we look for in an historian?' was not concerned, as the previous two papers had been, with the conditions that make history an independent manner of thinking. Rather, it contained Oakeshott's only extended consideration of historical style. This is distinguished at the outset from a biographical or sociological interest in historians as persons: 'I should be the last person to suggest that you should play the newspaper reporter and affect an interest in the colour of the ink Macaulay used or his size in hats.'[48] Instead, it is, as the previous chapter might lead us to expect, an interest in the character of the historian as revealed in his writings that Oakeshott was urging readers to cultivate. We cannot move on without noticing his justification, that 'any normal person . . . has some interest in history.' Such a remark immediately provokes the query 'what do you mean by normal?' And to this Oakeshott had a ready response; 'anyone who does not prefer his dog to his fellow human beings.' This raises a smile, but it is also a serious point. Anyone but a genuine misanthrope can be expected to take an interest in the past deeds of his fellow creatures.

In his published writings on the philosophy of history, Oakeshott was careful to insist that he was not imposing any particular method on the historian, and it now appears this was a view he held well prior to *Experience and its Modes*. As he observed, 'directly we start

---

[46]   Oakeshott, *On History and Other Essays*, Blackwell, Oxford, 1983, p. 56 n. 1.

[47]   Schweitzer, *Quest of the Historical Jesus*, p. 28.

[48]   Oakeshott, 'What do we look for in an historian?', LSE 1/1/47, p. 1.

talking about historians and their relation to history we are up
against this problem of how history *should* be written'[49] but the problem was insoluble, for the very good reason that there was no single
correct way in which to write history. This was not merely because
historical writing had developed in a number of stages or periods
since it came into existence; interestingly, Oakeshott seems to have
thought styles of historical writing were capable of being employed
across the centuries, in the same way as we might talk about a play as
a classical or modern tragedy. He put the point eloquently when he
declared 'The muse of history has no fixed caste of countenance, any
more than has the muse of poetry';[50] any style of historical writing
was acceptable so long as it was neither dull nor dishonest.

We can, then, talk about historical works from different periods as
if their authors were contemporaries, while still saying something
meaningful. In so doing, of course, we are not engaging in philosophy of history, in the strict sense of identifying the conditions of historical thought. But the fact that we can still say something
meaningful would presumably be explained, in Oakeshott's terms,
by the fact that all the events historians discuss are notionally part of
a single whole, the historical past. That there may be innumerable
different versions of the events in that past does not exclude there
being a single ideal account of events, from the standpoint of which
each particular account of events is more or less satisfactory. In fact,
as we shall see later, it is necessary that there be such an ideal if history as a discipline is to be capable of self-criticism.

Less technically, this idea prefigures the notion of a 'conversational' relationship that exists within and between forms of understanding. Oakeshott introduced the literary conceit of gathering
together a group of historians from different ages in a room, all scrib-
bling away, allowing us to talk to them directly. If one did so, he haz-
arded, 'one would soon discover that there were very few kinds of
human character unrepresented.'[51] Their character would express
not only their temperament; historians would not only be more or
less sceptical (Froude) or imaginative (Gibbon) or judgemental
(Macaulay). They would also be more or less talented, brilliant or
workaday, and we would enjoy hearing or reading some more than
others. There would also inevitably be one who tried to 'recount all the
schemes that had ever been tried or thought of, where they had been

---

[49] *op. cit.*, p. 3.

[50] *op. cit.*, p. 10.

[51] *op. cit.*, p. 5.

tried and who had thought of them'; this historian would be the one liable to make us want to 'make a dash for the door.'[52]

In one of those amusing but indefensible assertions that litter Oakeshott's earlier writings, he described this type of historian as 'a member of that singularly frivolous body of men who are known as antiquarians, — dead, and with their latest breath giving one brief moment more of life to things as dead as themselves.'[53] Antiquarianism is by no means the touch of death: as Oakeshott probably already knew, it was a vital force in the emergence of modern historical thought. He was on safer ground with his identification of Buckle as an example of the type of historian 'with a theory'. Oakeshott seems to have had in mind the tendency to explain everything in terms of a single cause or motivation, but he did not condemn this tendency so unequivocally as he would later on, saying that 'It is only when [the] theory is very fantastic indeed that we need get impatient.'[54] At the other end of the spectrum were those whose caution over committing themselves to any position had practically become a vice; Acton reappears here as one who had 'raised his natural diffidence into a philosophy: he it was who, after years of almost incredible research came to the conclusion that it was possible for the Pope to err.'[55]

In the second half of the paper, Oakeshott singled out two historians for particular attention — Gibbon and Macaulay. His description of Gibbon conforms closely to the criterion of an authentically historical view of the past he laid down several years later in *Experience and its Modes*. Gibbon's 'main aim, from first to last, was simply to describe the past. The ultimate meaning of it all did not interest him.'[56] On closer inspection, however, this view turns out not to be quite identical with the position that Oakeshott had adopted by the 1930s. He went on: 'History to [Gibbon] was a drama and not a problem', but this invocation of an artistic genre was something he later rejected. While Oakeshott always held to the view that there were important similarities between history and fiction — notions of agency were presupposed in both, for example — he came to think history could not literally be written by employing literary genres, as distinct from style.

[52] *op. cit.*, p. 7.
[53] *Ibid.*
[54] *op. cit.*, p. 9.
[55] *op. cit.*, p. 10.
[56] *op. cit.*, p. 12.

It is interesting to debate whether Oakeshott would still have thought in 1933 that Gibbon's 'wonderful turn for irony'[57] made him a better historian. Not, presumably, insofar as irony was employed in the service of genre — 'tragic irony', for example, would have no place in his later theory of history — but as a component of style, the deliberate expression of the opposite of the literal sense of a statement, it is not clear why he would have objected to it. Certainly, insofar as a sense of irony implies a feeling for the difference between the actual and intended or expected outcomes of events, his theory could be said almost to require it. Nor did this absence of genre from historical writing exclude the use of narrative, as we shall see in chapter four. It is unlikely, however, that by the 1930s Oakeshott would still have accepted Gibbon's use of the idea of decay as the organising principle of the *Decline and Fall* as properly historical. 'Decay' belonged to the world of practice, whereas 'history implies a world of positive events in which such negative concepts . . . have . . . no place at all.'[58]

In 1928, Oakeshott thought it praise to say of Gibbon that he had set 'his narrative marching steadily in one direction, with the inevitability of fate, like a Greek drama',[59] but the notion of inevitability came to seem as suspect to him as that of drama. Historical events were neither accidental nor inevitable, he would conclude, but contingent. To invoke 'accident' was another misapplication of a concept taken from practical life, and 'necessity' — mathematical, divine, or dramatic — was similarly foreign. Other grounds of praise were never retracted, however. It would certainly be odd of Oakeshott not to have admired an historian like Gibbon for his erudition, for the way that he 'writes with authority on everything he touches', but it is perhaps a little more noteworthy that he singled Gibbon out too on grounds of his imagination.

Simply because the historian is denied the use of literary genres (the 'tropes' of Hayden White's *Metahistory*) does not mean he does not draw on imaginative as well as rational resources in his work.[60] For Gibbon 'as for any artist, to know an event was not only to understand how it happened, but also to imagine it happening: and what is true of events is true, also, of characters'.[61] It is significant that Oakeshott thought that 'Like a dramatist, Gibbon tends to raise his

[57] *op. cit.*, p. 14.

[58] *EM*, p. 12.

[59] Oakeshott, 'What do we look for in an historian?', p. 13.

[60] The point is well made in Nardin, *op. cit.*, p. 148.

[61] Oakeshott, 'What do we look for in an historian?', p. 13.

characters above their own individuality and makes them types';[62] we saw in the previous chapter that he had approached historical figures in this way himself from a very early stage. By the 1930s he had begun to integrate this approach with his developing account of the history of political thought, and it was a manner of thinking that endured in him to the end. The tendency he identified in Gibbon to slide from character to caricature is also, as we shall see, something he was frequently in danger of himself.

The main contrast Oakeshott drew between Gibbon and Macaulay was that the latter was distinguished for his memory and judgemental style rather than his imagination. His weakness was a tendency to become lost in detail (not an accusation one can usually level against Oakeshott) which limited him to 'tableaux, or pageants' with no overall unity. His characters are more or less exclusively caricatures, though 'entertaining' ones. In the first instance, however, the point was not whether he was a better or worse historian than Gibbon, but to appreciate how he differed. 'Most of an historian's sins', Oakeshott concluded, 'particularly if he sins boldly and well, make his writing more interesting, and make him a better historian than he would otherwise be . . . save us only from the historian with no sins'. We shall shortly see this attitude exchanged for one less forgiving.

Philosophy, Experience and Modality

Experience and its Modes made no great impact in philosophical circles when it first appeared; the first print run of 1,000 copies took three decades to sell out, and Oakeshott himself recalled that 'Nobody took any notice, and it was soon forgotten'.[63] It is not true that nobody took any notice; his own collection of press cuttings shows the book was reviewed in the national press, including the *Manchester Guardian* and the *Times Literary Supplement*, as well as in a number of learned journals, and was often favourably received, though frequently as an eloquent restatement of the now unfashionable ideas of F.H. Bradley.[64] Thinkers whom he respected offered warm praise: R.G. Collingwood, for example, hailed it as 'original . . . important [and] profound'.[65] Others, though, were less complemen-

---

[62]   *op. cit.*, p. 14.

[63]   Oakeshott, Festschrift address, LSE 1/3.

[64]   Oakeshott's collection of letters and press cuttings relating to *Experience and its Modes* is at LSE 4/4/1.

[65]   R.G. Collingwood, Review of *Experience and its Modes*, *Cambridge Review*, vol. 55, 1934, pp. 249–50.

tary; Susan Stebbing's review has aptly been described as 'sniffy'.[66] She thought Oakeshott had merely repeated 'remarks made familiar to us by the writings of absolute idealists' and 'those who have not been convinced by Bradley are unlikely to be converted by Mr Oakeshott.'[67]

Collingwood and Stebbing differed greatly in their assessments of Oakeshott's philosophy of history. Collingwood thought 'the chapter on history . . . the real nucleus of [the] book' and pronounced it 'the most penetrating analysis of historical thought' yet written. Stebbing, although conceding that it was 'based upon a considerable knowledge of writings about history', found it 'extraordinarily confused.' The same extreme divergence of opinion has been evident ever since. Grant exclaimed that 'No-one who has pondered Oakeshott will ever again be able to see (e.g.) that standard freshman authority, E.H. Carr's *What is History?*, as anything more than a series of well-meaning howlers',[68] while Himmelfarb felt she had just been issued 'an invitation to historical nihilism',[69] and Meiland concluded Oakeshott's 'final position' was that 'historical knowledge is impossible.'[70]

To Oakeshott himself, *Experience and its Modes* had a dual purpose. The first aim was 'a study of the relationship . . . between experience as a whole and for its own sake [i.e. philosophy] and the various arrests which experience suffers.' That is, Oakeshott wanted to determine the relationship of philosophy to the several worlds or modes of experience, including science, history and practice.[71] He argued that philosophy was the more satisfactory form of experience because it was capable of arriving at 'concrete' definitions embracing experience as a whole, whereas the modes could know the whole of experience only from an 'abstract', partial perspective.[72]

[66] Grant, 'Inside the Hedge', p. 108.

[67] L.S. Stebbing, Review of *Experience and its Modes, Mind*, vol. 43, 1934, pp. 403–5.

[68] Grant, *Oakeshott*, p. 104.

[69] Himmelfarb, *The New History and the Old*, p. 182.

[70] J.W. Meiland, *Scepticism and Historical Knowledge*, Random House, New York, 1965, p. 62.

[71] *EM*, p. 4.

[72] In fact, Oakeshott claimed one of the central concerns of the book was with the place of philosophy in an age of science. He believed that this was one of the most important questions confronting modern philosophy, one which Dilthey, Husserl, Weber, Jaspers, Heidegger, Kierkegaard, and Nietzsche had all addressed. See Oakeshott, Review of W. Brock, *An Introduction to Contemporary German Philosophy, Cambridge Review*, vol. 57, 1936, p. 195. This belief is somewhat tangential to our theme, however, and cannot be pursued here, although Oakeshott's philosophy of science will be considered below.

The second aim was to 'study … the relationship of these arrests [i.e. the modes of science, history and practice] to one another', and to determine the specific character of each. This second enterprise, be it noted, is not entailed by the first. One might concentrate exclusively on the nature of historical enquiry, or the relationship of historical enquiry to practical life, without considering the relationship of history to philosophy. Oakeshott himself remarked that this second aim 'might be considered the main business'[73] of philosophy.

In this second enterprise, philosophy ensures the various forms of experience, such as science and history, are 'separated and kept separate' in the interests of avoiding the '*confusion des genres*' which led to 'the most insidious and crippling of all forms of error — irrelevance.'[74] The philosophy of *Experience and its Modes* has been described as 'water-colour . . . Hegelianism',[75] but, although Oakeshott certainly expressed a debt to Hegel and Bradley,[76] the enterprise being described here may perhaps be better understood as a neo-Kantian project. It was Kant's belief that 'we do not enlarge, but only disfigure the sciences, if we allow their respective limits to be confounded'[77] and, in Oakeshott's view, it was the task of philosophy to render the respective limits of the various modes as clear as possible, by identifying the distinctive postulates which 'imply, call forth and maintain'[78] the modes of history, science and practice. In a manner analogous to Kant's transcendental deductions, these postulates delineate the conditions of the possibility of the several modes of experience. So, when Oakeshott wrote of the 'logic' or 'structure' of historical enquiry, he should be taken to be concerned, as he put it in *On History*, 'not with the truth of [historical] conclusions but the conditions [of relevance] in terms of which they may be recognised to be conclusions'.[79]

In *Experience and its Modes*, however, the two enterprises remained enmeshed with one another. Consequently, Oakeshott's discussion of history attempted not only to discern the presuppositions of historical enquiry and its relation to the other modes, but also the features of history which rendered it abstract and defective in relation

---

[73] *EM*, p. 4.

[74] *op. cit.*, p. 5.

[75] E. Gellner, Review of C. Taylor, *Hegel*, *Encounter*, vol. 46, 1976, pp. 36–49.

[76] *EM*, p.7.

[77] I. Kant, *Critique of Pure Reason*, trans. N.K. Smith, MacMillan, London, 1983, p. 18.

[78] *EM*, p.74.

[79] *OH*, p. 5.

to philosophy. More — those very postulates, which from one point of view appeared as the distinctive characteristics of history, were from another point of view the features that rendered history an abstract mode of experience. 'What determines the world of historical experience as historical, determines it also as an arrest in experience.'[80]

Conventionally, 'experience' was not the watchword of Idealists but of empiricists, and in the 1930s of Cambridge realists and (logical) positivists. Perhaps, in making 'experience' such a central motif, Oakeshott was seeking to beard these lions in their own den. He had criticised the ambiguity of Locke's philosophy of experience that had been taken up by Bentham and the Mills.[81] The ambiguity, he believed, stemmed from the fact that 'experience' could stand either for 'experiencing' or for 'what is experienced', for either a subject or an object of experience.[82]

We saw that an absolute separation of the subject and object terms had led Oakeshott's earlier attempts at a philosophy of history into scepticism. He now argued that 'Experiencing and what is experienced are, taken separately, meaningless abstractions; they cannot, in fact, be separated.' The two elements mutually entail one another and 'the one side does not determine the other; the relationship is certainly not one of cause and consequent.' His argument that 'The character of what is experienced is, in the strictest sense, correlative to the manner in which it is experienced' did not deny that experience could be analysed into the two components of a thinking subject and an objective world. He wished to claim only that from a philosophical point of view this separation could never be absolute.

The book began by exploring this conception of experience. Oakeshott claimed that the knowing subject was incapable of 'direct, immediate experience'.[83] Equally, there were no objects capable of being experienced 'immediately'. So, sensation, perception, intuition and feeling all postulated some degree of thought or judgement. For example, for sensation to count as 'direct, immediate experience', it could involve no judgement or inference of any kind. An immediate object of sensation 'must be isolated, simple, exclusive and wholly unrelated; transient, inexpressible, unshareable and impossible of repetition.' Such an object would be 'utterly indeterminate,' 'a bare "this is," in which the "this" is . . . without name or character, and the "is" is limited to merely "here" and "now".' To

---

[80]   *EM*, p. 146.

[81]   Oakeshott, 'John Locke', p. 73.

[82]   *EM*, p. 9

[83]   *op. cit.*, pp. 10–13.

him, this was absurd; an object of experience must be 'regarded as
this sort of thing rather than that, as having these properties rather
than those' in order for it be an object of experience at all.[84]

Genuinely immediate experience also implied 'the absence of any
continuous or unified experiencing agent'. The subject becomes,
'like the object, a mere abstraction, now to be identified with sight,
now with hearing, and always devoid of continuity.'[85] Oakeshott
insisted the subject's thought must not be conceived of as a foreign
intrusion, 'the mere qualification of existence by an idea'. Rather,
thought 'is a qualification of existence by itself, which extends, in the
end, to a qualification of the whole of existence by its whole character.'[86] On this view, everything requires interpretation; 'what we
have, and all we have, is a world of meanings.'[87]

This by no means committed Oakeshott to an absolute scepticism
about the possibility of knowledge. Rather, he argued, meaningful
experience postulated 'knowledge', which could never be dismissed
as merely subjective. He did not deny the existence of 'a world of
ideas expressly characterised as mine . . . but it does not follow that it
is merely mine'. Whether my experience is coherent or not is never
simply 'by reason of its being my psychical state'. By the same token,
he was not concerned to dispute the existence of objective knowledge but its character. Objective knowledge was not a meaningless
idea, but it could not signify 'a world of existence outside experience'. His earlier equation of rationality with universal and timeless
truth was replaced by an identification of rationality with significance or meaning.[88]

'Truth', nevertheless, remained a postulate of experience.
Oakeshott's discussion of truth appears to owe something to
H.H. Joachim, whom he thanked for his criticisms of *Experience and
its Modes*. In *The Nature of Truth*, Joachim had contrasted a 'correspondence' theory of truth and a 'coherence' theory. The correspondence theory, he argued, saw truth as consisting in the agreement of
our ideas with an independently existing world. As both Joachim
and Oakeshott acknowledged, this view had some plausibility, but
neither could accept it without qualification. A 'mind-independent'
theory of truth, as Joachim called it, was quite correct to insist that
'We do not create truth, but only find it; and we could not find it if it

---

[84]   Meiland, *op. cit.*, p. 44.

[85]   *EM*, p. 13.

[86]   *op. cit.*, p. 24.

[87]   *op. cit.*, p. 61.

[88]   *op. cit.*, pp. 53–8.

were not there and (in a sense) independent of our finding'. But at the same time, he continued, 'we cannot separate truth and the finding of it . . . Truth . . . is not truth at all except insofar as it is the living experience of a mind.'[89] Oakeshott likewise rejected any suggestion that 'truth lies somehow outside experience,' or that it was 'an unknowable or inscrutable sum of knowledge'.[90]

Joachim believed this view of truth had implications for the study of history. The belief that 'a narrative is "true" if it "re-presents" . . . the real order of events' depended on the assumptions of the correspondence theory. Once it was recognised, however, that 'The sentient subjects of the past, their immediate experiences . . . have as such vanished for us' and are 'at best for us the precarious product of a most delicate inferential reconstruction' which 'can never actually reinstate them', this theory had to be abandoned.[91] Oakeshott would argue against the idea of historical writing as corresponding with an independent set of past events on very similar grounds. The significance of this is worth emphasising. Bradley had simply stated that 'we do not question that history apart from the historian does exist.'[92] Such 'realism' about the past had driven Oakeshott towards scepticism. If the historical past was 'there', it was entirely inscrutable. Once, however, one argues that historical understanding constructs a distinct kind of past, this problem is avoided.

For Joachim, the criterion of truth was 'conceivability', not in the psychological sense of a 'mental picture', but in the sense of 'being a significant whole . . . possessed of meaning for thought'.[93] Oakeshott's notion of a 'world of ideas' bears comparison with Joachim's concept of a 'significant whole' in which 'all [the] constituent elements reciprocally involve one another, or reciprocally determine one another's being'. On Oakeshott's view, a 'fact' only found its meaning in the world of facts to which it belongs, and the introduction of 'new' facts into that world (which is achieved by 'discovering the unity contained seminally or implicitly in what is given') has 'a transforming effect . . . To modify the system as a whole is to cause every constituent to take on a new character; to modify any of the constituents is to alter the system as a whole'. On this basis, he

---

[89] H.H. Joachim, *The Nature of Truth*, 2nd edn., ed. R.G. Collingwood, Oxford UP, Oxford, 1939, pp. 7, 14.

[90] *EM*, p. 31.

[91] Joachim, *op. cit.*, p. 15.

[92] Bradley, *op. cit.*, p. 9.

[93] Joachim, *op. cit.*, p. 64.

could explain why the discovery of a single new piece of evidence might prompt the revision of whole passages of the past.

Oakeshott, in effect, agreed with Joachim that truth 'must be sought, not . . . in isolated intuitions, but rather in the organised whole of a science [which] possesses at least relative self-dependence'. Even the coherence theory, however, was not held by Joachim to be finally satisfactory. As the 'work of a finite mind', it could not be completely true.[94] Oakeshott can be said to have evaded rather than resolved the difficulties involved in the concept, for as Nardin notes, he failed to define it. However, as Nardin also remarks, 'This failure can be explained, at least in part, by his commitment to the view . . . that different kinds of knowledge display different kinds of coherence'. Thus, for Oakeshott, 'the idea of coherence necessarily functions as a metaphor, not a technical concept'.[95]

There are also problems with Oakeshott's argument that there was a logical necessity in experience, so that 'We are forced by the nature of experience to what is absolute'.[96] The idea that experience could force or 'oblige' us to certain conclusions can be found in Bosanquet, for example, who had defined 'the objective' as 'whatever we are obliged to think'.[97] 'Obligation' nevertheless remained a metaphor drawn from legal or moral language. It did not help Oakeshott in establishing his belief that truth was necessarily coercive. Insofar as he had a justification for this view, it was that each mode implied a totality greater than the sum of its parts. Each mode, including history, suffered from a kind of hubris, claiming its 'relative' degree of truth as absolute,[98] whereas each was 'abstracted' from the concrete whole of experience. The modes were the result of 'arrests' or turnings aside from the pursuit of this concrete whole 'to construct and explore restricted worlds of abstract ideas'. In the concrete whole, the modes were both completed and superseded, for it was their 'logical ground'.[99]

In 1933, then, Oakeshott still thought of philosophy as aiming at absolutely satisfactory, because absolutely complete, definitions. Absolute or philosophical experience was 'absolved from the necessity in finding its significance in relations with what is outside itself'. It was 'whole', 'individual', and 'removed from change'. From this

[94] *op. cit.,* pp. 175–9.

[95] Nardin, *op. cit.,* p. 22.

[96] *EM,* p. 47.

[97] B. Bosanquet, *The Essentials of Logic,* MacMillan, London, 1928, p. 11.

[98] *EM,* p. 77.

[99] *op. cit.,* p. 82.

absolute standpoint, a mode such as history was an 'absolute fail-ure'.[100] One might wonder why philosophers should bother them-selves with the modes at all. In fact, Oakeshott gave several reasons.

Firstly, philosophy could show that 'the modes must be avoided or overcome if experience is to realise its purpose'. This is odd, for surely, in engaging in philosophical study of the modes, one has already escaped from them — one's standpoint is no longer that of the historian or the scientist. Oakeshott's desire to portray philoso-phy as not only distinct from but also superior to all other forms of thought gives one reason to think that it was his conception of phi-losophy, rather than any of the modes, which was suffering from hubris. His claim that philosophy was a more satisfactory form of experience than history was based on a contrast between the partial and limited standpoint of the historical mode and the absolute nature of philosophical experience. Since, however, all experience was limited or mediated in that it involved thought and judgement, and this was as true of philosophy as history, it may be doubted whether his arguments supported this contrast. Indeed, he decided eventually that philosophy was just as 'modal' as history, as we shall see later on.

Secondly, philosophy may determine 'the exact form of the modi-fication of each mode'. This is important, for Oakeshott believed that although history was 'defective' from a philosophical perspective, it 'had not ceased to be experience'. As experience, it rested on certain postulates which distinguished it and which it was possible for the philosopher to identify and examine.

Finally, philosophy may 'illustrate . . . the relation of abstract modes to one another'. Oakeshott argued that 'each abstract world of ideas is, as such and as a world, absolutely independent of any other.' It was impossible 'to pass in argument from any one of these worlds of ideas to any other.' The modes are not 'in any way depend-ent upon or directly related to one another.'[101] These latter two rea-sons belong to the second enterprise of *Experience and its Modes*, of identifying the distinctive postulates of each mode and determining the relations between modes. Oakeshott's argument for the superi-ority of philosophy to history was irrelevant to these questions, and he abandoned it after 1933.

Two notions of 'modes' in particular that Oakeshott wished to rule out were of modes as psychological faculties, and as 'stages in a development of experience'. Since psychology was itself a mode, a

[100] *op. cit.*, p. 149.
[101] *op. cit.*, pp. 75–6.

species of 'science', it could not be used in a philosophical explanation of experience. In rejecting the idea of modes as developmental
stages, Oakeshott differed from Hegel, and also Collingwood. While
it might be possible to arrange them in some sort of hierarchy, he
conceded, it was irrelevant to his enterprise to do so or to 'attempt to
determine the relative degree of abstraction belonging to each.' He
was not interested, for example, in whether history was more or less
abstract than or logically prior or posterior to science.

 Collingwood — who had presented history in *Speculum Mentis*
(1924) as one of a series of dialectical transitions, succeeding art, religion and science and preceding philosophy — focussed most of his
criticisms of *Experience and its Modes* on the notion of modality. He
rightly remarked that 'history for [Oakeshott] is not a necessary
phase or element in experience as such.' Because of this Oakeshott
'had failed to solve . . . the question why there is or should be such a
thing [as history] at all.' Collingwood qualified this, saying 'what I
call failing to answer the question he would describe as discovering
the question has no answer.'[102] Although Oakeshott did not think of
historical writing as necessary, Collingwood was wrong in thinking
he was without means of explaining its existence. Historical thought
could explain its existence by investigating its own history, on
Oakeshott's view. Before we can examine the historical mode, however, we must address the other two modes, the practical and the scientific. Since part of Oakeshott's aim was to determine how history
differed from the other modes, we will be better able to appreciate
the reasons he gave for its uniqueness if we begin by examining the
kinds of understanding he took it to exclude.

Practical Experience

The practical mode is important not least because a large part of historical study is given over to understanding actions performed
within it. In discussing religion Oakeshott had argued that the 'practical' world of morality was self-contradictory because 'out of every
moral success the further 'ought' springs up to condemn you once
more . . . it is a series without an end.' This view of practical experience meant that he could not accept philosophical pragmatism of
any sort. He was prepared to concede that practical experience was
'at once the most primitive and general' of all forms of experience,
but he would not assign it any logical precedence.[103] Although 'the

---

[102] R.G. Collingwood, *The Idea of History*, ed. T.M. Knox, Oxford UP, Oxford, 1989,
    p. 156.
[103] *EM*, p. 247.

larger part of mankind . . . find it impossible to entertain the idea that this practical world, within which they are confined as if in a prison, is other than the universe itself', Oakeshott believed his study of the postulates of practice revealed things to be otherwise.[104]

Despite being philosophically unsatisfactory, practical activity was undeniably a mode of experience. Further, it was not to be understood simply as the world of action, as distinct from thought. 'Action is not the product of thought, it is itself a form of thought. An "external" or "objective" world of doings and happenings which is not a world of ideas, is a mere fiction.'[105] For the same reasons, the practical mode was not simply the world of (irrational) will. 'Volition is itself thought', and as such, is rational. An important postulate of the practical mode is that the world is experienced '*sub specie voluntatis*' (under the category of will). This postulate, like any other, provided a criterion of coherence. Practical experience was 'a world of judgements, not of mere actions, volitions, feelings, intuitions, instincts or opinions.'[106]

Practical experience was 'distinguished . . . from all other worlds of experience in that in it the alteration of existence is undertaken.' The world to be realised is itself a practical world, not a world wholly different in kind. A further postulate of practical experience, the idea of value, was implied in a 'discrepancy' inherent in practical experience 'between what is and what we desire shall be', between this present and a future world.[107]

This gave a very broad meaning to 'practice', as Oakeshott acknowledged. A wide variety of characters might be recognised as practical persons. For example, the politician, the lover, the poet, the mystic and the evangelist were all attempting to bring about 'an unrealised idea, a "to be" which is — "not yet".' These practical selves were perpetually engaged in self-realisation, or the realisation of their wills in the world. Such selves may be said to be 'inherently free and self-determined', for a world of action presupposed such freedom. 'History assumes a world of unchanging past fact; practice assumes a world of mutable, transient fact' which is present.[108] Were present fact to be considered immutable in the practical world, he argued, change or action of any kind would be impossible.

---

[104] *op. cit.,* p. 273.

[105] *op. cit.,* p. 251.

[106] *op. cit.,* p. 256.

[107] *op. cit.,* p. 260.

[108] *op. cit.,* p. 263.

The past was significant in practical experience only insofar as it bore on present and future engagements. The 'practical' past might appear as an object of veneration or nostalgia, a source of advice, a means of persuasion, and so on, but in all cases, it is seen, so to speak, from over one's shoulder while facing forwards. Oakeshott did not consider any of these attitudes to the past illegitimate per se. He was concerned only to distinguish them from what he considered to be a distinctively historical view of the past. The difference between his view and a pragmatist perspective can be brought out by a brief glance at the *Logic* of the American philosopher John Dewey (1938).

While Dewey was at one with Oakeshott in opposing the positivist idea that historical enquiry 'simply reinstates the events that once happened', thinking instead of historical writing as the product of 'inferential enquiry' based on present evidence, he did not distinguish a peculiarly historical past. Rather, he wrote of a single 'historical continuum' combining past, present and future. Consistently enough, Dewey thought of historical study as providing 'new instruments for estimating the force of present conditions as potentialities for the future.' His view that 'intelligent understanding of past history' was a means of transforming 'the present into a certain kind of future' would be, from Oakeshott's point of view, a particular attitude towards the practical past rather than an authentically historical attitude.[109]

Scientific Experience

There is much truth in the remark that 'the section on scientific experience in *Experience and its Modes* was designed to free other worlds of experience from domination by it' and that Oakeshott's 'real interest was in the relations between history, practice and philosophy.'[110] Nevertheless, in order to understand Oakeshott's philosophy of history fully, it is necessary to contrast it with his philosophy of science. He was as little concerned to deny that science was a valid form of experience as he had been to deny the claims of practice.

Indeed, he thought his analysis of scientific experience 'not unlike' Kant's description of the kind of theoretical reasoning which dealt with the phenomenal realm.[111] Whereas some self-proclaimed followers of Kant, such as Buckle, had tried to assimilate historical

---

[109] J. Dewey, *Logic*, quoted in H. Meyerhoff, (ed.), *The Philosophy of History in Our Time: An Anthology*, Doubleday, New York, 1959, pp. 164–71.
[110] M. Cowling, *Religion and Public Doctrine in Modern England*, vol.1, Cambridge UP, 1980, p. 261.
[111] *EM*, p. 317.

enquiry to the (scientific) kind of thinking appropriate to the study of phenomena, Oakeshott wished to keep them apart.

Scientific experience, Oakeshott argued, was best understood as the world experienced *'sub specie quantitatis'*, under the category of quantity. Postulating that everything could be measured, science aimed to construct 'a world of absolutely stable, impersonal, communicable experience ... upon which universal agreement is possible.'[112] Thus, there are distinct similarities between Oakeshott's account of science and that of the logical positivists of the day. However, Oakeshott was in effect turning positivism against itself, using it to display its own limitations. Unlike A.J. Ayer, for example, who claimed there was 'no difference in kind between ... the laws of science (and) the maxims of common sense',[113] Oakeshott argued that in scientific experience, 'observation in terms of personal perception and sensation [is] superseded.' 'Apples and stones are not part of the nature of which science is cognisant: the law of gravitation does not refer to these or to any similar objects, but to the movements of mass.'[114] For Oakeshott, science did not deal with events of the kind known to practical experience. Where science attempts to extend its generalisations beyond what has been observed for predictive purposes, Oakeshott argued, they will take the form 'A has probability x relative to B', where x is a definite and invariable figure. Before predictive scientific hypotheses could be applied to practical ends, they require to be translated into non-scientific terms.

This was not to say that science dealt with an external, material or objective world, if by these terms was meant a world untouched by thought or judgement. 'The distinction between the "subjective element" and the "objective element" in scientific experience can be compared only with the worn-out fantasy of the primary and secondary qualities of matter', a 'fantasy' that belonged to Locke amongst others.[115] Oakeshott's rejection of a distinction between a 'subjective' and an 'objective' element in scientific knowledge is not without importance for his philosophy of history, as the question 'can history be objective?' has often been taken to be identical with the question of whether history can become a science analogous in form to the natural sciences. Although Oakeshott tended to eschew the vocabulary of 'subjectivity' and 'objectivity' throughout his

---

[112] *EM*, pp. 169–70.

[113] Ayer, *Language, Truth and Logic*, p. 49.

[114] *EM*, p. 194.

[115] *op. cit.*, pp. 172, 174.

career, his remarks suggest that his answer would depend very much on what was understood by 'objectivity'.[116]

Ayer had argued that the criterion of objectivity of scientific propositions was that they were verifiable (at least in principle) by observation. This claim that science could discover an objective reality through the method of observation is relevant to the philosophy of history, for some have hoped to make a science of history by the discovery of a similar method. Long before Ayer, J.S. Mill had set out to enquire 'Whether moral and social phenomena are really exceptions to the general certainty and uniformity of the course of nature; and how far the methods, by which so many of the laws of the physical world have been numbered among the truths irrevocably acquired . . . can be made instrumental to the formation of a similar body of received doctrine' in the moral sciences, including history.[117]

Mill's 'inverse deductive, or historical method' was intended to 'find the laws according to which any state of society produces the one which succeeds it.' After Mill, such thinkers as Windelband and Rickert rejected the identification of historical with scientific method, drawing a distinction between *Naturwissenschaften* and *Geisteswissenschaften*, but still attempted to base their theories of historical knowledge on 'the methodological ideal of idiographic knowledge', that is, on a method for the study of 'individual or concrete reality'.[118] For Oakeshott, by contrast, neither science nor history was distinguished by a method, shared or otherwise.

Scientific method, Oakeshott argued, only illustrated the general character of scientific enquiry, in that it was necessarily 'a method of measurement'. 'When we say that scientific observation is "exact," we mean no more than that it is conceived in terms of quantitative measurement' and that the propositions it produces about the relations between the objects it studies are ideally mathematically

[116] For the many and varied interpretations of the idea of 'objectivity' in the philosophy of history see J. Passmore, 'The Objectivity of History', in P. Gardiner (ed.), *The Philosophy of History*, Oxford, Oxford UP, 1974. The question of whether history can be 'objective' appears to date from the later nineteenth century when 'American historians detached Ranke's critical analysis of documents which suited their need to give history scientific respectability, from his idealistic philosophy', according to G. Iggers, 'The Image of Ranke in American and German Historical Thought', *History and Theory*, vol. 2, 1962, p. 18. Philosophers and historians then began to question whether one could indeed use documents to establish 'facts' about the past as Ranke was now alleged to have done.

[117] J.S. Mill, *A System of Logic*, 8th edn., Longmans, London, 1884, p. v.

[118] G. Oakes, 'Introduction' to H. Rickert, *The Limits of Concept Formation in Natural Science*, tr. G. Oakes, Cambridge UP, Cambridge, 1986, p. viii.

expressible.[119] In keeping with the generic character of experience, a scientific result is always a transformation of a given world of scientific ideas, and it was in this world, rather than in a method, that scientific enquiry found its logical beginning.

The world of scientific ideas offered 'the simplest or most economical [general] explanation' in terms of motion of any instance of observations concerning 'the relations of quantitative concepts.' It dealt not with the 'mere thisness' or particularity of an observation but with classes of observations. If the phrase 'the laws of nature' had any meaning, Oakeshott contended, it could only refer to the 'analytic generalisations [which] express the relations between these [scientific] concepts . . . inherent in the concepts themselves.'[120] So, for example, the propositions that gravity is proportional to inertia, or that the extension of a body is proportional to the force acting upon it, were derivable from the notions of gravity and inertia or force and extension themselves.

It was in the light of these 'structural concepts' of the world of scientific ideas that scientific hypotheses were advanced. Any hypothesis, scientific or otherwise, made 'the assertion in supposal that the character of a given and known world of ideas would appear, were it more fully known, to be of a certain sort.' In science itself, Oakeshott argued, a hypothesis always 'asserts a relation or consequence, and never the existence of what is related. It is concerned solely with adjectivals. What is asserted is not the existence of the subject or predicate (that is merely supposed) but a relation between the two.'[121]

This view had important implications for the sense in which science could be said to involve a search for causes. If 'the strict expression of all scientific generalisation is "if this, then that," or "Suppose A and B, then C",' then a cause must be a proximate or efficient cause. Science, if it uses the notion of a cause at all, assumes that a cause is 'the minimum antecedent circumstances sufficient to account for any example of a generalised result'.

To Oakeshott, such scientific causes were always conditional. The scientific judgement that 'A and B cause C' was a hypothetical, not apodictic, judgement. He admitted a difference between a hypothesis as such, 'a supposal about the world of scientific ideas', and a scientific conclusion that is a supposal about what is. Nevertheless, he denied absolute certainty to science, just as he did to history; no sci-

[119] *EM*, p. 176.

[120] *op. cit.*, pp. 182–3.

[121] *op. cit.*, p. 211.

entific conclusion was 'beyond the possibility of revision'.[122] Most important of all, though, scientific inductions in accordance with laws found their place in science alone.

Historical Experience

Like Oakeshott's view of the scientific and practical modes, his 'view of history' was not based on 'the standpoint of the historian' but that of the philosopher. Just as his studies of science and practice had not involved tips on scientific method or giving moral advice, his examination of history excluded 'advice as to how history ought to be written.'[123] This was not to say he thought it impossible to give such advice, only that he thought it none of his business. This is worth emphasising because, despite his explicit denial, it has been asserted that Oakeshott was covertly attempting to tell the historian 'what he should do.'[124] While Oakeshott's 'critical' approach to the philosophy of history aimed to specify the postulates of historical thought, the identification of such postulates is quite distinct from the provision of a set of positive guidelines about how to formulate historical statements.

Oakeshott's first task was to establish that history was a form of experience at all. Schopenhauer, we saw, believed that 'history has an inferior cognitive status because it fails to qualify as a science according to the criteria for scientific knowledge that Kant elaborates in his *Critique of Pure Reason*'.[125] History could not 'discover the necessary and universally valid laws that account for the properties of the phenomenal world.' It dealt only with 'the particular and the contingent', and lacked 'the fundamental characteristic of science . . . nowhere does it know the particular by means of the universal.'[126]

Oakeshott could not accept Schopenhauer's view of history as a 'mere series'. 'In this so-called historical series the terms are not merely successive, they offer criticism of one another.' Historical facts were not isolated particulars. 'Mere unrelated particles of data . . . are contradictions and lie in the region of the unknowable.' The corollary, that the historian was simply the passive recipient of impressions from the sources, was equally erroneous. 'No historian ever began with a blank consciousness, an isolated idea or a genuinely universal doubt, for none of these is a possible state of mind.'

[122] *op. cit*, pp. 208–11.

[123] *op. cit*, pp. 87–8.

[124] *The History of Ideas*, ed. P.T. King, Barnes and Noble, London, 1983, p. 122.

[125] Schopenhauer, *op. cit.*, pp. 439–40.

[126] Schopenhauer, ibid.

Historical enquiry transformed 'facts' or recorded events into historical narrative by judgement and inference, and 'judgement involves more than a series, it involves a world.'[127]

Historical understanding, then, shared in the generic character of experience. It was a 'world of ideas' undergoing perpetual transformation in the search for ever greater coherence. There remained the question of the *differentia* of historical experience, the 'system of postulates' it presupposed. Oakeshott denied that he was offering 'an exhaustive account of the system of postulates implicit in historical experience', and contented himself with listing five — 'the ideas of the past, of fact, of truth, of reality, and of explanation' in terms of change.[128]

The first postulate of historical enquiry was that the world be experienced '*sub specie praeteritorum*', under the category of the past. The historical past had to be distinguished, Oakeshott believed, from a number of other kinds of past. For example, the remembered past may form part of the material for history, but it is not itself the historical past. 'History is the historian's experience, but it is not the historian's autobiography, and it is not his experience merely as his.'[129] Again, the historical past was neither a merely hypothetical past — the past as it might have been — nor an apodictic past — the past as it had to have been. Further, the historical past could not be identified with a particular subject matter. To describe history as, for example, the study of the human or the political past might be convenient, but philosophically such distinctions lacked a principle. 'There is nothing in the human to distinguish it absolutely from the non-human past, nothing in politics to distinguish it finally from what is non-political.'[130]

Above all, Oakeshott wanted to distinguish the historical past from the past to be found in practical activities such as politics or religion, because he believed they were frequently confused. Strauss's *Life of Jesus*, for example, had expressed 'a disbelief in the Christian religion based upon . . . practical grounds . . . in the language of history' and thus had 'persuaded many who would otherwise have remained untouched.' In the present-future of practical engagement, the past was important only in relation to the tension between the world as it is and the world as it ought to be. By contrast, the his-

---

[127] *EM*, pp. 91, 95–7, 111.

[128] *op. cit.*, p. 101.

[129] *op. cit.*, p. 102.

[130] *Ibid.*

torical past was 'the past for the sake of the past. What the historian is interested in is a dead past; a past unlike the present.'[131]

We have already remarked that Oakeshott was no Actonian. Here he argued that 'History is not a bar of judgement; it passes no verdict; *die Weltgeschichte* is not *das Weltgericht*.'[132] Like Butterfield, who also opposed the Actonian desire to pronounce on the rights and wrongs of past events, Oakeshott saw moral judgement as beyond the limits of history. Butterfield, however, based this view on a principle of Christian charity; since we were all sinners, only God could pass judgement.[133]

Oakeshott did not enjoin historians not to deliver verdicts. Rather, he argued that, *qua* historians, it was actually impossible for them to do so. This was not a methodological point, but a consequence of the different postulates of the two distinct worlds of history and practice. The practical world was the world of will and value; it was there that judgements of right and wrong belonged. In taking up a moral relation to the past, any relation to the historical past was necessarily abandoned, even though the judgements of right or wrong made might be true.

Oakeshott's opposition to moral judgement of the historical past did not invoke the idea that historians were discoverers of a 'scientific' world of value-free 'objective' fact. Moreover, his argument allowed that morality was still a part of history; the persons historians study still have a moral character, constructed as they are on the analogy of practical persons. Past actions performed in the practical mode took place in a moral world, and this cannot be ignored.

Not only was the historical past not a moral tale, it was not useful either. It was not that the past could not be useful — only that the historical past could not be. 'History teaches no lessons . . . if . . . the past has taught us something . . . it is not the historical past which has been our teacher.'[134]

Oakeshott's argument that 'The historical past does not lie behind present evidence, it is the world which present evidence creates in the present' was not equivalent to the view that 'all history is contemporary history', if this latter phrase was taken to mean that history 'can only be written backwards'. Behind the belief that 'the present dominates the past,' lay, once more, the 'realist' view of the

[131] *op. cit.,* p. 106.

[132] *op. cit.,* p.158.

[133] H. Butterfield, *The Whig Interpretation of History,* W.W. Norton, London, 1965, esp. chapter six, 'Moral Judgments in History', and *Christianity and History,* G. Bell and Sons, London, 1949, p. 45.

[134] *EM,* pp. 141, 158.

past — the 'notion of a complete and virgin world of past events which history would discover if it could, but which it cannot . . . on account of some radical defect in human knowledge.' Oakeshott, we should emphasise again, wished to avoid any such scepticism.[135]

This emerges quite clearly in Oakeshott's treatments of the second and third historical postulates, 'fact' and 'truth'. The positivist view of historical facts had to be rejected for the same reason that the idea of isolated data of sense had to be rejected, namely, because such facts would be unknowable, outside all experience. 'In history there are no isolated facts, because there are none such in experience'. In his opposition to scepticism, however, he was careful to leave room for error — 'there are no historical facts about which mistake is impossible: where error is impossible, truth is inconceivable.'[136] It was in support of this criticism of positivism, rather than in anticipation of late twentieth century 'deconstructionism', that he insisted on the inseparability of fact or text from interpretation.

Historical truths were reached through inferences from present evidence. Oakeshott denied, in other words, both that historical truth was 'a matter of the correspondence of a present world of ideas with a past course of events' and that history could be 'the product of "pure reason" or a priori thought'. He had, in fact, grown considerably less sympathetic to speculative philosophies of history than he had been in the 1920s. Schlegel and Hegel were now described as having made at best 'selective simplifications', but 'to omit the detail involves the destruction of history.'[137] The best such works could provide was 'a diagnosis of the present condition of European civilisation and an assertion of a scale . . . which determines the relative value of human ideals and activities.' But it was not the business of the historian to disclose a Christian 'eternal significance' in the past, and such works were often merely 'superficial'.[138]

Of the fourth postulate, 'reality', Oakeshott argued that 'beyond its character as past, reality in historical experience [is] composed of events, things (or institutions) and persons.' 'The generic reality to which these abstractions belong' he called 'the historical individual'. Any such individual may be said to have a qualitative identity or 'character'. Like Bradley, Oakeshott used the idea of character 'to

[135] *op. cit.,* p. 110.

[136] *op. cit.,* p. 112.

[137] *op. cit.,* p. 155

[138] Oakeshott, Reviews of N. Berdyaev, *The Meaning of History, Cambridge Review*, vol. 57, 1936, p. 453; H. G. Wood, *Christianity and the Nature of History, Cambridge Review*, 1935, vol. 56, p. 248; L. Curtis, *Civitas Dei, Cambridge Review*, vol. 55, 1934, p. 450.

exemplify the notion of a concrete universal', or an individual embodying both particularity and genericity.[139] Character 'serves to establish the necessary sameness in difference which gives identity to an historical individual.'[140] According to Bradley's principle of the Identity of Indiscernibles, which Oakeshott rechristened 'the principle of continuity', 'what seems the same so far is the same'. Character could accommodate change, only provided that there was 'relative' continuity with what went before.

For example, the continuity exhibited by historical persons was not infinite. 'The persons of history are constructed upon the analogy of the persons of practical experience. Birth is the discontinuity which establishes their individuality, death the discontinuity which shatters it. The self in history is centred on the body; where the body is, there is the man'.[141] But they could be said to have a 'character' which provided them with an identity, in the form of a set of dispositions. 'The will for nothing in particular' was not a possible state of consciousness for Oakeshott. The subject or self in experience involves 'memory and . . . reflection . . . opinion, prejudice, habit, knowledge, is implied in every actual experience'.[142] Historical persons were not simply reliant on 'mere time and place'. Just as an historical event 'is never a mere point-instant,' 'an historical person is taken to maintain his identity from day to day and from place to place, so long as death does not intervene'.[143]

Perhaps the best known, because most notorious, feature of the philosophy of history presented in *Experience and its Modes* is Oakeshott's discussion of causality. No less a figure than Geoffrey Elton once claimed that 'The argument for abandoning the notion of cause [as a category of historical explanation] is most authoritatively stated in *Experience and its Modes*'.[144] If we look carefully, however, we will notice that Oakeshott himself warned against his argument that historical change was not explicable in terms of scientific causality being mistaken for a general criticism of the idea of cause.[145]

History, Oakeshott wrote, offered 'a rational . . . explanation of the world in terms of change, and an explanation of change in its world'.

[139] Boucher, 'The Creation of the Past', p. 212.

[140] *Ibid.*

[141] *EM*, p. 122.

[142] *op. cit*, pp. 26, 14.

[143] *op. cit*, p. 124.

[144] G. Elton, *Political History*, Penguin, London, 1970, p. 153 n. 16.

[145] *EM*, p. 132.

The method of explaining change most frequently attributed to history was explanation in terms of cause and effect. However, 'the notion of cause as a category of explanation . . . covers a variety of conceptions'. In science, a cause is an efficient cause, 'the minimum conditions required to account for any example of an observed result'.[146] Oakeshott did not assume that science was restricted to monocausal explanation, although Mandelbaum criticised his alleged identification of scientific cause in history with 'some specific prior event'.[147]

Mandelbaum wished to defend the use of a scientific conception of cause in history. He argued that since 'the explanations characteristic of the advanced sciences' relied on more than 'an appeal to directly observed regularities,' 'the gap between historical description and causal explanation is not . . . unbridgeable, as Oakeshott took it to be'.[148] However, Oakeshott had not reduced science to the observation of regularities. Nor did he regard scientific explanation as monocausal. He had clearly referred to 'minimum conditions' in the plural and was quite aware that a scientific cause could, as Mandelbaum stated, encompass a set of conditions. Oakeshott's point was not that historical explanation was not monocausal and therefore non-scientific; it was that historical explanation was not causal, in the sense that it did not rely on scientific causality at all. The number of causes, or of conditions composing a cause, was irrelevant.

After this, Oakeshott's rejection of the idea that it was the business of the historian to seek out general laws comes as no surprise. Historical generalisations, he believed, were perfectly possible, but they were not equivalent to scientific ones. The latter could claim genuine universality; the former were necessarily 'collective or enumerative'. A statement such as 'All the Reformation parliaments were packed' was an historical judgement, but it was not the product of a general law that allowed historical individuals to be 'reduced to instances of a principle'.[149]

'General' causes were also excluded from history. God, for example, could not be invoked as a cause in history because He could be used to explain any event whatever and hence explained nothing at all. So were 'decisive causes,' great events or turning points. A rela-

---

[146] *op. cit*, pp. 126–7.
[147] M. Mandelbaum, *The Anatomy of Historical Knowledge*, Johns Hopkins UP, Baltimore, 1977, p. 110.
[148] *Ibid.*
[149] *EM*, p. 161.

tive hierarchy of importance in explaining the causes of past events was one thing, but an absolute distinction 'between essential and incidental' events was another.[150] An event such as the Reformation might be called great, but this meant only that it 'concentrate[d] and include[d] within a single whole a number of . . . events'.

In fact, any explanation in terms of 'sole causes' like climate, geography, national character or 'the individual human will' was suspect. All were distinguishable factors, no doubt, but none could be 'relieved of all [their] connections, placed outside [the historical world] and then made the sole cause in it'. Thucydides, Oakeshott wrote, might have rested content with 'personal character and motive' as final explanations, but character or 'personality cannot be placed in this manner outside history without becoming irrelevant to history'.[151] In a slightly risqué sentence, deleted from the final version of *Experience and its Modes*, he observed that 'it would not be difficult to write an account of the world on the sole principle of *cherchez la femme*, but it would not be an historical account — not because it would be untrue, but because it would be unhistorical'.[152]

Oakeshott also criticised Bury's proposal that 'contingency' might replace 'cause'. Contingency, as Bury described it, was 'not mere chance, but a "coincidence"'.[153] To Oakeshott, this was a distinction without a difference. The idea of contingency as 'the meeting-point of two or more "strictly independent" series of events' was contradictory. How could such series be absolutely independent and at the same time have one or more events in common? Moreover, Bury's idea presupposed sequences of events 'each with a "natural" or "logical" development of its own, from which only a collision with another such course of events can cause it to diverge'.

There were, so far as Oakeshott was concerned, no 'norms' in the historical past. 'History knows nothing of the fortuitous or the unexpected'. These were practical ideas. 'In history there is nothing extraordinary, because there is nothing ordinary'. To evoke chance or accident was to forsake historical explanation. 'For himself and his friends the death of William I was an accident, for the historian it is no more accidental than if he had died in his bed'. The corollary of this view was that 'nothing in the world of history is negative or non-contributory'. For example, that the donation of Constantine was genuine was a false belief, for 'the document was a forgery'.

[150] *op. cit*, p. 129.

[151] *op. cit*, p. 131

[152] Oakeshott, *Experience and its Modes* (MS version), LSE 1/1/9, p. 127.

[153] *EM*, pp. 133–34.

Nevertheless, the belief that it was genuine was not a 'mere mistake' to the historian. It 'makes a positive contribution to our knowledge of the Middle Ages'.[154]

Oakeshott believed that 'Change in history carries with it its own explanation'. He again drew an analogy between the historian and the novelist, as he had when discussing the 'plot' of history. 'The historian,' he argued, 'is like the novelist whose characters . . . are presented in such detail and with such coherence that additional explanation of their actions is superfluous'. History, that is, 'accounts for change by means of a full account of change. The relation between events is always other events, and it is established in history by a full relation of the events'.[155] Shortly after *Experience and its Modes* was completed, Oakeshott wrote an essay attempting to illustrate this conception, recounting the circumstances leading to the English declaration of war on Spain in 1739.[156]

'A Declaration of War'[157] made no contribution to the larger view of the history of political thought Oakeshott was trying to develop, but it is worthy of attention for the way in which it cautioned against historical over-simplification. Truncated explanations, he argued, were usually available for any well-known historical event. Because in this case the event in question was a declaration of war, we might expect it to be explained by an identification of 'the parties concerned' and the assignation 'to one or other of the parties the responsibility or blame'. No doubt much of the appeal of this particular war for Oakeshott was the popular identification of its cause with a particularly quirky and grisly happenstance: 'the cutting off of the ear (or ears) of Captain Robert Jenkins by the Spanish customs office in Jamaica'.

Perhaps, too, Oakeshott liked this example as it was easy for him to show how the merest attention to detail began to explode the popular attribution of the war to this individual act of mutilation: 'Capt Jenkins's ear was cut off on April 9th 1731, he exhibited his severed ear at the bar of the H[ouse] of C[ommons] on March 16th 1738, but

---

[154] *op. cit.,* pp. 140–42.

[155] *op. cit.,* p. 141.

[156] Oakeshott, 'A Declaration of War', LSE 1/1/8.

[157] This essay is clearly the basis of one of the two short pieces of historical fiction, 'Robert Jenkins', which Oakeshott published in 1936. See A. Bryant et. al., *Imaginary Biographies*, London, Unwin Bros., 1936, pp. 73–81. The MS source for the other, Oakeshott's account of a day in the life of Jessie, 'The Servant Girl who burnt the MS. of the first Volume of Carlyle's *History of the French Revolution*', published in ibid., 61–72, has not been traced.

war was not declared until Oct 23rd 1739'.[158] The idea of a particular
cause of this sort operating at seven years distance, it went without
saying, was not further accounted for by the popular theory. Lecky
provided Oakeshott with an example of a historian explaining the
war in terms of a general cause, England's established colonial
rivalry with Spain. This was a slight improvement; at least it
explained 'War of some sort, with somebody . . . But what we have to
account for is *this* war, war with England'.

Of course, Oakeshott's emphasis on explaining an event as the
outcome of a multiplicity of other related events immediately raised
the question of where historical enquiry must begin. It was an
important feature of his account of history as a mode of understanding that it was carried on by a number of practitioners, and because
the practice of history was itself an historical entity, no historian ever
found themselves beginning completely from scratch in their work.
Here he suggested that the answers to the questions 'How far back
into the past . . . And into how much detail shall [the historian] go'
can 'be determined only empirically and by common sense'.[159]

The three areas Oakeshott selected to explain the war with Spain
were 'English parliamentary history and affairs at home . . . from the
accession of George II in 1727', 'Continental politics . . . from the
Treaty of Seville (1729)' and 'Colonial policy and politics, considered
from the Treaty of Utrecht 1713'. He was not, in fact, entirely happy
even with this account. His decision to explain the war as the outcome of three related chains of events that coalesced only in the
months before it began, he remarked, actually violated his own
requirements. The true historical genius 'would present these three
strands as a single whole and present them without confusion, and
he would not be content with so small a backward range.'

We do not need to follow Oakeshott's account in detail, but there
are some features of it that require notice. The first is, as we have
come to expect, an emphasis on character — Walpole's contemptu-
ous attitude to the opposition, for example, is singled out as a factor.
The second is an insistence on complexity — the short and the long
term, the economic and the political, the structural and the ephem-
eral, all had to be accounted for. This position is brought out in a
lengthy concluding passage, which is worth reproducing in full:

> The character of Walpole and Newcastle, the death of Caroline, the char-
> acter and motives of the opposition, the parliamentary situation in Eng-

[158] Oakeshott, 'A Declaration of War', p. 3.

[159] *op. cit.,* p. 4.

land, the Prince of Wales, the growth of popular opinion in favour of war, the inevitable reaction in favour of something exciting after this period of peace, the excitement of the mob, the merchants' desire for more extended trade, the conformation of European alliances, the S.S.C. [South Sea Company], the Spanish colonial system, the character of Keene, the fact that he was at once the British Ambassador in Spain and the agent for the S.S.C., the poverty of Spain, the effect of the movements of the British fleet, the fear of a Franco-Spanish alliance and the apparent imminence of such an alliance, and Jenkins's ear itself — together with his moving little speech in the H of C — all these, and much else, are parts of a single whole — a whole of which the declaration of War on 23rd Oct 1739 is also a part.[160]

Monocausal explanations of historical events, then, were inherently unsatisfactory. 'Nothing may be neglected; everything, perhaps, is not equally important; but every single thing is essential'. Although the essay was intended to illustrate the argument that 'History is the narration of a course of events which, insofar as it is without serious interruption, explains itself,'[161] Oakeshott did not make this 'narrativity' a postulate of historical understanding; what is postulated is an explanation in terms of change. As we saw in the discussion of historical style above, the finished product of historical enquiry takes the form of some kind of narrative presentation of its results. Nevertheless, historical reasoning is not itself 'following a story' — the story is the end product of historical thought. It is also important to realise that Oakeshott made no distinction between narration and analysis. On his view, narration, since it entailed judgement, was necessarily analytical.[162]

In the 1960s, W.B. Gallie claimed 'a new approach to ... the philosophy of history', arguing that understanding historical explanations entailed following a kind of narrative story.[163] This may be so, but Gallie, unlike Oakeshott, paid 'no attention to the epistemic particularities of history,' assuming that all narratives dealing with the past were 'historical'. Not only does this tend to elide any differences between history and fiction, it implies that historical research is determined by the categories of the narrative to be related, so that the inner logic of the story being told determines what may be

---

[160] *op. cit.*, p. 17.

[161] *EM*, p. 143.

[162] Cp. Elton, *op. cit.*, p.154 n. 28, and Mandelbaum, *op. cit.*, p. 26.

[163] W.B. Gallie, *Philosophy and the Historical Understanding*, Chatto and Windus, London, 1964, pp. 9, 21.

included in the account.[164] One may be forgiven for thinking that this
is putting the cart before the horse.

Oakeshott did not elaborate on the idea of change as a postulate of
historical explanation at any length. Simply stating that the relation
between events is composed of other events did not go very far in
elucidating either the nature of an historical event or the relations
between them. His suggestion that historical events depend for their
meanings on 'subsequent' terms in a series of events[165] was also
somewhat at odds with his idea that the historical past is 'the past as
past,' a fixed past which is not eligible to acquire new meanings in
the light of later events, unlike the practical past. But we must take
into account the fact that in *Experience and its Modes*, Oakeshott was
repeatedly distracted from explaining the logic of historical enquiry
by his efforts to establish history as unsatisfactory in comparison to
philosophy. He gave three main reasons for its 'defective' nature.

First, the 'form' of history 'contradicts the nature of its content'.[166]
Although historical reality 'appears to lie in the past,' the past is an
abstraction that forms no part of present reality and experience.
Why the structure of a form of experience that relies on a relation of
past and present should be contradictory rather than simply distinctive was not something Oakeshott explained satisfactorily. He wrote
that the historian 'supposes' the world of history 'actually' to lie in
the past, but such psychological terminology was inconsistent with
his own argument that he was not dealing with the psychology of
the historian but the logic of historical enquiry. While it might very
well be true that history postulates a relation to the past and philosophy does not, this alone does not support the argument for the defectiveness of history.

Second, Oakeshott alleged that history was defective because the
individuals of history fall short of (philosophical) definition. The
historical individual, be it a person, event, or institution, 'is . . . the
creature of designation . . . a defective mode of thought'. 'The end in
all experience is definition,' but since history is 'a world of merely
designated individuals, experience has fallen short of its own character'.[167] It has been remarked that it is hard to see how a philosophical definition of some of the historical individuals Oakeshott
mentioned, such as Napoleon or Cambridge, was even 'possible,'

[164] L. Goldstein, *Historical Knowing*, Texas UP, Austin, 1976, esp. chapter five, 'The
      Narrativist Thesis'.

[165] *EM*, p. 91.

[166] *op. cit.*, p. 146.

[167] *op. cit.*, p. 147.

and even if it were, 'it would require considerable argument' (which he did not provide) to show that a philosophical definition was 'more complete than a history of these things'. Indeed, 'precisely because the historical individual' such as Napoleon 'does not purport to be absolutely separate and complete, it is absurd to regard it as defective because it fails to be complete'.[168]

Third, Oakeshott contended that since historical understanding postulated its identities as changing, it was defective in relation to philosophy. In effect, this was simply a reformulation of his first claim that a mode of understanding which referred both to past and present was inferior to one that knew only a changeless present, and it was open to the same objection, that there was no reason to prefer the latter to the former on such grounds.

In fact, after *Experience and its Modes*, Oakeshott never again wrote of history as a defective mode of experience. It seems likely, then, that he realised that, of his two enterprises, only one, the enquiry into the logic of historical understanding, had proved fertile. The belief that history was defective in relation to philosophy, inherited from his earliest understanding of philosophy as metaphysical definition capable of penetrating to the ultimate nature of things, was slowly being abandoned even before World War Two.

A failure to recognise both the dual nature of Oakeshott's interest in history in *Experience and its Modes* and his later abandonment of one part of it is responsible for his reputation in some quarters as an absolute sceptic about historical knowledge. It will become clearer as we proceed that the belief that 'there is no suggestion in Oakeshott's later work that he meant to repudiate or significantly alter' what he had said about history in 1933 is simply false.[169] In the meantime, there is one aspect of Oakeshott's discussion of history that we have so far passed over, the relation of history to the social sciences.

History and the Social Sciences

We saw in chapter one that Oakeshott had a low opinion of the value of sociology for the study of politics. He also rejected it as a rival to historical study. His major criticism of the social sciences at large was that they suffered from 'a radical confusion between the scientific and the historical mode of thinking,' and consequently fell into

---

[168] J. Liddington, 'The Philosophy of Michael Oakeshott and its Relation to Politics', unpublished PhD Thesis, Balliol College, Oxford, pp. 65–8.

[169] Himmelfarb, *op. cit.*, p. 178.

irrelevance.[170] In *Experience and its Modes*, he concentrated mainly on psychology, economics and anthropology. Psychology and economics, he believed, were or could become genuine 'sciences,' but if they were to be so, they must be 'in conformity with the general character of scientific experience'.

That is to say, psychological or economic generalisations must result in probabilities, like those of physics. Both aimed to view the world quantitatively. Economics, for example, was 'concerned to measure the intensity of demand' and 'to generalise the phenomenon of price'. The corollary was that it bore no relation to either historical or practical experience. Economics was confined to stating the probability of the recurrence of a certain measurement within the system of its own observations' and did not refer 'directly to a 'human' world . . . of desires, feelings, wants and satisfactions'. It was 'not cognisant' of human desires as such.[171]

Psychology too was a view of the world in terms of measurement. It did not address a separate, 'mental' world any more than economics was concerned with a 'material' world. It was not concerned with the persons of historical or practical experience, 'the behaviour of living "personalities" as such.' Rather, it dealt with such 'quantitative concepts' as 'sensation' and 'attention' in terms of 'their duration, their relation to one another, their "threshold" . . . "intensity,"' and so on. Such a science was of no help in the conduct of practical life, nor was it 'psychology which is of assistance to the historian, but a knowledge of human character'.[172]

Anthropology, however, was a form of history, rather than a quantitative science. 'The men it is concerned with are historical persons, the societies it studies are historical facts, the events it records are historical events; in short, the abstractions it deals with are the abstractions of history'. The generalisations of anthropology were not, as Frazer had claimed, the general laws to which particular facts may be supposed to conform. 'No matriarchy has ever given rise directly to a full civilisation' was, like 'All the Reformation parliaments were packed,' an enumerative judgement. The use of a 'Comparative Method' made no difference to this. At the point at which this became a method of genuinely scientific generalisation, it was no longer of use in anthropology. For all that 'the anthropologist, intent upon developing the pseudo-scientific character of his subject, has in the past concentrated upon the observation of similari-

[170] *EM*, p. 178.

[171] *op. cit.*, pp. 221–30.

[172] *op. cit.*, pp. 236–41.

ties,' anthropology, like history, was 'regulated by the pursuit of differences'.[173]

On the one hand, it would appear that Oakeshott also thought of sociology as an historical science. Reviewing Mannheim's *Ideology and Utopia*, he placed it in 'an established tradition of great vitality in the recent history of social investigation . . . .which owes more to Marx and Nietzsche and Max Weber than to any other writers'.[174] He made no suggestion that Mannheim was engaged in quantitative scientific activity. On the other hand, Oakeshott seemed to admit the possibility of quantitative social science which was not limited only to economics and psychology, and in which 'each [past] event or situation [could] be transformed into an instance of a general rule'.[175] This was the view of a social science he put forward in a debate with M.M. Postan on 'History and the Social Sciences' in 1936.

Postan had lamented the 'anti-scientific reaction in modern historiography'. In the previous century, history had been 'studied . . . for the lessons it taught, or for the sake of the generalisations it suggested'. This was no longer the case.[176] He believed a reaction had been inspired by the distinction (unnamed) 'Neo-Kantian' philosophers had drawn 'between pure and practical reasons'. History was placed 'beyond science' and treated as 'an emotional and artistic exercise, aiming at . . . intuitive comprehension'. Oakeshott agreed with Postan that history was not a form of 'practical reason' at all. Yet where Postan went on to identify 'pure reason' or science with the whole of 'ordinary rational and positive knowledge,' Oakeshott balked. History, having been separated from 'science,' was not to be placed with 'practice', and conversely.

Any history that was not a science, Postan assumed, had to concentrate on the unique. If the objects of history were not universal, they had to be particular. If they were particular, historians were performing a 'descriptive' task only. The 'repudiation of all theoretical interest' which he took this to entail meant that historians were confined to 'the search for facts for their own sake'. Rather than uncritical positivism, Postan chose the attempt to achieve universal generalisations through the study of the particular. Despite his criticism of 'naive mid-Victorian attempts at social engineering,' social

---

[173] *op. cit.*, pp. 161–67.

[174] Oakeshott, Review of K. Mannheim, *Ideology and Utopia*, *Cambridge Review*, vol. 58, 1937, p. 257.

[175] Oakeshott, 'History and the Social Sciences', p. 79.

[176] M.M. Postan, 'History and the Social Sciences', in *The Social Sciences*, Le Play House Press, London, 1936, p. 61.

engineering as such could benefit: even the 'imperfect' generalisations of historical knowledge could make 'a contribution to our powers of social control'.

Oakeshott could not accept Postan's alternatives. Unlike Postan,
Oakeshott did not think that because history was not a form of practical reason, it must be reasoning of the kind found in the natural sciences. Nor, unlike the neo-Kantians Postan criticised, did he think
that the absence of scientific generalisation in historical understanding meant that history was non-theoretical or practical. Postan had
failed to see that there was no one single valid form for the understanding of the past. Postan's past was part of a process in which we
are still involved and which extended into the future, in accordance
with his desire for useful history. It was only by taking history to
mean either 'any and every way of thinking about the past' or 'a
course of events altogether independent of experience' that he had
been able to draw the conclusions he had.

Oakeshott nevertheless defended the possibility of 'the use of the
facts of the recorded past' by social scientists. Population or wealth,
for example, could be treated in quantitative fashion. Provided they
recognised that 'directly the facts of the past become instances of a
general rule they cease to be historical facts,' sociologists could get
on with their work. Here, however, he seemed to view sociology as
he had economics or psychology, an equivocation he did not resolve
prior to World War Two.

Oakeshott's Philosophy of History Before 1939

In his exchange with Postan, Oakeshott made no mention of history
as a defective mode of experience in relation to philosophy. Perhaps
he did not think his discussion of the different postulates of history
and science required any mention of the relation of either to philosophy. Yet the fact remains that he never again wrote of history in
those terms. There were many similarities with the views of *Experience and its Modes* in the last substantial piece he published before the
war, 'The Concept of a Philosophical Jurisprudence,' but it still
eschewed the vocabulary of defectiveness.[177] Although Oakeshott's
thoughts on jurisprudence did not involve him too heavily in the
philosophy of history, this article is worth mentioning if only
because it has been suggested that in it he flirted with a conception of
philosophy so different from any he had previously advanced or

---

[177] See Oakeshott, 'Philosophical Jurisprudence'.

would later hold that it would have had major implications for his conception of history.[178]

Oakeshott's suggestion that philosophical jurisprudence should be 'presented to us as a member of a scale or hierarchy of explanations of the nature of law' has been taken to indicate a move towards an account of experience in terms of a genetic hierarchy. Having criticised thinkers such as Hegel for philosophising in this manner, his statement that philosophy had the 'authority to create [a] hierarchy [of explanations]' in virtue of the fact that it stood at their head has been taken to mean that he was now doing likewise.[179] Obviously, if this were the case, we would want to know where history stood in this hierarchy. What would be 'above' and 'below' it? Would the position of a history of law in a hierarchy of explanations of law differ from the position of history as such in a hierarchy of explanations of experience at large?

On closer inspection, it becomes clear that Oakeshott's references to a hierarchy are rather misleading. Significantly, he did not place the various forms of jurisprudence he identified, the analytic, sociological, economic and historical, in order, or attempt to assess their satisfactoriness relative to one another. Rather than rejecting all he had said in *Experience and its Modes* about the 'biological' fallacy of arranging forms of experience in a necessary sequence, his only aim in introducing the idea of a hierarchy was to shore up his crumbling conception of philosophy as 'absolute' experience. He did not care what order other forms of jurisprudence were placed in, provided philosophical jurisprudence was recognised as the most satisfactory. And since he abandoned any attempt to make metaphysics the queen of the sciences after World War Two, we need not worry too much about a sudden major change in his view of the relation of history to philosophy.

Nevertheless, the article is not without relevance for our discussion of the other meaning of history, 'events'. Oakeshott ended with a call for a return to 'the tradition of Western philosophical jurisprudence'. His desire for a renewed study of this tradition, like the desire expressed in *The Social and Political Doctrines of Contemporary*

---

[178] T. Modood has argued that Oakeshott took a hierarchical approach to the modes of experience in 1933 as well as 1938 in 'Oakeshott's Conceptions of Philosophy', *Political Theory*, vol. 1, 1980, pp. 315–22. D. Boucher rightly criticises this view of *Experience and its Modes* but accepts Modood's claim that Oakeshott briefly experimented with the idea of a hierarchy of modes in 1938. See D. Boucher, 'Overlap and Autonomy', p. 79 n. 33.

[179] Oakeshott, 'Philosophical Jurisprudence', p. 352.

Europe for a distillation of the essence of Liberalism,[180] can be taken as a statement of a personal project. As he conceived of this tradition in 1939, it encompassed a variety of 'doctrines' and 'conclusions' but was 'single' in the sense that 'it is the universal context of every text in the history of philosophical jurisprudence'.[181] A shared assumption, in other words, that philosophical jurisprudence was concerned to answer the question of what law was, united writers as distant in time from one another as Aquinas, Hobbes, and Hegel. We shall see later that Oakeshott became much less confident about asserting the existence of such universal contexts for historical study, though he never lost his interest in the history and philosophy of law.

Since 'tradition' has become so closely associated with Oakeshott's name, largely thanks to those who accused him of imbuing it with 'mystical' connotations, we may pre-empt our next chapter and conclude this one with a few words about the meaning of the concept for him. It is very easy to exaggerate the importance it has in his work at large, and it is well to bear in mind that although he made use of it in his best-known essays, those of *Rationalism in Politics*, it had little place as an organising idea in his thought before the 1940s and was abandoned in favour of the idea of a 'practice' by the 1960s.

Insofar as 'tradition' played a role in Oakeshott's thought on history in either sense, it was a contextual idea. Like Collingwood, who proposed a 'logic of question and answer,' he believed that 'A's questions and A's answers cannot be understood without understanding the, perhaps, quite different questions and answers of B'.[182] The idea that a tradition was a perpetually changing identity, in keeping with his notion of the historical individual, was what ultimately undermined his belief in the kinds of universal historical contexts just mentioned. 'A tradition is not something which is merely conformed to, nor is it anything fixed and finished'. To the inseparability of text and interpretation, which was re-emphasised in 1939, we may add the inseparability of text from context or 'tradition'.

We should notice, however, that 'tradition' is an idea that tended to cut across some of Oakeshott's other distinctions, for example, the distinction between history and practice. He himself was most interested not in understanding the tradition to which he referred but in

---

[180] See chapter one, above

[181] Oakeshott, 'Philosophical Jurisprudence', pp. 357–59.

[182] Oakeshott, *op. cit.,* p. 360. Cp. R.G. Collingwood, *An Autobiography*, Oxford UP, Oxford, 1967, esp. chapter five, 'Question and Answer'.

using it to correct a contemporary tendency to inductive and positivistic (Austinian) jurisprudence with which he disagreed. What he neglected to spell out was that tradition in historical understanding (whether a tradition of philosophical thought or of anything else) was something different to a tradition in practical use. In the accounts he gave of the English political tradition after World War Two the confusion would be very visible.

Chapter Three

The History of Character, 1945-1958

Peace with Germany

World War Two ensured Oakeshott published nothing new between 1941 and 1946, though *The Social and Political Doctrines of Contemporary Europe*, having proved regrettably timely, was reissued twice during that period, selling well in America as observers across the Atlantic struggled to comprehend a continent plunging into self-destruction. Studying Oakeshott's thought during these years, then, has hitherto been difficult. However, the discovery in the LSE archive of a lengthy essay, written in mid-1943, alleviates the problem somewhat.[1] This piece addressed the terms of any future peace with Germany now that her eventual defeat had begun to seem assured. Italy was being invaded by the Allies, U Boat operations were being brought under control, and although D-Day was still some nine months away, Oakeshott was already anticipating it.

Historians have observed that 'After 1945, Europe rediscovered democracy',[2] and Oakeshott was no exception. In what was perhaps a comment on his own pre-war attitudes, he insisted that it was wrong to portray inter-war Europe as decadent because it did not immediately recognise the threat Hitler presented, and was not instantly ready to fight: 'It is an altogether false standard of values that condemns a civilization because it lacks the shrewdness to

---

[1]   Oakeshott, 'On Peace with Germany', LSE 1/1/11.

[2]   M. Mazower, *Dark Continent: Europe's Twentieth Century*, Penguin, London, 1998, p. 290.

recognise a barbarian when it sees one.' Oakeshott now declared
that 'It need be no part of our faith that everything in our civilization
is good; Western Europe has not found an ideal way of living . . . But
that its worst is not incomparably better than the best of what Germany has long desired to establish, nothing will persuade me.'[3]

In arguing that the Allied aim had to be to remove the danger Germany as a whole represented, Oakeshott was in effect coming out in
support of the policy of unconditional surrender first announced by
Roosevelt in January 1943. The Germans had attempted nothing less
than the destruction of European civilization in its existing form,
and in the aftermath of the fighting it was vital Europeans retained
confidence in what so many had died to preserve. Aneurin Bevan, at
that time the most important left-wing MP in the Commons, had
stated that 'the ordinary German was the first victim of Nazi aggres-
sion and when he lost his freedom ours was immediately threat-
ened.' Bevan's position rested upon a 'childish ignorance of the
nature and history of national socialism'. He had been blinded, in a
sense, by his own good nature: he simply did not 'understand a people that will make a slave of itself voluntarily . . . a people that derives
pleasure and satisfaction from suffering violence from its leaders.'

If the Oakeshottian account of the master-slave relationship
sounds rather sado-masochistic, that was probably intentional: one
of the sources of the instability of German society ultimately responsible for its slide into war was the 'profound sexual unrest that has
seized this people, dominating its social and political life and over-
flowing into and corrupting its way of conceiving all human relationships'. The war was not the result of anything so superficial as 'a
reaction against an ill-founded democracy', the Weimar republic.
Nor was the war simply the result of National Socialism and Prus-
sian militarism. As we shall see, Oakeshott saw the war as a
quasi-religious conflict, with roots that were hundreds of years old.

The true reason for the war, Oakeshott claimed, was nothing other
the character of the German people. The objections he anticipated
prompted him to become more explicit about what was involved in
attributing a character to an entire people. Firstly, as we saw in chapter one, there was no racial element involved. 'In no intelligible sense
are the Germans a single race, and what goes on in their bloodstream
is of no interest whatever.'[4] And, secondly, although this character
was an historical formation, it was not to be understood in terms of

[3]   Oakeshott, 'Peace with Germany', p. 7.

[4]   *op. cit.*, p. 22.

ancient history; it was useless to invoke, for example, Tacitus's notorious account of the Germani. It was 'the residue of the experience' of the last 'century or two' which had done most to shape German 'habits of mind and of feeling'. Thirdly, there was nothing inevitable or immutable about this idea of character. If individuals left one group and joined another, their character would change, and the character of their children would be even further removed from the character of the people they had left behind, because character is 'in the mind [which] is touched by every experience and every change in the physical and social conditions of living.'[5]

How, then, did Oakeshott view the German character? They had become a people so self-centred that they were self-deceived: 'the German people have a remarkable degree of self-consciousness and faculty for self-dramatization . . . joined with a peculiar inability to criticize themselves, a peculiar absence of self-knowledge, and a no less remarkable conviction that nobody else understands them.' They were, as his remarks on sexuality suggested, deeply divided against themselves. They had isolated themselves from other Europeans out of a sense of their own superiority and uniqueness, only to find that they nevertheless desired 'some relationship with the world outside other than that of mere power.' In a rephrasing of Hegel's concept of life as a perpetual struggle for recognition, Oakeshott observed that 'Even a German understands that to be liked adds something to being important.'

Europe had been visited with the consequences of the working out of an internal struggle within the German character, tormented by the same kind of religiously inspired emotional dynamic that had wracked Luther, 'a man who desired above all to feel himself in a state of grace, feel himself saved; just as the German character, in its weakness, desires to be accepted and loved.' Luther's sense of sin was so acute that it 'seemed to make forever impossible that redemption he desired; and it was only when he embraced the idea of redemption, not through goodness, nor through personal suffering, but through the suffering of someone else, vicarious suffering, that the way becomes clear.' Christ had suffered to redeem the world; now Europe would have to suffer to redeem the Germans, who had given in to 'an infantile megalomania which seeks to redeem its own sense of inferiority by the destruction of the world.'

There was little that could be done by anyone except the Germans themselves to alter this character; Oakeshott was sceptical of pro-

---

[5]   *op. cit.*, p. 24.

jects for reeducation, if that meant 'the attempt that must be made to rescue the German mind from the relics of National Socialism'. National Socialism was merely a symptom, and the 'diseased personality' which was the real cause of the German problem could only be cured by the efforts of the sufferers. 'If the peace of the world depends upon the education of Germany by outside influence then the peace of the world is a chimera.'[6] The main thing was to disarm the Germans thoroughly and permanently, for their own protection, and let the Germans themselves look after their own moral and spiritual rehabilitation.

Rationalism and the Peculiarities of the English[7]

Captain Michael Oakeshott of the Royal Artillery, service no. A501245,[8] ended nearly five years in a wartime army serving in Europe in the Allied Special Forces as a member of the glamorously named Phantom, a.k.a. F Squadron, a GHQ Liaison Regiment that acted as a signalling section for the SAS Brigade. Oakeshott later recalled that he 'used to say to the people I spent the war with, that if this is the world, I don't care for it much, and the sooner I am back in Cambridge the better pleased I shall be.'[9] When the end of the war finally came, a policy of unconditional surrender was indeed imposed, but a new fear now entered his mind, of having won the war only to lose the peace. On his release from military service Mr Michael Oakeshott, MA, was granted his wish to return to his beloved Cambridge, only to find the Labour party taking power and bent on establishing a fully-fledged welfare state.

Even the Conservative party, Oakeshott believed, had begun to resort to tricks of 'administrative technique' as a substitute for politics. Contemporary Rationalism was all-pervasive: 'The Beveridge report, the Education Act of 1944, Federalism, Nationalism, Votes for Women, the Catering Wages Act, the destruction of the Austro-Hungarian Empire, the World State (of H.G. Wells or anyone else) and the revival of Gaelic as the official language of the Eire, are alike the progeny of Rationalism.'[10] Although Oakeshott criticised

---

[6]   *op. cit.*, p. 39. This sentence is deleted in the MS, but Oakeshott appears to have endorsed the view it expresses.

[7]   With apologies to E.P. Thompson

[8]   A letter dated 6 September 1945 confirming Oakeshott's post-war right to the honorary rank of Captain is amongst papers relating to his wartime service at LSE 7/1.

[9]   Oakeshott, untitled and undated address to a Cambridge society, LSE 1/3.

[10]   *RP*, p. 11.

Hayek's *Road to Serfdom* on the grounds that 'A plan to resist all planning may be better than its opposite, but it belongs to the same style of [Rationalist] politics',[11] his own prophesies of coming 'tyranny' and 'despotism' in Britain as the result of a massive concentration of power in government hands aligned him with Hayek, who also saw 'totalitarians in our midst' in the later 1940s.[12]

If we disregard the transient and polemical elements in Oakeshott's account of Rationalism, however, we may see it as a continuation of his pre-war attempt to reduce the variety of European social and political doctrines to order. Communism, Fascism, National Socialism and much of modern 'liberalism' or 'Representative Democracy' were all dedicated to the planning of an ideal society, but in this they were simply continuing a trend that could be traced back to the Renaissance. Bacon and Descartes were singled out as 'the dominating figures in the early history of the project', and though Oakeshott did not wish to make them 'responsible for our predicament', nevertheless, he saw twentieth century Rationalism as the result of 'the exaggeration of Bacon's hopes and the neglect of the scepticism of Descartes.'[13] Karl Popper had just articulated a very different version of the history of political thought in *The Open Society and its Enemies*, but on Bacon and Descartes he seemed in agreement with his soon-to-be colleague at the LSE. Popper cited the 'optimistic epistemology' of Bacon and Descartes, according to which 'truth is manifest . . . there for everyone to see if only he wants to', as 'the basis of almost every kind of fanaticism'.[14] Oakeshott's Rationalist also found it 'difficult to believe that anyone who can think honestly and clearly will think differently from himself.'[15]

The ever increasing appeal of Rationalism in the modern world was due to the various 'types of political inexperience' that had arisen successively since the sixteenth century. These were 'that of the new ruler, of the new ruling class, and of the new political society — to say nothing of the incursion of the new sex.' The new ruler suffered the least from a lack of experience, for he had emerged in the sixteenth century, prior to the formulation of a 'general doctrine of Rationalism'. Not 'brought up or educated [to the exercise of] political initiative and authority', he nevertheless needed a guide to politi-

[11] *op. cit.*, p. 26.

[12] Oakeshott, 'Contemporary British Politics', *Cambridge Journal*, vol. 1, 1947, pp. 484–5. Cp. F.A. Hayek, *The Road to Serfdom*, Routledge, London, 1946, esp. chapter thirteen.

[13] *RP*, pp. 19, 34, 22.

[14] K. Popper, *Conjectures and Refutations*, Routledge, London, 1963, pp. 3, 8.

[15] *RP*, p. 6.

cal action, and it was to an instance of this need that Machiavelli's *The Prince* had been a response. Each subsequent group, however, had been increasingly liable to find plausible the idea that there was a 'method' which could be applied to politics.

Locke's second *Treatise* was Oakeshott's example of an attempt to provide for the second sort of political inexperience, that of the 'new social class'. Locke was the author of a 'long-lived' and 'valuable' political crib, which had not, unlike later efforts to provide for the political inexperience of later generations, covered up 'all trace of the political habit and tradition of [its] society with a purely speculative idea.' Since Locke wrote, however, political inexperience had become far more common; 'nothing can compare with the work of Marx and Engels . . . the authors of the most stupendous of our political rationalisms.' Communism had 'succeeded in inventing so plausible a method of covering up a lack of political education that even those who suffered from that lack were often left ignorant that they lacked anything'; the same might be said of National Socialism.[16]

This ignorance of ignorance was one of the reasons Oakeshott considered political Rationalism 'exceptionally' dangerous. Although it was based on 'an identifiable error' (taking technical knowledge for the whole of knowledge), it was 'unable to correct its own shortcomings; it has no homoeopathic quality; you cannot escape its errors by becoming more sincerely or profoundly Rationalistic.' Indeed, the Rationalist begins 'by destroying the kind of [practical] knowledge which could save him.'[17]

Oakeshott's alarm was so great not least because of his belief that 'The informality of English politics enabled us [the English] to escape for a long time putting too high a value on political action and placing too high a hope in political achievement — to escape, in politics at least, the illusion of the evanescence of imperfection.'[18] Now, however, this style of English politics was under threat, not least because those with socialist beliefs did not want the war to end — there was a 'belief . . . in the positive value of the effect of war upon society'. The English, just like the Germans, had constructed a myth or 'legend' of the war, expressed in the view that 'the people wanted a purpose in peace as cogent as that given them in war.'[19]

As Laski declared 'The war has shown us' what men can do 'when they unite together in the service of a common effort'; the difference

[16]   *op. cit.*, pp. 31, 35.

[17]   *op. cit.*, p. 37.

[18]   *op. cit.*, p. 26.

[19]   Oakeshott, 'British Politics', p. 477.

was that he admired a spectacle that filled Oakeshott with dread.[20] Long after he had ceased to be concerned with Rationalism, he remained convinced that the hallmark of a 'civilised' community was that its members were not, as such, joined in the pursuit of a common purpose. A wartime society was no model for 'civil association' for that very reason.

The socialist myth of the war, Oakeshott believed, drew on 'the fantasy of English history current in socialist circles'. This history had been distorted by the anachronistic use of the categories of 'left' and 'right,' products of continental politics after 1789 to describe the history of British politics since the seventeenth century. Later historians have in fact discerned 'a conscious attempt to provide an historical background for the Labour party' in the 1930s and 1940s on the part of historians such as R.H. Tawney, whose *Age of the Chartists* had just been reissued in 1947.[21] Yet the vision of English history that Oakeshott put forward was no more 'historical', by his own criteria, than that which he opposed.

According to Oakeshott, British democracy was 'a way of living and a manner of politics which first began to emerge in the Middle Ages.'[22] This emphasis on the medieval origins of contemporary British political practice allowed him to claim that 'Parliamentary government and Rationalist politics do not belong to the same tradition'. Whereas 'on the continent of Europe parliamentary institutions were in fact coeval with the full flood of rationalistic politics', English parliamentary institutions 'sprang from the least rationalistic period of politics, the Middle Ages, and were connected, not with the promotion of a Rationalist order of society, but . . . .with the limitation of the exercise of political power and the opposition to tyranny.'[23]

The English civil war, which had once appeared to Oakeshott as a conflict between progressive and reactionary forces, in which progress had (or was about to) come out on top, now seemed a presentiment of current problems. The attempts of sectaries such as the fifth monarchists to govern society by imposing a single purpose, in this case, 'to minister to the glory of God', was a situation that had horrified Hobbes; one might say Oakeshott believed himself faced with its modern counterpart. In the seventeenth century, the only escape

[20] H. Laski, *Faith, Reason and Civilisation*, Victor Gollancz, London, 1944, p. 12.

[21] J.P. Kenyon, *The History Men*, 2nd edn., Wiedenfeld and Nicholson, London, 1993, p. 252.

[22] Oakeshott, 'British Politics', p. 489.

[23] *RP*, p. 26, and Oakeshott, 'Scientific Politics', *Cambridge Journal*, vol. 1, 1947, p. 357.

from civil war between two competing strands of divine right belief, monarchical and popular, had been the institution at the Restoration of 'a government whose office was to maintain peace . . . by means of a substantively neutral legal order'.[24] In other words, the establishment of the rule of law, which Oakeshott's Hobbes favoured, and which Oakeshott himself was later to explore, had come to the rescue. But this manner of governing had 'reached its climax in the 'parliamentary' government which emerged in England . . . in the late eighteenth and early nineteenth centuries.' 'In England after 1867', he declared 'the new electorate was very little interested in the manner in which government was constituted, and very little interested in freedom, but it was vastly interested in a redistribution of wealth.'[25]

This view of English history may perhaps be described as a kind of inverted Whiggism. For the Whig, as immortalised by Butterfield, the aim history was 'to produce a story which is the ratification if not the glorification of the present.'[26] When Oakeshott reviewed the reissued version of *The Whig Interpretation of History* in 1950, twenty years after its original publication, he was highly complimentary.[27] He hailed Butterfield's criticism of 'the habit of reading the course of events backwards, and in this manner making history a success-story' (as he himself once had in regard to the English civil war) for its 'subtlety' and 'firmness'. Oakeshott, however, had only inverted his relation to the Whig history of England as a story of liberty, by regarding himself as in effect a late-comer. On his own account, English liberty had been lost, or had at least begun to disappear, a generation or so before his own birth. After centuries of 'success' in maintaining civil association, decline had set in. The Romantic optimism Oakeshott had been able to muster even after World War One was being considerably shaken in the years immediately before and after World War Two. Worst of all, he was forseeing the corruption of the English character. The English, a people 'nurtured not upon Oriental indifference or a Stoic philosophy, but upon a tradition of "nerve",' had 'achieved a combination of love of life and indifference to injury more profoundly balanced than any

[24] Oakeshott, *Morality and Politics in Modern Europe*, ed. S. Letwin, Yale UP, New Haven, 1993, pp. 94–5.
[25] *op. cit.*, p. 109.
[26] Butterfield, *The Whig Interpretation of History*, p. v.
[27] Oakeshott, Review of *The Whig Interpretation of History*, LSE 1/2/1. There are two reviews of Butterfield's *Whig Interpretation* in this folder, one slightly longer than the other, but it is not clear if either was published.

other', but Rationalism had put them in danger of becoming 'servile'.[28]

As soon Oakeshott's Rationalist made his appearance, critics argued that he was no more than a figment of Oakeshott's own 'terrified imagination,' a 'straw man' created just to be knocked down.[29] The charge has a certain truth; Oakeshott did sometimes write as if he saw Rationalists under the bed. 'Almost all politics today have become Rationalist or near-Rationalist', a state of affairs he described in pathological terms as an 'infection'.[30] Furthermore, such criticisms raise the important question of the historical status of the character of the Rationalist, who is, of course, a type, not an individual. Now, in *Experience and its Modes*, Oakeshott had argued that the objects of historical knowledge were individual; that is, they transcended the merely generic. By inference, then, the Rationalist is necessarily a less than fully realised historical character; there has never been a person who could be adequately described in historical terms simply by applying to them the label 'Rationalist'.

Indeed, we may ask whether the Rationalist is an historical character at all — in his essay on 'Rationalism in Politics', Oakeshott described 'the ambition of the historian' as 'to escape that gross abridgment of the process which gives [a new intellectual character] a too early or a too late and a too precise definition.' He immediately went on to state that his own 'ambitions are not pitched so high', proposing to 'foreshorten' his account of the history of modern Rationalism by concentrating on the moment of its emergence.[31] This is practically an open admission by Oakeshott that his description of Rationalism was at best equivocally historical.[32]

The same is true of Oakeshott's account of English history, which really ought to be regarded as an example of what he had called the 'practical' attitude to the past. Nevertheless, although Oakeshott sometimes wrote, as he himself said of another author, 'as if he knew of a golden age in the past . . . which . . . was strikingly more successful in dealing with its political problems'[33] than the twentieth century had been, he was never carried away by his own rhetoric for long.

---

[28]   Oakeshott, Review of J.W. Watmough, 'Cambridge Conversations', *Cambridge Journal* , vol. 3, 1950, p. 254.

[29]   Cp. e.g. Postan, 'The Revulsion from Thought', p. 153, and J.R. Archer, 'Oakeshott on Politics', *Journal of Politics*, vol. 41, 1979, p. 153.

[30]   *RP*, p. 25.

[31]   *op. cit*, p. 18.

[32]   Oakeshott, 'The Structure and Idea of National Socialist Society', unpublished lecture, c. 1936 ?, p. 10.

[33]   Oakeshott, Review of J. Bowle, *Western Political Thought*, *Spectator*, 1947, p. 626.

Rehabilitating Hobbes

In 1946, just after leaving the army, Oakeshott wrote his introduction to the Blackwell edition of *Leviathan*;[34] his work on Hobbes provides a useful foil for his contemporaneous portrait of the Rationalist. The nineteenth century Idealist and pluralist thinkers whom Oakeshott had admired in the 1920s had been unsympathetic to Hobbes's political philosophy. T.H. Green believed Hobbes had grounded the authority of the sovereign 'in the superiority of his power' so that the measure of his authority was simply 'the inability of the subjects to resist'.[35] Similarly, Gierke saw in Hobbes the threat of 'the utter extinction of any genuine public law'.[36] A.E. Taylor, writing in the first decade of the twentieth century, shared their views. He saw Hobbes as the author of an 'absolutist' political theory which was itself simply 'a body of corollaries from the principles of mechanics'.[37]

Conventionally, then, Hobbes was presented as 'a materialist imbued with the ideas of the "new" natural science' who had 'methodically applied . . . the laws governing bodies in motion and their deductive elaboration to . . . a civil and ethical theory.'[38] Indeed, this view of Hobbes as 'the prototype of a Utilitarian' whose 'political philosophy represented a deduction from egoistic psychology' in which 'obligation was explained as the enlightened calculation of individual self-interest' was still current in the 1960s.[39]

Oakeshott, however was attracted to a semi-medieval Hobbes, a Hobbes who echoed a 'Stoic-Christian tradition' in which 'pride or vanity is the passion against which all the force of civil society is expressly directed.' He argued that 'the scepticism and the individualism, which are the foundations of Hobbes's civil philosophy' drew on 'late scholastic nominalism', which had begun 'the displacement of reason in favour of will and imagination and the emancipation of passion . . . far before Hobbes wrote.' Hobbes had 'constructed a political philosophy that reflected the changes in the European consciousness . . . pioneered chiefly by the theologians of the fifteenth and sixteenth centuries.'[40]

[34] See the transcript of a conversation between Oakeshott and Kenneth Minogue in 1988 at LSE 8/4.

[35] Green, *Lectures on the Principles of Political Obligation*, p. 63.

[36] Gierke, *Natural Law and the Theory of Society*, p. 37.

[37] A.E. Taylor, *Thomas Hobbes*, Constable, London, 1908, pp. 5, 15.

[38] W.H. Greenleaf, 'Hobbes: The Problem of Interpretation', in *Hobbes-Forschungen*, ed. R. Koselleck and R. Schnur, Duncker and Humblot, Berlin, 1965, p. 8.

[39] Q. Skinner, 'Hobbes's Leviathan', *Historical Journal*, vol. 7, 1964, p. 321.

[40] *RP*, p. 278.

This description of Hobbes's medieval inheritance was vital to Oakeshott, because it allowed him to distinguish Hobbes's rationalism from the 'Reason' of Descartes and the 'Platonic-Christian' tradition which he was simultaneously criticising in his essays on Rationalism. According to Oakeshott, medieval thinkers, following Boethius, 'distinguished two elements in personality, a rational element and a substantial element. In later medieval thought, this definition suffered disruption. Emphasis on the rational element in personality resulted, finally, in the Cartesian doctrine of the primacy of cognition and of self-consciousness as the true ground of personality. By contrast, emphasis upon the substantial element [opposed] personality and rationality and resulted in what may be called the romantic doctrine of personality with its assertion of the primacy of will — the person is that which is separate, incommunicable, eccentric or even irrational.'[41] It was this latter emphasis, Oakeshott argued, that Hobbes shared with medieval nominalists, and consequently he 'does not normally speak of Reason, the divine illumination of the mind that unites man with God,' but of reasoning, a more modest business. The other conception of reason, of course, was typical of the Rationalist.

Rationality, on Oakeshott's view, did not exclude the use of imagination, as we have already seen in his account of historical understanding. It was natural, then, that he should also have been sensitive to the role of imagination in Hobbes's thought. Though he began by being somewhat suspicious of Hobbes's tendency to 'think in metaphors',[42] in his 'Introduction' he argued that in one respect at least the imaginative nature of Hobbes' style set his work apart. Indeed, he regarded Hobbes as almost unique in English philosophy on account of his 'power to create a myth', something for which he also venerated the memory of his old headmaster, Grant, in an obituary written that same year.[43] What Grant had done for his school, Hobbes had done for his country; *Leviathan* itself could be regarded as a myth, 'the transposition of an abstract argument into the world of the imagination'.[44] Should this seem eccentric, it is worth pointing out Oakeshott was not the first to understand *Leviathan* in these

---

[41]   *op. cit.*, p.280 and n. 1.

[42]   Oakeshott, 'Thomas Hobbes', p. 268.

[43]   Oakeshott, Obituary for Cecil Grant, Memorial Supplement to *The Georgian*, p. 12, LSE 5/3.

[44]   *RP*, p. 234.

terms. Carl Schmitt had already done so in a work with which Oakeshott was familiar, *Political Theology*.[45]

Like Schmitt, Oakeshott's sensitivity to the interaction of political and religious ideas affected his interpretation of Hobbes. Taking seriously Hobbes's description of the Leviathan as an 'ecclesiastical' commonwealth, he was one of the first modern critics to see the last two books as 'an intrinsic part of the larger logical whole',[46] portraying Hobbes as a 'civil theologian' whose sovereign was concerned not with the truth of doctrines but their effect on peace. What Hobbes sought from the sovereign, Oakeshott argued, was an authoritative interpretation of scripture which made no reference to the private beliefs of subjects but which offered an escape from the chaos which rules when all exercise their natural right to interpret scripture on their own behalf.[47] That, however, was not all he had to say on Hobbes and religion — Christianity was also important to the myth which Hobbes had created.

Oakeshott's understanding of *Leviathan* as a myth stemmed from his view that the book was not only a philosophical work but also a literary masterpiece. As such, it shared what he described as 'the office of literature' in any civilisation, 'to perpetually recall' or 'recreate . . . the collective dream' of that civilisation. Hobbes was an inheritor of the 'dream' or 'myth' which had 'distinguished medieval Christian civilisation' and which 'no subsequent experience or reflection has succeeded in displacing . . . from the minds of European peoples.' Oakeshott was referring to the myth of the Fall, the commission of the Original Sin of Pride in the garden of Eden, coupled with the promise of an 'ultimate salvation'. Hobbes, like his contemporary Milton, had sought to give this ancient story a form suited to a modern seventeenth-century audience.

It might seem, Oakeshott argued, that Hobbes was simply trying to replace the Christian myth 'by another and altogether different myth', the portrayal of a solitary 'inhabitant of a world which contains the material for the satisfaction of all his desires save one — the desire to continue forever in an endless series of satisfactions.' Indeed, in one sense this was the case, for Hobbes was writing after the Renaissance. It was then that 'A new image of human nature' had

---

[45] Oakeshott listed Schmitt's book in 'Thomas Hobbes', p. 264 n. For Schmitt's Hobbes see G. Weiler, *From Absolutism to Totalitarianism — Carl Schmitt on Thomas Hobbes*, 1994. Many years later, in 1980, Oakeshott discovered Schmitt had read his *Hobbes on Civil Association* with great interest: see the letters to Oakeshott from Ellen Kennedy and to Kennedy from Schmitt at LSE 1/6/3.

[46] Skinner, 'Hobbes's *Leviathan*', p. 329.

[47] *RP*, pp. 267–74, 288–91.

appeared; 'not Adam, not Prometheus, but Proteus — a character distinguished from all others on account of his multiplicity and his endless power of self-transformation.'[48] As we shall see, this change had a central place in the history of character. Yet, Oakeshott suggested, 'If we look closely at *Leviathan* we may find in it the emphasis, perhaps the over-emphasis, of one passage in the inherited myth.'[49]

Oakeshott found in the myth of the Fall a perception of the 'extremes' of human life — 'Pride and sensuality, the too much and the too little.' In both St Paul and St Augustine, he believed, there had been an emphasis in favour of the 'too much'. He quoted Berdyaev's remark that the Fall 'is at bottom a proud idea . . . if man fell away from God, he must have been an exalted creature, endowed with great freedom and power' who could at least hope for an eventual return to what could be thought of as his 'natural' condition. By comparison, Hobbes had emphasised man's 'littleness, his imperfection, his mortality, while at the same time recognising his importance to himself.'[50]

The difference between the two myths, or the two versions of the same myth, corresponded to the two main ways in which Oakeshott thought the human predicament had been conceived by philosophers and theologians. On the one hand, the human predicament had been thought 'to arise out of the nature of man'. On the other hand, it had been thought to arise 'out of a defect in the nature of man'.[51] For example, Plato and Spinoza had deduced society from human nature, whereas Augustine had deduced it from the defect of human nature he called sin. Hobbes might be thought to resemble Augustine, for he saw the human predicament arising 'from the egoistical character of man . . . it is vice and depravity that causes the chaos.' Nevertheless, this was not the case, for the egoism of Hobbes's solitary in the state of nature, Oakeshott argued, was 'neither moral nor a defect,' but 'only the individuality of a creature shut up, without hope of immediate release, within the world of his own imagination.' Although Hobbes considered 'the striving after power which is characteristic of the human individual' to be evil when it is directed by pride, he continued, this applied only when 'man is among men'. Only then may Pride inhibit felicity; it 'cannot produce chaos in itself'. For Hobbes, he concluded, it was out of the nature of

[48] *op. cit*, p. 366.

[49] *CA*, p .153.

[50] *op. cit.*, p. 154.

[51] *RP*, p. 278.

humanity rather than out of a defect in that nature that the human predicament arises.

The place Oakeshott gave to pride in Hobbes's new myth is worth further comment. In a 1958 essay on 'The Moral Life in the Writings of Thomas Hobbes', this disposition provided him with an answer to the question 'How did Hobbes bridge the gap between men's natural inclinations and what ought to be done about them?' At what he called 'the obscure heart of Hobbes's moral theory' lay 'the character of the just man', 'a character which actually appears in Hobbes's writings, and is moreover, recognised there as a just character.'[52]

This character Oakeshott also referred to as the 'proud' man. The nature of this connection between justice and pride must be made clear. Justice, for Hobbes, was a matter of keeping covenants. 'Injustice', he wrote, 'is no other than the not performance of covenant.'[53] Now, although keeping a contract is not necessarily a matter of pride, Hobbes had described one of the 'two imaginable helps . . . in man's nature . . . to hold [them] to the performance of their covenants' as 'a glory, or pride, in appearing not to need to break . . . their word.'[54] In a discussion of the 'justice of men' and 'the justice of actions', Hobbes declared 'That which gives to human actions the relish of justice, is a certain nobleness or gallantness of courage . . . by which a man scorns to be beholden for the contentment of his life, to fraud, or breach of promise.'

Hobbes, Oakeshott argued, 'recognised the twofold meaning which the word [pride] has always carried.' That is, Hobbes knew that the word had both positive and negative connotations. In Augustinian theology, for example, pride, 'the passion to be God-like' could mean 'either the endeavour to put oneself in the place of God, or the endeavour to imitate God.' The former was 'a delusive insolence . . . which provokes a destroying nemesis', but in the latter 'manner of being God-like . . . self-love appears as self-knowledge and self-respect, the delusion of power over others is replaced by the reality of self-control, and the glory of the invulnerability which comes from courage generates magnanimity, and magnanimity, peace.'[55]

According to Oakeshott, then, in Hobbes's philosophy pride supplied a motive for people to endeavour peace by being 'just', or keeping their contracts. On this basis, he tried to show how the passion of

---

[52] *op. cit.*, pp. 278, 312.

[53] Hobbes, *Leviathan*, Bk. 1 Ch. 15.

[54] The other was fear of the consequences.

[55] *RP*, p. 342.

pride could provide an answer to a difficult question traditionally associated with Hobbes's political philosophy. Notoriously, Hobbes's account of the creation of the sovereign raises the problem that 'he that performeth first, has no assurance the other will perform after.'[56] As Oakeshott put it, what is there in Hobbes's account to 'convince us that this covenant, unlike others made in the state of nature, will be kept?'

What Hobbes had to show, Oakeshott suggested, was that 'it is not unreasonable for any man to be the first performer in this covenant of mutual trust.' This did not entail demonstrating that it was a 'reasonable expectation that there will be a permanent body of particular persons who will always be disposed to requite . . . trust in them.' It would be enough, he claimed, if Hobbes could show that it was 'a reasonable expectation that at any particular time there will be enough who are so disposed.'[57]

In the case of the contract to create the sovereign, Oakeshott argued, Hobbes was entitled to claim that 'what one stands to lose is insignificant' compared to the possible gain — an end to the war of all against all. The possible benefits of peace, however, do not show that 'it is undeniably reasonable to be a first performer in this covenant to set up a sovereign authority (or even that it is undeniably not unreasonable to be such), but only that the risk entailed here is far more reasonable (or far less unreasonable) than the risk entailed in an ordinary covenant of mutual trust.'

This is so even if reason recognises that someone must be the first performer in order for the sovereign necessary to peace to come into existence at all. 'Since . . . what Hobbes is seeking is a demonstration of reasonableness, and not merely the probability of superior reasonableness', Oakeshott concluded, it would seem that his account is either 'faulty or incomplete'.[58] What, though, if Hobbes could make an additional supposition?

If Hobbes could assume 'a man (such as Hobbes understood Sidney Godolphin to have been) careless of the consequences of being bilked as the first performer in this covenant, a man of "pride" and not of "reason",' would this complete the demonstration of reasonableness at which he aimed? Oakeshott himself left the reader hanging, saying that to what extent this supposition did remedy the problem, 'the reader must decide.' One cannot help but feel, however, that Oakeshott himself had made up his mind.

---

[56]   Hobbes, *Leviathan*, Bk. 1 Ch. 14.

[57]   *RP*, p. 347.

[58]   *op. cit.*, p. 350.

We do not have to decide whether to accept or reject this ingenious interpretation to realise that Oakeshott was using characters, or imaginary *personae*, to address problems in the historical under-standing of a text. This is not to say he had simply invented the char-acter of the just man. He claimed to find it in Hobbes's writings.[59] Nor did he find it in Hobbes alone. The character of the just man, he believed, had 'its counterpart in the writings of other moralists' such as Spinoza and Hume.

Oakeshott's use of this character also sheds further light on his position in the history of Hobbes studies. Strauss had seen in the later writings of Hobbes, including *Leviathan*, the total or near-total abandonment of a 'feudal' morality and the adoption of what he called a 'bourgeois' morality. On this view, 'Hobbes's political phi-losophy is the most important testimony to the struggle which has been fought against the aristocracy in the name of bourgeois vir-tue.'[60] Hobbes's political philosophy, he believed, was designed to accommodate both the 'bourgeois' individual and the 'just man.' The Leviathan allowed them to live side by side, by supplying an external restraint in the form of the laws of the sovereign.

This had to be consistent, however, with Hobbes's statement that there was 'no obligation on any man, which ariseth not from some act of his own.' The rule of law could not operate on a man by mere force, for this constraint would not be 'self-imposed and conse-quently he cannot properly be said to be "obliged" to do what he is compelled to do or to desist from what he prevented from doing.' On this basis, Oakeshott argued that it was not because Hobbes wished to put forward an absolutist conception of the state or because he thought of politics as a 'competition of powers' that the concept of power was so important in his political philosophy. Rather, Hobbes's civil philosophy was 'a philosophy of power pre-cisely because to subject the civil order to rational enquiry unavoid-ably turns it into a mechanism.'

Despite Hobbes's use of the slogan *scientia propter potentiam* (which Oakeshott called the 'most dismal . . . of all sentiments'),[61] he argued that for Hobbes it was only through the agreement to create an artificial man, a legal *persona*, in the form of the office of the sover-

---

[59] Flathman, in a self-confessedly Oakeshottian reading of Hobbes, has argued that there are in fact at least two other characters portrayed in *Leviathan*; in addition to the character of the just man, he lists the man of false pride and the temperate man. See *Thomas Hobbes: Skepticism, Individuality and Chastened Politics*, Sage Publications, Newbury Park, 1993, pp. 85–6.

[60] L. Strauss, *The Political Philosophy of Hobbes*, Chicago UP, Chicago, 1963, p. 126.

[61] *VL*, p. 128.

eign, that obligation was possible at all. Hobbes believed, like Augustine, that no-one could have 'natural' authority over anybody else, and in seeking the authority necessary to enable beings in this condition to live together, he had had a 'vision of a state as an association ruled exclusively by law' in which the power of the sovereign, as such, 'has nothing to do with the obligation to observe the conditions of *lex* [law]'.[62] This remains a controversial interpretation — it is still possible to regard Hobbes as 'espousing an absolutism which would impose an equal subjugation on us all.'[63]

Nevertheless, in his own essay 'On Civil Association' in *On Human Conduct*, Oakeshott presented himself as following Hobbes in making 'Civil authority and civil obligation . . . the twin pillars' of civil association. He consistently argued that for Hobbes, the creation of civil laws was not tantamount to the establishment of a purpose or 'highest good' for a commonwealth. Hobbes's rejection of the concept of a *summum bɔnum* for either the state or the individual, reflected in his conception of life as an endless succession of desires, meant that the sovereign was neither to declare for nor aid his subjects in the pursuit of an ultimate goal. The office of the sovereign was simply to abate the 'unconditional competition' or war of all against all that characterises the state of nature.

In this sense, 'Hobbes, without being himself a liberal, had in him more of the philosophy of liberalism than many of its professed defenders.' It was Oakeshott's contention that 'Hobbes is not an absolutist precisely because he is an authoritarian.' Hobbes's scepticism extended to the power of the 'artificial reason' of the sovereign, and this separated him 'from the dictators of this or any age.' Rather than fostering absolutism, Hobbes had been trying to forge a middle way 'between those who claimed too much for Authority and those who claimed too much for Liberty.'[64]

Hobbes's *Leviathan*, Oakeshott concluded *contra* Gierke, described a form of association that could 'comprehend individuals . . . without destroying them.' The generation of the Leviathan was not destructive of individuality, for 'to authorise a representative to make a choice for me does not . . . compromise my individuality; there is no confusion of wills, so long as it is understood that my will is the authorisation of the representative and that the choice he makes is not mine but his on my behalf.' Far from destroying indi-

---

[62] *OH*, pp. 150, 157–8.

[63] P.T. King, 'Introduction' to *Thomas Hobbes: Critical Assessments*, vol. 1, Routledge, London, 1993, p. xiv.

[64] *RP*, pp. 281–3.

viduality, Hobbes's *Leviathan* was 'the minimum condition of any settled association among individuals.'

Hobbes, then, would have found the insistence of the Rationalist on the unconditional right of the individual to be the sole and final judge of his actions as destructive of the conditions of the enjoyment of any individuality at all. Like Hobbes, the Rationalist sees 'nothing so firmly rooted that he hesitates to question it and judge it by . . . .his "reason",' but unlike Hobbes he is not sceptical about reason itself. Hence his optimism — he 'never doubts the power of his reason.' Where Hobbes saw no *summum bonum* inherent in political activity, the Rationalist is engaged on a quest for political perfection, because 'he cannot imagine politics which do not consist in solving problems, or a political problem of which there is no rational solution at all. Such a problem must be counterfeit. And the "rational" solution to any problem is, in its nature, the perfect solution.'[65]

Again like Hobbes, the Rationalist is an 'individualist'. Where Hobbes's individualism was 'aristocratic,' however, the 'moral ideology' which 'inspires the Rationalist' in the twentieth century is only 'the desiccated relic of what was once the unselfconscious moral tradition of an aristocracy' — the Rationalist has become 'vulgar'. The source of this vulgarity, at least in part, is the Rationalist attitude to experience. For example, the Rationalist 'always insists on (experience) being his own experience (wanting everything to begin *de novo*)'. The detail of experience is overlooked by the Rationalist, who 'reduces the tangle and variety of experience to a set of principles which he will then attack or defend only upon rational grounds'. Unlike the Hobbesian individual with his touch of negligence, who might be expected to appreciate that 'a touch of shabbiness is joined with every real convenience', the Rationalist believes that 'the remedy for any particular ill is as universal in its application as it is rational in its conception.'

This belief was at least in part the product of a distinctively Rationalistic attitude towards the past. A Rationalist has 'no sense of the cumulation of experience . . . .the past is significant to him only as an encumbrance.' He is a character belonging to an age 'which thinks that what it has discovered for itself is more important than what it has inherited . . . over-impressed with its own accomplishments and liable to the illusions of intellectual grandeur which are the characteristic lunacy of post-Renaissance Europe; an age never at peace with itself because never reconciled with its past.' With no sense of

[65] *op. cit.*, p. 16.

what Burke called the partnership of past and present, Oakeshott
wrote, 'the conduct of life' for the Rationalist 'is a jerky, discontinu-
ous affair.' This was in contrast to the life which recognises tradition,
the principle of which was 'continuity.'[66]

This attitude to the past was reflected in its turn in the Rationalist
attitude to politics in particular. 'Nothing is of value' to the Rationalist 'merely because it exists (and certainly not because it has existed
for generations)'; to him, political activity 'consists in bringing the
social, political, legal and institutional inheritance of his society
before the tribunal of his intellect'. He commits the 'error' of 'identifying the customary and the traditional with the changeless',
whereas 'a tradition of behaviour is not a fixed and inflexible manner of doing things; it is a flow of sympathy'.[67]

In contrast to his treatment of Hobbes, Oakeshott tended to assert
rather than argue when describing the Rationalist, simply attributing traits and dispositions to him without much show of evidence.
The suspicion that rhetoric had taken over from argument is
strengthened by the use he made of 'tradition'. In his discussion of
the tradition of thought to which Hobbes belonged, he had been concerned with the ancestry of Hobbes's thought, whereas in his essays
on Rationalism, 'tradition' took on an unannounced normative
emphasis in addition to its genealogical usage. A neglect of tradition
became a matter for rebuke, and by Oakeshott's own lights, where
there is rebuke, there is a practical concern of some sort or other.

Religious considerations were as important to Oakeshott's view
of Rationalism, as they were to his understanding of the German
character, and of Hobbes. He attributed a 'gnostic' bent to Rationalism, and amongst the 'deeper' and more 'obscure' reasons for the
development of Rationalism he reckoned the decline of Christian
belief, to which *Leviathan* had been another response. Rationalism
was 'closely allied with a belief in Providence: a beneficent and infallible technique replaced a beneficent and infallible God'. In place of
the Christian myth which Oakeshott described in discussing
Hobbes, the Rationalist had placed the 'myth' of 'the assimilation of
politics to engineering' in which he 'claims for himself the character
of the engineer, whose mind (it is supposed) is controlled throughout by the appropriate technique, and whose first step is to dismiss
from his attention everything not directly related to his specific
intentions.'

---

[66]   *op. cit.*, pp. 6, 23, 41, 6.

[67]   *op. cit.*, p. 8.

The Rationalist, it might be said, suffered from the kind of pride Hobbes had rejected, the desire to usurp the place of God. It has been noted that 'Rationalism is itself a sort of passion, one of intellectual pride' and that a 'concern with pride . . . .characterises Oakeshott's own project, as it does his treatment of Hobbes.'[68] Indeed, Oakeshott thought that the morality of the Rationalist involved 'what other peoples have recognised as idolatry', the worship of false gods. He even hinted that Rationalism had been even more destructive in religion than in politics, when he wrote that 'If we except religion, the greatest apparent victories of the Rationalist have been in politics.'[69]

Thanks to the polemical nature of Oakeshott's portrait of the Rationalist, and his attribution of the persistence of Rationalism to a 'hidden . . . doctrine about human knowledge', some critics received the impression that he was attacking reason or knowledge as such. Popper, for example, believed at one time that the 'Cambridge historian' (as Oakeshott still was in 1947) had used 'tradition' as a 'big stick' with which to attack reason as such.[70] Others believed that an exaltation of tradition over reason had carried Oakeshott into a kind of mysticism.[71] This, however, was more due to the tone than the content of Oakeshott's writings. Even before World War Two he had criticised 'misology', or making a philosophy out of 'doubting the competence of reason to give reality',[72] and in 1948 he wrote to Popper to disabuse him, telling him that 'when I argue against rationalism, I do not argue against reason. Rationalism in my sense is thoroughly unreasonable. That reason has a place in politics I do not doubt at all, but what I mean by Rationalism is the doctrine that nothing else has a place in politics.'[73] In the same letter, he remarked to Popper that 'I do not believe either that reason is capable of excluding violence (even in the long run) or that, because reason can't, nothing can. I think I know of a "method" of politics which is not either truly or falsely Rationalist but which is the opponent of violence.'[74] Oakeshott called this method 'the politics of conversa-

---

[68] B. Frohnen, 'Oakeshott's Hobbesian Myth: Pride, Character and the Limits of Reason', *Western Political Quarterly*, vol. 43, 1990, p. 795. I am grateful to Dr. Tregenza for drawing this piece to my attention.

[69] *RP*, pp. 41, 8.

[70] Popper, *op. cit.*, p. 121.

[71] Cp. e.g. N. Wood, 'A Guide to the Classics; the Scepticism of Professor Oakeshott', *Journal of Politics*, vol. 21, 1959, pp. 647–62, and Crossman, Review of 'Political Education', pp. 60–1.

[72] Oakeshott, Review of L. Chestov, 'In Jacob's Balance', *Scrutiny*, vol. 2, 1933, p. 101.

[73] Oakeshott, Letter to K. Popper, 28 January 1948, Hoover Institution, California.

[74] *Ibid.*

tion', an image for political activity (and indeed, for life as a whole) which played an increasing role in his work from the 1950s onwards.

Faith and Scepticism

From the mid-1950s onward, as Oakeshott's thought entered its final phase, elements of all these ideas flowed into his argument that there had been two opposing conceptions of the proper activities or 'office' of government at work in European history since the Renaissance. He experimented with different terms for this opposition. In the Harvard lectures mentioned above, for instance, he talked of 'individualism' and 'collectivism'. In his LSE lectures in the 1960s, he used terms derived from Greek, '*telocracy*' and '*nomocracy*', and as we shall see in chapter five, when he published *On Human Conduct* in the 1970s he chose two Latin words, '*societas*' and '*universitas*'.

The most fully worked out version of this thesis prior to *On Human Conduct* was published posthumously in 1996 as *The Politics of Faith and the Politics of Scepticism*. Quite why Oakeshott decided not to publish it during his lifetime is unclear. Perhaps he decided that what he called his attempt 'to speak informally, in no manner in particular,' neither as philosopher, historian, nor 'man of affairs',[75] was unsuccessful; after all, he later declared that 'I do not myself know where to place an experience released altogether from modality'.[76] Nevertheless, the main theme of the work, the two conflicting understandings of the role of government that had been expressed in European political theory and practice, is identical with that of *On Human Conduct*, and for that reason it is worth examining the earlier study at some length.

Oakeshott's insistence on the dual character of European politics was a means of emphasising their complexity. European politics were not 'monolithic',[77] and they were not the outcome of a design or plan of any kind. The fact that they were ambiguous was not, from the practical point of view, necessarily a defect: 'ambiguity of language has served to conceal divisions which to display fully would invite violence and disaster.' Insofar as this ambiguity did pose a problem, it was 'mainly philosophical: the ambiguity makes it difficult for us to think clearly about our politics'. It affected all the doctrines Oakeshott had wrestled with before 1939, and more. 'Liberalism, Capitalism, Socialism, Romanticism, Classicism, all

---

[75]   *PF*, p. 1.

[76]   *RP*, pp. 492–3, 512.

[77]   *PF*, p. 8.

these events, processes and movements . . . are themselves ambiva-
lent . . . complex and self-divided.'[78]

The labels of 'The Politics of Faith' and 'The Politics of Scepticism'
were intended, Oakeshott stated, to denote 'at once the poles of an
activity and the poles of our understanding of an activity.' They
were at once historic and theoretic extremes, but 'each is a process as
well as a condition', and there had been 'a variety of versions' of each
over the last five hundred years.[79] He was quick to emphasise that he
did not aim at replacing this variety with a single style of politics,
though as we would expect, he clearly preferred the sceptical
approach. Nevertheless, scepticism itself was not free from defects,
and each style could be expected to prove its own nemesis if left
unopposed.

The politics of faith, as its name suggests, had been inspired initially by religious ideas. Indeed, Oakeshott thought that much of the
ambiguity in European politics stemmed from the fact that Christianity 'has never completely assimilated to itself the civilization we
enjoy',[80] and different elements of its inheritance pointed in different
directions. The politics of faith, then, was a 'Pelagian' tradition; it
believed that man was 'redeemable in history'. The human perfection at which it aimed was 'to be achieved by human effort, and confidence in the evanescence of imperfection springs here from faith in
human power and not from trust in divine providence.'[81] Though
Oakeshott did not explicitly say as much, it would seem that Rationalism had been reduced to no more than an aspect of this style of
politics.

Oakeshott's study of the Rationalist had emphasized the sixteenth
century as the point at which a new conception of knowledge
emerged. He now stressed the material effects of this change; it was
an era that witnessed the 'appearance in a remarkably short space of
time, of greatly increased quantities of power',[82] unprecedented in
the medieval period. Until the means to impose a single purpose on
their subjects became available, it had never occurred to governments to do so; since the Renaissance, however, various forms of this
project had been attempted. Initially religious in inspiration —
regarding government as an instrument for the pursuit of some form
of Christian salvation — the politics of Faith had quickly acquired an

[78] *op. cit.*, pp. 21, 15.

[79] *op. cit.* pp. 17–18.

[80] *op. cit.*, p. 13.

[81] *op. cit.*, p. 23.

[82] *op. cit.*, p. 46.

economic character. It was no longer the view of knowledge in Bacon's *Novum Organum* but his utopian goal of 'the restoration of what the race lost at the Fall'[83] in the *New Atlantis* which interested Oakeshott. Whatever the precise form of this style of politics, however, it could be expected to be impatient with formalities. A 'nice observance of rules and constitutions will readily be felt to hinder its impetus'. Consequently, 'Rights, the means of redress, will be incongruous, their place being taken by a single, comprehensive Right — the right to participate in the improvement which leads to perfection.'[84]

This change in focus required Oakeshott to reassess the place of various major thinkers in the history of political thought. Machiavelli, for example, once the ancestor of Rationalist attempts to found a science of politics, was now notable mainly for his unspoken assumptions about the character of the state. Machiavelli's 'attention was usually centred upon the enterprise of founding and maintaining a state in difficult circumstances,' but 'it never occurred to him to doubt that the state to be founded and maintained' was an 'association of persons joined, not by choice in the pursuit of a common purpose, but in the recognition of the authority of a law administered by a powerful ruler.'[85]

The sceptical style of politics which Oakeshott discerned in Machiavelli was 'not to be identified with anarchy or the stark individualism which is often the partner of anarchy.' Nor did it entail the rejection of the pursuit of perfection; only of the use of government as a means to it. It premised the inevitability of conflict in human affairs, and regarded the state as an evil necessary for its mitigation. The debt he now owed to Hobbes is transparent in his remark that 'The Sceptic understands order as a great and difficult achievement never beyond the reach of decay and dissolution . . . when it collapses life rapidly becomes "solitary, poor, nasty, brutish, and short".'[86]

Both this 'primarily judicial'[87] conception of government, concerned mainly with maintaining the relevance and guaranteeing the enforcement of legal rights and duties in the rapidly changing circumstances of modern European societies, and its opposite, were made vital to the understanding of English history. England had

---

[83] *op. cit.*, p. 53.

[84] *op. cit.*, p. 29.

[85] *HC*, p. 244.

[86] *PF*, p. 32.

[87] *op. cit.*, p. 109.

been 'more rapidly and conclusively centralized than anywhere else in Europe' by the end of the sixteenth century, with the church being placed under the power of crown and the creation of an apparatus of local government 'under the hand and direction of the King's Council and its subsidiaries'.

While this enhanced public order, it also inspired minute government, and 'the apparatus of banking and book-keeping, the records, registers, files, passports, dossier and indexes' were all brought to bear with previously unknown thoroughness. So little did Oakeshott think things had changed by the twentieth century that he remarked 'the only overwhelmingly important additions which have appeared in modern times have been the by-products of electricity,' though he added, somewhat tongue in cheek, that without the telephone 'the politics of Faith would long ago have lost half their charm by losing most of their impetus.'[88]

No sooner had Bacon set down his description of Bensalem than the English Puritans appeared. In a manner characteristic of the politics of faith, they 'opposed all other religious beliefs than their own, not because a variety of religious beliefs was observed to be liable to provoke disorder', which of course was why the sceptical Hobbes demanded that the sovereign be able to settle religious questions, 'but because all but their own were identified with "error".' All that remained for the European *philosophes* to do by the eighteenth century was systematise these earlier English examples.

Yet England had never been without an answer to the politics of faith. Hobbes in theory, Cromwell in practice,[89] were amongst those who sought to contain the excesses of Puritanism in the seventeenth century. 'The earliest triumph of the politics of Scepticism was the recognition of the distinction between politics and religion . . . implicit in early Christianity'.[90] The American revolution had been carried out in the same sceptical style, and had produced 'the most profoundly sceptical constitution of the modern world', though the French revolution had soon departed from the sceptical path. Eighteenth-century thinkers who had done their best to adhere to it included Hume, Burke, Adam Smith, and (marking a considerable change from Oakeshott's view of him in the 1930s) Bentham.[91] All these thinkers saw government 'not [as] the exercise of an undefined

---

[88]   *op. cit.*, pp. 50–1.

[89]   Although Oakeshott did remark that Cromwell was one of those 'politicians who in other circumstances were more likely to find themselves in the camp of Faith than that of Scepticism': see *op. cit.* p. 71

[90]   *op. cit.*, p. 81.

[91]   *op. cit.*, p. 73.

guardianship over the activities of the subject, but the performance of certain public duties' that were to be as narrowly specified as possible.

The connection between this view and the morality of individuality is hinted at in Oakeshott's claim that early modern sceptical politics was distinguished by a sense of mortality which recognized the earth 'not as a world to be exploited but as a "player's stage".' A sense of the finitude of human existence, of its limits, coupled with a self-conscious acknowledgment of the dramatic character of 'human conduct' (a phrase that now began to occur regularly in Oakeshott's work), was unlikely to produce a personality that would make the state a tool of mundane redemption. Nevertheless, it did not render even the most profound sceptic immune from ambiguity, to judge from the political thought of John Locke.

Locke, who in the 1930s had been the spiritual father of a kind of parliamentary democracy which Oakeshott thought had reached a dead end, was now presented as a prime example of the way in which faith and scepticism could combine even within a single thinker. Locke was a committed defender of the rule of law against royal absolutism; but his attempt to protect the rights and duties of Englishmen by basing his arguments on natural law drew him away from this sceptical position. The 'impulse to assure ourselves that our arrangements and authorized manners of behaviour represent not merely fact and habit, but "justice" and "truth," and that they have a "certainty" which is out of reach of the vicissitudes of time and place, has always been strong. But it is an impulse which belongs properly to faith.'[92]

A similar confusion had emerged in the sceptical attachment to Republicanism of, for example, Paine. The belief that a particular constitutional arrangement, however sceptical its inspiration might be, could permanently guarantee that governmental power would never be yoked to the pursuit of perfection, implied an abandonment of 'the reading of human behaviour which makes political Scepticism intelligible.'[93] No constitutional device, Republican or otherwise, be it the separation of powers or the universal suffrage desired by Bentham and James Mill, had ever provided such a guarantee.

Political scepticism, however, had not only been defeated by a lurch towards faith. It carried within itself the seeds of its own destruction. Precisely because the political sceptic was in the habit of

---

[92] *op. cit.*, p. 82.

[93] *op. cit.*, p. 84.

'being exact, and never excessive' in performing the duties associated with maintaining public order, he was in danger of underesti-
mating both the speed and the scale of the response required when
faced with exceptional circumstances; just, in fact, as Oakeshott
thought Europe had miscalculated when faced with Nazi Germany.
By contrast, the politics of faith tended to result in a permanent state
of emergency, a politics of perpetual crisis. The attempt to impose
total control it involved, when pushed to its logical conclusion – as
it had been in Germany – 'awakens the politics of Terror which
sleeps in every version of government as the pursuit of "perfection"', especially when imposed on societies like those of modern
Europe, whose citizens did not appreciate being distracted from
their own highly diverse array of activities. Government became so
all-pervasive it became indistinguishable from anything else.
Duguit, one of the pluralist authors Oakeshott had admired in the
1920s, was now criticised for the claim that 'government has no special character'; it was the very nemesis of the politics of faith to 'stand
for all forms of legitimate activity and so none in particular.'[94]

   It is worth reiterating that Oakeshott did not believe either style of
politics could stand by itself. 'Each is not less the partner than the
opponent of the other; each stands in need of the other to rescue it
from self-destruction' and defeat of its own purposes. If the politics
of scepticism could be accused of reducing politics to 'play', in the
sense described by Huizinga's *Homo Ludens*,[95] of an 'activity pursued on certain specified occasions, at fixed times and in a place set
apart and according to exact rules', the politics of faith were, left to
themselves, inclined to become exclusively 'earnest'. The visions of
symmetry replacing chaos that had tantalised Europeans since at
least the seventeenth century were themselves illusions generated
by the politics of faith, and Marxism was only the latest of them.[96]

   Oakeshott's own preference, he declared, was for 'Neither Diony-
sus nor Apollo, but each in his place and season.' Nevertheless, he
believed that of the two styles of politics he had described, it was the
politics of faith that had gained the upper hand. In particular, it had
become 'the most notable political gift of Europe to the world.' Yet,
at this time, he did not believe all was lost. In a metaphor recalling his
days as a racing man, he remarked that 'the punters who have made
[faith] the favourite have sadly misjudged it. The pedigree, by Power

[94] *op. cit.* pp. 95, 94 and n.
[95] J. Huizinga, *Homo Ludens A Study of the Play Element in Culture*, Paladin, London,
      1970 (1938).
[96] *PF*, pp. 119–20.

out of Fond Hope is not reasoning; gross stamina allied to mere speed, oddly enough, never got a satisfactory animal.'[97] We shall see in chapter five that as time wore on, he became increasingly unsure that faith was not going to be first past the post after all. The jocular remark made at the end of the 1960s as he accepted a *Festschrift* from former pupils that 'we all have our own dates for the end of the world [and] mine is about 1950' masked an increasing cynicism and despair at the modern world.

The History of Character

So far, we have allowed a theme of great importance for Oakehott's future work on the history of political thought to remain in the background, namely, his claim that there were discernible character types corresponding to these two conflicting political styles. Clearly, this idea had been implicit in all the various writings we have looked at in this chapter. Oakeshott had moved from the consideration of the characters of particular historical and fictional figures, to the study of the character of groups, both national and supra-national. In doing so, he had confronted the presuppositions of his own enquiry. The Germans, we saw, had become 'a people that derives pleasure and satisfaction from suffering violence from its leaders'; the Rationalist desired government that would impose an overall plan on society; and Hobbes's scepticism limited his conception of government to supplying an external restraint on subjects in the form of the laws of the sovereign.

What Oakeshott now embarked on was a re-examination of the history of modern political thought in the light of the histories of the various types of personalities he had detected in his writings of the 1940s and early 1950s. For example, the character-type he believed the writings of Montaigne, Hobbes, Spinoza, Hume, and many others described, he soon began to refer to as 'the individual'. The similarity between Hobbes's proud man, described by Oakeshott as 'a man not at all without imperfections and not deceived about himself, but who is proud enough to be spared the sorrow of his imperfections and the illusion of his achievements' and his own character of the individual is unmistakable. Hobbes's proud man, 'not exactly a hero, too negligent for that, but perhaps with a touch of careless heroism about him', like the individual, knows, 'in Montaigne's phrase . . . how to belong to himself'.[98]

---

[97] *op. cit.*, pp. 124, 126.

[98] *RP*, pp. 350, 359.

The concept of 'character' has been conspicuous by its absence from the work of most historians in the latter half of the twentieth century. One of the few to make it a central motif, J.H. Grainger, acknowledged that his *Character and Style in English Politics* had been inspired in part by Oakeshott himself.[99] In 1955, Knowles gave his inaugural lecture as Cambridge Regius Professor of Modern History on 'The Historian and Character', remarking that 'historians are notably less concerned with personalities and their characters than they were a century ago.'[100] Oakeshott himself grew up at a time when the idea was still common currency, as a glance at his school magazine with its reviews of the 'characters' of the 1st XI will testify. However, it was only in the late twentieth century that historians began to investigate the role of the idea of character in nineteenth century thought, including political thought.[101]

The idea of a history of moral character was a familiar one in the later nineteenth century, and it was well-known to Oakeshott himself. (He suggested to his LSE students that they read Lecky's work on the *History of European Morals from Augustine to Charlemagne* even as he was working on his own version of the history of character.) In the writings of so prominent a thinker as J.S. Mill, 'character' played an important role. Mill's 'famous plea for individuality was couched as a protest against what he called "the pinched and hidebound character" which he took to be enjoying an insidious popularity in the moral reflection of the time.'[102]

As Black has pointed out, Mill fully shared the belief of later Idealist and pluralist writers that 'The ultimate aim of all political procedures is to enable the human personality to develop its moral and intellectual qualities to the full.'[103] It was certainly not Mill's intention to foster the 'excessive' individualism for which utilitarian thought was later criticised; in *Utilitarianism*, he contrasted a 'customary morality' with the rational moral 'principle of utility' which he believed was grounded in 'the feeling of unity with our fellow creature . . . deeply rooted in our character'.[104]

[99]   J.H. Grainger, *Character and Style in English Politics*, Cambridge UP, Cambridge, 1969, p. 9.

[100] D. Knowles, 'The Historian and Character', Cambridge UP, Cambridge, 1955, p. 1.

[101] See, for example, Collini, 'The Idea of Character in Victorian Political Thought', pp. 28–50.

[102] Collini, *op. cit.*, p. 31.

[103] Black, *Guilds and Civil Society*, p. 192.

[104] J.S. Mill, *Utilitarianism, Liberty and Representative Government*, Dent and Sons, London, 1948, pp. 24–5.

In his first essay on the history of moral character, 'The Tower of Babel', published in 1948, Oakeshott contrasted a morality of custom with one of self-conscious ideals. The similarity was very likely the result of design. We have already seen that Oakeshott's philosophy of history was a lineal descendant of Mill's search for a logic of the social sciences; his views on the history of political thought also developed in relation to Mill's. In the notes Oakeshott appended to his inaugural lecture at the LSE on 'Political Education', he presented his own work as 'a further stage' in an enquiry on which Mill had also been embarked.

Mill had sought an 'explanatory device' in 'a "theory of human progress" and what he called a "philosophy of history".'[105] Oakeshott's own work, by contrast, rejected 'any general theory about the character and direction of social change [as] an adequate reference for explanation.' His own history of character, in other words, could not be used in the application of what Mill called the 'inverse deductive, or historical method'. Nevertheless, Oakeshott's relation to Mill may perhaps be described in the terms Collingwood used to describe Bradley's relation to him. Oakeshott, like Bradley, was 'a rather disillusioned and cynical follower [who] continuously subjected Mill to sharp criticism; but his aim ... was not to annihilate Mill's doctrines, it was to amend them into a form ... he could find acceptable'.[106]

In the later 1940s Oakeshott was clearly searching for an approach more plausible than he found Mill's psychological generalisations. The most concrete result of an abortive attempt at a study of Nelson, for which Oakeshott seems to have been collecting material in his last years at Cambridge, was a draft of a paper on 'The Interpretation of Character in Human History'.[107] Neatly illustrating his own contention that thought moves seamlessly between different levels of understanding, he was, typically, driven by his meditations on Nelson's character to a consideration of what it meant to attribute a character to an historical figure. Strikingly, he argued that 'To study evidence (words, actions, poetry, painting etc.) with a view to the detection of the human character they belong to is neither history nor biography but something else.' While historians, as such, might sometimes engage in the study of character, their main purpose was the relation of events. The tension, even conflict, between these two

---

[105] *RP*, p. 69.

[106] Collingwood, *An Essay on Metaphysics*, p. 154.

[107] Oakeshott, 'The Interpretation of Character in Human History', LSE 3/10.

enterprises was never completely resolved in his own work, even in *On Human Conduct* — as he himself was aware.

Some positive conclusions, however, were reached. There was a complex historic vocabulary describing emotions, attitudes, and relationships which had to be accounted for.[108] They had to be understood as 'Historical emotions; as distinct from the mechanism of emotion psychology as a science', with which he associated J.S. Mill. They also had to be distinguished from any anthropological or utilitarian concept of 'the abstract emotions so-called the "simple pleasures and pains" which no man actually feels, the "sensations" which no man ever enjoys, the "feelings" no man has ever experienced, — because they are abstractions, abridgements of experience'.

Oakeshott's treatment of the idea of character was a plea for the recognition of the complexities involved in understanding human action of the sort encountered in the 'Declaration of War' he had written in 1933. However, an unpublished paper on 'The Idea of "Character" in the Interpretation of Modern Politics', [109] probably written around the same time as the one we having just been discussing, makes clear he was aware he was dealing with an idea that had become unfashionable: 'We have learned to be suspicious of the word "character,"' he remarked 'because it has so often been used in a manner that implies, or seems to imply, beliefs that we would like to avoid — the belief, for example, in real essences'. No such metaphysical baggage was necessary to make sense of the idea, however. A person's character could be defined as 'a balance of dispositions'. It is what 'we ordinarily think we can discern when we are given the opportunity of observing and reflecting upon . . . conduct', that is 'actions . . . and utterances, in a variety of situations'. To have knowledge of a person's character was 'to have beliefs about his dispositions and expectations.'[110]

There is an ambiguity at work here which we have so far only touched on. Knowles believed that 'a dilemma' from which the his-

---

[108] Oakeshott's list of these terms was as follows: 'Sullen admiration reserved charm *habilité* chagrin Peevish respect secretive *virtu honnête* Reverence forgiving melancholy Fearlessness merciful magnamonious Dread generous pity Patience friendship nobility affable kindness Fortitude comradeship affection reflective Faithfulness joy pleasure self-conscious constancy perseverance.' See 'The Interpretation of Character in Human History,' LSE 3/10.

[109] Oakeshott, 'The Idea of "Character" in the Interpretation of Modern Politics', LSE 1/1/35. This paper is undated but the style and vocabulary is that of the later 1950s or perhaps the 1960s.

[110] *MP*, pp. 29–30.

torian 'cannot perhaps ever . . . fully [escape]' was 'whether to judge a man's achievement by his ideals and preferences . . . or by the generally accepted standards of human behaviour.'[111] Yet he was in no doubt that the historian still had to judge. He was using character in what has been called its 'evaluative' sense. As well as this moral or evaluative sense, however, there is a 'descriptive' sense which 'refers us to an individual's settled dispositions . . . but does not itself involve a judgment on the goodness or otherwise of these dispositions.'[112]

In contrast to Knowles, Oakeshott was interested in the descriptive sense of character. Moral judgements of character, according to his own philosophy of history, lay outside the provenance of historical enquiry. The question arises, however, of whether he consistently pursued this descriptive approach, or whether he blurred the two senses from time to time. In our final chapter on the history of political thought we shall argue that such blurring did occur and identify the precise points at which he ceased simply to describe the ethical qualities of his subjects and broached the limits he had himself identified.

Bearing these problems in mind, we may now turn to the relationship Oakeshott saw between the history of character and the history of political thought and practice. By assuming that 'dispositions' or character provide one means of explaining the whole field of human activity, Oakeshott was able to understand the past by looking for and examining changes in dispositions. Corresponding to these changes in disposition or character, he believed, would be changes in the conduct of politics, science, art, morals, and any other activity one cares to name. There was no limit to the period of time which could be studied in this way. Indeed, the longer the period of time, the more fundamental the changes in dispositions were likely to be.

Once humanity has escaped from 'a natural necessity which binds all . . . to act alike,' people must engage in 'conduct to which there is an alternative', moral conduct.[113] Although 'in any manifestation of the moral life, form and content are inseparable' and 'neither can be said to determine the other', it was possible, Oakeshott argued, to make abstraction from the concrete reality and study the form alone. It was the 'form' which moral conduct had taken in which he was particularly interested. From such a study, he insisted, both 'The

[111] Knowles, *op. cit.*, p. 9.

[112] Collini, *op. cit.*, p. 33, from whom the convenient labels of 'descriptive' and 'evaluative' senses of character are borrowed.

[113] *RP*, p. 466.

practical question, What kinds of human enterprise should be designated right and wrong' and 'the philosophical question, What is the
ultimate nature of moral criteria', were excluded.[114]

In the lectures Oakeshott gave as a visiting professor at Harvard in
1958, he told his audience that the history of morality provided 'a
context to which [ideas about government and politics] may be
referred in order to make them more intelligible.' However, just as
morality does not 'cause' political belief, 'character' does not 'cause'
action.[115] Rather, a moral character finds 'a counterpart in an appropriate understanding of the constitution and office of government,'
and the two 'may be used to elucidate one another as text and context'.[116] His hypothesis that 'modern European politics . . . has a
"character"' resolved itself into the claim that in the modern period,
'political activity and the activity of governing' have shown themselves 'to have certain dispositions which are used, exploited, perhaps cultivated but not significantly added to.'

The only unusual aspect of this hypothesis so far as Oakeshott
himself was concerned was that he was using it over a period of several centuries. 'The proposition that the politics and government of a
particular European state during a short period may reveal a "character"' was 'a commonplace'. For example, 'British government in
the mid-eighteenth century discloses an unmistakable "character,"'
as does 'the *ancien régime* in France'.[117] This is further evidence that
Oakeshott did not think of himself as doing anything innovative
with the idea of character. He believed that other writers had
attempted to 'ascertain 'the dispositions of [the] new political character' which he was concerned with as early as the eighteenth century. Montesquieu, in particular, had made 'ideal models . . . of the
dispositions of this character' in *The Spirit of the Laws*. In fact,
Oakeshott went so far as to say that 'Montesquieu's "*Esprit*" is . . .
what I have called "character".'[118]

Oakeshott believed that to make good his claim he had to show
'first, that somewhere about the beginning of [the sixteenth century]
. . . significantly new political conditions had come to establish themselves, conditions likely to provoke new political aspirations,

---

[114] *op. cit.*, p. 467.

[115] *MP*, pp. 29–30.

[116] *op. cit.*, pp. 18, 27–8.

[117] *op. cit.*, p. 31.

[118] *op. cit.*, p. 36. See also Plato, *Republic*, Bk. II, 369 ff.; Aristotle, *Politics*, Bk. III. ch. iv.
It is somewhat surprising Oakeshott did not invoke Adam Smith's *The Theory of
Moral Sentiments* in support of his claim.

beliefs, projects and practices; and secondly that these have since remained relatively unchanged.'[119] Elaborating the substance of this claim was a cornerstone of all his subsequent forays into the history of political thought, as we shall see in our final chapter on the subject.

Oakeshott's history of character took in the best part of a millennium. He concentrated on the medieval and modern periods, now identifying three, rather than two, moral traditions. Hobbes and the Rationalist had their place in this arrangement too; in fact, it was first formulated in the later 1950s with the context of Hobbes's writings in mind. Again employing the analogy of a language, Oakeshott claimed that since roughly the tenth century, three moral 'idioms' had 'followed one another . . . without ever quite superseding one another.'[120] He referred to them as 'idioms' because 'all of them use a single moral vocabulary', with the consequence that 'the words and expressions of that vocabulary have acquired a notorious ambiguity'.[121]

The first was 'the morality of communal ties'. The second was 'the morality of individuality'. The third, and final, 'idiom' was 'the morality of the common good'. In one form or another, this was the arrangement which underlay all Oakeshott's subsequent accounts of the history of political thought as well as of the history of morals, though it did not achieve its final form until the later 1960s. We have yet to make plain, however, the connection between these two histories in his writings; we will begin to do so with a brief exposition of his revised version of the history of morality.

The morality of communal ties recognises 'human beings solely as members of a community', and all activity whatsoever is understood to be communal activity. In it, 'separate individuals, capable of making choices for themselves and inclined to do so are unknown.' For as long as the morality of communal ties held sway, as it did in medieval Europe between the tenth and twelfth centuries, 'circumstances in which individuals might have appeared' were absent. Nevertheless, this idiom still represented genuine moral activity, for it was 'the product, not . . . of design, but of . . . long-forgotten choices.'[122] Insofar as this was an unreflective moral idiom, it had something in common with what Oakeshott had described as the habitual form of morality. However, the character belonging to that

---

[119] *op. cit.*, pp. 31–2.
[120] *RP*, p. 298. Oakeshott's increasing use of the analogy of a language in his philosophy of history will be discussed in the following chapter.
[121] *MP*, p. 18.
[122] *RP*, p. 297.

morality, the man of *amour-propre*, was now seen as a much later event, coming into being only with the second of the moral idioms Oakeshott now described.

The morality of individuality emerged out of the break-up of the medieval order, although 'it was not until the sixteenth century that it had appeared unmistakably over the horizon.'[123] Leaving on one side the reasons Oakeshott gave for this change until our final chapter on the history of political thought, we should note that this morality assumes persons who 'have come to recognise themselves in the character of separate and sovereign individuals, associated with one another, not in the pursuit of a single common enterprise, but in accommodating themselves to one another as best they can.'

With this change came the Protean image of human nature and the new philosophical and theological understanding of human personality Oakeshott had found reflected in Hobbes, and it was within this idiom of morality that he now placed *Leviathan*. Hobbes was 'the first moralist of the modern world to take candid account of the current experience of individuality'[124] by giving a philosophical account of an already established manner of life. Although the form of morality Hobbes was exploring was a post-feudal one, Oakeshott described it as 'aristocratic' — he insisted, as he thought Montesquieu had, that honour was 'an aristocratic virtue but one which need not be confined to an aristocracy'.[125]

The morality of the common good was in turn a response to the morality of individuality becoming widespread. Here, persons are still 'recognized as independent centres of activity, but approval attaches itself to conduct in which this individuality is suppressed whenever it conflicts, not with the individuality of others, but with the interests of a "society" understood to be composed of such human beings. All are engaged in a single common enterprise.'[126] Hobbes, for Oakeshott, had excluded this morality in principle by denying the existence of a *summum bonum*; the Rationalist, though Oakeshott did not explicitly make the connection, could be expected to subscribe to it insofar as a common enterprise to be engaged in was thought discoverable by reason.

Oakeshott gave a further reason why Hobbes could not have been an exponent of this third morality — it was more recent than his writings. 'For Hobbes (or any other moralist in the seventeenth and

[123] *MP*, p. 20.
[124] *RP*, p. 367.
[125] *MP*, p. 38.
[126] *RP*, p. 344.

eighteenth centuries) to have undertaken to explore either the morality of communal ties or the morality of the common good would have been an anachronism.'[127] It was too early for one and too late for the other. Again we see Oakeshott trying to divorce Hobbes from association with the rise of a class devoted to economic prosperity; the pursuit of wealth as a common enterprise belonged to the morality of the common good rather than the morality of individuality.

Oakeshott did, however, qualify this assertion when he admitted that even though Hobbes was 'primarily concerned with motives for obeying civil law' and did not take much interest in 'what a man might otherwise do with his life' such as engaging in trade and commerce, Hobbes did sometimes 'intimate and point towards the notion of a "common good" . . . a single approved condition of circumstances for all.'[128] It was the interaction of these two latter forms of morality that he had identified which interested Oakeshott the most. He was concerned with the medieval morality of communal ties, as he called it, mainly because it had been the seed-bed of individualism. What subsequently preoccupied him, even in On *Human Conduct*, was the tension between the second and third of the moralities he had delineated.

---

[127] *op. cit.*, p. 298.
[128] *op. cit.* pp. 343–4.

Chapter Four

The Philosophy of
History, 1947–1975

History and Other Modes

After 1945, Oakeshott retained the four major categories of thought
he had employed since the 1920s, namely, scientific, historical,
philosophical, and practical or ordinary understanding. We have to
ascertain how he now arranged these categories and the place of historical study in this arrangement. We have already noticed the arguments that 'There is no suggestion in Oakeshott's later work' on the
philosophy of history that he wished to 'significantly alter' his earlier views and that his later work 'adds nothing' to his earlier writings.[1] Now, it is true that 'Historiography is the only topic on which
Oakeshott seems never to have shifted his ground', insofar as 'the
essence of his position throughout is a rejection of all realist, Rationalist, positivist, transcendental or reductionist views of history.'[2]
What did change markedly, however, were the strategies for effect-
ing this rejection. In this latter sense, the suggestion that Oakeshott's
philosophy of history remained unchanged in the fifty years
between *Experience and its Modes* and *On History* contradicts the path
we have suggested for his intellectual career.

A strong indication that Oakeshott intended *On Human Conduct* to
incorporate and supersede what he had said earlier is provided by
his own assertion of a difference between his earlier and later work
on the philosophy of history. He wrote that 'historical understanding, which appears in *Experience and its Modes* as a determinate arrest
in experience, appears in *On Human Conduct* as the theoretical
engagement in which we seek to understand assignable actions and

[1]   Himmelfarb, *The New History and the Old*, p. 178, and King, p. 105.
[2]   Grant, *Oakeshott*, p. 99.

utterances . . . in terms of contingent relations'. Oakeshott was quite explicit that he wanted 'such changes' to be 'read back into what I had written earlier', because, he claimed, 'they make it more exact'.[3] This passage indicates clearly that he no longer regarded history in quite the same way as he had in *Experience and its Modes*. In particular, he thought the introduction of contingency as a postulate of historical understanding necessitated a revision of his earlier views.

Nevertheless, even those who accept that Oakeshott's later philosophy of history represents a self-conscious revision of his earlier ideas do not agree on what has changed. For example, it has been argued that in *Experience and its Modes* philosophy had been presented as at the head of a hierarchy of modes. The essays of *Rationalism in Politics*, particularly that on 'The Voice of Poetry in the Conversation of Mankind' are said to mark a break with this position. In *On Human Conduct* Oakeshott is alleged to have changed his mind again and to have returned to his earlier view of philosophy at the head of a hierarchy of modes.[4]

Obviously, were this interpretation correct, it would have implications for the status of historical enquiry, as we saw in chapter two. We need not reiterate the reasons for denying that Oakeshott saw philosophy as standing at the head of a hierarchy of modes in *Experience and its Modes*, but we have now to tackle the assertion that he took this view of philosophy in *On Human Conduct*. Oakeshott's essay on 'The Voice of Poetry in the Conversation of Mankind', his first major post-war statement on the nature of philosophy, is alone enough to undermine it.

According to the metaphor of conversation, the whole of life may be understood as a conversation composed of various 'modes' or 'voices,' including those of philosophy, history, science, poetry and practice. Oakeshott wanted to direct attention to the voice of poetry in particular because 'In recent centuries the conversation has become boring because it has been engrossed by two voices, the voice of practical activity and the voice of "science".'[5] He wished, then, to introduce 'poetry' (which he used as a synonym for art of all kinds) as a distinct mode of experience, in contrast to *Experience and its Modes*, where he had asserted that in 'art, music and poetry' we are 'wholly taken up with practical life.'[6]

---

[3]   Oakeshott, 'On Misunderstanding Human Conduct', *Political Theory*, vol. 4, 1976, p. 364.

[4]   See chapter two, above.

[5]   *RP*, pp. 488–93.

[6]   *EM*, p. 297 and n. 1.

Oakeshott now described the relationship between the various voices as 'conversational,' to distinguish it from an argumentative or inquisitive relationship. A conversation has no predetermined outcome, nor is it the business of any one voice to attempt to silence all of the others. The various voices may differ without disagreeing and they do not compose a hierarchy of any kind: 'in it different universes of discourse meet, acknowledge each other and enjoy an oblique relationship which neither requires nor forecasts their being assimilated to one another.'[7]

The status attributed to philosophy in this essay is that of one voice amongst others; it enjoys no greater (or lesser) status than any of the other voices. In Oakeshott's eyes, this revised view marked a clear break with 'one of the most notable traditions of European thought in which all activity was judged in relation to the *vita contemplativa*', the philosophical life of reason. That this change in his view of philosophy was carried over into *On Human Conduct* is evident from Oakeshott's comments on Plato's metaphor of the cave. For Plato, Oakeshott argued, 'the intelligibility of the cave-dweller's world seems . . . at once so complete . . . and so minimal that he is disposed to write it off as nescience' by comparison with the knowledge enjoyed by the philosopher. In contrast to this, Oakeshott, determined no longer to use the contemplative life of philosophical Reason as the yardstick of the adequacy of 'practical' or 'cave' understanding, argued that the cave-dwellers 'are not at all inadequately equipped for understanding and dealing with the world in which they live.'[8]

This was also a self-criticism. In *Experience and its Modes*, Oakeshott had thought philosophical experience could escape the limitations of 'mediate' experience. We saw in chapter three that he rejected the idea of 'an experience released altogether from modality'; this rejection included philosophical experience, now demoted to the position of just another mode.[9] The implication of this change for Oakeshott's philosophy of history should be clear. Since philosophy no longer had a superior status to any of the other voices, it no longer had a superior status to history. History, in other words, was no longer a defective mode of experience in relation to philosophy.

In *On Human Conduct*, then, philosophers, like historians, were seen as particular species of theorists. They were distinguished from historians in that philosophical 'questions are asked not in order to

---

[7]   *RP*, p. 490.

[8]   *HC*, pp. 27–30.

[9]   *op. cit.*, pp. 492–3, 512.

be answered but so that they may themselves be interrogated in respect of their conditions.' In another sense, however, the philosopher is recognisably the same character as in *Experience and its Modes*, in that he appreciates that 'the character of the engagement of understanding' is that of 'an unconditional adventure in which every achievement of understanding is an invitation to investigate itself', whereas others simply participate in this adventure without recognising its proper character.

In this sense, it was still possible for Oakeshott to talk of 'arrests' in experience; in an argument familiar to us from writings composed as early as the 1920s, he claimed that the historian, as such, must necessarily stop short of investigating the postulates of the activity of being an historian in order to write any history. But, since philosophy is 'an investigation which denies or questions its own conditions', it 'surrenders' the 'opportunity of achieving . . . conditional perfection' open to a 'specific undertaking to understand a this' of the sort historical enquiry is committed to.[10] On our interpretation of *On Human Conduct*, then, Oakeshott cannot possibly be said to have placed philosophy at the head of a hierarchy of forms of explanation. Nor can his ideas on the philosophy of history be said to have remained unaltered once the idea that all other modes are defective in relation to philosophical experience had been abandoned.

It has also been claimed that *On Human Conduct* 'appears to constitute [a] departure' from Oakeshott's earlier views, not because of a change in his view of philosophy, but because *On Human Conduct* assimilates historical and practical understanding. *On History* is then presented as the book in which Oakeshott 'reverts' back to the views of *Experience and its Modes* that history and practice are distinct.[11] This interpretation acknowledges that there was some change in Oakeshott's philosophy of history, but it does not sit easily with our arguments about that change. Oakeshott was always critical of any attempt either to subsume history under, or grant it pre-eminence over, any other form of study. In *Experience and its Modes*, it had been a common feature of all of Oakeshott's modes, including history, that they tended to claim too much for themselves. It was on just these grounds that he criticised Collingwood's posthumous work, *The Idea of History*, in 1947. Oakeshott received *The Idea of History* with the same mixture of praise and criticism with which Collingwood had greeted the philosophy of history of *Experience and its Modes*.

---

[10]   *HC*, p. 11.

[11]   Boucher, 'Overlap and Autonomy', pp. 85–6.

Collingwood, Oakeshott wrote, 'with the single exception of Croce', was 'the only philosopher of first-class ability to give prolonged and concentrated attention' to the philosophy of history; 'if he had been unhindered by ill-health and early death', he 'could have done for historical knowledge . . . what Kant did for natural science.' Nevertheless, Collingwood's philosophy of history seemed to Oakeshott to have become 'a philosophy in which all knowledge is assimilated to historical knowledge, and consequently . . . a radically sceptical philosophy.'[12]

Oakeshott's criticism of Collingwood's philosophy of history on the grounds that it assimilated all understanding to historical understanding leads us to expect that he would have attempted to avoid such 'radical scepticism' in his own work by keeping history distinct from other forms of thought, including what he had called the practical mode of experience. How, then, did Oakeshott now see the relation between historical study and what he had earlier called the 'practical' mode? We saw in chapter three that the distinction between practical and historical attitudes to the past was of continued importance in Oakeshott's post-war thought, even though he blurred it himself in his polemical critiques of Rationalism. Had he not continued to insist on this distinction, it would be impossible to explain his alarm at the thought that practical attitudes to the past might overwhelm historical thought altogether. 'We live in an intellectually corrupt age', he declared in 1948, 'and the writing of history has not escaped the general corruption.'[13]

Oakeshott believed the 'corruption' he attacked in the 1940s and '50s had arisen because 'contemporary history is centred upon the use to be made of it, upon the dogma that it can be made to prove; concerned only with the future, we pervert history to our own purposes.' He took E.H. Carr's *The Bolshevik Revolution* to be an example of the 'corruption'. Carr's book 'degenerated into a peculiarly simple exercise in whiggish history'; he had 'achieved the remarkable feat of "going native" without being a Communist', writing history from the perspective of Lenin and the Bolsheviks themselves. Carr's 'prejudice in favour of success' ensured that 'Russia before the Revolution is never allowed to enter in detail into the story of the Revolution.' 1917 appeared as 'the creation of a world *ex nihilo* by a

[12]   Oakeshott, Review of Collingwood, *The Idea of History*, pp. 84–5.

[13]   Oakeshott, Review of K.B. Smellie, *Why We Read History*, *Cambridge Journal*, vol. 1, 1948, p. 766.

demiurge who came from Switzerland' and 1905 'is treated as an incident in pre-messianic history.'[14]

No doubt some of Oakeshott's criticisms were a little disingenuous; reading them, one could be forgiven for thinking that in the 1940s and early 1950s it was only the Labour party and socialist historians who engaged in (by his standards) unhistorical rhetoric about the past, which was certainly not the case. One would certainly be left unaware of such works as Barker's multi-volume treatise on *The Character of England*, or the 'consensus history'[15] of G.M. Trevelyan, intended to promote national harmony at a time of immense strain. All that we have sought to establish, however, is that in the post-war period of *Rationalism in Politics*, Oakeshott continued to insist in principle on the distinction between the practical and the historical past. That he tended to blur it himself is true, but does not affect the latter point.

The question is whether Oakeshott maintained this separation of history and practice in *On Human Conduct*. In fact, there is good reason for thinking that he did; that there has been doubt on the matter has been largely due to the changes in his philosophical vocabulary. Oakeshott declared that in future he would restrict the use of the term 'practical' to 'participation in or subscription to a "practice"', because to 'speak of the understanding implicit in conduct as "practical" understanding . . . might falsely suggest that the only understanding implicit in conduct is knowing how to participate in practices'.[16]

The identification of 'practical' with 'traditional' knowledge in *Rationalism in Politics* had given just this impression to some critics; it had suggested a mindless conformity to the dead weight of the past, and this was not what Oakeshott had had in mind. In his view, 'knowing how to participate in a "practice" . . . is not exclusive to conduct. It is present also . . . in both "historical" and "scientific" enquiry, both of which are engagements in theoretical understanding released from the considerations of conduct'.[17]

The assertion that historical understanding is a kind of 'theoretical' understanding 'released from the considerations of conduct' confirms Oakeshott still regarded history as distinct from what he had earlier called 'practical' understanding and now referred to as

[14]   Oakeshott, 'Mr Carr's First Volume', *Cambridge Journal*, vol. 4, 1951, pp. 346–52.

[15]   J. Hernon, 'The Last Whig Historian and Consensus History: George Macaulay Trevelyan', *American Historical Review*, vol. 81, 1976, pp. 66–97.

[16]   *HC*, p. 57 n. 1.

[17]   *Ibid.*

'the understanding implicit in conduct'. It is true that he talked of history as one of several 'idioms' within the same 'order' of theoretical understanding which are ultimately reducible to one another. Since, however, practical understanding or the understanding implicit in conduct is not a theoretical understanding, whatever other forms of theoretical understanding history might be reducible to (anthropology or sociology, perhaps), it is certainly not reducible to 'practice' or 'conduct'. And although history is a 'practice' of a sort, with its own methods and so forth, what it aims at is not action, but the creation of a theory. Thus, we may conclude that although it underwent some reformulation, Oakeshott's basic distinction between history and the practical mode remained unchanged between 1947 and 1975.

What of the relationship of history to science? In *Experience and its Modes*, science and history were portrayed as distinct worlds of experience, supported by postulates which were entirely different in each case. Oakeshott had insisted on this in order to make clear that historical study was not a scientific enterprise on the model of the natural sciences. He had distinguished 'causation' in history from the concept of 'causation' employed in the natural sciences, and had denied that historical study involved the use of, or search for, 'general laws' akin to those to be found in science. In doing so, he had been criticising writers such as Buckle, Comte and J.S. Mill who had authored positivistic conceptions of history.

The enterprise of understanding history on the model of the natural sciences, however, had not disappeared with nineteenth-century positivism. For example, the philosopher Hempel, in his 1942 essay on 'The Function of General Laws in History', had no doubt at all that 'general laws' had a 'function in scientific historical research . . . quite analogous' to that of 'the natural sciences'.[18] In claiming this, Hempel may be said to have been 'approaching history with an already formed conception of explanation to some extent affected by Hume's analysis of causation.'[19]

Hume had argued that we are simply 'determined by custom to transfer the past to the future, in all our inferences.' When we say that one event is caused by another, we are in effect merely asserting that 'no instance has ever yet been found' of the latter event not occurring after the former. The only alternative Hume could see to this explanation of causality in terms of habits formed by experience

[18]   C. Hempel, 'The Function of General Laws in History', *Journal of Philosophy*, vol. 39, 1942, p. 35.

[19]   Goldstein, *Historical Knowing*, p. 207.

was the existence of 'a medium, which may enable the mind to draw an inference' from the former to the latter. Only thus could inductive thought be made to rest on 'reasoning and argument'.[20] Although Hume himself confessed that he was unable to see what such a medium would be like, later writers (such as Hempel) believed that a 'general law' would fill the gap.

As Goldstein remarks, writers like Hempel have simply assumed the applicability to historical thought of the argument that we cannot assert x is the cause of y without making use of some such proposition as, 'if x then y'. The task of the philosopher of history is then said to consist in identifying the propositions of the latter sort which have been or ought to be used. From Oakeshott's point of view, of course, this begs the question, for historical thinking does not employ scientific inductions in which kinds of event are related according to mechanical laws. In his essay 'On the Activity of Being an Historian', he rejected once more the 'idea that there was a manner of understanding the past which leaves it completely intelligible' by 'revealing past events as example of general laws.'

Historians in this period nevertheless continued to be attracted by the identification of history with natural science. Cobban, a respected historian of France and fellow Caian, was severely critical of Oakeshott's arguments to the contrary. In a discussion of 'History and Sociology'. Cobban, like Postan before World War Two, saw the historian as a species of social scientist, whose activity would be impossible without scientific 'general laws'. Because Oakeshott did not accept this, Cobban believed he must be committed to a belief that past events were 'irrational'; Oakeshott had reduced the historical past to 'meaninglessness'.[21]

Cobban had, in fact, simply misunderstood what was entailed in Oakeshott's rejection of the argument that historical study shared the logic of a natural science; a non-scientific meaning was not automatically equivalent to no meaning at all, as he assumed. History and science, Oakeshott argued, were to be understood as two distinct responses to present experience. Both treat the present as evidence for what does not itself appear, but science does so in terms of general and necessary relations, whereas the historian sees the present as evidence for 'a world composed wholly of contingencies . . . which . . . are intelligible . . . on account of the circumstantial relations

[20] D. Hume, *An Enquiry Concerning Human Understanding*, sec. 4 pt. 2, sec. 6, in D. Hume, *Enquiries Concerning Human Understanding and Concerning the Principles of Morals*, 2nd edn., ed. L.A. Selby–Brigge, Clarendon, Oxford, 1936, pp. 372.
[21] A. Cobban, 'History and Sociology', *Historical Studies*, vol. 3, 1961, pp. 1–4.

which have been established between them.'[22] This argument was developed in more detail in *On Human Conduct*. There, Oakeshott made clear that science and history are not only different kinds of responses to the present; they are also responses to kinds of present that are different to begin with.

The 'goings-on' that present themselves before my eyes, Oakeshott now claimed, will be recognised implicitly or explicitly, to belong to one of two specifiable 'categories of identity.' 'To the first category belong "goings-on" the identification of which includes the recognition that they are themselves exhibitions of intelligence' and 'To the second category belong "goings-on" recognised ... not themselves to be exhibitions of intelligence.' For each of these two categories of identity there is an appropriate 'order of enquiry.' Furthermore, 'Identities in respect of their categories and enquiries in respect of their "orders" are . . . exclusive of one another.'[23] Oakeshott was reasserting, in other terms, the notion of modal irrelevance familiar from *Experience and its Modes*. This version, however, was preferable insofar as it avoided the problems associated with the concept of absolute experience.

In 1975, as in 1933, Oakeshott insisted that the modes or orders of enquiry could not be reduced to one another; 'the understanding of identities recognised as themselves exhibitions of intelligence cannot be reduced to the understanding of identities not so recognised.' For example, the historian presupposes in his investigations that what he is dealing with is present evidence for past intelligent goings-on or 'human conduct,' and therefore is precluded by his own assumptions from offering a scientific explanation of this evidence in terms of non-intelligent processes. The relationship between history and natural science in *On Human Conduct* is the same as in *Experience and its Modes* — mutual irrelevance. In the later work, Oakeshott refined the distinction by subsuming history and science under the distinction between the theoretical understanding of the intelligent and the not-intelligent.[24]

We do, however, have the choice of whether to theorise human actions as instances of intelligent conduct or not-intelligent behaviour, whereas we do not, except in purely playful or artistic moments, have the option of regarding instances of non-intelligent behaviour (a leaf falling) as intelligent conduct. As Nardin puts it, Oakeshott rephrased the identification of the real with the meaning-

[22]   *RP*, pp. 153, 182.

[23]   *HC*, p. 15.

[24]   See Nardin, *op. cit.*, p. 135.

ful made in *Experience and its Modes*, but distinguished 'two kinds of meaning in understanding: that which belongs to the object to be understood and that which the observer brings to the study of the object. Intelligent things have meaning in both senses, not-intelligent things only in the latter.' Oakeshott came to think that genuine social sciences, particularly psychology, make the latter choice, understanding action in not-intelligent terms.

In both *Experience and its Modes* and *On Human Conduct*, Oakeshott regarded it as 'beyond reasonable doubt' that 'there is a genuine science of psychology' which studies 'such goings-on as feeling . . . wanting . . . playing . . . not as states of consciousness or exhibitions of intelligence, but as observable processes.' Such processes are 'understood in terms of theorems which denote regularities which are not themselves exhibitions of understanding and do not have to be learned in order to be operative.' What Oakeshott regarded as spurious was explanation of goings-on supposedly recognised as intelligent in terms of 'a so-called psychological type, of the ur-experiences of infancy, biological urges, genetic inheritance, repressed anxieties or of environmental pressures — anything but the ideas [an individual] has learned (but might not have learned) to think.'[25] This was a categorial error, a confusion similar to a modal misunderstanding in that it could only produce irrelevance.

'Psycho-historical speculations', in Cohn's phrase, were in vogue in the 1960s and 1970s, but Oakeshott had little sympathy with them.[26] In a remark that is perhaps a reference to Cohn's work, *Europe's Inner Demons*, Oakeshott argued that 'The prevalence of astrology, magic, witchcraft, and Satanism in fourteenth-century Europe is not explained by being identified as "the normal psychological reaction to circumstances of unusual danger and physical suffering"'; this would involve treating such beliefs as if they were a matter of stimulus and (non-intelligent) response.[27] If psychology were a science in the mould of the natural sciences, then, it represented a different order of enquiry to history.

The same was true of economics; Oakeshott consistently held that a genuine science of economics was possible, composed of theorems dealing with processes and regularities, but that these bore no direct relation to the theoretical understanding of human conduct.[28] The case of sociology, however, was different. In the 1930s, Oakeshott

---

[25] *HC*, pp. 20–3.

[26] N. Cohn, *Europe's Inner Demons*, Paladin, St. Albans, 1976, p. 258.

[27] *HC*, pp. 22–3.

[28] *op. cit.*, pp. 19, 45.

had been unsure whether to class sociology with psychology and economics, or with anthropology, which he regarded as a form of history. In *On Human Conduct*, he gave a clear answer. 'Sociology' was not a 'science' in the same sense as psychology. Rather, it was 'an engagement of historical understanding of a certain limited sort.' Sociology, he argued, was the attempt to understand a 'going-on' recognised as an intelligent illustration of human conduct 'in terms of the conditions imposed upon it by the multiplicity of more or less durable relationships of human beings [practices]', and to understand 'these relationships in terms of their postulates'.

Thus, sociologists become involved in a categorial confusion if they attempted to explain a 'society' as a 'system' or 'process . . . in terms of . . . regularities or . . . causal conditions, and not as a procedure whose postulates are reflective intelligence, contingent beliefs and acknowledgments of authority or utility.'[29] It need hardly be emphasised how different this conception of sociology is from that held by an influential founder of the discipline like Durkheim. The latter 'left [history] only with the auxiliary role of finding, cleansing and presenting the raw material for the generalisations of sociologists.'[30] Oakeshott, by contrast, saw these cherished generalisations merely as attenuated historical propositions.

Although we have been particularly concerned to emphasise that Oakeshott persisted in keeping history separate from all the other areas of experience which he identified, we should not ignore Oakeshott's efforts to display history as one member of a family of theoretical activities. In his later writings on the philosophy of history, history still shares with philosophy (and natural science and poetry) the status of an 'escape from the conduct of practical life' that was attributed to it in *Experience and its Modes*.[31] In an unpublished paper, which from its argument seems to post-date the point at which Oakeshott's changed view of philosophy became unambiguously apparent, we may find a detailed exploration of this idea of history and other voices as escapes from practice.

The paper, entitled 'Work and Play', was left undated, but judging by its style as well as its argument, it belongs to the years we are now considering, the later 1950s and 1960s. Escape from 'the world' and a release from 'work' were themes that had figured in some of Oakeshott's earliest writings on religion.[32] Here, religion is still

[29]   *op. cit.*, p. 24.

[30]   E. Breisach, *Historiography*, 2nd edn., Chicago UP, Chicago, 1994, p. 277.

[31]   *EM*, pp. 296–7.

[32]   *ML*, p. 32.

important, but the dichotomy is no longer between a religious and a worldly life. Oakeshott believed, like Hobbes, that the wants and desires of the practical self, which stem from the human 'ability . . . and propensity, not merely to accept what the world happens to offer in satisfaction of needs, but to seek for what it does not immediately offer', are inherently inexhaustible, terminable only by death. This was so because wants, unlike needs, 'are related to no fixed condition of things'. 'Work' was simply the 'effort to achieve the sort of happiness which is to be had from satisfying human wants.'[33]

This kind of activity absorbed an enormous amount — nearly all — of our intelligence, effort and ingenuity. Nevertheless, as Hobbes had pointed out, a 'creature whose satisfactions generate new wants endlessly, is a creature of unavoidable anxieties.' There is no final satisfaction to be had in the happiness that comes from the fulfilment of wants.[34] For Oakeshott, 'to be a creature of wants is itself a curse, a condemnation to a life in which every achievement is a frustration.' It was for this reason that he was convinced that 'Doing is a deadly thing.' There was, however, the possibility of at least a temporary and partial escape from 'the deadliness of doing' in 'another form of activity, peculiar to human beings, which does not suffer from the defect inherent in work and the satisfaction of wants: "play".'

We saw in the previous chapter that Oakeshott followed Huizinga in defining 'play' in a very extended sense; he did not refer simply to games. 'Play' was a kind of 'activity which, because it is not directed to the satisfaction of wants, entails an attitude to the world which is not concerned to use it, to get something out of it, or to make something out of it.' We will not be surprised to discover that Oakeshott classed history as a form of 'play' in this extended sense. 'Philosophy, science and history are different adventures into this realm of understanding and explanation', in which we are 'emancipated' from work. Whereas life in the practical world is 'a dream followed by an effort to make it come true', history is 'a dream enjoyed for its own sake', an 'end in itself'. Historical study is one of the activities in which 'human beings have believed themselves to enjoy a freedom and an illumination which the satisfaction of wants can never supply.'[35]

In an address to the LSE history society, Oakeshott remarked 'I do not want to make too much of it; but the truth is that life . . . is apt to have some tiresome passages.' When in the army, he reminisced, he

[33]   Oakeshott, 'Work and Play', LSE 1/1/48.

[34]   *op. cit.*, p. 9.

[35]   *op. cit.*, pp. 11–12, 15.

had been given an 'escape kit': 'a knife disguised as a bar of choco-
late, a tin of porridge and a soldiers cooker and a benzedrine tablet.'
An 'escape kit' of this sort was exactly what reading and studying
history provided for the lay person and professional alike, though
Oakeshott was quick to emphasise that by it he did not 'mean anything so trivial as . . . a hobby; I mean something commensurate with
the dignity of an immortal soul.' He even went so far as to say that
'the escape outfit [history] provides is immeasurably superior to any
other', though given our observations above, we may regard this as
the expression of a personal preference rather than his considered
philosophical position. He would, though, definitely have been willing to defend his statement that 'the historical past forbids us to project our own current enterprises into it, and it discourages even the
projection of our loves and hates. It is conspicuously different; it is
infinitely various, it awaits us, it is full and not empty, and (best of
all) we can do nothing about it.'[36]

No doubt there are similarities between Oakeshott's views and
those of earlier Romantics such as Schiller, who thought of play as
'the highest human activity' and anything but a game.[37] Yet however
successful the metaphors of 'play' and 'conversation' in indicating
the role and use of history in Oakeshott's scheme of things, they
remained figurative notions. The use of these metaphors was characteristic of a period of his thought in which he had finally abandoned his earlier ideas about the status of philosophy, but had yet to
work out the consequences of this move. In his later writings such as
On Human Conduct, he deliberately sought to translate the images in
which he had initially attempted to express his changed view of
things into philosophical terms, and it is useful to bear them in mind
when construing some of the more intricate passages.

History and Contingency

The logic of historical enquiry, as Oakeshott portrayed it in *On
Human Conduct*, postulated recognition of human beings as agents
in pursuit of contingent wants, contingently related to one another
in terms of various practices. It postulated, in other words, what he
called 'human conduct'. He did not think it made sense for historians to treat the past events they sought to understand in the same
way as they would if they were actually required to respond to similar kinds of things happening in the present. Nevertheless, there is
an important similarity between the kind of understanding

---

[36]   Oakeshott, Address to the LSE History Society, undated, LSE 1/3, p. 3.

[37]   E.F. Carrit, *The Theory of Beauty*, 5th edn, rev., Methuen, London, 1962, p. 10.

employed in performing and responding to actions, and the kind of understanding involved in historical enquiry.[38] Both historical understanding and the 'understanding implicit in conduct' presuppose that they are dealing with goings-on that involve reflective intelligence. This is also true of the novelist, whose characters are also intelligent agents; Oakeshott believed history, literature and life all involved a kind of understanding which he called 'event-making'.

This view was made explicit in an unpublished LSE seminar paper from the early 1970s, much of which would be published in somewhat revised form in *On History* a decade later. Oakeshott presented the similarity between historical and what he had previously called 'practical' understanding as follows. The understanding in conduct, he argued, draws on 'the past' as it appears to memory and to the deliberate effort to remember, recollection. The historical past is like the past of recollection rather than memory in the sense that it has to be evoked (a memory may come to me unbidden). However, it is not 'my own' past.

Oakeshott used the following example. 'I see a piano being moved into the house next door. This is an identified and an intelligible occurrence. But if I am curious I may try to turn it into an "event".' To do so is to understand this occurrence 'as the outcome of a series of contingently related occurrences.' This understanding is arrived at on the basis of evidence, in this case in the form of the answers I receive to such enquiries as 'Has Mr Smith taken up the piano?' Although 'an historian has to undertake this business of "event-making" in somewhat peculiar and difficult circumstances', because he is not dealing with goings-on present before him, but only with present evidence for past goings-on, the understanding involved in conduct and in historical understanding may both be said to involve 'event-making' of this sort.

Even before he published *On Human Conduct*, then, Oakeshott had come to see the 'event making' undertaken by historians as an understanding in terms of contingent relationships. In his essay 'On the Activity of Being an Historian', Oakeshott had contrasted the natural sciences, which make events intelligible in terms of 'general laws' and 'necessary and sufficient conditions', with historical understanding, in which events belong to 'a world composed

---

[38] Perhaps it is this similarity which leads Boucher, for example, to think that Oakeshott actually made historical and practical understanding reducible to one another. While Oakeshott made 'human conduct' a postulate of both, that does not alter the fact that he considered history to be theoretical, which practical understanding was not.

wholly of contingencies . . . which are intelligible . . . on account of the circumstantial relations which have been established between them.'[39]

Oakeshott's use of the idea of 'contingency' in this 1958 essay indicated the beginnings of a further change from the ideas of *Experience and its Modes*. In his discussion of Bury in 1933, the 'contingent' was simply a synonym for such practical conceptions as chance or accident. It symbolised a failure in historical explanation. In 1958, the 'contingent' referred to a distinctive kind of intelligible relationship investigated by historical understanding. There is reason to suspect that this change owes more than a little to Oakeshott's reflections on the concept of *fortuna*; a frustratingly incomplete paper tracing the history of this idea from Aristotle through Boethius and Dante to Machiavelli survives amongst his papers at the LSE.[40] Machiavelli, Oakeshott suggested, observed that 'it is a feature of earthly life that events are apt to take quite unforeseen turns' and 'are subject to dramatic, revolutionary, apparently capricious changes', yet are not therefore unintelligible. To say that historians aim to render intelligible the workings of *fortuna* would seem to be no different from saying that they aim to understand an event in terms of its contingently-related antecedents.

Detailed exploration of contingency, however, is only to be found in the first essay in *On Human Conduct*, 'On the Theoretical Understanding of Human Conduct', and in *On History*. There, contingency was made to denote 'a kind of relationship which specifies the character of what is related.' It denotes, in other words, the 'category of identity' with which it deals; human conduct or intelligent action. Like a 'causal' relationship, it claims to be a 'significant' relationship 'such that the recognition of it enhances the intelligibility of the "goings-on" concerned'. It is 'neither a merely factual juxtaposition of "goings-on" in terms of "when" or "where" nor a mere correlation of "goings-on" in terms of likenesses or arbitrarily chosen common characteristics.'[41]

Contingent relationship, Oakeshott argued, is a 'contiguous' relationship, a relationship of 'touching,' in the sense that there is an 'absence of interval' between the identities it relates. 'There is only an unbroken continuity of occurrences.' Moreover, this continuity 'is not merely the absence of interval; it is the congruity of what came after with what went before'. Oakeshott, who had once thought of

[39]   *RP*, pp. 153, 182.

[40]   Oakeshott, 'Fortuna', undated, LSE 1/1/34.

[41]   *HC*, p. 101.

historical events as intelligible in terms of events that come after those we seek to understand, reversed this view completely. Contingent relationship is a relationship 'of each occurrence to the one before.'

Oakeshott acknowledged that 'every antecedent is itself a subsequent and every sequel is an antecedent', but this argument that an event has a different character depending on whether it is regarded as an outcome, or as preceding other events, does not affect the point that an historical understanding of any given event must be *exclusively* in terms of antecedent events. On these grounds, he declared that 'understanding in terms of contingent relations is contextual: what has to be understood and the terms in which it is understood are not two different kinds of identities (like a "law" and examples of its operation), they are individual occurrences made to elucidate one another in an investigation of their evidential relationships.'[42]

There are obvious similarities here with the philosophy of history of *Experience and its Modes*. The emphasis on continuity and the individuality of historical events, for example, are familiar. That should not obscure the fact that Oakeshott had not previously described the kind of relationship between historical events in such detail; he had said almost no more than that the relations between events were themselves events. The product of historical investigation of contingently related events, he now argued, was a 'narrative' in which an event is 'understood neither as a fortuitous happening, nor as a necessary consequence, but as . . . intelligible.'[43]

The argument that narratives of contingent events are the products of historical enquiry did not involve the suggestion that such narration excludes, or is opposed to, analysis and interpretation. We have already seen that for Oakeshott, unlike, for example, Mandelbaum, the narration of events inescapably involves understanding and interpreting them. The significance of 'contingency' was, rather, that it rescued history from the 'irrationality' and 'meaninglessness' which Cobban, for example, feared, in the absence of a scientific 'causal' relationship.

Let us sum up. In his essay 'On the Theoretical Understanding of Human Conduct', Oakeshott presented historical understanding as an idiom of one of two orders of theoretical enquiry. The order of enquiry to which it belonged was dedicated to the understanding of intelligent goings-on, postulating 'human conduct' and contingently related events. 'The theoretical understanding of a

[42]   *op. cit.*, p. 105.
[43]   *op. cit.*, p. 106.

substantive action or utterance is . . . in principle, a "historical" understanding.'[44] What history cannot supply is an understanding of the category 'human conduct' itself; that is the task of the kind of theorist known as the philosopher. 'A platform of conditional understanding' such as history is 'constituted by its conditions which, from different points of view, may be recognised as assumptions or postulates.'

It was, however, as impossible, in Oakeshott's view, simultaneously to make use of an assumption and question it, as it is to specify simultaneously the position and momentum of a subatomic particle. Looking at the thing one way precludes you from looking at it another, he argued. An historical understanding of chivalry or Stoicism postulates, and therefore does not question, the identity 'human conduct'; it is the philosopher who does that.[45] It cannot, therefore, be held against history that it is 'untheoretical' in this sense — though of course Oakeshott thought it possible for historians to break from their task to query the ideas with which they were working. Most importantly of all, however, Oakeshott remained convinced of the autonomy of historical enquiry; he presented it as an idiom 'constituted in theorems exclusively its own' and 'capable of its own conditional perfection.'[46]

History as a Language

Even before the war, Oakeshott had hinted at the importance of language for a philosophical understanding of historical enquiry. In *Experience and its Modes*, he had argued that much of the evidence confronting historians belonged to the world of 'practical' activity; evidence of political activity, for example, necessarily does so. What the historian does with this evidence is not to ask whether any of statements it might contain are 'true', in the sense of deciding whether to accept or reject the testimony they offer as authoritative, but to make them intelligible in historical terms.[47] Oakeshott went further still; since 'the idiom of happening is always that of practice, and the record of happening is usually in the idiom of practice', he argued, 'an "historical" event is something that never happened,

---

[44] *op. cit.*, p. 105.

[45] *op. cit.*, pp. 9, 56.

[46] *op. cit.*, p. 17.

[47] Oakeshott, 'Mr Carr', p. 348.

and an "historical" action something never performed . . . an historical character is one that never lived.'[48]

Shortly after World War Two, Oakeshott fixed on the simile of the
translator as a way of characterising the task of making evidence of
past practical activity historically intelligible. An immediate difficulty with this analogy of translation, Oakeshott acknowledged,
was that 'The historian has no vocabulary of his own; he is obliged . . .
to use the language of morals and politics.' In this situation, the only
thing that could be said was that 'he should be wary of [the] implications' of the language he was forced to use.[49] Nevertheless, he
insisted that historians who 'believe themselves to be dealing with
things, not words' were under an illusion.

Reviewing Duncan Forbes' essay on *The Liberal Anglican Idea of
History* in 1953, Oakeshott concluded that that the most 'fruitful line
of thought in respect of the nature of history' was to regard it 'as a
manner of speaking about the world, a particular language not to be
confused with any other. And when we reflect upon this manner of
speaking, what we are on the look out for is the categories which
belong to it.'[50] This 'linguistic turn' mirrored developments elsewhere. As a contributor to the first series of *Philosophy, Politics and
Society* in the later 1950s, he was present at the beginning of 'the historical resolution of political discourse into . . . idioms and "languages" . . . that has transformed the historiography of political
thought.'[51] Yet in his introduction, Laslett exempted Oakeshott from
the class of 'linguistic philosophers' such as 'Russell and
Wittgenstein, Ayer and Ryle', whom he thought had indirectly put
paid to the 'traditional ethical systems . . . of Bosanquet's time, or
even Harold Laski's'.[52] He was right to do so, for Oakeshott's linguistic self-consciousness did not lead him to share the pessimism
about the state of the humanities in general and of historical knowledge in particular which was endemic in this period.[53]

Nevertheless, Oakeshott's use of linguistic-cum-literary analogies
— writing of history as a certain 'reading' of the present and as one
amongst a number of 'voices' composing a conversation —

---

[48] *RP*, p. 180.

[49] Oakeshott, 'Mr Carr', p. 349.

[50] Oakeshott, Review of *The Liberal Anglican Idea of History*, *Cambridge Journal*, vol.
      4, 1953, p. 251.

[51] J.G.A. Pocock, *The Ancient Constitution and the Feudal Law*, rev. edn., Cambridge
      UP, Cambridge, 1990, p. xi.

[52] P. Laslett, 'Introduction' to *Philosophy, Politics and Society*, 1st ser., Blackwell,
      Oxford, 1956, pp. viii–ix.

[53] See Plumb (ed.), *Crisis in the Humanities*.

prompted an increasing number of comparisons between his views and those of the later Wittgenstein. Ever since the publication of *Rationalism in Politics*, commentators have repeatedly pointed out the similarity between Oakeshott's ideas and those of the *Philosophical Investigations* as well as with 'ordinary language' philosophy. For example, to Pitkin, Oakeshott's description of the scientific and the practical modes as two distinct 'universes of discourse' suggested a parallel with the idea of 'language games' or different regions of language devised by Wittgenstein. [54] To others, the critiques of Rationalism that Oakeshott was also producing at the time intimated 'a parallel with the neo-Wittgenstinian attack on logical positivism'. [55]

The similarities are indeed striking, but there is little doubt that we are dealing with a conceptual similarity rather than an historical influence. Although Wittgenstein and Oakeshott were at Cambridge together for much of the time before the war, there is no evidence that they ever spoke. Yet, although Laslett was right to regard Oakeshott as removed from the Wittgenstinian interest in 'ordinary language' that characterised English, or at any rate, Oxford, philosophy in the 1950s and 1960s, this theme cannot be ignored entirely. Indeed, as we shall see, Wittgenstein's indirect impact on the history of political thought made itself felt in the seminar series which Oakeshott began convening in at the LSE in 1964-5 as part of a new one year MSc degree in political thought. This new MSc had been imposed on the Professor of Political Science by an 'administrative dictat,'[56] but he had responded enthusiastically, writing to a former pupil that 'I have spent most of the summer getting ready for this new MSc' and 'I am beginning to see how good it might be'.[57]

The seminar soon became the main forum in which Oakeshott developed his ideas on the philosophy of history. Some idea of the subjects raised can be gained from the reading lists Oakeshott supplied for students. [58] One such list began by listing works which dealt

[54] H. Pitkin, *Wittgenstein and Justice: On the Significance of Ludwig Wittgenstein for Social and Political Thought*, California UP, Berkeley, 1972, pp. 50, 142, 201, 329, 338.

[55] D.H. Munro, 'Godwin, Oakeshott and Mrs Bloomer', *Journal of the History of Ideas*, vol. 35, 1974, p. 613. The comparisons of Oakeshott and Wittgenstein are too numerous to list them all. See, for example, C. Falck, 'Romanticism in Politics', *New Left Review*, vol. 18, 1963, p. 70; Crick, *op. cit.*; K. Minogue, 'Michael Oakeshott and the History of Political Thought Seminar', *Cambridge Review*, vol. 112, 1992, p. 117; Wells, *op. cit.*, p. 141; Nardin, *op. cit.*, p. 232.

[56] Minogue, 'Michael Oakeshott and the History of Political Thought Seminar', p. 114.

[57] Oakeshott, Letter to N. K. O'Sullivan, 26 September 1964, private collection.

[58] Syllabuses, reading lists, and seminar programmes relating to Oakeshott's MSc course are at LSE 8/3.

in a general way with 'history as a mode of thought', introducing the idea that historical enquiry was itself an historical phenomenon with a history and identifying some of the common organising ideas of historical writing which would receive more extended treatment in *On Human Conduct* and *On History*, such as 'past events, identity, change, continuity, contingency, context' and so on.

We have already met many of the works Oakeshott suggested as introductory reading material for the course – Collingwood's *Idea of History*, Butterfield's *Whig Interpretation* and Gallie's *Philosophy and the Historical Understanding* were all amongst them. Using these works to familiarise his students with the idea that historical enquiry was a distinct form of understanding, he went on to the problems associated with the various forms of the 'history of ideas'. Histories of philosophical, scientific, economic, legal, artistic, literary, religious and moral ideas were all up for discussion, and in all cases he made sure that a wide variety of works were represented. Nineteenth century authors such as Lecky, Schweitzer, Hallam, Maitland, Hegel, and Bosanquet rubbed shoulders with distinctly more modern names such as Pocock and MacIntyre.[59]

The seminar itself soon began to attract some illustrious participants. As well as Elie Kedourie, Maurice Cranston, and Kenneth Minogue – all senior figures in the study of politics at the LSE – historians such as C.B. Macpherson, Shirley Letwin and J.G.A. Pocock all attended at least once.[60] One participant who was about to become extremely important in the study of the history of political thought was Quentin Skinner, who presented an early version of his influential paper on 'Meaning and Understanding in the History of Ideas' to that seminar in 1968.[61]

In the published version of 'Meaning and Understanding in the History of Ideas', Skinner argued that 'the understanding of texts' in historical study 'presupposes the grasp both of what they were intended to mean, and how this meaning was intended to be taken.'[62] His 'emphasis on intentions [was] inspired by Collingwood and substantiated with arguments from Austin's . . . and . . . Wittgenstein's philosophies of language.'[63] This in turn involved a stress on the need to understand texts in the contexts in which they

---

[59] Oakeshott, Reading List.

[60] Minogue, *op. cit.*

[61] Professor Skinner in conversation.

[62] Q. Skinner, 'Meaning and Understanding in the History of Ideas', *History and Theory*, vol. 8, 1969, p. 48.

[63] Boucher, *Texts in Context*, p. 198.

were written; we can only discover what the author intended to say if we know, as Collingwood put it, the question to which his work was an answer.[64] Skinner's views have in turn been accepted by leading English historians. Burrow, Winch and Collini, for example, have accepted that the historian's task ought to centre on the recovery of intentions.[65]

There are, then, two main aspects to the view of historical study that Skinner advocated. First of all, it stressed the need for contextual understanding. Secondly, it stressed the need for the recovery of authorial intentions.[66] On the first point, there would have been little for Oakeshott to disagree with. Reviewing two works of ancient history, he wrote that 'the study of a text is a study of its words, and no text will reveal its meaning unless the interpreter goes to it with the questions, "Why this word and not that?" and "what precisely, in this literary and historical context, is the connotation of this word?"'[67] Texts require contexts, for the 'whole answer' to a question about meaning 'is never supplied by the text itself'. Such an attitude, which recalled his insistence on the inseparability of 'text' from 'interpretation' in *Experience and its Modes*, had early led him to accept that texts must be understood in their contexts if they were to be understood historically.

Over the second point, the question of intentions, however, it might appear that Oakeshott and Skinner part company. It has been said that Oakeshott 'denies that history concerns itself with the intentions, purposes, reasons . . . of an agent.'[68] Yet although Skinner places much greater emphasis than Oakeshott on intentions, making them the 'main focus' of historical enquiry,[69] Oakeshott cannot be said to have ignored their importance in historical enquiry. He made his general position clear in criticisms of Collingwood's argument that the task of the historian was to re-enact the ideas of the agents involved, a task which included recovering their intentions.[70]

Reviewing W.H. Walsh's *An Introduction to Philosophy of History*, Oakeshott described 'the view [of history] favoured by Collingwood' as 'the enterprise of resurrecting or reconstructing the

[64] Collingwood, *An Autobiography*, pp. 29–44.

[65] S. Collini, D. Winch, and J. Burrow, *That Noble Science of Politics: A Study in Nineteenth Century Intellectual History*, Cambridge UP, Cambridge, 1983, p. 5.

[66] This summary of Skinner's views owes a great deal to Boucher, *Texts in Context*.

[67] Oakeshott, Review of R. Barrow, *Introduction to Augustine*, *Cambridge Journal*, vol. 4, 1951, p. 570.

[68] Boucher, 'Overlap and Autonomy', p. 89.

[69] Skinner quoted in Boucher, *Texts in Context*, p. 204.

[70] A view apparently shared by Boucher, 'Overlap and Autonomy', *ibid*.

thoughts, feelings and emotions of the past'. He was critical of this because the enterprise of 'reconstructing' the past assumed a relationship of correspondence between the historically reconstructed thought and an independently existing past. The 'main difficulty of the re-enactment thesis' was that it did not recognise that 'an historical account of the past at least purports to present something which was never in the mind of anybody at the time.' The historian does not produce a representation of our vanished past but constructs a new kind of past, the outcome 'of a way of thinking about the past which would have been impossible for anyone who lived in that past.'[71]

That is not to say, however, that the intentions of participants are to be ignored. It was not the relevance to history of intentions as such, but their status as psychic acts capable of being recovered or 're-enacted' in the mind of the historian, which Oakeshott rejected. In *On Human Conduct* he made it clear that an understanding of intentions was a crucial element in the understanding of action.[72] To the philosopher, human conduct involves intelligent human actors or agents who are (or were) 'historic' continuing identities, the authors of actions which seek satisfactions in the responses of others. In the performance of such actions, both intention and motive are to be reckoned with.[73]

If intentions and motives are inseparable from human conduct, and historians understand action in terms of human conduct, then intentions — for example, what an author meant to do in writing — cannot be ignored. Oakeshott wished only to emphasise that the meaning of 'an action is not tied to the achievement of what is meant in performing it. If it were frustrated of its intention it would not cease to be an action or become another and a different action'.[74] If this seems obvious, we must remember that Collingwood believed that if an agent 'did not succeed in carrying . . . out [a plan] . . . no-one will ever know what it was.'[75]

History and Morality

Oakeshott's rejection of the idea that the historian's task could be identified primarily with the recovery of intentions has ramifications for his philosophy of history which extend beyond his differ-

[71] Oakeshott, Review of W.H. Walsh, *An Introduction to Philosophy of History, Philosophical Quarterly*, vol. 2, 1952, p. 277.

[72] *HC*, p. 32.

[73] *op. cit.*, pp. 36–9, 55–9.

[74] *op. cit.*, pp. 39–40.

[75] Collingwood, *An Autobiography*, p. 70.

ences with Collingwood and Skinner. At least in part, the reasons for his rejection rested on his philosophy of action, and it is also via the notion of action or 'human conduct' that the idea of 'character' entered into his philosophy of history.

For Oakeshott, 'human conduct' was a postulate necessary to the historical understanding of past actions. The concept entailed intelligent agents who are the authors of actions. In understanding any action, any instance of human conduct, he argued, 'two inseparable but distinguishable considerations' are involved. Firstly, actions are 'adventures to procure wished-for substantive satisfactions in the responses they achieve'. Therefore, the 'self-disclosure' of one's intentions is necessary in order that others may be able to respond to my aims. Secondly, actions are also 'exploits in self-enactment', performed with certain 'sentiments or motives'. Self-enactment concerns what we might call the spirit in which an action is done. Both considerations are relevant to historical understanding. Actions must be understood both 'in terms of the motives in which they are performed' and in terms of the intention with which they are performed; the historian must try to understand both what a past actor was aiming at, and that actor's reasons for doing so.[76] Of course, as we shall see in chapter six, the understanding of motives and intentions was for Oakeshott only a step on the way to the construction of an historical event.

We may bring out the significance of the distinction between self-disclosure and self-enactment by noticing how Oakeshott related it to the writings of other philosophers. On the one hand, he thought that J.S. Mill had attempted to base his moral philosophy exclusively on considerations of 'justice'. That is, Mill's utilitarian philosophy focussed on actions as 'self-disclosures', as the products of intentions to satisfy wants. Mill had not ignored self-enactment, but he had denied it any moral significance.[77] On the other hand, both Kant and Aristotle made 'self-enactment', or the 'honour' aspect of morality, 'that to which the term "moral" exclusively refers'. For example, Kant made the morality of actions depend solely on the presence of a good (disinterested) will. This was equally unsatisfying to Oakeshott, who thought that while either

---

[76] *HC*, p. 74.

[77] Oakeshott's judgement of Mill may have been over-hasty on this point. Mill's appeal to 'nobleness' in *Utilitarianism*, for example, may be read as an appeal to a consideration of self-enactment. And as we have seen, it was partly from Mill that Oakeshott inherited (via British Idealism) his concern with 'character'. Cp. Mill, *Utilitarianism, Liberty and Representative Government*, p. 11.

self-disclosure or self-enactment might be given more weight in any particular moral practice, neither could be ignored entirely.[78]

What relationship did Oakeshott see between considerations of justice and honour, right and nobility, self-disclosure and self-enactment? He argued that 'The sentiment in which an action is performed and its intended outcome are . . . not . . . related in such a manner that the one implies, or is even a signal of the other'. On this view, there is no necessary relation between motives and intentions; the motive or 'sentiment has no direct relation to the action as an intention to procure a satisfaction . . . Spite, greed, jealousy, or benevolence [all sentiments or motives] do not specify actions.' It is an important consequence of this that while intentions might be frustrated, for example, because others failed to respond in the desired fashion, our motives cannot be frustrated in this way.

The exercise of agency involved in forming and attempting to carry out intentions, Oakeshott argued, involved 'movement about a world where achieved satisfactions breed wants'; a world to which work, amongst other things, belongs. However, 'where the consideration in doing is not what is intended to be achieved but the sentiment in which it is done, conduct . . . is emancipated from liability to the frustration of adverse circumstances. For, what the agent chooses to think is related to his understanding and respect for himself, to the integrity of his character, and not at all to a contingent situation to which he must respond by choosing an action.'[79]

An example is provided by Oakeshott's reading of Hobbes. The intention in making a civil covenant is to set up an artificial man, the sovereign. But the motive for covenanting may either be pride or fear. In the case of Hobbes's just man, his pride is not lost if his intentions are frustrated. In *On Human Conduct*, Oakeshott described 'self-enactment' as having the power to qualify 'the unresolved and inconclusive character of human conduct'. 'There is at least the echo of an imperishable achievement when the valour of the agent and not the soon-to vanish victory . . . are the considerations.' Nevertheless, this echo of immortality is always distant; 'the enacted self is itself a fugitive; not a generic unity but a dramatic identity without benefit of a model of self-perfection.'[80]

The point of dwelling on the nice distinctions of Oakeshott's philosophy of action is that wherever historians are dealing with actions, with 'self-disclosures' and 'self-enactments', they will be

---

[78]   *HC*, p. 71 and n. 1.

[79]   *op. cit.*, pp. 72–3.

[80]   *op. cit.*, p. 84.

faced with such moral considerations as 'honour' and 'justice'. The problem is then to explain how historians relate past actions so as to take account of this moral aspect of action, while preventing the moral dimension of their own language from interfering with their interpretation of the evidence.

In *Experience and its Modes*, Oakeshott had argued that moral judgement was necessarily excluded from historical enquiry because it belonged exclusively to the practical mode. His remark in a review published shortly after the war that 'Acton's dictum to "judge character at its worst"' was 'a precept so preposterous, so myopic, so sadly corrupting that without the aid of any other error it has the power of transforming history into a gallery, not of rogues, but of moral abstractions'[81] indicated that he had not changed his mind on the irrelevance of moral judgement to the historical past.

This distinction between a practical and an historical past did not prevent misunderstanding. For example, when fellow Caian and historian of France A.J. Cobban declared that Oakeshott's essay 'On the Activity of Being an Historian' was 'a description which could hardly be bettered of the ideals of the contemporary historian', he did not mean this to be flattering. Contemporary historians, Cobban argued, were led by their desire for 'objectivity' to attempt to exclude moral judgements from their historical writing.

Cobban believed that 'many contemporary historians . . . do in fact manage to live up to this austere standard, and by refraining from implied moral judgements have largely succeeded in assimilating massacres into the norm of political events'. Oakeshott, he was convinced, was contributing to this trend by saying, in effect, that 'we cannot help describing massacres as massacres,' but that 'the important point is to avoid any suggestion that massacres are a bad thing, because this would be a moral judgement, and therefore non-historical.'[82]

Cobban's example is unconvincing. Surely, to describe an event as a massacre is not only to have made a statement of 'fact' but to have recognised the 'wrong' involved. The subjects of a massacre, a large-scale unlawful killing, are properly described as victims. If the term 'massacre' is both factually descriptive and contains an ethical element, any extra 'implied moral judgment' added by the historian above and beyond the description of an event as a 'massacre' would then appear to be superfluous. Yet Cobban's intuition that there were some difficulties with Oakeshott's position was not altogether

[81] Oakeshott, Review of K.B. Smellie, p. 766.

[82] Cobban, *op. cit.*, pp. 1–4.

mistaken. Why are historians necessarily excluded from using the moral language they employ in their non-theoretical activities?

In *Experience and its Modes* and his essay 'On the Activity of being an Historian', Oakeshott had answered this question by arguing that it was the illegitimate intrusion into historical writing of an attitude belonging to the practical mode that was the source of the confusion. In *On Human Conduct*, however, he ceased to talk of a practical mode, and this had an effect on how he now dealt with the problem. He wrote that 'the short-coming (it is not of course error) of a historian who laces his narrative with . . . "moral judgements" is not on account of his concern to understand performances in terms of a moral practice, but on account of his concern to understand performances in terms of a practice of any sort.'[83]

In order to understand Oakeshott on this point, we must outline briefly what he meant by a 'practice', a notion which, as Nardin observes,[84] was a refinement of the idea of 'tradition' in *Rationalism in Politics*. He first raised the idea that being an historian involved knowing how to participate in a 'practice' in the late 1950s, but it was only given an extended elaboration in *On Human Conduct*. There, he described a 'practice' as 'a set of considerations, manners, uses, observances, canons, maxims, principles, rules and offices specifying useful procedures or denoting obligations or duties which relate to human actions and utterances.' The important point about such practices is that they provide 'a prudential or an authoritative adverbial qualification of choices and performances, in which conduct is understood in terms of a procedure.' Like the 'traditions' of *Rationalism in Politics* from which they developed, 'practices' do not prescribe what to say, but only the terms in which utterances can be made. The postulates which are the terms or conditions of the practice of historical enquiry, such as 'human conduct', cannot themselves be used to arrive at an account of past events; they are concerned only with the kind of account to be given.

A 'practice' is or involves 'a relationship between agents articulated in terms of specific conditional prescriptions'.[85] Practices may overlap; 'all verbal utterances . . . are subscriptions to the language in which they are spoken, and they participate in one or another (but not more than one) of the practices which constitute distinguishable *mores* of utterance . . . *historice, oratorice, philosophice* etc.' The idea of a 'practice' may be taken as a more formal account of the 'conversa-

[83] *HC*, p. 99 n. 1.

[84] Nardin, *op. cit.*, p. 28.

[85] *HC*, pp. 55–6.

tional' character of intellectual life; it explains how, despite their lack of a distinctive vocabulary or unified voice, historians are able to form a certain language community, united and distinguished by its shared postulates.

The question is, then, how the practice of historical understanding relates to the practice of moral intercourse in which historians participate in their non-theoretical activities. Oakeshott argued that moral judgements of the past involved an attenuated understanding of a past action in the same way that the 'sociological' understanding of actions did. The sociologist, Oakeshott argued, may explain the reasons for an action in terms of the actor being 'middle-class, unemployed . . . deprived, immigrant, orphaned'. This, however, is not an understanding of the action but only the action 'in respect of the reflection of a practice it throws back', in terms of its 'conventionality'.

Similarly, understanding an action exclusively in terms of its 'rightness' or 'wrongness' will fall short of the kind of account of actions and events that historians aim at. 'Right' and 'wrong' are abridgments from a moral practice; in a fully historical enquiry, 'no action or utterance is what it is' simply in terms of its subscription to the practice of rightfulness and wrongfulness and 'no agent in any of his actions is merely a practitioner'. In historical enquiry, 'practices' themselves (including 'institutions') are recognised as historical; they appear as 'footprints left behind by agents responding to their emergent situations . . . which are only somewhat less evanescent than the transactions in which they emerged.'[86]

Oakeshott acknowledged that moral judgements about the past cannot be said to be wrong or false simply because they are judgements about the rightness or wrongness of past actions. It is only that they are inadequate as historical judgements. There are various kinds of statements about the past it is possible to make, and in certain practical situations a judgement of right or wrong, guilt or innocence, may be the appropriate one — as in a court of law, for example. However, attempts at exculpation or condemnation of the sort which might take place in a court, Oakeshott believed, could not be classed as examples of theoretical reasoning. Rather, they employ an *ex post facto* persuasive discourse of a type appropriate to conduct; but since the historian is not trying to understand actions with a view to responding to them, this persuasive speech is irrelevant.

This is presumably why Oakeshott came to think it a 'shortcoming' rather than an 'error' for historians to describe past events in

---

[86] *op. cit.*, pp. 96–100.

their own moral language. The historian is one who has escaped the self of conduct. In effect, then, Oakeshott's position in *On Human Conduct* is not that saints and rogues are not visible in history — 'Villainy abounds', as he put it in a talk given to the LSE history society [87] — but that to treat historical persons only as saints or rogues is to lapse into moral abstraction.

History as an Aesthetic Fiction?

Our discussion of history and morality explored Oakeshott's distinction between the motives and intentions involved in action. In turn, these motives and intentions go towards the composition of a person's character. 'An agent is a "character", composed of substantive beliefs, affections, understandings, wants etc.; that is, exhibitions of intelligence.'[88] But we also encountered his argument that such characters or selves are dramatic creations. Having initially defined character in the context of dramatic criticism, Oakeshott eventually decided that character itself was 'dramatic'.

On the one hand, this notion of the self as a dramatic creation is an expression of a robust scepticism. While acknowledging that 'human beings are apt to be disconcerted unless they feel themselves to be upheld by something more substantial than the emanations of their own contingent imaginations',[89] Oakeshott insisted on a view of 'agents as historic persons', composed entirely of such contingent self-understandings.

On the other hand, the dramatic self may also be taken as an aesthetic notion. Indeed, in addressing 'self-enactment', where one is concerned with the quality of the action, the motive rather than the intent, the likelihood of an aesthetic perspective being adopted is high. Because the qualities of motives are divorced from criteria of practical success, they are readily transformed into the impractical objects of delight which belong to Oakeshott's mode of aesthetic contemplation. Oakeshott's own accounts of the past, one might argue, were inclined to pay more attention to self-enactment than self-disclosure.

Oakeshott's interpretation of Hobbes, which, as we saw, fixed on the 'moralisation of pride' as an explanation of how the original contract may come about, is based on what, in the vocabulary of *On Human Conduct*, is a consideration of self-enactment. This seems to

---

[87]   Oakeshott, untitled address to the LSE history society, p. 5.

[88]   *HC*, p. 93.

[89]   *op. cit.*, p. 80.

be confirmed by the comment in *On Human Conduct* that Hobbes thought 'a "just" action might be performed in a variety of different motives . . . but that the word "justice" also stood for a "virtue," that is, a particular sentiment in which an otherwise "just" action might or might not be performed, which he identified as a contempt for being unjust.'[90]

When we recall some of the other characters populating Oakeshott's pages such as the religious man, or the individual, the impression that these characters have been created more with a view to the sentiments in which their actions are performed (their self-enactments) than to the outcomes these actions were intended to secure (their self-disclosures) is reinforced. Even in the early case of the religious man, that character's concern for his integrity represents, like Hobbesian pride, a motive rather than an intention. The same may be said of the later character of the individual whom we encountered in the previous chapter. Oakeshott, it would appear, was tempted to see individuality as tied less to the success of one's self-disclosures than to the quality of one's self-enactments, notwithstanding his criticisms of Kant and Aristotle.

Oakeshott was aware that lack of caution in the use of historical types such as the individual could lead to overstepping the 'conditions of relevance' of historical utterance. Just as he had criticised Thucydides in *Experience and its Modes* for resting content with personality as a final explanation, he argued in *On Human Conduct* that to understand an action in terms of an ideal character 'representing a single dominant demeanour' (such as pride) was an arrest in historical understanding. We never, in other words, meet merely with 'individuals' (or 'anti-individuals') in history; and at least some of the time, Oakeshott knew it.

More particularly, Oakeshott was aware of the danger for historical understanding in treating historical characters from a dramatic–aesthetic perspective, a danger that was only heightened by the fact that both history and fiction were both conventionally presented as narratives of contingently related events. He himself compared the task of the historian to that of the novelist. For example, a novelist recounting the fortunes of a group of characters may allow these characters to speak a certain language between themselves. 'But the novelist himself is not a character in his book; he is the creator of his characters' and novelists should not be expected only to speak the language that their characters speak between themselves. The relationship of the historian to the past actors he studies, Oakeshott

---

[90] *op. cit.*, p. 76.

argued, is analogous to the relationship of the novelist to the characters he creates in the sense that 'The historian is the maker of his
events; they have a meaning for him which was not their meaning
for those who participated in them . . . He is the creator of his characters; and to reveal only what their contemporaries thought of them
or what they thought of themselves (though this is of great importance) is to show an imperfect mastery over them.'[91]

Nevertheless, Oakeshott did not wish to turn either life or history
into an art form. 'I am a little doubtful about the enacted self as a
work of art', he wrote in a letter following the publication of *On
Human Conduct*.[92] The work of art closest to a piece of historical writing, the historical novel, was still writing of a different kind. In his
essay on 'The Voice of Poetry', he described 'poetic' activity (by
which he meant any form of artistic endeavour) as responding to
what we see before us without treating it as evidence for past or
future happenings; the historical attitude, by contrast, always treats
the present as evidence for a past that does not appear. Since the first
essay in *On Human Conduct* is almost exclusively concerned with
practical and theoretical activity, artistic activity is mentioned only
once, briefly, as artifice or making undertaken for its own sake.[93]
However, it is quite clear that Oakeshott still thought historical theorising and artistic 'making' (including the writing of 'historical' nov-
els) distinct, although both represent 'escapes' from doing.

The difference between historical and other kinds of narrative,
including the fictional, is capable of even more precise formulation.
We are familiar with Oakeshott's argument that the kind of past historians study is not the past of which our present is a continuation.
This conclusion separated him even from philosophers of history
who reached similar conclusions in other respects. For example,
A.C. Danto's *Analytical Philosophy of History* took a 'constructionist'
view of the past similar in important respects to Oakeshott's.
Because the past cannot be observed, Danto argued, 'historians are
obliged to aim, not at a reproduction but at a kind of organisation of
the past'. Furthermore, Danto reached this conclusion after observing that historical works contain narrative sentences; 'History tells
stories'.[94]

[91]   Oakeshott, 'Scientific Politics', pp. 347–8.

[92]   Oakeshott, Letter to N.K. O'Sullivan, 28 June 1977, private collection.

[93]   *HC*, p. 35.

[94]   A.C. Danto, *Analytical Philosophy of History*, Cambridge UP, Cambridge, 1965,
       p. 111.

However, Oakeshott and Danto parted company over the nature of historical narratives. Historical events, Danto believed, 'are continually being re-described, and their significance re-evaluated . . . in accordance with what different sets of later events [they] may be connected.'[95] By contrast, Oakeshott argued that the peculiarity of historical narratives is that they describe events in terms of events that occur sometime before. In his view, the narratives which order our practical lives and those that occur in fictions may indeed describe events in terms of subsequent events. However, the case of history, he believed, must be different. In order to understand historically how past events came about, we cannot study events subsequent to those we seek to understand. That is not to say that looking back on an ever-receding past event cannot give it new meaning, but that, since doing so involves viewing a passage of the past in the light of our present rather than in light of its past, the meaning is not an historical one.

What allowed Oakeshott to break with Danto's position was his identification of the historical past as a unique kind of past distinct from the kinds of past found in fiction and practical life. Like Dewey, Danto appears to have thought of the past historians study as related to the temporal process in which we are involved. His belief that 'our common ways of thinking about the world are historical'[96] involved no distinction between our 'ordinary' historical thought and the kind of historical thinking involved in the practice of historical enquiry. It is because of this that he suggests historical events are to be understood in terms of what came after them.

Let us spell out the consequences of Danto's position.[97] If it were correct, then the past events it is presumably the business of the historian to understand must be assumed to be already understood — otherwise, we could not know that the events that succeeded them had any relation to them, i.e., we could not know these subsequent events as consequences of the earlier events. But Oakeshott's point is that to assume that the past events with which we are concerned are already understood is either a fictional device or, as we shall see in chapter six, the hallmark of a present-minded view of the past. For Oakeshott's historian, unlike the novelist and the practical person, past events acquire meaning exclusively in terms of what came before, not what came after.

---

[95]   *op. cit.*, p. 11. Author's italics.

[96]   *op. cit.*, p. vii.

[97]   It is in fact very similar to W.B. Gallie's, discussed in chapter two, and indeed Gallie regarded his work as an extension of Danto's.

Thus, when Oakeshott wrote that 'To understand a substantive performance in which an agent discloses and enacts himself is to put it into a story in which it is recognised to be an occurrence contingently related to other occurrences',[98] he did not mean to imply that the narratives of the historian are identical to those of the novelist. To say that there is no difference between historical and fictional narratives would indeed be an admission of absolute scepticism about the possibility of historical knowledge. Yet he made no such claim.

For Oakeshott, even where we are dealing with historical novelists, who use 'the past' as a backdrop to the story they have to tell, the way in which the historian and the historical novelist treat the materials they use will be different — even though 'the same' documents may be used in the writings of both. Goldstein remarks that 'It is easy to imagine that entire sentences . . . identical in every linguistic respect might appear both in some historical novel and some proper work of history.' Because Oakeshott distinguished an historical from an artistic past, however, he would undoubtedly have endorsed Goldstein's conclusion that nevertheless 'Their statuses would be different'.[99]

In our final chapter on the philosophy of history we shall examine Oakeshott's almost unstudied final work, *On History*, in the light of our conclusions so far. We will begin by addressing the question of the relationship between the philosophy of history as it appears in *On Human Conduct* and as it is presented in *On History*. Beforehand, we must return to history in the sense of events, in our final chapter on the history of political thought.

---

[98]   *HC,* p. 105.

[99]   Goldstein, *op. cit.,* p. xviii.

Chapter Five

Modern European Politics, 1958-1975

The Origins of Modern Politics

Oakeshott's writings on the history of political thought in the 1960s and 1970s contained no more polemical assaults on the governments of the day to match the one he had launched at the Attlee administration. Nonetheless, there was still a pessimistic tone to be heard, no longer shrill, but perhaps more radically despondent. 'The repetition of *idées reçus*,' he believed, had 'taken the place of reflection' in modern political thought.[1] Although Oakeshott was still concerned with the same post-Renaissance period, he now explicitly acknowledged that Rationalism was no longer the object of his attention. 'The word is never used [in *On Human Conduct*] and what it stands for is never mentioned: I am concerned with something else'.[2] But he was not only revising his own earlier work. As he remarked, 'what the historian does is to make a contribution to a story which he is not the first to tell'.[3]

In fact, even in the 1970s, Oakeshott was still developing his arguments in relation to works he had known since his youth. Lord Acton's essays on the 'history of freedom' (which he recommended

---

[1]   *HC*, p. 311.

[2]   Oakeshott, 'On Misunderstanding Human Conduct', p. 357.

[3]   Oakeshott, Review of G.J. Renier, *History, its Purpose and Method*, *Philosophical Quarterly*, vol. 1, 1951, p. 284.

to his undergraduates) were, he believed, addressing nothing other than the history of the state understood as a non-purposive association which he himself wanted to relate.[4] Maitland and Barker, as well as Gierke and Acton, were included on the reading list which accompanied his lectures. Oakeshott's interpretation of modern political life and thought continually harked back to the works of these historians. For example, he explicitly rejected Gierke's belief that modern European politics 'is so like the politics of the ancient world that it is illuminating . . . to speak of an antique-modern political experience, contrasting it with that of the middle ages.'[5] Although Oakeshott believed Greek and Roman history were important for understanding modern politics, he preferred to see modernity as continuous with the medieval period rather than as a sharp break with it.

Even when Oakeshott did not make the objects of his criticism explicit (which was frequently the case), it is still not hard to discern points at which he differed with other, perhaps more well-known and influential, commentators. For example, Strauss saw Plato and Aristotle as having given a 'classic form' to political philosophy. For Strauss, ancient political philosophy was distinguished from later political thought by the absence of a mediating tradition 'which acted like a screen between the philosopher and political things.'[6]

Strauss's Hellenism was by no means unique. Arendt's work, *The Human Condition*, was an attempt 'to understand the political in the sense of the polis.' Voegelin made 'attempts to return to the Greek conception of politics as embracing all human activity and as concerned with the "highest good".'[7] Oakeshott, by contrast, acknowledged the Greeks as 'the inventors of "politics"' but did not conclude from this that they had arrived at a definitive understanding of politics which subsequent historians and philosophers were obliged to accept.[8] This lack of Hellenism was amply compensated for, however, by his admiration of the Romans 'the only European people who have shown a real genius for politics.'[9]

---

[4]   *HC*, p. 245.

[5]   *MP*, p. 23.

[6]   L. Strauss, *What is Political Philosophy ?*, Free Press, Glencoe, 1959, p. 27.

[7]   Arendt and Voegelin quoted and cited in K. Minogue and A. de Crespigny (eds.), *Contemporary Political Philosophers*, Methuen, New York, 1976, pp. 229, 115–6.

[8]   Oakeshott, 'The Political Experience of the Ancient Greeks', Lecture 2, LSE 1/1/21, pp. 4, 16.

[9]   Oakeshott, 'The Political Experience of the Romans', Lecture 13, LSE 1/1/21, p. 1.

The reason for this admiration is not difficult to discern. If Oakeshott regarded the Greeks as the inventors of 'politics', he saw the Romans as the inventors of 'by far the most comprehensive and elaborate system of law that any people, save in modern times, has elaborated for itself.' Rome 'became a legally organised society in a manner which even Athens never became.'[10] He went so far as to claim that Rome (in both its Republican and Imperial periods), had been 'what may be called a civil association . . . a set of private persons joined in the recognition of a law to which they, all alike, owed obedience.'[11]

The significance of this description will hardly escape us. 'Civil association' was the kind of association Oakeshott had found in Hobbes and made the subject of his own political philosophy. He was claiming, in effect, that Roman history and Roman law provided the first examples of non-purposive understandings of a state, examples subsequently handed down to the medieval and the modern worlds. But, given that it is a fact that 'Roman law existed as an authoritative tradition'[12] in political thought between 1200 and 1600, we need to know precisely which features of it Oakeshott seized upon.

Obviously, Oakeshott was not interested in the Stoic development of ideas of natural law which took place in the Roman period. He looked to *lex*, the 'positive' law of the Romans, and it was the form rather than the content of *lex* which interested him. 'In *lex* [the Romans] discovered a means of modifying, and even abolishing, ancient custom' which came to be thought of 'as itself *lex* and therefore capable of being emended in a law-making process.'[13]

The Roman belief Oakeshott saw implied in *lex*, 'that, by means of a known process of making law, they had command over their own rules of order', was, he claimed, nothing other than 'an elementary belief in what later came to be called "sovereignty"'. A sovereign authority is not merely one that has no contemporary superior, but one which is emancipated from the past.' A sovereignty of this sort, he believed, was one of the definitive characteristics of the modern European state.

Oakeshott seems to have arrived at this view through the study of histories such as C.H. McIlwain's *The Growth of Political Thought in*

[10]   Oakeshott, 'Roman Political Thought (iii)', Lecture 15, LSE 1/1/21, p. 1.

[11]   *op. cit.*, pp. 8, 10b.

[12]   M.P. Gilmore, *Argument from Roman Law in Political Thought, 1200–1600*, Harvard UP, Cambridge Mass., 1941, p. 7.

[13]   Oakeshott, 'Roman Political Thought (iii)', p. 8.

the West and *Constitutionalism: Ancient and Modern*. Both were included on his LSE reading list. McIlwain, discussing 'The Constitutionalism of Rome', attacked, like Oakeshott, Gierke's view that 'Modern absolutism was a return to Roman autocracy' and that 'liberty was solely a retention . . . of the freedom of the primitive Germanic peoples.'[14] Whatever the medieval period learnt from Roman law, both believed, it was not 'autocracy'.

The medieval world could be said to have begun with 'the unmistakable collapse of the Roman Imperial administration' around the year 400 and ended with a transformation of medieval realms into modern states largely completed by 1500, although Oakeshott regarded the dating of these events as 'so approximate' that each date could be 'moved a century either way.' But however long the medieval period was thought to last, 900 years, 1300 years, or something in between, he was insistent that it should not be seen as 'the dark ages'. 'The view that this was a period of European history of even comparative stagnation has nothing whatever to be said in its favour.'[15]

'The problem of government' that early medieval peoples faced 'was how to impose and maintain the rudiments of law and order in a world in which the *pax Romana* had been destroyed, in which a single, recognised 'law of a territory' had not yet emerged (but in which many different laws were current), and in communities in which there were recognised to be "noble" families, families of free men, and serfs and slaves.'[16] What government there was began from 'the exercise of "lordship"; the authority to rule in virtue of ownership. All authority was connected with landed property.'[17]

Out of this lordly style of rule, there had developed a 'somewhat hesitating distinction between rulership and the lordship from which rulership had circumstantially emerged'[18] which Oakeshott regarded as comparable in its significance to the Greek creation of politics and the Roman invention of *lex*. Again, Oakeshott's 'research' into this story of the separation of the authority of rulers from proprietary right is likely to have consisted in reading the works of historians. Maitland's mentor Vinogradoff, for example, related how 'the Emperor Frederic . . . asked whether [he] was not by

---

[14]   C.H. McIlwain, *Constitutionalism: Ancient and Modern*, Cornell UP, New York, 1947, p. 41.

[15]   Oakeshott, 'Medieval Political Experience', Lecture 16, LSE 1/1/21, pp. 1, 13.

[16]   *op. cit.*, p. 5.

[17]   *op. cit.*, p. 6.

[18]   *HC*, pp. 218–9.

right lord (*dominus*) of everything held by his subjects', only to be told that 'he was lord in the political sense, but not in the sense of an owner.'[19]

Oakeshott remained convinced of the importance of these Roman and medieval ideas and practices to the last. In an essay in his final work, *On History*, he wrote that 'we owe [the rule of law] not to the theorists, but to the two peoples who, above all others, have shown a genius for ruling: the Romans and the Normans.'[20] More than once, he quoted Lord Acton's remark that 'Modern history tells how the last 400 years have modified the medieval conditions of life and thought.'[21] Modernity, he asserted, 'is a tumult of emotional and intellectual activity which emerged...from the recesses of the culture of twelfth-century Christendom.'[22] This in itself is not controversial. 'The modern state', wrote J.R. Strayer, 'is based on the pattern which emerged in Europe in the period 1100–1600.'[23] Nor is Oakeshott's view — that two characteristics in particular distinguished the modern European state from the medieval kingdom — the 'sovereign' quality of the authority of their rulers, and the degree of power at their disposal — unusual.[24]

The sixteenth-century rise of the sovereign state is an accepted fact. Bodin's philosophical definition of sovereignty as 'that absolute and perpetual power vested in a commonwealth which in Latin is termed *majestas*', we are told, 'marks the break' with medieval kingship that had already been accomplished in practice.[25] So is the growth in power of the early modern state. 'No-one would wish to deny', wrote Elton, that 'the physical power of monarchs increased' in the sixteenth century and after.[26] The singular and doubtless also controversial aspects of Oakeshott's view emerge only when we pay attention to its details. What is peculiar is his presentation of modern political thought and practice in quasi-medieval terms, as the history of attempts to establish the distinction of 'rulership' from 'lord-

---

[19] P. Vinogradoff, *Roman Law in Medieval Europe*, Oxford UP, Oxford, 1929, p. 62.

[20] *OH*, p. 64.

[21] Oakeshott, Review of H. Butterfield, *The Origins of Modern Science*, *Times Literary Supplement*, 1949, p. 762; *PF*, pp. 1–2.

[22] Oakeshott, 'The Emergence of the History of Thought', LSE 1/1/23, p. 8.

[23] J.R. Strayer, *On the Medieval Origins of the Modern State*, Princeton UP, Princeton, 1970, p. 12.

[24] *HC*, p. 189.

[25] J. Bodin, *Six Books of the Commonwealth*, trans. M. J. Tooley, Blackwell, Oxford, 1953, pp. xxiv, 25.

[26] G.R. Elton, *Reformation Europe, 1517–55*, Collins, London, 1963, p. 301.

ship' more securely and of a tendency to relapse into treating government as in effect the exercise of 'lordship', or *dominium*.[27]

Oakeshott had already drawn attention to the increased power of modern governments in *The Politics of Faith and the Politics of Scepticism*; *On Human Conduct* restated his view that this increase in power gave political reflection 'a new centre of gravity'.[28] In the medieval period, the main concern of political thought had been with authority, with the form and derivation of the right to rule. But the participation of governments in the general increase since the sixteenth century in 'the ability to control men and things' had resulted in their acquiring an 'apparatus of power . . . shared by all governments regardless of their constitution.'[29] These developments had raised questions largely unique to modern political thought, concerning the office of governments, or the kinds of activities they ought to undertake.

In the medieval period, 'the pursuits of government' had lain 'very little within the field of choice'. 'To maintain peace and order, to guard the laws and customs of the community, when necessary to organise defence, when propitious to embark upon conquest or migration, and to deal with social and economic change when they produced an emergency' was the narrow 'round of engagements' to which 'the activity of governing was confined'. With the emergence of the modern state, however, 'the pursuits which governments could entertain ceased to be confined within the relatively narrow limits of a strict convention.'[30]

This novel concern with the activities of powerful governments had come to predominate in modern political thought, Oakeshott believed, to the point where even writers ostensibly concerned with the authority of governments were in fact addressing the office or activities of governments. For example, when Kant 'approved of a republican constitution' on the grounds that 'a government of this sort would automatically pursue peace', this 'was really a concern with the activities of governments disguised as a concern with the constitution of governments.'[31]

In this redirection of attention, Oakeshott argued, the ambiguous character of the modern state was revealed. For example, in the six-

---

[27] *HC*, p. 219.

[28] *HC*, p. 193; *MP*, p. 11.

[29] *HC*, p 195. Cp. *MP*, p. 33; Oakeshott, 'The Character of the Modern European State', Lecture 21, LSE 1/1/21, p. 9; and Oakeshott, 'The Office of Government (i)', Lecture 29, LSE 1/1/21, p. 6.

[30] *MP*, p. 11.

[31] *op. cit.*, pp. 10–12.

teenth century, the beginning of the modern period, 'free' and 'sovereign' European states such as France, England, and Spain, could all be recognised as associations 'in terms of law' with governments 'not subject to any superior external authority' and having 'the authority and the procedures to emancipate [themselves] continuously from [their] legal past.' Yet all these characteristics were ambiguous.[32] Was law, for example, 'a system of prescriptive conditions indifferent (. . . not merely impartial) to the satisfaction of wants, to be subscribed to in making choices about what to do or say, or . . . a set of prudential managerial conclusions specifying a common purpose and the manner in which this purpose shall be contingently pursued'?[33]

Similarly, the identification of government as sovereign 'does nothing whatever to specify its office.' The adjective 'sovereign,' Oakeshott argued, describes a quality of authority. It has nothing to say about whether the engagement of government is 'that of a guardian of a system of prescriptive conditions to be subscribed to in making choices' or whether it is 'an engagement concerned with the choice or the custody of a common purpose and the direction of its pursuit'. It was in an attempt to answer such questions, Oakeshott believed, that the terms *societas* and *universitas* had been pressed into service, and it is to them that we shall now turn.

Societas and *Universitas*

Oakeshott's stress on the ambiguous nature of the modern state separates his own interpretation of political modernity from so-called 'monistic' views. Strauss, for example, believed that the 'modern' was characterised by a single 'project' in which Machiavelli, Hobbes, Locke, Rousseau, Hegel, Marx, and Nietzsche were all involved. This was 'to enable man to become the master and owner of nature through the intellectual conquest of nature. Philosophy or science should make possible progress towards ever greater prosperity.'[34]

Oakeshott saw no such unilinear trend. That was why in *On Human Conduct* he proposed to use two terms from Roman law, *societas* and *universitas*, 'in the tensions of a partnership' to convey

---

[32] *HC*, p. 253.

[33] *HC*, p. 231.

[34] D. Germino criticised Strauss (as well as de Jouvenel and Voegelin) for their 'monistic' views of the history of modern political thought in *Machiavelli to Marx: Modern Western Political Thought*, Rand McNally, Chicago, 1979, pp. 11–14. The quotation from Strauss is taken from Germino, p. 14.

the ambiguity of modern politics.[35] Independent scholarship confirms that Oakeshott was correct in believing that *societas* and *universitas* were familiar terms in medieval and early modern political discourse.[36] Of course, that in itself does not support his interpretation of their meanings, which changed considerably over the centuries. In order to appreciate his interpretation of these terms, it is best to begin at the beginning, with their Roman, legal, meanings.

A *societas* was a form of contract; it formed part of the Roman civil or private law of obligations and required only the agreement of the *socii* or contractors, and their *bona fides* to come into existence. A *universitas* was 'a corporate body created by the [Roman] state, such as municipalities or the guilds (*collegia*) of different trades.' Although 'both the state and corporate bodies might have property which they held exactly like individuals', so that, for example, 'some *universitates*, such as municipalities, had things which they owned for the use of the public . . . *res universitates*', in the eyes of Roman private law the *universitas* was not itself a person.[37]

It is important to understand that despite their juristic origins, Oakeshott did not think of the two forms of association described by *societas* and *universitas* as purely legal in nature. As inherited by the medieval world, each also implied contrasting moral and political values. Again, he was not alone in this belief. Most recently, Black has argued that the contract of *societas* implied 'the notion of human society as an arena of relatively free-floating relationships, in which people were involved in buying, selling . . . marrying and entering partnerships.'[38] This conception of social life contributed to 'the early diffusion of liberal ideas about person and property' (which Black calls 'the values of "civil society"') in the medieval period. Although Black argues that the degree of continuity between Roman

---

[35] *HC*, pp. 199–200.

[36] For example, in his work *Universitas*, Librairie J. Vrin, Paris, 1970, the French scholar Michaud-Quantin remarks that the term *universitas* 'est sous la plume du juriste le nom générique de la communauté' in the middle ages: see p. 7. He also argues that theologians and jurists made much use of *societas*: see pp. 64–9.

[37] *The Institutes of Justinian*, trans. T.C. Sandars, Longmans, London, 1922, p. 92.

[38] Black, *Guilds and Civil Society*, p. 35. In his introduction to this work Black acknowledges (p. xiv) that his model of 'civil society' was partly suggested by Oakeshott's *societas*. In *Community in Historical Perspective. A Translation of Selections from Das deutsche Genossenschaftsrecht (the German law of Fellowship)*, ed. A. Black, Cambridge UP, 1990, p. 258 n. 5, he also suggests that in certain respects Oakeshott's *societas* was identical with Gierke's notion of a *Rechtstaat*, and in fact Oakeshott did discuss 'the idea of a *Rechtstaat*' (though without specific reference to Gierke) in an unpublished and undated paper on 'Law'. See Oakeshott, 'Law', private collection, pp. 4–5.

universitates and medieval guilds is 'unclear', he believes that both invoked values quite different to those assumed in the contract of *societas*. Roman and medieval guilds, he claims, placed great importance on 'brotherhood' and 'mutual aid'.[39] Black, like Oakeshott, believed that a tension between individuality and community, civility and equality, was present in European political thought from classical times.

Societas and *universitas*, Oakeshott wrote, had come into use again with the medieval rediscovery of Roman law — 'from the twelfth century they had become familiar wherever argument had to do with the legal specification of associations.' Their meanings subsequently changed as both began to extend beyond the legal sphere, but they had eventually gone out of use in the modern era, because neither had been able to 'sustain itself' as an adequate analogy for the character of a modern state; 'their English equivalents ("partnership" and "corporation") came to be used indifferently.' It seems peculiar, then, that Oakeshott should have wished to apply *societas* and *universitas* to the modern period in which they had gone out of use. He believed, however, that the kinds of association they denoted had not. It was still possible to treat Hegel, for example, in this light, even though he never used these terms, because he was addressing the kinds of association they had once been used to understand.

Oakeshott, distinguishing between philosophical and historical 'ideal types', placed *societas* and *universitas* in the latter category. He had long ago ceased to approach the history of political thought by asking how closely a particular thinker approximated to some timeless ideal definition of the state. He would doubtless have agreed that the 'search for approximations to [an] ideal type' of that sort tends to 'yield a form of non-history'.[40] Presumably, he preferred *societas* and *universitas* to his earlier contrasts between 'faith' and 'scepticism' and 'individualism' and 'collectivism' precisely because of their historical basis. They did not represent 'single proposition[s] or principle[s]', like A.O. Lovejoy's 'unit ideas' moving unchanged through time.[41] The kinds of association for which each stood had found historical expression in a succession of different forms; there had been, for example, at least three 'idioms' of the understanding of a state as a *universitas* since it first emerged.

---

[39]   Black, *Guilds and Civil Society*, pp. xi, 6.

[40]   Skinner, 'Meaning and Understanding in the History of Ideas', p. 11.

[41]   A.O. Lovejoy quoted in P.T. King, *The History of Ideas*, Barnes and Noble, London, 1983, p. 189.

Our understanding of the significance of Oakeshott's deliberately anachronistic application of *societas* and *universitas* to the modern period will benefit from noticing J.L. Auspitz's perceptive remark that Oakeshott was using these terms in 'an improvisation on a theme from Maitland.'[42] Maitland, in his introduction to his translation of Gierke, *Political Theories of the Middle Age*, had cautioned that 'an Englishman will miss a point in the history of political theory unless he knows that in a strictly legal context, the Roman *societas*, the French *societé* and the German *Gesellschaft* should be rendered by the English "partnership" and no other word.'[43]

Maitland wanted to prevent confusion between 'partnerships' (*societates*) and 'corporations' (*universitates*) in the study of a period in which the application of both concepts was widening. He credited Gierke with discovering that the expansion of the idea of *universitas* by attributing to it a personality, albeit a fictional one, originated in the mid-thirteenth century. At the same time, Maitland noted, there had been a corresponding extension of the meaning of *societas*. 'Before the end of the Middle Ages, the Roman word for partnership (*societas*) was assuming a vastly wide meaning, and, under the patronage of Ciceronian comparisons, was entering the field of politics.'[44]

As we saw earlier, Maitland and Gierke believed that the post-medieval period had been dominated by the idea of the state as a *societas*. In their view, the group life offered by medieval *universitates* had been destroyed by the increasing prominence of contractarian conceptions of state association. Gierke in particular deplored this development; in Maitland's words, he believed that the state itself 'had become a merely collective unit — a sum of presently existing individuals bound together by the operations of their own wills.'

To Gierke, Hobbes's *Leviathan* was an instance of this kind of theory — his sovereign rested on 'mere naked power'. Having 'made the individual omnipotent', Hobbes had to force him 'to destroy himself instantly in virtue of his own omnipotence' by subjecting him to the 'man-devouring monster' of *Leviathan*.[45] Hobbes, moreover, was only one example of the burgeoning individualism of the early modern period. Gierke believed that all associations had

[42] J.L. Auspitz, Review of *On Human Conduct*, *Commentary*, vol. 61, 1976, p. 94.

[43] F.W. Maitland, 'Introduction' to O. Gierke, *Political Theories of the Middle Age*, Cambridge UP, Cambridge, 1951, pp. xxii–xxiii.

[44] Maitland, *loc. cit.*

[45] Gierke, *Natural Law and the Theory of Society*, pp. 52, 61.

increasingly come to be seen from an individualistic perspective. In part, he attributed the success of *societas* to the 'unphilosophical' character of the classical and medieval concept of *universitas*. 'A merely fictitious personality, created by the state and shut up within the limits of Private Law, was not what the philosopher wanted when he went about to construct the state itself.'[46] The emergence of the joint-stock company sustained only by its share-holders gave this development further impetus. Whether individualistic modern states had developed towards a monarchical absolutism, or a 'mere collectivism' (which as Maitland remarked, was simply another name for 'democratic' individualism) Gierke believed they were 'condemned to be "atomistic" and "mechanical"' associations.

Oakeshott agreed with Maitland and Gierke that 'political theory . . . borrowed the contract of partnership . . . rather than the . . . act of incorporation' as an analogy for the state; 'by the fifteenth century *societas* had become the commonest reading of the character of a realm.'[47] But he explained both the reasons and the results of this event differently. The story of modern Europe as a 'quest for community' consequent on the destruction of 'a civilisation of . . . persons who knew themselves as partners in communal solidarities' by 'the cold and hostile world of transactional engagements' held no appeal for him.[48] To appreciate his reasons for disagreeing, however, we must say a little of his own understanding of *societas* and *universitas*.

We will begin with Oakeshott's discussion of the medieval usage of these terms, taking *societas* first. When *societas* slipped loose from its strictly legal meaning, he argued, 'this constitutive pact became the description of an outcome; *socii*, each pursuing his own interests or even joined with some others in seeking common satisfactions, but related to one another in the continuous acknowledgment of the authority of rules of conduct indifferent to the pursuit or the achievement of any purpose.'[49] 'Friends or neighbours, suitors to a court or speakers of a common language' and even the human race could all be thought of as associations of *socii*. And so, of course, could the state.

The place that will or choice has in Oakeshott's account of *societas* is important. Although membership of a *societas* may be the outcome of a choice (as in friendship) 'what is intrinsic to this mode of association is not the choice to be related but the recognition of understood

---

[46]   Maitland, *loc. cit.*

[47]   *HC*, p. 213.

[48]   *op. cit.*, p. 320.

[49]   *op. cit.*, p. 201.

terms of relationship — the acknowledgment, for example, of a common linguistic or moral condition.'[50] This is particularly significant where *societas* is used as an analogy for a state, an association with 'a law and office of authority'. If the members of a state understood as a *societas* are said to be 'free', this cannot be in virtue of their having chosen to belong. The freedom of *socii* lies elsewhere, in the fact that 'they are not joined in the pursuit of any common purpose but only in respect of their common acknowledgment of the authority of a law which does not and cannot specify substantive conduct and does not require approval of the conditions it prescribes.'[51]

A *universitas*, by contrast, involved 'persons associated in respect of some identified common purpose, in the pursuit of some acknowledged substantive end.' Corporate association, Oakeshott insisted, must be in terms of a purpose. Associates in a corporation can 'give an intelligible account of their relationship . . . only by specifying the object, the purpose or the interest in terms of which they are related.'[52] Moreover, choice was intrinsic to this kind of association. 'The corporate associate is free in respect of his association . . . being a choice of his own.'[53] As an analogy for the character of a state, *universitas* suggested 'a many of intelligent agents become one in the joint pursuit of a common substantive purpose and in the enjoyment of the means necessary for undertaking the managerial decisions entailed.' The state understood as a *universitas* is an 'enterprise association,' and the 'laws' appropriate to it are 'prescribed conditions of conduct deemed to be instrumental to the purpose pursued.'[54]

Like Gierke, Oakeshott thought that one of the circumstances hindering the use of *universitas* as an analogy for the character of a state was that, legally, the *universitas* was 'the creature of an already recognised superior legal authority.' But he gave another reason, not considered by Gierke — that states were manifestly compulsory organisations, whereas membership of a *universitas* was a matter of

[50] *op. cit.*, p. 202.

[51] *op. cit.*, p. 251.

[52] *op. cit.*, p. 116.

[53] *op. cit*, p. 251. It might be thought that Oakeshott was innovating in making 'voluntariness' a feature of *universitas*, because the pluralists he had admired in his youth had not tended to regard *universitas* as an individualistic form of association. This however is an error; the kind of group Gierke valued, for instance, was precisely one to which members had chosen to belong, one of which they were not merely naturally (as with the family) or compulsorily (as with the state) members. The kind of 'voluntariness' pluralists disliked and associated with corrosive individualism took the form of acts of will by persons acting solely in their own interests with no regard for a wider community.

[54] *op. cit.*, p. 205.

choice. The corporate associate 'is free because his situation is a choice of his own and because he can extricate himself by choosing to do so',[55] but this was not so with the state, membership of which was neither a matter of choice nor possible to relinquish. In other words, a state understood as a *universitas*, Oakeshott believed, necessarily lacked the kind of freedom characteristic of all other *universitates*.

We cannot leave these terms without noticing that Oakeshott's account of them retained the connection between individual character and modes of government that he had first made before World War Two. He argued that both *societas* and *universitas*, used as analogies for a state, assumed an appropriate *persona* belonging to those associated in that state. The analogy of *societas* assumes persons with a 'disposition to make choices for [themselves] to the maximum possible extent.' As an association in terms of non-instrumental law, it would be contradictory for the associates to desire that the state direct them in their choices. By contrast, the analogy of *universitas* assumes persons who wish to have decisions taken for them, to be directed and managed. In the following two sections we shall examine the evidence he presented for this connection.

The State as a *Societas*

What we must examine now is Oakeshott's account of 'the intimations of *societas*' in the late medieval realm and the modern state. Amongst the circumstances which he considered had encouraged the usage of this term as an analogy for the character of a state were the nature of kingship and the extension of law, finance, war and 'foreign relations'. A medieval king, Oakeshott argued, 'was not distinguished from his fellow landlords by the magnitude of his proprietary estate but by the occupation of an office of authority identified by a title, some conditions of legitimate succession to it, a ceremony of induction, some expectations about his conduct, and some beliefs about the source of his authority . . . .His realm . . . could hardly be thought of in terms of territory.'[56] Thus, it could not easily be thought of as a resource to be developed. Rather, the primary engagement of the king was 'to promote himself from being a military leader and the custodian of an ill-defined "peace" closely related to his presence and his person to being a ruler and the supreme dispenser of justice among his subjects.'

---

[55] *op. cit.*, pp. 157–8.

[56] *op. cit.*, p. 207.

In extending their legal authority, kings not only constituted their realms; they also 'discovered that [they] could not [themselves] escape from it, that *lex facit regem.*' This situation reflected, at least in part, the influence of Roman law. The rediscovery of the *Corpus Juris Civilis* made possible a contrast between 'a medieval realm . . . an association in terms of specified *libertates*, themselves the creations of [a] law . . . [which] was merely a totality of fluctuating *privelegia'* and an association in terms of 'a system of rules of conduct specifying formal relationships between *cives* and thus enclosing and protecting an area of activity which it did not itself occupy.'[57] Here again we see Oakeshott arguing that Roman law had favoured 'limited' rather than 'absolutist' government.

Oakeshott acknowledged that 'This gradual and often interrupted extension of royal justice was concerned as much with the maintenance of the rights of the ruler and with the collection of the revenue due to a king as with doing justice between his subjects, and it was an indistinguishably judicial, financial and administrative undertaking.'[58] The income that was raised might be spent upon administration, military engagements, 'the pursuit of dynastic ambitions or the prosecution of family quarrels', but however much the king's subjects might resent this, 'it did not suggest that a realm was itself a piece of real estate . . . or that ruling was itself estate management.'[59]

Nor did the military engagements of kings provide grounds for thinking of the realm as a corporation; by the late medieval period, 'The king's military estate was an important means of maintaining his authority within his realm, but it was no longer possible to think of the realm as itself a military enterprise.' This was reflected in the abandonment of the legal duty of the magnates to supply the king with fighting men or its conversion into money payments. Finally, 'the authority of the ruler had to compete with that of powerful rulers from without', notably the Pope and Emperor. But in England, France and Spain, by the fifteenth century 'even the church had been reduced to the status of a corporation within the realm.'[60]

All these circumstances promoted an understanding of the inhabitants of a realm 'united (in so far as it was united) in acknowledging . . . royal authority, and the . . . jurisdiction of royal courts of law' and of the king as 'a ruler of subjects, a *defensor pacis*, whose office was to

---

[57] *op. cit.*, p. 208 and n. 1.

[58] *op. cit.*, p. 208.

[59] *op. cit.*, p. 209.

[60] *op. cit.*, p. 212.

perform certain public duties distinguished (though still with some difficulty) from his private concern.'[61] The diversity to be found in the early modern state provided further encouragement for this view. It was 'composed of persons, communities and fragments of communities, strangers to one another, separated in respect of language, moral imagination, customs, aspirations and conditions of living, moved by local affections and animosities, exhibiting the differences of religious belief commonplace in Christendom since the twelfth century.' In such circumstances, 'Was anything more to be expected than that they should be joined in respect of a common law and a single ruler?'[62]

This diversity, Oakeshott believed, was closely connected to the history of character. The final and perhaps the single most important event which lent strength to the belief that the modern European state was best understood on the analogy of *societas* was, in the dramatic language of character, the appearance of a 'new kind of drama' in which the *persona* of the individual came to the fore. This was an 'event of supreme and seminal importance in modern European history',[63] and although we have touched on it already, it was in *On Human Conduct* that it received the fullest treatment.

There, Oakeshott argued that since classical times there had been 'a reading of the human condition in which the race of men is recognised to be saddled with an unsought and inescapable "freedom" which in some respects they are ill-equipped to exercise.' That is, a human being had been thought of as a 'free' agent 'as distinguished from a composition of biological or other urges.' But in the late medieval and early modern period, 'What has to be reckoned with is a historic disposition to transform this unsought "freedom" of conduct from a postulate into an experience and to make it yield a satisfaction of its own . . . the disposition to recognise imagining, deliberating, wanting, choosing and acting not as costs incurred in seeking enjoyments but as themselves enjoyments.'[64]

Over a century ago, Burckhardt had drawn attention to such a change in moral character in *The Civilisation of the Renaissance in Italy*, and he dated it to: 'the close of the thirteenth century [when] Italy began to swarm with individuality.' In Hegelian terms, he had described this event as the subjective side of human consciousness asserting itself against the medieval understanding of self 'only as a

---

[61] *op. cit.* cit.

[62] *op. cit.*, p. 233.

[63] *RP*, p. 382.

[64] *HC*, p. 236.

member of a race, people, party, family or corporation — only through some general category.'[65] The outcome had been a host of new human types — 'the private man' and the 'all-sided man', *'l'uomo universale'*, were of particular note. In 1975, Oakeshott still believed Burckhardt was the 'most perceptive historian' of this change.[66]

In the past generation, the thesis that 'a profound change in social attitudes began around 1100' with 'the beginnings of individualism' arising from 'the breakdown of the feudal order' has had plenty of defenders.[67] Morris has argued that *The Discovery of the Individual* was taking place between 1050 and 1200.[68] Skinner began his work on *The Foundations of Modern Political Thought* with the observation that 'As early as the middle of the twelfth century the German historian Otto of Freising recognised that a new and remarkable form of social and political organisation had arisen in Northern Italy. One peculiarity he noticed was that Italian society had apparently ceased to be feudal in character.'[69]

Whenever this change has been thought to have occurred, it has been recognised to have had political and economic implications. It meant the end of what Ullman called 'the absorption of the individual by the community', and it marked the first emergence of citizens of modern states.[70] MacFarlane found *The Origins of English Individualism* in the medieval period as an alternative to the account of 'the major shifts in European . . . society and economy over the period from the thirteenth century' offered by sociologists, philosophers and historians such as Macaulay, Marx, Weber, and R.H. Tawney. For these writers, MacFarlane notes, the crucial event was a 'change-over' in the sixteenth and seventeenth centuries 'from a subsistence to a market economy, from a "distributive" Catholic ethic to an "accumulative" Protestant one, from an integrated and hierarchical society to a ruthless and competitive one.'[71] Here, the

[65] J. Burckhardt, *The Civilisation of the Renaissance in Italy*, Penguin, London, 1990, pp. 98 ff.

[66] *HC*, p. 240.

[67] See A. Black, in *The Cambridge History of Medieval Political Thought, c. 350–c. 1450*, ed. J. H. Burns, Cambridge UP, Cambridge, 1988, p. 589; and Black, 'Society and the Individual from the Middle Ages to Rousseau', p. 145.

[68] C. Morris, *The Discovery of the Individual, 1050–1200*, Society for the Promotion of Christian Knowledge, London, 1972, pp. 188.

[69] Q. Skinner, *The Foundations of Modern Political Thought*, vol. 1, Cambridge UP, Cambridge, 1978, p. 3.

[70] W. Ullman, *The Individual and Society in the Middle Ages*, Johns Hopkins, Baltimore, 1966, pp. 5, 32.

[71] A. MacFarlane, *The Origins of English Individualism: The Family, Property and Social Transition*, Blackwell, Oxford, 1978, pp. 52, 54.

connotations of individualism are mainly negative, as they were for Gierke.

Oakeshott used the contention that 'individualism' was nurtured in and by the medieval period rather than succeeding it in a similar way to MacFarlane, questioning the rise of what C.B. MacPherson called *The Political Theory of Possessive Individualism* in the early modern period. For MacPherson, the twentieth century 'liberal democracy' had its roots no further back than seventeenth century England. It was then that 'the principles' of the modern state 'were all developed'. Chief amongst these principles was 'a new belief in the value and rights of the individual' conceived 'as essentially the proprietor of his own person or capacities'. The 'freedom' which accompanied such individualism was, he believed, simply 'a function of possession'.[72]

For Oakeshott, the roots of individualism were much older, and were moral as well as economic. 'Of course, this disposition displayed itself in commerce', he agreed, but he added (rather rudely) that 'anyone who believes . . . that it was of "possessive individualists" that Pico della Mirandola, or Montaigne or Hobbes or Pascal or Kant or Blake or Nietzsche or Kierkegaard wrote is capable of believing anything.'[73] But 'Individualism,' it has been said, 'is a word that has come to be used with an unusual lack of precision.'[74] To appreciate the full significance of the character of the individual in Oakeshott's later writings on the history of political thought, we must be clear about what it excludes.

The 'disposition or quality of character' which Oakeshott called 'individualism' was 'not to be understood as a surrender to a so-called "subjective will," or as a relapse into the effortless indulgence of inclination, or as the canonisation of conscience.' It did not 'imply the worship of non-conformity, a devotion to arbitrary so-called "self-expression", or a resolution to be different at all costs.' The disposition that arose in the medieval period, the 'spring-time of the European spirit',[75] represented 'a difficult achievement. The self here is . . . the outcome of an education . . . and conduct is recognised as the adventure in which this cultivated self displays its resources', not as a series of 'unconditional choices'. Being an 'individual' in this sense 'does not require indifference to

[72]   C.B. MacPherson, *The Political Theory of Possessive Individualism: Hobbes to Locke*, Oxford UP, Oxford, 1962, pp. 1–3.

[73]   *HC*, p. 242 n. 1.

[74]   S. Lukes, *Individualism*, Blackwell, Oxford, 1973, p. ix.

[75]   *HC*, pp. 236–7, 239.

moral or prudential practices or aversion from any but self-made rules . . . the independence or originality of . . . conduct lies not at all in an unconcern for the conditions which specify the arts of agency.'[76]

Particularly important for Oakeshott's history of political events and ideas is his insistence that 'Persons understanding themselves and understood in terms of this disposition postulate a state understood in terms of *societas*.'[77] This did not exclude *cives* or *socii* from choosing to become members of any number of *universitates* contained within the state. 'Chosen corporate association is so far from conflicting with their character that they may confidently be expected to undertake it as a device for satisfying common wants.'[78] However, the state of which *personae* of this kind are members is not itself a *universitas*. That was appropriate to an altogether different type of character, as we shall now see.

The State as a *Universitas*

There were, Oakeshott believed, definite 'features of a medieval realm which might . . . suggest that it should be understood in terms of the analogy of a *universitas*.'[79] For example, corporate association 'was a familiar feature of medieval life from the twelfth century' and there were numerous 'political' bodies which were 'deliberately incorporated *collegia*', such as 'the provincial *Cortes* of Spain, the *Parlement de Paris* or that of Toulouse (incorporated in 1483), the Exchequer of Normandy'. There were also 'assemblages, self-perpetuating, elected or appointed (but not by an authority capable of awarding corporate status and not to represent the members of a corporation) to perform in common certain duties and specified in

---

[76] *op. cit.*, p. 237.

[77] *op. cit.*, p 242.

[78] Although Black has argued that Oakeshott's view of the history of political thought is 'implicitly anti-corporatist' (*Guilds and Civil Society*, p 235), the use of the analogy of *societas* to describe the modern state did not, so far as Oakeshott was concerned, involve any hostility to community. The desire of individuals to form *universitates*, communities or corporations, was entirely compatible with an individualistic understanding of the state as a *societas*. In his own words, 'the only "animosity" I have ever entertained towards "community" or association in terms of the pursuit of a substantive purpose is concerned with the attribution of this character to a state or the attempt to impose it upon a state.': see 'On Misunderstanding Human Conduct', p. 376. Since Black himself raises the question (in *Guilds and Civil Society*, p. 217) of whether 'the ultimate horror endured by Europe' under National Socialism was not 'the state as guild', Oakeshott's position may not be as different from his own as he believes.

[79] *op. cit.*, p. 214.

terms of this purpose', such as the Grand Council of Venice. All of
these examples might suggest that the state be understood in corporate terms. The 'survival of an unpurged relic of lordship in the office
of a king' only added further weight to this view.[80] Wherever ruling
was not clearly distinct from lordly, proprietary right, there was at
least a 'remote intimation of a realm as a corporate enterprise.'[81]

In a revealing aside, Oakeshott confessed that this version of modern European political history 'owes much to Ranke and . . .
Neurankeaner historians . . . who held that the dominant theme of
modern European history is the tension between religious and civil
association, continuously transformed.'[82] Ranke's appeal may well
have been due to what Oakeshott called his concern 'with the inter-
national history of modern times...distinguished by a "European"
detachment from nationalistic...interests', reflecting his own
pan-European focus. He believed that Ranke's later followers, such
as Max Lenz, had located the 'principle of modern German domestic
history...in the unresolved tension between secular and religious
authority.'

Lenz, according to Oakeshott, had taken the Reformation to be a
'proto-occurrence of this tension'; by 1958, Oakeshott had decided
that 'the politics of collectivism' (in the language of *On Human Conduct*, a state understood as a *universitas*) 'emerged first in a religious
idiom' at the time of the Reformation. Oakeshott also attributed to
Lenz another view he would make his own, that 'in ever changing
forms' this style of politics had left its mark on 'the whole of modern
history'.[83] It seems, then, that in *On Human Conduct* Oakeshott
self-consciously set out to re-tell the story of modern European politics as the tale of a confusion between the 'heavenly' and 'earthly' cities. It was, of course, the state as a *universitas* which represented the
attempt to realise the heavenly city on earth.

The outcome of the Reformation, 'not merely the expropriation of
the alleged undesirable authority of the *sacerdotium* but the appro-
priation of the very desirable and extensive authority by the civil
ruler', encouraged the understanding of a state as a *universitas*. It
was crucial, Oakeshott argued, to realise that 'the sacerdotal authority which in part thus fell to the *regnum* was different in kind from

[80] *op. cit.*, p. 219.

[81] *op. cit.*, p. 220.

[82] *HC*, p. 286, n. 1.

[83] Oakeshott, Review of Herkless, *The Historiography of Max Lenz*, undated
      typescript, LSE 1/2/6. It is not clear whether this piece was published.

that which a civil ruler already enjoyed.'[84] In particular, the acquisition of the Papal *potestas docendi*, the authority to be 'the director of
the education of Christendom, the guardian of learning and the arbi-
ter of knowledge . . . intimated a transformation of the office' of rulers who appropriated it.

In the attempt to quell religious anarchy, rulers everywhere
attempted to ensure their 'teachers and preachers' would 'speak
with one official voice'. Where Catholicism survived, they began the
'disciplinary and managerial undertaking' of defending it 'against
the intrusive novelties of "protestant" belief and the cosmopolitan
culture of "humanist" education.' In the Lutheran state 'the cultural
and religious norm was itself to a large extent novel and in choosing
it the ruler was displaying his newly acquired authority as the
guardian of his subjects' moral and spiritual welfare.'[85] In doing so
the Protestant 'godly Prince...acquired a command over his subjects
which no Catholic king ever enjoyed'; all 'lived under the threat of
deviation'.[86] But in either case, '*temporalia* and *spiritualia* were assimilated to one another not merely jurisdictionally but substantively.'
Governments had become 'seriously concerned with the religious
and cultural integration of their subjects.'[87]

The belief that 'Ruling was to have the custody of the material,
moral and spiritual welfare of a community with a teleology of its
own into which that of the individual soul had been assimilated'[88]
pre-dated the Reformation. Oakeshott thought it already present in
Aquinas and Dante. However they differed over Papal and Imperial
claims, each had 'understood ruling to be something more than having custody of a law and courts designed to ensure the *temporalis
tranquilitas* of subjects each of whom has a "final cause" of his own.'
Their 'attribution of "mission" to the office of ruler', however, was
not nearly so strongly reflected in 'the activities of rulers' of the later
medieval period as it would be in the modern era. The power of governments 'to match such an engagement' was yet lacking.

On account of this lack of power, and because of the medieval tendency 'to extend the notion of corporate association and the honorary status of a *universitas* to almost any "multitude of men" joined in
pursuing a common purpose', one should not, Oakeshott warned,
assume that because a medieval writer used the word *universitas* in

[84]   *HC*, p. 222.

[85]   *op. cit.*, p. 283.

[86]   *op. cit.*, pp. 283–4.

[87]   *op. cit.*, p. 280.

[88]   *op. cit.*, p. 223.

connection with a political association, he was writing of a nascent corporate state. As an example, he offered Marsilius of Padua's *Defensor Pacis* (1324). 'Marsilius is reputed to have made substantial use of the analogy of corporate association' — he 'writes of a realm as a *universitas*.' Nevertheless, his 'argument does nothing to sustain it in that character'.

Marsilius's concern with 'the authority to make law,' Oakeshott argued, led him to write of a realm as a '*universitas* civium'. He believed that only incorporation allowed 'the contingent assemblage of ... agents' composing a *civitas* to 'acquire an imprescriptible authority' to make rules which can satisfy the need for order 'which they could not possess as individuals'. But he had assigned this *universitas* 'No "end" other than that satisfaction of the common need for a compulsory order.' Thus, Marsilius's use of *universitas* 'turns out not to have the essential characteristic' it has when used as an analogy for the character of a state; 'it is not a many joined in pursuit of a common substantive satisfaction.'[89]

In the modern state, 'the tireless extension and elaboration of a central apparatus of ruling' had made this vision far more plausible. This apparatus was the source of government power, but it was 'totally indifferent' both to the constitution of a government (the terms of its authorisation to rule) and to 'the "sovereignty" of states; "sovereign" authority has nothing to do with competence'. Created to deal with administrative matters 'such as the collection of authorised revenue or the suppression of local disorder', employing procedures which were 'not those of a court of law' and 'agents' who were 'not themselves judicial officers', this apparatus had usually 'represented a disposition to regard all conduct in terms of its threat to public order rather than any design to "manage the lives of the people"'. However, 'its appearance as a common feature of European states ... beckoned imagination towards an understanding of them in terms of enterprise association.'[90] In the absence of such an apparatus, Oakeshott believed, no government would have been able to undertake a managerial office.

European colonialism and imperialism had added force to the analogy of *universitas* from a wholly new direction. The early modern conquest and colonisation of the 'new world', for example, proceeded by 'the extension of the lordship of the ruler under whose protection or license [colonies] were established.' The fact that plantations and settlements were themselves often corporations was less

---

[89] *op. cit.*, p. 217.

[90] *op. cit.*, pp. 267–8.

important, Oakeshott argued, than that 'the notionally uninhabited lands . . . were understood to belong, by right of conquest or occupation, to the rulers of the state whence the settlers came.' The Europeans who left for Spanish and Portuguese South and Central America, French North Africa and the first British Empire were all 'agents of an enterprise.' He thought this less true of later African and South Pacific colonies which 'were not, for the most part, licensed adventures in pursuit of substantive satisfactions', although the Belgian Congo was an exception. But in general, 'the consequence of this colonial experience was to familiarise modern Europe with states which were, in some significant respect, enterprises.'[91]

War, often in connection with colonial and imperial activity, had played a similarly important role in fostering the idea of the enterprise state. It is mystifying how Anderson could write that Oakeshott 'could never afford to register the logic of military competition for state construction.'[92] Such a conclusion is possible only if one wilfully ignores his statement that 'the five centuries of modern times have been a period of continuous warfare,' or that 'to be preparing to make war or to repel an enemy, or to be at war, or to be counteracting the consequences of the belligerence of others . . . has been the *normal* condition of every European state.'[93]

Oakeshott called war 'the enemy of civil association', because he believed that a state at war 'is indisputably turned in the direction of association in terms of a substantive purpose'; consequently, 'the status of "subject" recedes before that of . . . role-performer in an enterprise.' However, his argument that 'belligerence is alien' to the philosophical model of civil association hardly supports Anderson's view that he could find no place for the part war had played in the history of the ambiguous states of modern Europe. If anything, he believed that it had become increasingly important.

Sooner or later, any review of the circumstances which Oakeshott believed had rendered the modern state eligible to be understood as a *universitas* must come back to the history of character. There had been a change in moral character, he argued, corresponding to the emergence of individualism. There emerged, first, the 'individual *manqué*' and then the 'anti-individual'. The individual *manqué* had emerged concurrently with the disposition to individuality. The 'desuetude of a communally organised life . . . excited some,' but it 'depressed and discomforted others'. 'The counterpart of the agri-

[91] *Ibid.*, pp. 268–72.

[92] Anderson, 'The Intransigent Right', pp. 7–11, p. 10.

[93] *HC*, pp. 272–3. Italics mine.

cultural entrepreneur . . . was the displaced labourer; the counter-part of . . . the *libertin spirituel* was the dispossessed believer.'[94] Whatever 'combination of actual loss, debility, ignorance, timidity, poverty, loneliness, displacement, persecution or misfortune' had created this character, he found himself without the ability or 'confidence . . . to make choices for [himself] in matters of belief, language, conduct, occupation, relationships and engagements of all sorts.'

As the morality of individuality became more prevalent, that of the individual *manqué* underwent a transformation. 'What had been no more than an inability to hold his own in belief and conduct became a radical self-distrust . . . the discomfort of ill-success turned into the misery of guilt . . . and in the course of time his natural submissiveness prompted the appearance of "leaders"' who could tell him 'what . . . to ask for and to do'.[95] The anti-individual, as Oakeshott described him, was 'a *persona* . . . that could be accommodated only in the sort of association which the analogy of *universitas* suggested for the character of a state'. In the twentieth century, Germany and Russia had produced leaders who 'evoked' in their followers 'the character of the determined 'anti-individual,' one intolerant not only of superiority but of difference, disposed to allow in all others only a replica of himself.' Such modern figures as Hitler, however, had their ancestors in the sixteenth century; Oakeshott drew an explicit comparison between National Socialist Germany and Calvinist Geneva, arguing that both involved understanding the state as a *universitas*.

In contrast with Oakeshott's description of the individual, the sources he acknowledged as having inspired the characters of the anti-individual and the individual *manqué* were not historical. He drew on Burckhardt again, but he cited *Force and Freedom* rather than his historical works.[96] Hoffer's *The True Believer*, the other work he mentioned, was more of a sociological study (subtitled *Thoughts on the Nature of Mass Movements*) than an historical one. Hoffer's argument that all mass movements, from Christianity to National Socialism, attract a similar sort of personality characterised chiefly by the 'desire to escape [the] self' and 'the willingness to dissolve it . . . in a compact collective whole' would obviously have struck a chord

[94] *op. cit.,* p. 275.

[95] *op. cit.,* p. 277.

[96] Also known as *Reflections on History,* Liberty Press, Indianopolis, 1979 (*Weltgeschichtliche Betrachtungen,* ed. J. Oeri, 1905); cp. *HC,* p. 278 n. 1.

with Oakeshott, who described the 'anti-individual' as requiring 'the warmth of a solidarity' in which he would 'be told what to do'.[97]

It is, nonetheless, still possible to find support in the works of other historians for such views. One work that Oakeshott may have been drawing on was Cohn's *The Pursuit of the Millennium*, which he read as 'a sixteenth-century chapter in the history of Gnostic belief'.[98] Cohn's work described the attempts of millenarian sects to achieve a final, collective salvation in life, led by 'would-be prophets or would-be messiahs', whom he described as 'half-intellectuals' with a sense of 'mission' that would recognize 'no other claims'. It is not hard to see how Oakeshott could have identified such figures with his own 'anti-individual'. Similarly, Cohn's account of those who took part in such movements as people who had experienced the collapse of traditional social and kinship groups and who had no 'recognized and assured place in society', forming an 'unorganized, atomized population', fits Oakeshott's description of the 'individual *manqué*' quite neatly. Cohn even included 'peasants without land' and 'journeymen and unskilled workers living under the continuous threat of unemployment' in his description of the 'amorphous mass' caught up in millenarianism.[99]

Oakeshott did emphasise that the individual *manqué* and the anti-individual were not simply to be identified with 'the poor', 'the peasantry' or 'the "proletariat' as such. 'The ingredient of spiritual indigence is not less important . . . than the absence of possessions; and the true vagabond does not belong here', he wrote. If, as he himself had proposed in 1962, these characters were identified with a 'mass man' or 'the masses', 'then it must be understood that what is being referred to is not their numbers but their incapacity to sustain an individual life and their longing for the shelter of a community'.[100] For all that, Oakeshott's character of the 'anti-individual' bore much the same relationship to 'the individual' as the 'Rationalist' had to Hobbes. He is a dependent, derivative figure, and all the tensions we have identified between Oakeshott's 'descriptive' and 'evaluative' uses of character come home to rest in him.

Behind Oakeshott's use of these characters in *On Human Conduct* lie the religious interests which had figured in his work since his earliest essays. For example, he described the individualism of

---

[97] E. Hoffer, *The True Believer: Thoughts on the Nature of Mass Movements*, Harper and Bros., New York, 1951, p. 58. Cp. *HC*, pp. 276–7.

[98] N. Cohn, *The Pursuit of the Millenium*, 3rd edn., London, 1984.

[99] *op. cit.*, pp. 13–15, 282–6.

[100] *HC*, p. 276.

Montaigne as the spirit of 'Augustine come again to confound both Gnostics and Pelagians.'[101] Indeed, to both the individual and the anti-individual Oakeshott ascribed an appropriate theological understanding, in which we recognise once more the two kinds of pride that Oakeshott found in Hobbes as well as Augustine. The God of the individual was 'an Augustinian god of majestic imagination, who, when he might have devised an untroublesome universe, had the nerve to create one of self-employed adventurers of unpredictable fancy . . . and thus acquire *convives* capable of "answering back" in civil tones with whom to pass eternity in conversation.' The God of the anti-individual is 'the Proprietor of an estate of vast resources who, although he may be suspected of being somewhat niggardly, is nevertheless . . . a "providence," not the author of rules . . . but the source of substantial benefits.'[102]

Oakeshott himself recognised that in the use of his characters he was yielding to 'the temptation to seek a more general explanation than a historical understanding can provide.'[103] When he hypothesised that if the individual 'had been the only character who walked the world in which the states of modern Europe emerged, then . . . they might have become unequivocal civil associations', we may suspect him of a contradiction. If we have understood him aright, 'civil association' was an ideal character, an abstract mode of association detached 'from the contingencies and ambiguities of actual goings-on in the world.'[104] As no more than an instrument 'which may be used in seeking to understand complex, ambiguous, historic human associations', it is not capable of actualisation. His mention of unequivocal civil association is surely an expression of longing or regret rather than an historical proposition.

In *On Human Conduct*, then, Oakeshott's characters had left him at an impasse. Even though he acknowledged that he was going beyond the bounds of historical thought by raising the possibility that 'hidden in human character there are two powerful and contrary dispositions, neither strong enough to defeat or put to flight the other',[105] he did so regardless. At the least, it must be said that Oakeshott's own efforts sometimes lacked the virtue for which he had praised Shakespeare long ago, of creating characters who can stand alone and villains who 'do not inevitably depend for their *rai-*

[101] *op. cit.*, p. 241.
[102] *op. cit.*, p. 325.
[103] *op. cit.*, p. 323.
[104] *op. cit.*, p. 109.
[105] *op. cit.*, p. 323.

son d'être upon . . . heroes.'[106] For example, writing of the leaders of the anti-individual as 'half-men,' offering a 'warm, compensated servility', seems to go beyond the historical, descriptive use of character.

When that has been said, however, the claim that Oakeshott's characters are simply reducible to 'caricatures of the transformations which . . . Burckhardt tried to capture'[107] might still be thought to go too far. Oakeshott expanded the history of individuality throughout the whole of the modern period in a way without parallel in Burckhardt's *Civilisation of the Renaissance*. The dialectical necessity which Burckhardt saw in the emergence of the individual was also absent from Oakeshott's account. Nor is it quite true to say that 'All of Oakeshott's imposing erudition ends in the bathos of this small parable of the divided soul of economic man.'[108] If anything, what marred Oakeshott's version of the history of political thought was quite the opposite problem; his Romantic tendency to elevate it into a drama of cosmic proportions. We might even say that his own works exemplified the tension they described.

Philosophers of *Societas*

We have surveyed the events Oakeshott believed encouraged the understanding of a state as a *societas*. The place he assigned to this analogy in the works of particular thinkers remains to be seen. He believed that it was 'commonly to be met with at the level of implicit assumption',[109] not only in Machiavelli, but in Hume, Burke, Paine, de Tocqueville and Ranke. Contrary to his earlier view of the documents of 1776 and 1789 as the product of Rationalist politics, he now found this assumption in the American Declaration of Independence, the Federalist papers, the American Constitution and the *Déclaration de Droits de l'Homme et du Citoyen*.[110]

Of course, this argument for the existence of a shared set of implicit assumptions immediately arouses suspicions; it is not readily susceptible of proof. It should be said, nevertheless, that Oakeshott was not arguing that unity of assumption about the character of the state involved agreement in other areas. He could quite happily admit that Burke and Paine, for example, had little else in

[106] Oakeshott, 'Shylock', p. 61.

[107] Boucher, 'Politics in a Different Mode', p. 728.

[108] Anderson, *op. cit.*, p. 10.

[109] *HC*, p. 243.

[110] *op. cit.*, pp. 245–6, 252.

common. All the writers he mentioned, he was careful to point out, were usually mainly 'concerned with other matters . . . the constitution of governments . . . the "derivation" of the authority of rules and rulers, with contrivances for limiting the alleged menace of "sovereign" authority', and so on.[111]

However, Oakeshott claimed to find the idea of a state as an association in terms of non-instrumental rules of law made explicit in the canonical 'great texts' of political philosophy. Bodin, Hobbes, Spinoza, Montesquieu, Kant, and Hegel, and, more ambiguously, Locke, Fichte, Bentham, and J.S. Mill, were all united by 'their recognition . . . of a state in terms of *societas*'. Again, to understand the extent of Oakeshott's claims, it is important to notice his qualifications. None of these authors 'is without minor equivocation' and they 'often divided' over 'other matters . . . the so-called "origin" of civil association . . . the authority of rulers and the constitution of historic governments.'

Oakeshott's way with political thinkers was remarkably synthetic. It would seem from the names mentioned above that nearly every 'canonical' political thinker between the sixteenth and mid-nineteenth centuries, with the possible exception of Rousseau and the definite exception of Marx, had assumed, characterised, or theorised the state as a *societas*. In this sense, his claim that his own interpretation of modern political thought broke up 'the conventional grouping of writers and establishe[d] new lines of communication'[112] seems justified.

When we look more closely, however, we may find Oakeshott's interpretation more familiar than it appears at first sight. Virtually all the thinkers he had admired either in his youthful Idealist phase or as upholders of 'representative democracy' now reappear as theorists of *societas*. It is also striking that Oakeshott's list of these theorists overlaps with perhaps more familiar selections made by others. For example, fully two-thirds of those selected by Plamenatz as liberal writers, including Locke, Montesquieu, Burke, Constant, Mill, Hume, Acton, and Bentham are also included in Oakeshott's pantheon.[113] The writers traditionally presented as part of the story of the change from status to contract or of the struggle of liberty against equality here become the upholders of 'civil' against 'enterprise' association.

---

[111] *op. cit.*, p. 244.

[112] *MP*, p. 47.

[113] J. Plamenatz, *Readings from Liberal Writers*, Allen and Unwin, London, 1965, pp. 240.

A great deal of the coherence of Oakeshott's interpretation rests not on any similarity between the thinkers he mentioned (as he himself acknowledged, they were often in disagreement) but on the identical questions he asked of them. In each case, he would begin by asking how an author conceived of the individual human being, and then enquire what manner of government they thought suitable for such persons. Of course, it was a cardinal tenet of his philosophy of historical understanding that it made available a view of the past not present at the time. But there will always be those who will argue that he imparted greater coherence to his evidence than it could be made to bear.

Critics will also find the lack of detail hard to excuse in an author who insisted on it as a feature of historical understanding. Oakeshott may have felt that the republication of his essays on Hobbes compensated for the curious absence of any lengthy treatment of him in *On Human Conduct*, but he made no attempt whatsoever to defend his castings of, for example, Spinoza, Hume, or Fichte as theorists of *societas*. Even where he did offer more extended discussions, there is a lack of textual references that can be extremely frustrating. None of the other authors (such as Wolin, Germino, MacPherson, and Skinner) offering synoptic histories of modern political thought in the same period neglected to provide a full critical apparatus of footnotes, bibliography and so on. Oakeshott blithely ignored such technical considerations, and at the very least this makes it difficult to work out on which passages of a given work he was basing his interpretation. Obviously, we have no space to go through his views on each of the thinkers he mentioned. Instead, we shall take just one example, Hegel. We have selected him because, with the exception of Hobbes, he appears to have been the political thinker who meant most to Oakeshott.

The few pages which Oakeshott devoted to Hegel in *On Human Conduct* represent his only extended published thoughts on him. In light of the importance Idealist thought had had for him in the 1920s and 1930s, it is worth paying close attention to what he had to say. Recognising that by the 1970s Oakeshott had long abandoned his Idealist vocabulary, Anderson wrote that 'Hegel is still received in *On Human Conduct*, but he is out of place.'[114] In his view, Hegel's presence was simply an 'echo' of Oakeshott's earlier Idealism. This, however, is misleading. What distinguished Oakeshott's reading of Hegel was that there was no longer much that was Idealist about it at all. Hegel's *Philosophy of Right* was 'a dreadfully miscellaneous piece

[114] *Ibid.*

of writing.'[115] It was, however, also the 'most sophisticated' under-standing of a state as a *societas* to be found in the history of modern political thought.[116] Hegel, like Hobbes, had become a theorist of the rule of non-instrumental law. This was an extremely controversial position to take. For Anderson, Hegel was 'the supreme theorist of the state as a substantive, goal-directed community,' and Oakeshott's reading of him was 'a whim even by the measure of his Hobbes'.

It is certainly true that for most of this century Oakeshott's Hegel would have received little support. The nadir of Hegel's reputation in the English-speaking world came with Popper's *The Open Society and its Enemies*, which dismissed his 'bombastic and mystifying cant' at length.[117] By the 1980s it was possible to declare that 'Hegel is back',[118] but even so it is doubtful whether more recent interpreta-tions would have been congenial to Oakeshott. Taylor,[119] for exam-ple, portrayed him as the founder of a Romantic 'expressivism' which found little resonance in Oakeshott's interpretation.

Oakeshott began, as always, by asking how the author in question understood a human being. Hegel, he argued, conceived of persons as 'individual exhibitions of *der Geist* . . . not . . . a substance or an impersonal "force" . . . [but] reflective intelligence rather than Rea-son.'[120] The view that 'in Hegel's interpretation of history it is the nation, rather than the individual . . . that forms the significant unit'[121] was one he could not accept. *Der Geist*, like his own 'conver-sation,' was 'a procedure of "criticism" (dialectic) rather than a pro-cess, and if it may be said to exist anywhere it is in the characters, the adventures, the works and the relations of human beings.'

Der Geist also turns out to involve, in effect, the recognition of goings-on in the world in terms of 'human conduct'. In the exercise of *der Wille*, one is 'imagining the not-self (the "natural" world) to be other than it is and resolving to change it from what it is to what it is imagined to be.' In *Experience and its Modes*, Oakeshott's own 'practi-cal mode' had drawn on this Hegelian transformation of an 'is' into

[115] Oakeshott, Review of S. Avinieri, *Hegel's Theory of the Modern State, European Studies Review*, vol. 5, 1975, p. 219.

[116] *HC*, p. 252.

[117] K. Popper, *The Open Society and its Enemies*, vol. 2, 5th edn., Routledge, London, 1966, p. 28.

[118] I. Hacking, in *Philosophy in History: Essays on the Historiography of Philosophy*, ed. R. Rorty, J. B. Schneewind, and Q. Skinner, Cambridge UP, Cambridge, 1984, p. 107.

[119] C. Taylor, *Hegel*, Cambridge UP, 1975.

[120] *HC*, p. 257.

[121] G.H. Sabine, *A History of Political Theory*, Henry Holt, New York, 1944, p. 621.

an 'ought' for its basic structure. In turn, Hegel was drawn into the Oakeshottian scheme of things in *On Human Conduct*. Action was said to consist for Hegel, as for Oakeshott, in a formal and a substantive element. The latter element was concerned with the pursuit of concrete satisfactions, the former with the practices or conditions of the relationships in terms of which these satisfactions were to be pursued. Furthermore, for Oakeshott, as for his Hegel, action could involve differing kinds of relationships or modes of association.

One such mode was Hegel's *bürgerliche Gesellschaft*. This phrase Oakeshott wrote, 'has unfortunately come to be translated as "civil society"', 'unfortunately' because *bürgerliche Gesellschaft* is an economic mode of association, a *universitas*, rather than a *societas*. Hegel considered it a part of ethical life, but he followed classical economists such as Adam Smith in considering it 'a conditional ... mode of association' which 'postulates another mode of association',[122] the state. For Hegel, the mode of association in a state was a relationship in terms of *das Gesetz*, non-instrumental law. This was also a moment in ethical life, but it is 'not composed of contrivances for satisfying wants'. Instead, it takes the form of 'a system of known, positive, self-authenticating, non-instrumental rules of law ... which postulate "free" agents as their subjects.'

In his twenties Oakeshott had attempted to describe Hegel's view of the relation of philosophy to historical events. Fifty years later, reflecting on essentially the same question, he concluded that '*Der Geist* is a philosophical idea and so is the conditional mode of *der Geist* which [Hegel] calls *der Wille*, but the self-recognition of persons in terms of *der Wille* is a historic achievement ... *der subjektive Geist* is not only a philosophical idea but may also be a contingent human disposition ... notably displayed in the self-understanding of modern peoples.'[123] Yet for Hegel, as for himself, Oakeshott believed, 'no modern European state could be identified as an unambiguous example of the idea' of civil association. What grounds there were for such an identification rested on the degree to which '*der subjektive Geist*' or 'individuality' was present.

Unlike Gierke, Oakeshott believed, Hegel knew that 'the last place to look' for a theory of the state 'was among the peoples of what had once been called the Empire of the German Nation.'[124] Like the *socii* of civil association, the inhabitants of Hegel's *Staat* were not, as such, 're-

[122] *HC*, p. 261.

[123] *op. cit.*, pp. 262–3.

[124] Oakeshott, Review of Avinieri, p. 218.

lated in terms of..."national consciousness"...love...virtue...or...
their concern to satisfy their contingent wants.' They were *cives*.

Philosophers of *Universitas*

One of the peculiar features of Oakeshott's history of modern political events and ideas which he did not make explicit was that the tension he discerned both in events and in ideas was weighted
differently in each case. So far as events were concerned, governments had increasingly behaved as the managers of corporations.
But in the realm of ideas, the 'canon' came out strongly on the side of
the view that the state was a non-purposive association. Of course,
he had always insisted that historical and philosophical thought
bore no direct relation to practice. It was not that there was no relation between ideas and events, but the two did not determine one
another. A philosophical understanding of the state as a *societas* did
not, as such, affect the events which increasingly led particular, historical states to take on the character of *universitates*.

Some may well find the apparent consequences of this view ironic.
However well Oakeshott (or Hobbes, or Hegel) constructed their
philosophical models of 'civil association', the logic of their own
work meant that it could do nothing to promote the practical realisation of such an association. On Oakeshott's own account, it was a
half-century or so before his own birth that the idea and practice of
the state as an 'enterprise association' finally became endemic. In the
twentieth century, this 'Servile State' had become almost universal.
Yet without changes in the rules and mores of modern European
states (for which his own work could offer no direct help, since rules
for, or courses of, action could not be deduced from them) there was
nothing for it but to sit and watch the rot spread. A theory cannot act.

Others will find this unkind. Simply by writing and teaching as he
did, it might be said, Oakeshott reminded all who were willing to lis-
ten that the current manner of government was complex, and that
the dominant elements in it ought not to be allowed to obscure its
other features, even if he did not spell out a way to realise an alternative. But whichever side one takes on the issue, what he actually
made of the thinkers who had understood the state as a *universitas*
remains to be seen. It need hardly be said that all the difficulties associated with his treatment of those he regarded as theorists of *societas*
were reproduced here. If anything, the problems are even greater,
not least because of his obvious dislike for this idea of the state.

It is striking that the successive versions of the idea of a state as a
universitas which Oakeshott identified — religious, productivist and

distributionist or 'welfarist' — all involved what *Experience and its Modes* had called 'speculative' philosophies of history, or 'practical' understandings of the past. All were, in the language of *Rationalism in Politics*, 'myths' of various sorts. Take, for example, J.S. Mill. The ever closer approximation to 'perfection' which Oakeshott believed Mill, at least in his moods as a theorist of *universitas*, saw it as the task of government to promote coincides neatly with Mill's belief in 'progress' which Oakeshott had rejected in his philosophy of historical understanding, not to mention his political philosophy.[125]

Similarly, Calvin, whom Oakeshott believed to be one of the earliest writers to develop the 'religious' version of telocratic government, is said not only to understand the office of a government as the imposition of the glorification of God on its subjects, who are united in a state for this purpose, but to explain this understanding in terms of an expectation of future salvation for the Elect.[126] Oakeshott's model of historical enquiry disbars this view of things from being described as authentically historical; on his view, this would be an example of a practical past constructed to meet present needs.

Although the rulers of Geneva 'were not themselves thought of as agents of salvation' (which was predestined), their business was to ensure 'the conduct of each of their subjects conformed at all times to the purpose of the enterprise [of] the glorification of God'. To do so, they used 'commands which, appropriately, recognised no distinction between "public" and "private"', and an 'apparatus of government' involving 'courts of morals, sumptuary regulations, inquisitions, informers, secret agents, censorship, overseers of schools and universities, threats' and so on.[127]

Bacon, influenced by Calvinist theology, was another notable early modern contributor to the understanding of a state as a *universitas*. Oakeshott once remarked that 'the most important texts for the understanding of the modern world are . . . the two passages in the book of Genesis in which human beings are recognised to be free of the world and as having to exert themselves in the practice of freedom — dominion and work.' These Biblical stories, he claimed, were 'the spring of Bacon's understanding of the exploitation of the resources of the world which he both observed and preached.'[128] The Fall had 'done nothing to qualify' God's gift to mankind, recorded in

---

[125] *MP*, pp. 81–2.

[126] *op. cit.*, p. 95.

[127] *HC*, p. 284.

[128] Oakeshott, Review of H. Marcuse, *Reason and Revolution*, *Spectator*, 1 Apr. 1955, p. 404.

Genesis, of all the resources of the earth, 'except to make "work" a condition of its enjoyment.' In the post-lapsarian world, this exploitation was 'the chief (and perhaps the only) way mankind has of glorifying God.'

Bacon's *New Atlantis* imagined a state as 'a corporation aggregate concerned with the exploitation of the resources of a state and of the office of government as that of estate management.' But the enterprise itself aimed not so much at 'satisfactions for felt wants' as the production of 'votive offerings' — 'the "well-being" corporately pursued was recognised as the fulfilment of a "calling" to conquer the natural world . . . *laborare est orare*.'[129] What Bacon had recognised as an 'act of worship,' however, later became a purely productive undertaking. He was 'the progenitor of that understanding of the character of the modern European state in which it is recognised to be, and not merely to have, an "economy".'[130]

The religious idiom of the state as a *universitas* had been translated 'by about the end of the seventeenth century . . . into secular terms.' The Baconian and Calvinist ideas of the state came together 'in a version of corporate association which . . . established itself as the favoured modern idiom . . . a many made one in devotion to a pattern of "enlightened" conduct.'[131] The type of the 'enlightened' prince supplanted the 'godly' prince, but the idea of 'enlightened' government, Oakeshott believed, was 'itself a blend of moral and religious and "lordly" engagements attributed to the office of government.'[132]

Enlightened despotism 'was prefigured in much that went before'; the 'managerial and tutorial undertaking' it implied, Oakeshott believed, date back at least to the Reformation. As in *The Politics of Faith and the Politics of Scepticism*, he saw the '*vertu* of the philosophe' as 'analogous to Puritan "righteousness" in being a pattern of substantive performances instrumental to an imagined satisfaction and allowing only functional variations.' It differed 'in being a programme . . . directed by "reason" in place of spiritual authority or divine inspiration' and in aiming at 'the continuous promotion of an interest rather than the enjoyment of a final earthly or heavenly salvation.' But neither of these differences explained 'the real novelty of *le despotisme éclairé* . . . the clear recognition that the manage-

---

[129] One is tempted to add, *arbeit macht frei*, so close does Oakeshott seem to come to making National Socialism a direct descendant of Baconianism in this respect.

[130] *HC*, pp. 287–8.

[131] *op. cit.*, p. 297.

[132] *op. cit.*, p. 286.

ment of a corporate enterprise requires an apparatus of lordship commensurate with the undertaking.'[133]

It was German Cameralists such as von Justi who supplied the outline of the detailed apparatus necessary to the French philosophes' vision of Enlightened government. Again, Oakeshott saw the roots of Cameralism lying deep in the past — they 'drew upon the considerable products of administrative inventiveness of . . . rulers since the fifteenth century and what they achieved was . . . novel in its totality rather than in its detail.' In their state, 'composed of boards, commissions, organisations, agencies, *bureaux*' and the like, 'Judicial offices occupied an inconspicuous place, and (like the philosophes) Cameralists had little use for *parlementaires*.' From Cameralism one could trace the direct line of descent to the 'managerial engagements' of twentieth century governments. 'All the lineaments of the Servile State' were 'already half-revealed' in the eighteenth century.[134]

As late as Saint-Simon Oakeshott still found Christian echoes, 'but the reverberations of theology became less distinct in the utterance of each successive generation' despite leaving traces in Comte and Marx. Marx's 'mythology . . . view of world history and . . . political vocabulary',[135] he believed, amounted to little more than a secular Calvinism. He saw in Marx only a quasi-theological tale of redemption at the hands of the elect. Of the twentieth century, Oakeshott had almost nothing to say. In sharp contrast with Berlin, for example, who believed it was a 'fallacy' to regard ideologies such as communism and fascism as 'only more uncompromising and violent manifestations of . . . a struggle discernible long before',[136] he was adamant that what he had once called 'the social and political doctrines of contemporary Europe' — National Socialism, Communism etc. — held no novelty. They were simply more destructive variations on the medieval theme of lordly rule. Any idea of a decisive break with the past reflected in phrases such as 'the end of history', 'the end of modernity', or 'post-modernism' was conspicuously absent.

It should be said that if Oakeshott believed this was the predominant understanding of a state in the twentieth century, he did not think it the only one. Although 'two world wars . . . and the techniques of control . . . devised' in them had given further encourage-

[133] *op. cit.*, p. 299.
[134] *op. cit.*, pp. 300–01.
[135] *MP*, pp. 95–6.
[136] I. Berlin, *Four Essays on Liberty*, Oxford UP, Oxford, 1969, p. 7.

ment to the idea of a state as a *universitas,* European states remained 'still-puzzling' ambiguous associations: the tension that had persisted for hundreds of years remained as unresolved as ever.

The Philosophy of History, 1975–1983

Human Conduct and History

Neither *On Human Conduct* nor *On History* attracted the public attention *Rationalism in Politics* received. *On Human Conduct* was at least thought worthy of a symposium in the pages of *Political Theory* (which Oakeshott was largely unhappy with, feeling once again that he had been misconstrued),[1] but *On History* sank almost without trace after mixed reviews. The austere style in which both books were written was presumably too great a deterrent after the flowing essays of *Rationalism in Politics*. Consequently, the relationship between the philosophy of history in *On Human Conduct* and in *On History* has had little discussion beyond that already noticed. In addition, although the first three essays in *On History* are unmistakably essays in the philosophy of history, the essay 'On the Theoretical Understanding of Human Conduct' has rarely been examined for what it has to say on this subject.[2] Yet in that essay, Oakeshott reached the conclusion that 'The theoretical understanding of a substantive action or utterance is . . . a "historical" understanding.'[3]

When the essay is seen in this light, we are in effect confronted with a choice. We may go on to the second essay in *On Human Conduct*, 'On the Civil Condition', in which 'human conduct' is treated, not as a postulate of historical understanding, but as an assumption of the relationship Oakeshott called civil association. Or, we may open *On History* and begin reading from the first page. If we take the latter option, we find an almost seamless continuity of discussion on

[1]   See *Political Theory*, vol. 4, 1976.

[2]   Nardin, *op. cit.*, is perhaps the first writer to highlight its significance in this respect.

[3]   *HC*, p. 105.

the philosophy of history. This chapter is, in part, an account of what results when we do so. Let us begin, then, by stating the relationship between the two books more exactly.

In *On Human Conduct*, historical study was described as 'an arrest in the unconditional engagement of theorising' which makes the attempt 'to understand in terms of its postulates a "going-on" identified in terms of its characteristics.'[4] The goings-on historians seek to understand, we know, belong to the 'category of identity' which embraces exhibitions of reflective intelligence. One of the postulates in terms of which goings-on belonging to this category are understood is 'human conduct', and as the title of *On Human Conduct* suggests, it was with this postulate in particular that Oakeshott was then mainly concerned.

Now, in *On Human Conduct* it was also argued that for each 'category of identity' there is a corresponding 'order of enquiry'. This view may be regarded as a technical rephrasing of the earlier claim in the essay 'On the Activity of Being an Historian' that 'what we see is relative to how we look.' If we identify what we see happening as belonging to the category of intelligent goings-on, we cannot, without falling into confusion, error or irrelevance (which are practically equivalent terms for Oakeshott), make sense of it using an order of theoretical enquiry appropriate to understanding unintelligent goings on such as chemical reactions. In *On History* it is the order of enquiry 'history' rather than the category of identity 'human conduct' which is the centre of attention. Since, however, Oakeshott believed that kinds of identity and orders of enquiry mutually entail one another, the two books may be said to be complementary.

The two books were both products of the same period of Oakeshott's career. He remarked in a letter to his publisher that 'Earlier versions of what I have to say [in *On History*] were composed for a seminar on the history of political thought with which I was concerned for about 10 years in the London School of Economics',[5] the same seminar on political thought which was so useful to him in working out the ideas of *On Human Conduct*. The unpublished seminar papers which survive from this period, some of which are effectively drafts of the first three chapters of *On History*, and other sources such as the seminar notes published by M.P. Thompson,[6]

[4]   *op. cit.*, p. 18.

[5]   Oakeshott, Letter to Basil Blackwell, 30 December 1981, LSE 11/6.

[6]   M.P. Thompson, 'Michael Oakeshott: Notes on "Political Theory" and "Political Thought" in the History of Political Thought, 1966-9', *Politisches Denken Jahrbuch*, vol. 2, 1991, pp. 103–19.

will provide valuable additional evidence as we work through these final writings. We will see that the ideas of the two books on the philosophy of history overlap to the extent that the arrangement of them into the essay 'On the Theoretical Understanding of Human Conduct' and the 'Three Essays on History' between the covers of separate books can be misleading. Oakeshott might just as easily have placed these four essays together between the covers of a single work.

Before we examine the ideas of *On History* in detail, it is worth asking how the single enterprise revealed in this comparison of *On History* and *On Human Conduct* related to Oakeshott's earlier writings on the philosophy of history. Oakeshott had been concerned to spell out 'the postulates and presuppositions in terms of which [historical experience] is constructed and maintained' since 1933, [7] and it is quite right to say that 'In *On History*, as in *Experience and its Modes*, Oakeshott aims to present historical understanding as *sui generis* and entirely distinct from the modes of understanding found in practical life or science',[8] or for that matter, philosophy.

In *On History*, the detection of these same postulates is described, in the terminology of *On Human Conduct*, as 'theorising the conditions of relevance' of historical understanding. The starting point is the recognition of the 'identifying marks' of history (such as a recognition of its subject matter as 'past'). These are then resolved into an 'ideal character' or an 'ideal mode of understanding' understood 'in terms of its necessary conditions'.[9] Yet in *Experience and its Modes* these postulates of historical reasoning had been evidence to Oakeshott that history was not 'experience itself in its concrete totality', but merely an 'abstract mode of experience'.[10] Neither of the later two works betrays the slightest interest in the opposition of abstract and concrete experience so central to *Experience and its Modes*.

This change is reflected in the use of the term 'modality'. It is true that in both *On History* and *Experience and its Modes*, history is referred to as a 'mode'.[11] In fact, Oakeshott had never abandoned the use of the term 'mode' entirely. [12] Its meaning for him, however, had changed significantly; this is why it is a mistake to suppose that the

[7]   *OH*, p. 5.
[8]   J. Gray, Review of *On History*, *Political Theory*, vol. 12, 1984, p. 450.
[9]   *OH*, pp. 6, 34.
[10]   *EM*, p. 87.
[11]   *OH*, p. 2.
[12]   *RP*, p. 488.

ideas of his first and last works are identical. 'Modality' in *On History* signifies nothing more than 'an autonomous manner of understanding, specifiable in terms of exact conditions . . . logically incapable of denying or confirming the conclusions of any other mode of understanding.'[13] It had, of course, meant this in Oakeshott's earlier work. But it had not meant only this. There, 'modality' had been contrasted with a superior kind of non-modal (philosophical) experience. Where *Experience and its Modes* had sought to arrange all else in relation to philosophy, *On History* does not even bother to announce itself as a philosophical essay but dives in *in medias res*.

On History only raises the question of the relative status of history and philosophy, so important in *Experience and its Modes*, briefly, and at the very end. Oakeshott contented himself with remarking that 'neither is subordinate to the other'; the historian is not dependent on the philosopher (or any other species of theorist) for a method, nor is the philosopher dependent on the actual existence of persons who conduct theoretical enquiries into past events, that is, historians, in order to be able to specify the postulates of such an enquiry.[14] We must conclude, then, that the same status is attributed to historical enquiry in *On History* as in *On Human Conduct*. In both works, history is one of many modes conversationally related to one another. It is a kind of theorising, as distinct from doing. Like all theorising, it represents what Oakeshott had earlier called an 'escape' and now jokingly referred to as a 'holiday' from 'the business of life and death and dinner'.[15]

Past

On History begins with two definitions of 'history'. They are not, however, *a priori* definitions of the sort Oakeshott had been attracted to in his scholarly youth, but acknowledgments of two ordinary usages of the term 'history' — the same usages we have been examining in his own work. In one of its senses, history means 'the notional grand total of all that has ever happened in the lives of human beings', or a particular 'passage of somehow related occurrences distinguished in this grand total by being specified in terms of a place and a time and a substantive identity.' This is history in the sense of 'events'. But there is another meaning, in which the term refers to 'a certain sort of enquiry into, and a certain sort of under-

[13] *OH*, p. 2.

[14] *op. cit.*, p. 118.

[15] *op. cit.*, pp. 24–6.

standing of, some such passage of occurrences; the engagement and the conclusions of an historian.'

These two meanings are 'distinct but . . . not discrepant'. They are frequently combined in the titles of historical works: Oakeshott gave the example of Mommsen's *Romische Geschichte*, 'an understanding of occurrences set down by Mommsen as the result of [the] sort of enquiry . . . that distinguishes an historian.' Mommsen had no hand in making the Roman Republic, but he may be said to be one of the makers of the history of the Roman Republic.[16] These usages, Oakeshott remarked in a paper on 'Present and Past,' were 'paralleled in the common use of the word "science"'. For example, an expression such as 'Gray's science of anatomy' indicates both a certain stock of information about the structure and working of the human body assembled by Gray and the manner in which Gray assembled and displayed this information.

It is, of course, with the second sense of 'history', 'history as an enquiry', that *On History* was concerned. Oakeshott had toyed with the idea of calling the book 'On Historiography' to make this plainer, but decided that this was 'far too pompous', telling his publisher 'I should like to take advantage of the ambiguity of the word 'history' and call it simply: On History.'[17] As the description of Mommsen as one of the makers of Roman history implies, Oakeshott remained committed as ever to the view that the historian creates or constructs the past. The historian undertook the 'construction', not the 'reconstruction', of the past, as he put it in his paper on 'Present and Past'.[18] The 'historical past is a past which . . . .was never itself present. It can neither be found nor dug up, nor retrieved, nor collected, but only inferred.'[19] As in *Experience and its Modes*, it is the outcome of an historical enquiry.

The arguments used to establish this in *On History* differ from those of *Experience and its Modes*. In 1933 Oakeshott had argued that since all experience is present experience, there could be no past which is not in some sense tied to the present. It followed from this that the historian could not be regarded as creating a representation of an independently existing past. Consequently, he had spent a great deal of time in 1933 examining the difference between the historical and practical pasts. *On History* was still in accord with the proposition of *Experience and its Modes* that all experience is present

[16] *op. cit..*, pp. 1–2

[17] Oakeshott, Letter to Basil Blackwell, 30 December 1981, LSE 11/6.

[18] Oakeshott, 'Present and Past', LSE 1/1/26, p. 7.

[19] *OH*, p. 33.

experience of some sort, but it devoted more space than the earlier work to contrasting the historical and practical presents. It attempted to identify the postulates or 'conditions of relevance'[20] which constitute an enquiry as historical by following the course of an ideal process of historical reasoning. This ideal process, as we will see, commences with an encounter with evidence that takes place in the present before proceeding to the composition of a passage of historical events.

Before we embark on our discussion of the kind of present in which historical thinking begins, and its differences from the kind of past found in the practical realm, we should perhaps make a brief remark on the term 'practical' to forestall any confusion. This relates to one of those changes of vocabulary which have sometimes caused Oakeshott's readers some perplexity. In *On History*, Oakeshott reverted to speaking of a 'practical' mode. The reason for this return to a terminology abandoned by *On Human Conduct* was not made explicit. It is possible that he thought because *On History* was not dealing in depth with the idea of a 'practice' there was less danger of readers mistaking his meaning. Be that as it may, the important thing is that we are clear that what is meant in *On History* by 'practical understanding' is what had been called 'the understanding implicit in conduct' in *On Human Conduct* and the 'practical mode of experience' in *Experience and its Modes*. It is the satisfaction of wants, moral and instrumental, that is important in our ordinary 'universe of practical discourse', which is always linked to an ever-receding future.[21]

If the idea that there may be more than one kind of past was necessary to Oakeshott's philosophy of history in order to ensure the autonomy of history, the corollary of this view, which we shall now examine, was that each kind of past entails an appropriate notion of the present. An 'imaginary' past, for example, has a corresponding present also composed of 'images' such as a poet (or an 'historical' novelist) might create. In his essay 'On the Activity of Being an Historian', Oakeshott had argued that the historian attempts to assemble a present composed not of poetic 'images' but of objects seen exclusively as evidence for past events.[22] In *On History*, he refined this, writing that 'The present in historical understanding . . . is itself . . . a recorded past, which means only a past which has itself survived

---

[20]   *op. cit.*, p. 2.

[21]   *op. cit.*, pp. 10–11.

[22]   *RP*, p. 170.

and is present.'[23] Alternatively, one might say that the starting-place of historical enquiry is composed of 'objects . . . assembled as themselves answers to historical questions about the past.'[24]

The 'survivals' (or pieces of evidence) which compose this 'past-present' of historical enquiry will have a certain character. For example, they may be recognised as 'themselves performances . . . the utterances and fabrications of . . . human beings . . . engaged in transactions with others . . . and expressing themselves, their thoughts and beliefs.' Translating the language of *On History* into that of *On Human Conduct*, historical evidence is assumed to be what survives of goings-on belonging to the category of identity covering intelligent action. That is to say, historical evidence is evidence of past 'human conduct', of intelligent practical and theoretical doings. Whether one is writing histories of theoretical enquiries (such as historical writing itself) or of practical endeavours seeking the satisfaction of wants, it is assumed that one is dealing with evidence of 'human conduct'.[25]

Oakeshott insisted, as he had in *Experience and its Modes*, that historical enquiry postulates the critical treatment of evidence. Collingwood's question 'Can we believe Gildas?', Oakeshott remarked, was 'unfortunately phrased'. It implied — what was not the case — that the historian is in the position of simply having to decide whether to accept or reject what an author says as 'true'. For Oakeshott, not only must historians criticise their evidence, they may also be just as interested in what evidence 'may incidentally disclose . . . its asides, what it lets fall, what is there but is not part of the design, what it may be perceived to take for granted' and even in 'what it leaves unsaid' as in its 'authentic utterance'.

Oakeshott acknowledged that such 'Inference *e silentio* is notoriously speculative', but he believed that 'in intellectual history, where what is not said may circumstantially be recognised as intentionally not said, its yield has been great.' When one thinks of the discussion provoked by the absence of 'historical' arguments referring to an ancient constitution in Locke, for example, this is a reasonable point.[26] One might also say that Oakeshott could hardly refuse 'inference *e silentio*' a role in interpretation given the way he himself

---

[23] *OH*, p. 30.

[24] *op cit.*, p. 46.

[25] *op. cit.*, pp. 13–4.

[26] P. Laslett, 'Introduction' to J. Locke, *Two Treatises of Government*, Cambridge UP, Cambridge, 1990, p. 76.

had practiced a kind of 'reading between the lines' in his earlier essay on 'The Moral Life in the Writings of Thomas Hobbes'.

In that essay, Oakeshott had raised the problem of how to account for the fact that in Hobbes's writings 'there appear (not side by side, but almost inextricably mixed) a theory of moral obligation at once original and consistent with the other philosophical novelties to be found in them, and another account of moral obligation the vocabulary and the general principles of which are conventional.'[27] For example, Hobbes 'uses the expression "natural laws" both when he means to denote the hypothetical conclusions of human reason about self-preservation and to denote obligations imposed by God upon all men except atheists(?), lunatics and children'. This struck Oakeshott as 'a manner of speaking which is almost a confession of a design to confuse.'[28]

The presence of these contradictory lines of argument would be explained, Okeshott argued, if it were the case that 'Hobbes's writings on civil obedience (and *Leviathan* in particular) may be taken to have a twofold purpose.' The first was 'an exercise in logic . . . appropriately conducted in the vocabulary which Hobbes had made his own.' The second was 'to show his contemporaries where their civil duties lay and why they lay there, in order to combat the confusion and anarchical tendencies of current thought and conduct.' This latter enterprise had to be 'framed in the idiom and the vocabulary of current political theory' to allow it to be 'assimilated to current prejudices about moral conduct.'[29]

Either we accepted this 'explanation of . . . important discrepancies in Hobbes's writings . . . in terms of artful equivocation', Oakeshott argued, or we were left with 'mere confusion'. The corollary of accepting it, however, is the view that Hobbes had both an 'esoteric' and an 'exoteric' doctrine, the latter for 'the ordinary man who must be spoken to in an idiom and a vocabulary he is accustomed to', and the former for 'the initiated (those whose heads were strong enough to withstand the giddiness provoked by his scepticism).' This argument is reminiscent of views Strauss had put forward in *Persecution and the Art of Writing*. There, Strauss had argued that philosophers were frequently driven to employ 'a peculiar manner of writing . . . to reveal what they regard as the truth to the few',

---

[27] *RP*, p. 333.

[28] *op. cit.*, p. 335.

[29] *Ibid.*, pp. 336–7.

distinguishing 'between the true teaching as the esoteric teaching and the socially useful teaching as the exoteric teaching'.[30]

While it would be wrong to number Oakeshott amongst the Straussians, as they have become known, Strauss's suggestion shows that the idea that a political philosophy may contain a 'hidden meaning' was not peculiar to him alone. In fact, Oakeshott thought that there were several other thinkers, including Plato, Machiavelli and Bentham, to whom this interpretation might reasonably be applied. For example, he came to think Bentham's philosophy 'so untidy, so riddled with inconsistencies and half-constructed arguments', that it was best to see it as the product of a 'designed untidiness' in which 'an elaborate philosophical facade' had been thrown over a 'pragmatic and empirical' defence of individualism.[31]

Although Oakeshott recognised that such explanations 'in the nature of the case . . . cannot be demonstrated to be true',[32] the important point is that he was willing to consider such an explanation at all. Of course, he did not believe that one should assume from the outset that a thinker had an 'esoteric' doctrine and that the task of interpretation was to recover this doctrine. He was no advocate of producing interpretations without an evidential basis — he inveighed against what he called 'the lunacy of decoding' or 'deconstructing' texts.[33] 'Reading between the lines' was justifiable only insofar as it contributed to the interpretative goal Nietzsche had laid down of 'understand[ing] an author better than he understood himself.'[34]

In this regard, it is important to observe that for Oakeshott, the use of a piece of evidence in one history does not exclude it from being used in others; the meanings of historical evidence are by their nature unquantifiable and inexhaustible, a corollary of the view that historical enquiry is inherently interminable. In an historical enquiry, 'every survival is a heterogenous object, without any exclusive reference or utterance.'[35] This does not mean, of course, that evidence is anything the historian wants it to be. Those survivals which are 'fragments of transactions in which their authors sought to satisfy their wants' belong to the 'mode . . . of present-future, and their

---

[30] Strauss, *What is Political Philosophy?*, p. 222.

[31] *MP*, p. 73.

[32] *RP*, p. 337.

[33] *VL*, p. 68.

[34] Oakeshott, Review of W.T. Jones, *Masters of Political Thought, Cambridge Journal,* vol. 1, 1948, p. 637.

[35] *OH*, p. 57

survival to occupy the present of historical discourse does nothing to qualify this mode'. So, a 'Minoan pot was made to cook a dinner or to carry water from the well, not in order to inform Sir Arthur Evans about a Minoan civilisation which has not itself survived', but Sir Arthur or anyone else may use the pot to aid in answering as many different historical questions as they can come up with about Minoan civilisation.

The view of the past implied in the historical present that the historian assembles, then, is of the past as a problem. This idea of the past, Oakeshott argued, may be contrasted with the remembered or recollected past. If we rack our brains for some precedent which could help us with our present problems, a precondition of this search is that the desired example is not itself problematic. The useful past cannot be more baffling than the present situation it is meant to illuminate or it will not be useful. In his seminar paper on 'Events', Oakeshott used the metaphor of the mirror image to describe the relation between the practical and the historical past; the two are exact opposites in the sense that the one presupposes a past which is precisely what is to be explained and the other a completely unproblematic past. It is the latter, the 'living' or 'didactic' past, which Oakeshott believed Bolingbroke's *Letters on the Study of History* had effectively addressed when the latter described history as 'philosophy teaching by examples'.[36]

The purpose of the distinction of the historical from the practical past remained unchanged; it was to protect the autonomy of historical knowledge from reduction to a pragmatic view of the past. In *On History* Oakeshott singled out Heidegger as an example of a holder of pragmatist views entailing the belief that there was only one kind of past and that this past was also the past known to historical enquiry. Three separate sets of notes on Heidegger amongst Oakeshott's papers suggest that he had *Being and Time* in mind.

Sein und Zeit, first published in 1927, included an account of 'Temporality and Historicality' which distinguished the same two meanings of history with which Oakeshott began *On History*. Heidegger wrote that an 'obvious ambiguity of the term "history"' resulted from the fact that 'this term may mean the "historical actuality" as well as the possible science of it'. In complete contrast to Oakeshott, however, he wished to 'eliminate' from his discussion 'the signification of "history" in the sense of a "science of history"'.' Heidegger dismissed the work of neo-Kantians such as Simmel and Rickert as

---

[36] Bolingbroke, *Historical Writings*, ed. I. Kramnick, Chicago UP, Chicago, 1972, p. 9.

'only aiming at the "epistemological" clarification of the historiological way of grasping things' and at understanding 'the logic with
which the concepts of historiological presentation are formed.' The
meaning of 'history' which Oakeshott devoted *On History* to discussing was the meaning of 'history' set aside by Heidegger in *Being
and Time*.

Heidegger was claiming, in effect, that historical study is justified
by the utility it has for our practical world. Later on in the same chapter of *Being and Time* he went on to discuss (and endorse) Nietzsche's
view of all historical study as justified only in the service of life. Consistently, he believed that history 'like any science, is . . . factically
dependent at any time on the "prevailing world view".' That is to
say, the historian in writing history cannot escape the presuppositions of the practical world he or she currently and contingently
inhabits. Oakeshott's complaint was that Heidegger's view of history led to 'history as enquiry' being entirely ignored, reducing historical writing to the circumstances of its production.[37]

Oakeshott's notes on Heidegger, as well as his published criticisms in *On History*, show him rejecting this elision of the distinction
between the practical and the historical past. To Heidegger, it was
impossible to escape the demands of what Oakeshott called the
practical realm. But for Oakeshott 'We may think historically only
when we bracket off our own *Dasein*'.[38] Heidegger's belief that history necessarily has 'an intrusive, qualifying component of an original practical understanding' was rejected as a category mistake.
Although the lawyer and the historian might use the same copy of
Magna Carta, for instance, the historical meaning of that document
cannot be 'discerned in and abstracted from' any meaning it might
have for our 'present future of practical engagement'. For
Oakeshott, it was logically impossible for objects of any kind to be
transferred from the world of practice to that of history because 'an
object constituted in terms of one set of conditions cannot itself be
transformed into an object which owes its character to a categorially
different set of conditions.'[39]

Nor, finally, could the writings of historians (or indeed, any theoretical or artistic productions) be reduced to functions of the various
practical contexts in which they were produced. Although 'every
engagement to understand' was 'a practical performance',
Oakeshott argued that history was not distinguished as a form of

---

[37] Heidegger, *Being and Time*, p. 430.

[38] Oakeshott, notes on Heidegger, LSE 3/5.

[39] *OH*, p. 24.

enquiry by such considerations. Historical enquiries take time, can be hindered by poor health and so on, but it is not in virtue of such considerations that they are recognisable as historical.

Oakeshott's and Heidegger's discussions of history both explicitly claimed to have been influenced by Dilthey. Heidegger claimed to be continuing the latter's work on a logic of the human sciences, including history. According to its author, the discussion of history in *Being and Time* was simply 'furthering [the] adoption . . . [of] the [pioneering] researches of Dilthey'. If Oakeshott did not see himself in quite this light, he nevertheless had a strong admiration for Dilthey; in the mid-1960s, he cited him (together with Hegel and Aristotle) as one of those from whom he had 'learnt most' – though he did also remark that 'no man who ever put pen to paper succeeded in being more obscure.'[40]

Their common acknowledgment of Dilthey as a predecessor should not conceal the fact that Oakeshott and Heidegger differed radically over his significance. Oakeshott wanted to amplify Dilthey's thesis that 'the human sciences form an independent whole alongside the natural sciences' with particular reference to historical enquiry. Heidegger, by contrast, was interested in the place of 'history' (Oakeshott's 'practical past') in the life-world. Consequently, Dilthey's 'psychological' work on subjects such as 'the perception of the external world'[41] interested him more than anything Dilthey had to say on the nature of historical enquiry. If anything, Heidegger remained truer to Dilthey than Oakeshott, for he, like Dilthey, separated history from natural science but not from the practical 'life-world'. By contrast Oakeshott's notes on Dilthey, also preserved at the LSE, show that he thought of himself as having gone beyond Dilthey in theorising the logic of historical enquiry. Dilthey's hermeneutics had come to rest at 'the reconstruction of a past historical situation as it occurred and was understood by those who participated in it'; he believed 'the business of the intellectual historian was to find out not what a man had thought, but what he had thought he thought.'[42] Oakeshott, by contrast, conceived of historians as aiming 'to uncover connections which were not observed at the time', and indeed could not have been observed at the time.[43]

[40] Oakeshott, 'A Reply to Professor Raphael', p. 90. Cp. Oakeshott, 'The Emergence of the History of Thought', p. 21.

[41] Cp. Dilthey, *Introduction to the Human Sciences*, pp. 354 ff.

[42] LSE 1/1/23, p. 21.

[43] Oakeshott, notes on Dilthey, LSE 3/3, p. 2.

We should not, however, make the difference between Oakeshott and Heidegger appear total. Oakeshott regarded Heidegger's description of the 'life-world' as unobjectionable provided it was taken for no more than an account of what he himself called 'a present-future of practical engagement'. Indeed, he appeared to sympathise in his notes with Heidegger's concept of *Angst*, assimilating it to his own sceptical account of 'the deadliness of doing'. *Angst* was the result not of 'a feeling of failure to achieve this or that, but the feeling that in every this or that there is failure even if there is achievement' — a feeling, he believed, from which impractical activities such as history offered at least temporary relief.[44] His complaint was that Heidegger took for an exclusive description of the past what was only an understanding of the past in terms of one 'conditional universe of discourse' or 'mode of understanding' amongst others, thereby threatening the autonomy of theoretical thought, including science and philosophy as well as history.

Unlike Heidegger, Oakeshott argued that although 'awareness of past' is a familiar experience, it is not an undifferentiated one. Certainly, we have a remembered past which is a component of our 'every-day experience'. Our memory gives us 'continuous and unsought access' to past, and in doing so provides us with continuity that is essential to personal identity. In addition, we may make a deliberate effort to remember. We do this when we try to recollect. Nevertheless, the historical past is not to be identified with either the remembered or the recollected past, both of which belong to the 'practical' self. To the historian, memories and recollections are simply further forms of evidence. The question for the philosopher of history is, 'How can I get to know and evoke a past which is not and never was my own? Or a past which is perhaps my own but the significance of which is not that it is my own ?'[45]

This way of describing the question which the philosopher of history asks explicitly allows the historian to figure in the historical past he relates. Pocock, however, has argued that Oakeshott will not allow this. Reviewing *On History*, he wished 'to enquire whether the relation between the "practical" and the "historical" modes may not be made to appear less exclusive.' Pocock wanted to defend the position that 'the historian may . . . find himself describing sequences of change which have a present tense, which are still going on in his own world and defining . . . the pursuit of practical objectives by

[44]   Oakeshott, notes on Heidegger.

[45]   Oakeshott, 'Present and Past', p. 4

himself and others.'[46] In other words, he wished to defend the claims of contemporary history.

In fact, Oakeshott's essay 'On the Activity of Being an Historian' had made the point that it was not at all logically impossible to write contemporary history, and there is nothing in *On History* to suggest that he had changed his mind on this question. His historian may indeed write history about a present of events which he may still be living through, or even, at the extreme, participating in. It was, however, circumstantially very difficult to do this. The reason concerns the kind of present the historian inhabits. Presumably, if I am to write the history of contemporary events in which I have taken part or at the extreme in which I am still taking part, Oakeshott's point is that I must alter my attitude to them just insofar as I am writing history.

In other words, as an historian I am no longer an actor but a critical spectator of the deeds of the recent past, even my own. The etymology of the vocabulary of 'theorising' which Oakeshott provided in *On Human Conduct* tends to reinforce this point. In Greek, a *theoros* or 'theorist' was 'a spectator concerned to follow and understand . . . a *thea* . . . a spectacle [or] a "going-on".'[47] This idea of the theorist as a non-participatory observer was reflected in the way in which Oakeshott regarded all theorising, including history and philosophy. When Pocock wrote 'There is really nothing sacrosanct about my practical objectives if they entail a presentation of history which can be shown to be either mythical or false', he does not seem to have appreciated that for Oakeshott 'my practical objectives' may make reference to the past but they can never 'entail a presentation of history', simply because 'history' in Oakeshott's sense is found only in history books, never in the practical, persuasive, discourse to which political speech, for example, belongs.

Pocock also claimed that Oakeshott's distinction of 'objects composing the practical present . . . defined by their use in a present-future of practical engagement' and objects 'composing the historians present defined as survivals from, and evidence of, a past or pasts . . . seems not to make much of the possibility that these are the same objects differently regarded'. On the contrary, the idea that 'the same' object may be viewed in more than one way, depending on whether it is viewed practically, historically or scientifically is crucial to Oakeshott's modal distinctions. The comparison of the

[46]   J.G.A. Pocock, Review of *On History*, *Times Literary Supplement*, 21 October 1983, p. 1155.

[47]   *HC*, p. 11.

practical use of Magna Carta as a source of analogies in a modern law court with its status as a piece of historical evidence addressed precisely this point.[48]

A related point, well made by Nardin, is that Oakeshott's theory explains how the works of historians are capable of mutual criticism. Gray's review of *On History* claimed that Oakeshott, lacking a criterion of truth, could not decide between conflicting accounts, so that 'we are unable to arbitrate between two coherent but incompatible pieces of historical reconstruction.'[49] As Nardin points out, in order for two historical narratives to be seen as incompatible in the first place, the Oakeshottian criterion of internal coherence within the world of historical understanding already has to have been applied. Gray's desire for 'an independent standard of historical truth to which our various accounts must correspond' is underpinned by nothing other than 'the same uncritical attachment to realism, with its definition of truth as correspondence' that Oakeshott had been hammering away at since *Experience and its Modes*.[50]

Occurrences and Situations

Oakeshott's aim in *On History* was to display the ideal stages through which historical reasoning moves, beginning with the unique character of the historical present and culminating with the construction of a passage of historical events. It should be stressed that, like Oakeshott's philosophy of civil association, which described not an actual state but an ideal mode of relationship, this movement from a present of historical survivals to a properly historical past was meant only to represent an 'ideal' process of historical enquiry. The mind of any particular historian might leap forward and backward between the various stages outlined, perhaps even omitting some of them.

In the first essay, Oakeshott had argued that a present-past composed of survivals may be seen as one of the presuppositions of a properly historical past. The historian begins in what he called a 'present-past' of performances, things done, which have survived in the form of artefacts. The first part of the second essay, on 'events', is devoted to explaining the transition from the present of historical enquiry to an historical past. What the historian must do first is 'distinguish and understand these performances in terms of their con-

---

[48]   *OH*, pp. 42–3.

[49]   Gray, *op. cit.*, p. 452.

[50]   Nardin, *op. cit.*, pp. 148–49.

nections with others to which they may be circumstantially related.' This involves two things.

Firstly, 'every such performance has a language'. A particular piece of evidence may be understood 'in terms of its subscription to a practice' or practices. In *On History*, as in *On Human Conduct*, 'practices' are seen on the analogy of languages, each with a 'vocabulary and syntax of its own'. So, Oakeshott acknowledged Pocock's identification of the 'language' of Harrington's *Oceana* as that of 'civic humanism' as an understanding of the book in terms of a 'practice'.[51]

Secondly, each piece of evidence is more than simply a subscription to a practice. For example, if it belongs to the practical mode, it is also 'a substantive action or utterance which belongs to a transaction and seeks a satisfaction, that is, a future', and must be understood 'in terms of . . . transactional relationships' with other performances. Again, we see the similarity between Collingwood's 'logic of question and answer' and Oakeshott's position. Both argued that we have a less than satisfactory understanding of a piece of evidence if we cannot see it as an action in response to certain other actions which itself invites a particular response. We may call this a variety of 'contextualism', provided we bear in mind that, for Oakeshott, the other performances to which we relate our piece of evidence 'are not the "scene" in which it took place, or the "background" against which it was performed . . . they are the conditions which constitute its character, just as it is amongst the conditions which constitute their characters'.[52]

In distinguishing the language of a piece of evidence, and the relation it has to other such pieces, the transition occurs. The initial investigation was concerned with the character of the pieces of evidence themselves, but in studying these it has been transformed into an investigation in which pieces of evidence become the basis of inferences 'about a past which has not survived', something about which the evidence as such can say nothing.[53] We have entered upon the construction of what Oakeshott called 'occurrences' or rudimentary historical 'situations'. Such 'occurrences' lie mid-way between a concern with fragments of present evidence and a past of historical events. An 'occurrence' is 'an anatomised fragment of past circumstances'. A 'situation' differs from an 'occurrence' in being made up of related occurrences; it is 'a composition of notionally contemporaneous, mutually related, historical occurrences.'

[51] *OH*, p. 50.

[52] *op. cit.*, p. 51.

[53] *op. cit.*, p. 52.

The titles of historical works, Oakeshott argued, may sometimes be recognisable as 'labels' identifying historical 'situations' of this sort. Macaulay on 'the condition of England in 1685', Namier's work on *The Structure of English Politics on the Accession of George III*, Stone's *The Family, Sex and Marriage in England 1500–1800*, and Braudel's *Mediterranean* could all be seen as pieces of historical writing which described an historical situation. Or, an example from an earlier paper, Maitland's sketch of English public law at the death of Henry VII could be seen, in a photographic metaphor, 'as one of a series of "stills"' to be found in his *Constitutional History of England*.[54] Oakeshott also applied the idea of a "situation" to intellectual history or the history of ideas. A *mentalité*, for example, designates a particular situation. Burckhardt's *Griechische Geist*, and presumably also his *Civilisation of the Renaissance in Italy*, are likewise labels for a situation. Of course, such situations 'are not, and do not purport to be, expressions which denote the self-understandings of persons who occupied these situations.'

One of the noteworthy features of these examples is the unfamiliar connections they allowed Oakeshott to make between historians. One does not normally associate Namier, the student of the micro-structures of eighteenth-century English politics, with Braudel, the historian of social and economic forces distributed over *la longue durée*. Yet here they can be seen as employing an identical structure for their work; differences in subject matter appear as inessential in relation to the common attempt to anatomise a frozen moment in time, of whatever duration. Moreover, the large claims made for both the Namierite and the Braudelian approaches seem somewhat exaggerated when seen in this light. Oakeshott's account of the logic of historical situations suggests that supporters of both Namier and Braudel took for the only legitimate form of historical writing what was only a particular form, and not even the most sophisticated form at that.

Historical occurrences and situations, Oakeshott argued, represent 'an unstable level of historical understanding'. They are unstable because they are relatively static. Both exclude change from their accounts while at the same time implicitly recognising it. For example, in acknowledging that a situation had a beginning and an end, it is admitted that it is 'evanescent', but this changefulness is excluded in the interests of intelligibility. 'The only change an historical situation . . . can accommodate is some minor shift in its tensions . . . .an historical enquiry thus oriented will be disposed to seek situations of

---

[54] Oakeshott, 'Change', LSE 1/1/26, p. 3.

almost structural immobility, and to find them either in situations so brief that they may be represented as in fact changeless, or else . . . in situations so extended and anatomised on so large a scale [*la longue dureé*] that they display almost "geological" stability.'[55] Thus, a 'situation' may be criticised in its own, historical, terms.

Relating Events

The kind of historical understanding which might supersede an understanding in terms of situations was an historical understanding in terms of 'events'. To begin with, an historical event is not simply 'a somewhat extended understanding of an historical situation'. The historian does not take an already understood situation and simply attach to it 'a past alleged to have promoted its appearance upon the scene'. Oakeshott gave the example of 'the abolition of the British slave trade'. This situation 'may . . . be made more intelligible by attaching it to a past which conceptually reflects this identification (a past composed of slavery, the trade, the activities of its opponents, etc.)'. However, this will not transform the occurrence into an event. That 'requires . . . the situation itself to be transformed by being understood as the outcome of an uncovenanted circumstantial confluence of vicissitudes which will certainly include events which had nothing to do conceptually with slavery or the trade.' Just as evidence is transformed when used to infer situations, so situations are transformed when they are used to infer events. Static situations become dynamic events.[56]

Like a situation, 'An historical event . . . is not an assignable performance and therefore it cannot be understood in terms of the intentions of a performer.' Unlike a situation, however, an event is not simply the interactions of people according to their diverse understandings of a shared context. Rather, it is concerned with 'the unintended eventual by-products of such transactional engagements . . . which may be understood in their relation to antecedent by-products of human engagements.' An historical event, then, is a situation that has been transformed by being 'understood in terms of the mediation of its emergence', or, what is the same thing, 'a past constituted not in terms of its situational immobility but of time and change.' Naturally, this immediately raises the question of the nature of the relationship between historical events.

[55]   *OH*, pp. 60–1.

[56]   *op. cit.*, p. 64.

There were certain relations which Oakeshott was adamant could not be considered to hold between historical events. The relationship of similarity or comparison has had a certain amount of popularity with historians; 'comparative' history is a familiar notion. Oakeshott did not want to deny that subject to certain conditions comparison of otherwise unrelated situations may be a 'valuable heuristic device'. He did not, however, wish to include comparison in the logic of historical enquiry as such. As we saw above with the example of the abolition of slavery, relationships of likeness between antecedent and subsequent events are no doubt observable, but it is not on account of such similarities that one event may be said to follow from another.

Nor is the relation between historical events 'correlative'. 'A correlation is a mutual relationship in terms of which dissimilars are observed to be linked in a certain (usually measurable) respect without there being any recognisable reason for this connection.'[57] So, H.T. Buckle observed a link between the price of corn and the number of marriages in a parish, but in itself this was not a significant relationship. Buckle had to transform this correlation into such a relationship by viewing it in terms of the cost of maintaining a household.

Oakeshott certainly thought it possible 'to anatomise an historical situation, to abstract quantified features from it and, if they were sufficiently numerous and plotted on a graph, to display the situation as structure composed of correlations.' However, 'cliometrics' of this sort could give 'no answers, although it might suggest interesting questions to pursue.' Moreover, although quantification may be useful in the study of historical situations, 'where the enquiry is concerned with events, the observation of correlations can have no place at all.' The relation of antecedent to subsequent which exists between historical events is excluded in correlations, which are mutually related.

Oakeshott's evaluation of the role of quantification in historical understanding looks exceedingly moderate when set against the outlandish claims sometimes made, for example, by more incautious members of the *Annales*. Le Roy Ladurie, for instance, wrote that 'history that is not quantifiable cannot claim to be scientific' and that by the 1980s 'the historian will be a programmer or he will be nothing.'[58] This wild exaggeration represents the crest of the great

---

[57]   *op. cit.*, p. 90.

[58]   Le Roy Ladurie quoted in L. Stone, 'The Revival of Narrative', *Past and Present*, vol. 85, 1979, pp. 5, 13.

wave of interest in social and economic history after World War Two, which was closely connected with quantificatory enterprises of the sort Oakeshott wished to put in theoretical perspective. As we saw earlier, Hempel's development of his 'covering law' theory had given new impetus to the idea that history uncovers 'causal' relationships after 1945. 'The controversies surrounding causative history . . . have proved to be one of the more marked continuities in the twentieth century philosophy of history.'[59] Murphy's remark in 1986 that the debate over Hempel's 'covering-law model [also known as the 'deductive-nomological'[60] theory of history] has not been resolved in forty years and it will not be resolved in the near future'[61] proved prophetic, for at the beginning of the twenty-first century, this kind of desire for 'scientific' history remained strong.[62]

In neither *On History* nor *Experience and its Modes* did Oakeshott suggest that historians should not use the word 'cause' to indicate a certain sort of significant relationship between events. In *On History* Oakeshott made it explicit that the occurrence of the word 'cause' in a piece of historical writing usually signified little more than either 'noteworthy antecedents', as he put it, or an attempt to relate actions to their outcomes in order to establish responsibility. The former was entirely unobjectionable; the latter represented a judicial or moral form of enquiry inappropriate to historical study. In neither case, however, was history confused with a natural science. That confusion again attracted most of Oakeshott's attention when discussing 'causality' in *On History*, where he examined the idea that historical events were related by 'causes' of the sort to be found in the natural sciences more closely than he had done previously.

Though not without a hint of mockery, Oakeshott argued far less stridently than he had done in *Experience and its Modes*. He now distinguished two rather different versions of the thesis that historians are interested in the detection of causal relations. In the first, an historical event was seen as an example of a general 'law'. In the second, an historical event is demonstrated to have been the effect of a 'cause'. In the first version of this claim, it is the discovery of the laws

[59]   C. Condren, *The Status and Appraisal of Classic Texts*, Princeton UP, Princeton, 1985, p. 129.
[60]   Gray, *op. cit.*
[61]   M.G. Murphy, 'Explanation, Causes and Covering Laws', *History and Theory (Beiheft)*, vol. 25, 1986, p. 56.
[62]   Nardin asserts, almost certainly correctly, that Oakeshott's 'view of historical explanation . . . is not the view . . . that most historians or philosophers of history hold' today. The most common model of explanation still 'relies on causality, as it is understood either in ordinary or scientific discourse'. See Nardin, *op. cit.*, p. 166.

behind the 'historical process' itself which is proposed. In other words, historical enquiry is said to proceed by understanding events as examples of general laws which it may also be the task of the historian to formulate. Here, the laws with which the historian must equip himself are the result of 'a procedure of examining (and perhaps comparing) a number of occurrences and situations and coming to perceive them as structures composed of regularities.'[63] This version of the thesis, it should be noted, is not narrowly tied to the idea of history as a natural science, as Oakeshott's examples illustrated.

Oakeshott took Trotsky's view that 'an historical work only completely fulfils its task when occurrences unfold themselves upon its pages in their full natural necessity' as a modern restatement of the Augustinian view of the past as a story of redemption culminating in the birth of Christ. The Trotskyite and Augustinian standpoints, however, were equally inadequate as philosophical accounts of historical understanding. Oakeshott did not deny that the 'laws' which may be abstracted from past survivals may be genuine laws, but he argued that if they were, by the same token, they could not be historical, because historical evidence is neither composed of models or examples, nor understood exclusively in terms of regularities. There was 'an unresolvable categorial distinction' between explanation in terms of laws and historical explanation.[64]

The second version of the claim that the relations between historical events are causal was 'more circumspect: it has nothing to say about an "historical process" or about "laws" of historical change'. Rather, it undertakes 'to spell out exactly the logical structure of causal explanation' and to show that historical enquiry has this logical structure. Here it was Popper and Hempel that Oakeshott had in mind.

According to Oakeshott, both thinkers identified three main elements to a causal explanation. These were, firstly, 'an observed object, identified in terms of its kind, whose existence is to be explained'. Secondly, 'some other observed objects, also identified in terms of their kinds'. Finally, 'a universal "law" (capable of being empirically falsified) which states that there is a constant, regular or systematic relationship between the existence of the kind of object whose existence is to be explained and the existence of these other kinds of objects, thus identifying them as its causal conditions and

[63]   *OH* , p. 75.
[64]   *loc. cit.*

allowing its existence not merely to be observed but to be deduced.'[65]

Oakeshott accepted this 'Popper-Hempel thesis' as an account of the logic of causal relationship, but he did not accept that it was an account of the relation between historical events. In fact, Popper distinguished history from the natural (and social) sciences because it was less interested in establishing law-governed causal relations between events than in the description of specific events.[66] As a description of Hempel's position, however, Oakeshott's account seems accurate. In order to apply this account of causality to historical understanding, Oakeshott argued, Hempel had to modify it.

This involved recognising 'the object whose existence is to be causally explained and the objects invoked as its causal conditions' as survivals from the past. These survivals were to be further identified in terms of their kinds and regarded as separated from one another by intervals of time of which 'causality itself knows nothing'. In addition, instead of attempting 'to deduce the existence of an already empirically observed kind of object by joining it to its causal conditions', the aim of causal explanation in historical enquiry is (in effect) to 'retrodict the occurrence of an already reported kind of happening by relating it to antecedent happenings recognised as its causal conditions, the premise of this recognition being an expressly or tacitly invoked universal "law".'[67]

Even when these modifications in the original account of causality have been made, however, Oakeshott still objected to the idea that historians are interested in causation in this sense as a denial of 'the elementary conditions of historical enquiry'. Since an historical enquiry understood as an enquiry into causes must begin with an empirically observable past, it must begin in a present of survivals from the past of the sort he had outlined in the first essay. 'But its alleged concern to explain the occurrence of such a "given" (survived) past would condemn it to the absurdity of explaining the survival (that is, the occurrence in the present) of these survivals.' To avoid this, causal explanation attempts to jump 'directly into a past which has not survived by beginning in a present of alleged informative statements reporting and asserting the occurrence of certain kinds of happenings.' This, however, was impossible.

It was impossible not only because the character of historical evidence was not what Hempel assumed it to be, but also because the

---

[65]   *OH*, p. 77.

[66]   K. Popper, *The Poverty of Historicism*, 2nd edn., Routledge, London, 1966, p. 144.

[67]   *OH*, p. 78.

events which compose the historical past were not 'already described and understood kinds of happenings' lacking 'only deductive proof of their occurrence'. Hempel had assumed a realist view of the past, with the consequence that the 'concern . . . to understand the character of a not yet understood passage of a past which has not survived . . . is dismissed as a nugatory engagement.' Instead, Hempel's model raised 'the occurrence of an alleged already described and understood kind of happening from the status of a report to that of a retrodicted necessity'. In other words, 'it assumes to be already known what it is the purpose of an historical enquiry to ascertain.'

Finally, rather than treating historical events as individual mixtures of genericity and particularity, Hempel's view of history as the search for causes is concerned 'only with the occurrence of happenings abstracted and identified in terms of their kinds'. Not only may a cause only be sought for 'an already known and understood effect', it may 'only be attributed to an abstraction: only an event of the kind E' may be said to be regularly accompanied by "events of the kinds C_1, C_2 etc".'

Oakeshott's final position on causality, then, was that the historian 'does not and cannot claim to be invoking any of the Aristotelian "causes" or the conceptions of causality argued by philosophers (like Leibniz) who have considered the matter: these are not relationships between events separated by an interval of time.'[68] He had identified that kind of relationship in *On Human Conduct* as a contingent relationship. There, contingency was described as a relationship of 'proximity and of "touch"'. It was an 'immediate relationship', in the sense that no law was required to relate the existence of an event to its causal conditions. Further, it was a 'circumstantial relationship . . . of evidential contiguity' in which the significant antecedents of an event 'impart not themselves but a difference'. As we saw earlier, this understanding in terms of contingent relationships shares certain characteristics with our ordinary understanding. Both may be described as a kind of 'event-making'. The events which are 'made' by historians, however, are distinguished by being in the past, and by being understood exclusively in terms of previous events.

On History pursued the idea that 'contingent' relationship is not a necessary relationship. It 'has no place for extrinsic general terms of relationship' of any sort. As a circumstantial relationship, it connects

---

[68] *op. cit.*, p. 85.

an event to those prior events which are 'significantly related to it, because, in touching, they impart not themselves but a difference'. It is not, however, an 'exclusive' relationship — 'antecedents are not absorbed in this subsequent' but 'remain eligible to be significantly related' to other subsequent events.[69]

Contingently related historical events, Oakeshott concluded, have 'no necessary character', each being a 'conflation of accessories' which themselves have 'no exclusive characters but are the difference they made in a convergence of differences which compose a circumstantial historical identity.' As Nardin observes, 'the concept of contingency is more precise than the concepts of "configuration" and "colligation"' proposed by Mink and Walsh to describe the relationship between historical events.[70] The 'configuration' of events, or their location within a larger pattern of events, and their 'colligation', or arrangement into a coherent account, are certainly part of the process of historical thought as Oakeshott described it. But neither concept is able to 'exclude the attempt to make sense of events by interpreting them in the light of subsequent events', a crucial error from the point of view of both *Experience and its Modes* and *On History.*

It is wrong to suggest that Oaksehott's historical, contingently related 'events' are the outcomes of an 'arbitrary' exercise.[71] There is nothing arbitrary about reasoning from evidence. When Oakeshott described the relation between historical events as contingent, he meant not that history was arbitrary but that it was 'conditional', in the sense that no piece of historical writing is capable of being a final or exclusive account. He did not mean that historians can write anything they like about the past, which would indeed be arbitrary. What is truly striking about his 'events' is not their arbitrariness but their linguistic nature; Oakeshott took his argument that the historical past exists nowhere save in historical works to its logical conclusion and treated historical events as semantic constructions.

There is, then, a great difference between the 'events' of historical and practical experience. Historical events are 'conclusions of enquiries . . . answers to historical questions about the past which admit of no other kind of answer.' By contrast, the 'events' of our practical experience belong or belonged to a sensible present; they may go on before our eyes. But it is never possible to witness historical events in

---

[69]   *op. cit.,* pp. 94–5.

[70]   Nardin, *op. cit.,* p. 163.

[71]   G. Leff, Review of *On History, English Historical Review,* vol. 100, 1984, p. 914.

the same way; they are the meanings in authentically historical narratives. *On History*, in effect, enlarged on Oakeshott's earlier argument that an historical event is one that never 'happened'. An historical event is not itself a 'happening' but a construction. Such constructed events 'could not have survived', for they were never 'there' to be observed in the first place.[72]

Change

The last of the three main postulates of historical enquiry which *On History* dealt with was 'change'. Change, Oakeshott argued, may be regarded as a presupposition of historical writing in the sense that an historical event is the outcome of other, previous events, and thus 'an historical enquiry invokes the idea of change'. There was, however, no such thing as 'change as such'. Just as he would admit no unqualified ideas of 'the past' or of 'events', he saw only different modes of change, each with 'its counterpart in a different mode of understanding the past'.[73] In particular, practical and historical modes of change were to be distinguished from one another, in the same way that practical and historical modes of present and past and practical and historical kinds of events had been distinguished in the preceding essays.

All change involves a paradox, Oakeshott argued, because in change 'the notion of alteration' is 'combined with the notion of remaining the same'. The idea of change most familiar to us and most frequently to be found in the practical world is 'that in which differences are attributed to something which itself remains unaltered'. For example, if I am asking for change for a sum of money, 'I shall expect to be given coins whose value is the same', and here 'the unaltered identity' is the value. In the practical world, change 'is a difference of place, time, use, order, colour, size, and so on, attributed to an unaltered identity.'[74] This was a useful idea of change, doubtless indispensable in our daily life. It was not, however, a suitable candidate for historical change.

In historical enquiry, we are dealing with 'A past composed entirely of historical events and their relations', and this is 'a past composed entirely of differences: it is a past from which . . . an unchanged identity' of the kind to be found in the practical idea of change 'has been expressly excluded'. It should be emphasised that

---

[72]   *OH*, p. 95.

[73]   *op. cit.*, p. 116.

[74]   *Ibid.*, p. 99.

'This does not mean that the components of an historically under-stood past are incessantly changing; nor does it mean that no recog-nition be given to relative durabilities.' What it does mean, however, is that 'the notion of historical change is not that of difference attrib-uted to some changeless item in the situation'.[75] We have seen that Oakeshott found Lovejoy's notion of a 'unit idea' unsatisfactory; the reason for his dissatisfaction was that such a concept seemed to imply that there were genuinely changeless components in an his-torical enquiry.

The exclusion of any of the Aristotelian causes from historical enquiry must necessarily exclude teleological change. The kind of change in which a potential becomes actual, in which a 'nature' is realised, is a 'genuine conception of change: there is difference and there is identity.' It could not serve as an historical conception of change, however, because 'instead of the identity being a separable item in the situation . . . it is an unchanging purpose or destiny which is present from the beginning, which determines the differences and their sequential succession, and which is achieved when the process of change is completed.'[76]

The idea of teleological change in historical enquiry was a notion Oakeshott had been critical of since his very earliest writings on the philosophy of history. In the 1920s, he had taken the 'historical' writ-ings of Hegel, Schlegel, and Spengler as examples of attempts to import teleological change into historical understanding. Spengler reappeared in *On History*, with Toynbee, Kant, St Augustine, and Trotsky, as examples of thinkers advancing teleological understand-ings of past events. Oakeshott was quite clear that all he was claim-ing was that these accounts of the past were not historical. For example, an historical past does not deny that the human race is embarked, as Kant thought, on a purposeful journey, but it does exclude such a view.

Organic change, in which a 'law or normality' provides the unchanging identity 'which specifies the general character of the dif-ferences and perhaps the order of their occurrence', was also rejected by Oakeshott as an account of the kind of change to be found in his-torical study. Evolutionary change, change in virtue of a 'law of development' is certainly open-ended change, involving no teleol-ogy, but 'the impossibility of distinguishing in an [historical] past an identity which even plausibly corresponds to an organic species, and the consequential impossibility of formulating an evolutionary

[75] *loc. cit.*
[76] *OH*, p. 102.

law in terms of which to understand the differences which compose a passage of historical change' meant that it must be set on one side.

What, then, is the kind of change which may be found in an historical enquiry? It has been noted that Oakeshott 'relies heavily upon Aristotle' for his account of change.[77] This might seem peculiar. After all, so far as we know, and excluding a few remarks like those in the *Poetics*, Aristotle never gave his attention to what we would call the logic of historical enquiry. Oakeshott, though, was not the only reader of Aristotle this century to find in him some implicit ideas about historicity. For Popper, 'historicist doctrines . . . directly follow from Aristotle's essentialism.' The 'historicist doctrines' Popper found in Aristotle, however, were clearly teleological. Popper believed, using an organicist metaphor of his own, that the consequences of this 'fertile' Aristotelianism 'were slumbering for more than twenty centuries' before they awoke once again in the philosophy of Hegel.[78] However, since Oakeshott had already excluded this teleological account of historical change from his view of historical change, the historicist doctrines which Popper found in Aristotle are of no help to us in understanding *On History*.

In fact, it was Aristotle's *Physics* which interested Oakeshott. Obviously, he was less concerned with exposing Aristotle's thought than with making use of it for his own ends. Provided we bear this in mind, however, it is interesting to see just what he made of Aristotle's ideas. He quoted the remark from Book V of the *Physics* that 'The continuous is a kind of contiguity . . . It is found in things whose nature is such as to make them one when they are in contact.'[79] Why should Oakeshott have found this of significance for the logic of historical understanding?

The answer is perhaps most clearly visible in his earlier paper on 'Change'. In that paper, Oakeshott had already begun to make use of what he called Aristotle's 'masterly review of different conceptions of change and identity'. In particular, he was interested in the view that 'A succession of occurrences . . . may be recognised to be "change" if it is continuous and solely in virtue of its continuousness. That is, "continuity" of change is itself a form of identity or sameness.' Since Aristotle thought this continuity to be a kind of con-

---

[77]   D. Boucher, Review of *On History*, *History of Political Thought*, vol. 5, 1984, p. 165.

[78]   Popper, *The Open Society and its Enemies*, vol. 2, pp. 7–8.

[79]   Oakeshott appears to have been quoting *Physics*, 227a10 ff.

tiguity, 'There is continuity "when the edge of one thing touches the edge of another without interval, and they hold together".'[80]

Oakeshott stressed that such continuity was not to be confused with simple succession. 'What constitutes continuity as a special type of "contiguousness" is not merely that two things touch one another edge to edge without interval, but that they "hold together" when they touch.' As Oakeshott read Aristotle, it was 'the character of the things concerned' that determined whether, in touching, these things also 'held together' to form an identity.[81] Aristotle's discussion of change, however, was conducted 'in the language of physics'. In order to be of use for the philosophy of history, Oakeshott thought it necessary to 'translate it into the language of time — a translation Aristotle did not himself make. "Occurrences" must be substituted for "things"'. When this was done, he argued, we find that 'A following-on of "occurrences" may be recognised to have an identity, and thus to be an example of "change", if they are shown to follow one another without interval . . . .and if they are such that when they touch one another they "hold together", each with the next, in such a way as to compose a recognisable "one", an intelligible "event"'. In other words, we may recognise an historical change as such 'simply in virtue of the alteration being continuous or uninterrupted'.[82]

An historical past 'cannot be recognised as a passage of change' simply because it resulted in a certain outcome. No outcome can 'be known in advance of its antecedents being assembled and . . . like its alleged antecedents, is itself only another difference.'[83] This is because 'An historian is never in a position to look back from an already understood historical situation and to conclude what must have been its components or significant antecedents.'[84] We are already familiar from *On Human Conduct* with the argument that the kind of relationship between historical events is a contingent relationship, a relationship of immediate contiguity. It is precisely this continuity or contiguity, Oakeshott argued in *On History*, that provides the sameness or identity necessary to historical change.

On Human Conduct and *On History* were more forthcoming both on the relation between historical events and on the nature of historical change than *Experience and its Modes* had been. Yet the idea that

---

[80]   *OH*, p. 113.

[81]   Oakeshott, 'Change', pp. 11–12.

[82]   *op. cit.*, p. 13.

[83]   *OH*, p. 113.

[84]   *op. cit.*, p. 95.

historical change derives its identity simply from its continuity can be seen as an expression in other terms of the view advanced in 1933, that the historian explains change by giving a full account of it. The identity of 'an assemblage of historical differences' is to be found 'in its own coherence; that is, in its character as a passage of differences which touch and modify one another and converge to compose a subsequent difference.'[85]

This relation of touching, of course, was the contingent relationship Oakeshott described in his discussion of historical events. It is perhaps worth re-stating that this was not a 'merely fortuitous or accidental relationship'. To see it as such is possible 'only at the cost of its rationality'.[86] Nor is it a 'conceptual' relationship. The historical past, which is a 'continuity of heterogenous and divergent tensions', is not a past in which events are understood by relating them to events of similar kinds.

Oakeshott's considered view of historical understanding was that it supplies 'a past understood in terms of its past'. The historian 'infers a past of which there can be no record and one necessarily unknown in default of such an enquiry.'[87] The lack of such an understanding may not be consequential, in the sense that the historical past is 'useless' and even liable to mislead as a source of advice about what to do. Yet these are not grounds for arguing that the practice of historical enquiry and the products of such enquiry are without value. All historians have, on Oakeshott's view, are 'shapes of [their] own manufacture . . . something more like a tune than a neatly fitted together, solid structure.' But this should not be mistaken for a belief that historical enquiry is of no account. The music of Clio is available nowhere else.

The History of Thought and the History of Political Thought

The three essays Oakeshott published in *On History* do not exhaust the questions he discussed at the LSE seminar. It is clear from his opening statement in a version of 'Present and Past', dated 1973, 'We are setting out to make a study of historical writing about political thought', that he conceived the published essays as part of a larger investigation. In fact, he was concerned not just with the history of political thought, but with the more general topic of the history of

[85] *op. cit.*, p. 114.
[86] *HC*, p. 102.
[87] *OH*, p. 63.

thought at large, as two unpublished papers make clear.[88] The first, on 'The Emergence of the History of Thought', dates from the later 1960s; the second, on 'Political Thought as a Subject of Historical Enquiry', from 1979-80. Much has been made of the importance of these seminars; M.P. Thompson, for example, believes that the conclusions which emerged from the several seminars Oakeshott gave on the latter subject were 'quite devastating for any engagement with a general history of political thought.'[89] However that may be, they fit very neatly together; both belong to the final phase of his thought on historical understanding, and by concluding with a discussion of them, we may get a better idea of how Oakeshott conceived the context and importance of his own work.

The first paper addresses the way in which the enterprise of intellectual history emerged out of a 'concern to establish and to explore a past relationship for a present understood in terms of intellectual engagement and achievement.' Over the last several hundred years of European history, Oakeshott contended, every discipline, be it physics or history, had constructed a 'practical' past for itself. Every one of the human and natural sciences had had its own pantheon of founders, of heroes and villains, fools and saviours; and the aim of such versions of the intellectual past was to be useful, like any other kind of practical past. When in his *Physics* 'Aristotle gives some account of the ideas of his predecessors', he was 'locating himself, identifying himself and his own enterprise by evoking an intellectual past, an epic of physical speculation, to which he as a physicist claims to belong.'[90]

What Oakeshott had once called 'ideology', and later came to think of as 'myth', was essential to society; it allowed the existence of a popular self-understanding. This phenomenon was replicated within each intellectual community, where such myths gave 'authority and confidence' to its undertakings. 'Spratt's *History of the Royal Society* is a story of doings, of the circumstantial encounters of enquirers in which they lay before one another their "finds" . . . a lineage of performances and performative utterances', just as 'The understanding of ourselves offered us in the writings of Karl Marx, no less than that presented in Otto of Freising's *Chronicle of the Two*

---

[88] Oakeshott appears to have taken the 'history of ideas', 'intellectual history', *Kulturgeschichte*, and *Geistesgeschichte* as synonymous.

[89] Thompson, *op. cit.*, p. 106.

[90] Oakeshott, 'Emergence of the History of Thought', pp. 1, 5.

Cities or in the writings of Joachim of Fiore, is in terms of a past composed of symbolic events.'[91]

The construction of such a 'practical' past for an intellectual discipline might seem to be less of a pressing need than in the case of a political movement, because beliefs, theories, ideas, and so on 'are self-sustaining or self-defeating in a way in which actions are not.' A theory can be proved true or false, but action always remains evanescent even when successful. Moreover, whereas a past of events is in some way indispensable to self-understanding, a past of beliefs is arguably less so. Even a philosopher, however, may wish to express his pride in the intellectual achievements of his predecessors, as Plutarch did in his *Lives*.

Throughout most of European history, moreover, there have been 'whole generation[s] of associates . . . disposed to self-recognition in . . . intellectual terms.' As Oakeshott saw it, there had been three notable attempts since the fifteenth century by intellectuals to seek 'the confirmation of their identity in a past of a corresponding character'. The first was developed by the Humanists, 'the beneficiaries of a slowly accumulated intellectual estate', who found a mirror of the new self-confidence of the Renaissance in their vision of the ancient world. Both the humanists and the Protestant Reformers saw antiquity 'as a dazzling world of intellectual achievements', and 'the centuries which intervened . . . as an age of darkness, ignorance and intellectual corruption . . . which must be swept away if the human race was to tread once more the path of truth.'[92]

In the seventeenth century, a new legend of Europe's intellectual past emerged, the product of the controversy between the ancients and the moderns. This was the 'Baconian' vision of the past. Suited to 'a generation . . . completely absorbed in the absolute novelty and fruitfulness of its own methods of enquiry', it saw the past in an even more negative light than the humanists had done. Although 'a complete absence of intellectual debts' was an impossibility, the Baconians did their best to reject their medieval heritage and convince themselves of their own absolute originality. For them, the past was 'a legend of simpletons among whom Aristotle was *simplicissimus*'. In seeing the past in this way they produced 'a reversal of convention which displayed a breath-taking touch of genius' by seeing 'the "modern" age, the current world', and not the ancient

---

[91] *op. cit.*, p. 4.

[92] *op. cit.*, pp. 6, 8. At this point the latest version of the manuscript ends. The following references are to an earlier manuscript version, the first half of which appears sufficiently similar to the surviving text of the later version to justify treating the second half of it as at least very close to what would have been said.

world, as the one which 'supplied mankind with its intellectual heroes'.[93]

The third and final legend of the past Oakeshott discussed was the product of the Enlightenment. We observed earlier, in relation to Marx, how views of the past Oakeshott regarded as unhistorical tended to be held by those with whose political theories he also disagreed. The same point is made here in relation to the *philosophes*. He regarded their Enlightened view of the past as closely related to the Baconian version; the aim of much of their interest was to allow themselves 'to celebrate more confidently the novelty and superiority of their own achievements, and to win an intellectual identity for themselves by placing their own gigantic activities in an appropriate context'. This was not, however, the whole story. Within Enlightened intellectual culture, there was some recognition 'of the intellectual struggles of men . . . trying to hold back the tide of error and superstition', and even of 'the whole intellectual past [as] a single, often slow and uncertain, but progressive movement towards the glories of Enlightenment'. Lessing, for example, understood the past as '*die Erziehung der Menscheit* — "the education of mankind"', a process in which 'the man of the Enlightenment' could recognize himself 'as a graduate'. Turgot, Voltaire, Kant, and Condorcet also subscribed to similar views.[94]

Oakeshott believed this Enlightened legend of the intellectual past to be still current; perhaps rather harshly, he instanced C.P. Snow's *The Two Cultures* as 'a composition based upon some of its cruder themes'. There were those who had kicked against it; notably, he thought, Joseph de Maistre. In this context, however, its main importance was that, like the humanist and Baconian legends, it 'generated an enhanced awareness of an intellectual past' which could be regarded as authentically historical.[95] While none of the pasts these three great intellectual movements created were historical in themselves, their activities contingently promoted the development of an understanding of the past that was.

The legendary intellectual past of the European Enlightenment had told the story of a unilinear process, embodied in the deeds of 'a single hero — "the Human Mind", or "Human Reason", a unique changeless identity, like that denoted in the parallel expression "Human Nature"'. This hero leapt from peak to peak in a series of

---

[93]　*op. cit.*, pp. 9–10.

[94]　*op. cit.*, pp. 11–13.

[95]　*op cit.*, pp. 13–16. These pages appear to constitute Oakeshott's only discussion of de Maistre in his writings, published or unpublished.

miraculous leaps, with no attention being paid to the land between them, or the geology of the terrain over which he moved. All of these notions had to change in order for intellectual history as we have it today to emerge. Oakeshott thought it characteristic of these early attempts at the history of philosophy that 'philosophers were distinguished from one another, not in respect of their problems, but merely in respect of the answers they give to perennial problems.'[96]

Oakeshott singled out Hegel's *History of Philosophy* as particularly important in promoting change, though he conceded Vico and the Scottish, as distinct from French, Enlightenment, had already played a significant part. Hegel recognised that in intellectual history 'the questions being asked, as well as the answers, change', and that from this point of view there was no such thing as mere 'error'. The past is one in which every 'intellectual adventure provokes another and in which adventures turn out to be either more or less fruitful'. There is development, but not teleological development, or a scheme imposed from without; instead, 'the starting point of one thinker is [seen as] the point to which an earlier thinker had brought a particular enquiry'. Oakeshott remarked that this point of view is 'perhaps, not quite "history"; but it is certainly not the legend of the Enlightenment of the Baconians or of the "humanists"'.[97]

Savigny and his followers, Oakeshott believed, had attempted something similar in the field of law. But before this new historical perspective could become more than the preserve of the specialist, the 'intellectual past had to be released from its servitude to the current intellectual condition of Europe'. The idea of the march of mind had to be replaced by 'Men thinking in specific, local intellectual circumstances'. Moreover, the materialistic metaphor which attributed 'solid, timeless characters' to ideas, treating them 'as quasi-physical objects, inherited, passed on, possessed or rejected', had to be replaced by an understanding of them as 'thoughts capable only of provoking thought'. The truth or falsity of the events of intellectual history needed to be regarded as an irrelevance; instead, 'the intellectual adventures of mankind had to be understood in terms of Lessing's maxim — as each man saying what appears to him to be true and leaving truth itself safely in the hands of God.'[98]

The single most important change, however, was the recognition that the historian does not have direct access to thought itself. The

[96] *op. cit.*, pp. 17–18.

[97] *op. cit.*, p. 19.

[98] *op. cit.*, pp. 19–20.

thoughts of the past have to be created, like any other historical event, through the use of evidence such as 'pieces of writing, sermons, prayers, speeches, proceedings in courts of law, rituals, works of art, compositions, buildings, institutions, accounts of actions' and so on.[99] Only when all these changes had taken place did Oakeshott think that history as we have it today, the discipline on which his own works, including the first three essays of *On History*, were a meditation, had appeared.

Oakeshott regarded all that he had to say on the history of thought as applicable to the history of political thought in particular. 'Political Thought as a Subject of Historical Enquiry' began where 'The Emergence of the History of Thought' ended, by outlining 'The formal characteristics of a subject of historical enquiry'. Any historical subject belongs not merely to a specifiable place and time, but to a context, and is 'recognised not merely to have occurred but to have come into being and to be an outcome or event.' The subject of historical enquiry is 'to be understood in terms of the changes which made its eventuality', that is, 'other and antecedent events' to which it is related on the basis of evidential continuity. In other words, the subject in historical enquiry is a contingent outcome, and this excludes viewing it as the effect of a cause or causes, as an actualised potential, and so on.[100]

As he had done ever since *Experience and its Modes*, Oakeshott insisted that even the starting place of an historical enquiry presupposes some criticism or judgement. In 'the first stage in an historical enquiry' the historian is offered an identity which is simply 'recognised in terms of some distinguishing marks'. These are usually little different to the 'marks of identity used in common discourse'. For example, 'an historian of the exploration of Africa will not be expected to identify either "exploration" or "Africa" in other than the commonly accepted terms.' Writing about African exploration may of course involve the historian in making some distinctions 'not always observed in common speech'; between, for example, 'travellers, traders, prospectors, missionaries, and explorers properly speaking', but on the whole these identities need little transformation or 'translation' from ordinary speech in order to be historically serviceable.[101]

---

[99] *op. cit.*, p. 20.

[100] Oakeshott, 'Political Thought as a Subject of Historical Enquiry', LSE 1/1/27, pp. 1–2.

[101] *op.cit.*, p. 3.

Sadly, however, the historian's task is not always so straightforward. Some subjects of historical enquiry, Oakeshott argued, may prove more ambiguous than others. For example, 'education . . . although it is pointed to in an expression of ordinary discourse, is nevertheless dreadfully indistinct and notably ambiguous.' Education as such is an identity 'without a context to bring it down to earth and locate it', and the historian 'may be expected to stay away from it as something quite unmanageable, saying perhaps "I can identify 'English grammar schools in the sixteenth century', 'the cloister schools of the Carolingian Empire' . . . .or 'the education of a Mandarin in Confucian China' — none of these require me to identify 'education'. But if you want from me a history of 'Education', where do I begin?"' This identity, in other words, carries within itself no particular time or place to which it is tied.[102]

Such a problem, Oakeshott argued, arose whenever the historian was faced by an inherently 'speculative and uncertain' term like 'education'. He offered a comparison with the problems faced by a historian of literature interested in '*die Novelle*', a literary genre which emerged in early nineteenth-century Germany. The simple fact that certain authors announced their works as *Novellen* was 'insignificant'; an historically useful identity requires 'some recognisable marks of identity' and 'this identity cannot be determined by inspecting pieces of writing unless we know already what we are looking for, and an historian cannot merely stipulate an identity in terms of arbitrarily chosen marks of recognition.' Yet at the same time the historian of *die Novelle* needs an identification of his subject which is flexible enough to recognise that 'a piece of writing may have some but not all (these marks of identity) and still be recognisable as a *Novelle*'. Most of all, the identity must be one which can accommodate change, 'For, whatever else it is, *die Novelle* for a literary historian is something on the wing; it is something that . . . changes.'[103]

'The predicament of an historian of . . . "political thought"', Oakeshott went on, was 'more severe than that of any other historian.' 'Political thought' was even more difficult to translate into a fit identity for historical enquiry than 'education' or *die Novelle*. He set about establishing the point by analysing the titles of some of the works on the history of political thought which had appeared on his LSE reading list; Sinclair's *A History of Greek Political Thought* and Allen's *A History of Political Thought in the Sixteenth Century*.

[102] *op.cit.*, pp. 3–4.
[103] *op.cit.*, pp. 4–5.

Sinclair's use of 'Greek' presented no difficulties; it refers to a language and to a rough geographical area. 'Sixteenth Century' is likewise transparent; it allows us immediately to identify a passage of
time. 'Political thought', however, was 'the main identifying mark'
in both titles; it is 'the chief indication of the something the historian
has distinguished and proposes to explore', and at the very least 'it is
an announcement of a concern with "intellectual history" — a history of man thinking.' But what, in detail, should we understand by
it?[104]

The expression 'political thought' is 'composed of an adjective
purporting to qualify a noun.' In this sense it is comparable to such
expressions as 'Christian theology, Cartesian philosophy, Newtonian physics, Greek medicine', but Oakeshott found it vaguer than
these. 'The noun "thought" is woefully imprecise when compared
with the words "theology", "philosophy"' and so on, and 'the adjective "political" does little to alleviate the mystery; it is dreadfully
vague when compared with the words "Christian", "Cartesian",
"Newtonian".' Although 'politics' and 'thought' are identities
which are common in ordinary speech, if the historian simply
accepts them in the form they are offered, as 'Africa' was accepted,
confusion will be the likely result.[105]

It is not that we cannot recognise a politician or distinguish political utterances from other kinds of utterance; Oakeshott believed that
'in general we have a not wholly unreliable set of marks of identity to
distinguish "politics".' Nor is what is meant by 'thought' totally
obscure. In common parlance, 'thought' may at least be taken to
exclude 'merely physical movements or organic impulses, and . . .
natural objects as such'. It is still 'vague and informal'; it may refer to
'sentiments, beliefs, opinions, doubts, visions, exclamations, ideas,
systems of ideas, doctrines, manifestoes, propositions, ideologies,
guesses, arguments, scientific theorems, designs, plans, ideals,
wants, intentions, etc — in short mental dispositions, constructions
and exploits of all kinds, usually expressed in words.' The 'rough
identifications of "political" and "thought" which common discourse has to offer' were not worthless.[106]

Oakeshott thought that historical works had actually been
attempted on something like this basis, using only these ordinary
identities. He gave as an example Sabine's *A History of Political Theory*. While Sabine had not been 'totally indiscriminate' in what he

[104] *op.cit.,* pp. 6–8.

[105] *op.cit.,* pp. 8–9.

[106] *op.cit.,* pp. 9–10.

had included, his work was 'always on the verge of disintegration'; his book 'contains pretty well everything that has ever entered anybody's head' on every subject that could conceivably have ever had anything to do with 'political thought', 'from Nominalism to the price of bacon.' There was simply no way that 'an intelligible continuity of historical change' could be detected in a work structured on such premises.[107]

To go to the opposite extreme, however, and make concepts or definitions of 'politics' and 'thought' the subjects of historical enquiry, a solution Oakeshott believed Dilthey had suggested, was equally unsatisfactory. If 'politics' was defined, for the sake of example, as 'the authoritative allocation of values in a society', then the task of the historian is 'to turn over the records of human thought looking for beliefs, opinions, doctrines, dreams . . . and adventures concerned with . . . the authoritative allocation of values in a society.' Similarly, if we define 'thought', we might come to 'the conclusion, which Skinner and some other historians of political thought seem to have reached, namely that all political thought is necessarily ideological thought: propositions and arguments designed to justify and make respectable the pursuit of the satisfaction of "political" wants.' However we choose to define our terms, we will find we have 'taken the wrong road'.[108]

Oakeshott believed historical enquiry presupposes the attempt 'to understand and display an intellectual situation in terms of the antecedents which made it historically what it was, which converged to constitute its historical character'. However, 'when this intellectual situation is conceptually defined, the only relevant antecedents will be those which are conceptually affiliated to it. And in place of a passage of intellectual change composed of contingently related intellectual events', we 'will have only a changeless situation surrounded by other situations recognised solely in terms of their approximation to or divergence from it.'

Ever since he had first reviewed it in 1934, Oakeshott had believed Gierke's *Natural Law and the Theory of Society* illustrated this defect. Gierke had taken Althusius' idea of contractual government as an 'ideal model', so that 'The writers before Althusius were taken to be trying but failing to achieve what Althusius had achieved; and the writers who came after were considered only according to how closely they adhered to the model contract theory in all its logically necessary parts.' By contrast, an authentically historical account

[107] *op.cit.*, p. 10.
[108] *op.cit.*, p. 12.

would have moved from the observation that there were 'a number of writers using the language of contractualism' to asking what each individual author was 'trying to do with this language and why?' Gierke's definition had ensured he 'could only see ... writers circling round this single ... concept of a contract of government.'[109]

'Political thought', then, does not itself identify 'a separable and coherent continuity of intellectual change'. To treat it as if it did so will leave us with nothing better than 'scrap-books of deceptively similar intellectual adventures'. Oakeshott went so far as to advise his audience to forget the expression altogether – 'it has become a portmanteaux expression meaning next to nothing.'

Did Oakeshott's final comments on writing the history of political thought imply a radical scepticism about the enterprise itself? We have seen that his own later reflections on the history of political thought were tinged with a certain pessimism. Did he arrive at a similar position with respect to historical enquiry? The answer must be in the negative. Oakeshott did not come to think there was nothing to be done other than to simply give up trying to write history about past politics. Although he thought that his reflections and the efforts of past historians had shown that there was no resolution to the 'predicament' of writing 'the history of political thought' as such, he held that it was at least possible to 'avoid [this predicament] in some intellectually respectable manner.' Consequently, he concluded by suggesting several ways in which historical writing about politics might be organised so as to avoid both the vagueness of ordinary notions of 'politics' and 'thought' and the ahistorical rigidity of definitions. The various approaches he explored were all ones he believed historians had actually employed. They are worth noticing, however, for they constitute a rare foray into 'methodology'.

Firstly, one might concentrate on a single text or a closely related group of writings and attempt 'to understand ... its various ideas, arguments and manners of argument as an example of a man thinking in the exact continuity of intellectual change which it itself demands in order to be historically understood.' This is nothing other than an elaborate statement of what is involved in understanding 'texts in context'. Gewirth's work on *Marsilius of Padua* or Dietze's history of *The Federalist*, for example, did not ask 'Is this a piece of political thought'; they restricted themselves to asking 'what are these writers thinking about and how did they come to be thinking about it ?' We might say that this is the approach Oakeshott had taken to Hobbes.

[109] *op.cit.*, p 12–13.

Secondly, rather than fixing on a single text, one 'might identify a continuity of intellectual change in terms of a theme or a doctrine'. Such a 'theme' might be difficult to identify, but a definition of politics will be no help. Cohn's *Pursuit of the Millennium*, 'a sixteenth century chapter in the history of gnostic belief', and Letwin's *The Pursuit of Certainty* were two works 'concerned with a continuity of intellectual change specified in far more direct, exact and local terms than any concept of "politics" suggests.'

Thirdly, the historian might 'identify his continuity of intellectual change in terms of an argument or a passage of an extended argument; that is, assignable writers addressing themselves to the exploration of a common problem.' Oakeshott believed Pocock had done this in *The Ancient Constitution and the Feudal Law*. As another example, he cited Shapiro's 'study of nineteenth century Russian writers concerned with what they identify as the "autocracy" of the Tzars', which 'does not seek a well-grounded concept of autocracy [but] is concerned only with how these writers use the word.' This may also be recognised as the approach employed in *On Human Conduct*, where Oakeshott dealt with the 'common problems' of identifying the character of a state and the office of government.

What all these kinds of historical writing about politics shared was the absence of a need for 'any general identification of "the political", much less a concept of "politics".' Oakeshott did not intend them to be exhaustive classifications; one would hardly expect him to, given his insistence on the problematic, ambiguous, and indeterminate quality of words like 'politics' and 'political'. What is important about Oakeshott's suggestions is that they are evidence of his belief that historical writing about politics, however understood, could be successfully carried on in a variety of ways. He never diverged from his earliest thoughts on the inappropriateness of prescribing a single style of writing history. Nor did Oakeshott's last thoughts on the possibility of writing about 'the history of political thought' involve him in any pyrrhic varieties of scepticism. Historical writing may be difficult, but was manifestly not impossible.

Conclusion

We began with the view of Oakeshott as a Tory propagandist, a common assessment of his work by critics in the 1960s and 1970s. We saw that this verdict was being revised in the 1980s and 1990s, when those outside Oakeshott's immediate circle began to regard him as a major political philosopher. Although welcome, this reassessment did not go far enough. Recent students of Oakeshott's ideas had changed their opinion of his writings on politics, but had continued to concentrate on these at the expense of his other works, particularly those on history. After following the development of Oakeshott's philosophy of history and his ideas on the history of political thought from their inception to their final formulation, we may say with some certainty that he has little place in the history of twentieth-century British politics. Despite the claims of *Le Figaro* and *The Times*, evidence of Oakeshott's influence on government and practical politics has yet to emerge. He finds his true place in the intellectual rather than the political sphere. In this concluding section, it is appropriate to review his work on history and to ask which elements of it have endured. We will begin with his writings on the history of political thought and then turn to his views on historical enquiry.

Oakeshott's work on Europe's political past contained two unifying themes — the history of 'character' or morals and the history of liberal thought and practice. Both of these were present in his writings before World War Two, as we saw in chapter one. However, as chapters three and five made clear, both themes underwent considerable transformations during his time at the LSE, and again in his retirement.

To take the history of morals first, we saw in chapter one how Oakeshott began by analysing the characters of particular historical and fictional individuals. In the 1930s, he began to make explicit the connection between the *personae* of his various characters and differ-

ent kinds of government. Chapter three showed that this linkage
was greatly reinforced in the 1940s and 1950s. In the 1940s, for example, he argued that Hobbes's *Leviathan* was a philosophical account
of the kind of state most suited to the character of the 'individual'
typical of the Renaissance and early modern periods. The Germans,
by contrast, had given themselves up to slavish domination, in a
manner not dissimilar to, though more brutal than, the kind of government envisioned by Rationalism. These contrasts were broad-
ened and formalised into the contention that there were two
opposing conceptions of the proper office of government corresponding to the contrast between the two main types of personality
visible in European history. In his retirement, this position was
stated in terms of an opposition, discussed in chapter five, between
'individuality' and 'anti-individuality' which Oakeshott suggested
was characteristic of the entire post-medieval period.

The second theme, the history of liberal political thought and
practice, underwent a similar broadening of scope over the years. In
chapter one, we saw that before 1939 Oakeshott regarded liberalism
as a phenomenon post-dating the French revolution of 1789. In the
twentieth century, it had become one of a number of competing 'ideologies' including communism, fascism and national socialism.
Chapter three described his post-World War Two work on Hobbes
which persuaded him that the author of *Leviathan* was a liberal *avant
la lettre* with a political philosophy which reconciled law, liberty and
authority. In his last writings on liberal thought and practice, dealt
with in chapter five, he claimed to detect the principles which
remained characteristic of modern liberalism even earlier than the
seventeenth century, in medieval *societates*.

For the sake of clarity, let us maintain this separation of the two
themes of the history of morals and the history of liberalism and
assess each in turn, beginning with the former. Oakeshott's history
of morals made much of the medieval origins of the morality of modern individualism. This certainly connects him to contemporary
debates, for the question 'Did the twelfth century discover the individual?'[1] is still being asked. Those who defend the idea of medieval
individualism still complain that most non-medievalists 'commonly
understand medieval people to be little more than automatons:
slaves to oppressive norms . . . medieval man . . . is . . . the person we
can congratulate ourselves on having transcended'.[2] Whatever the

[1]   C.W. Bynum, 'Did the Twelfth Century Discover the Individual ?', *Journal of
       Ecclesiastical History*, vol. 31, 1980, pp. 1–17.
[2]   W.I. Miller, 'Deep Inner Lives, Individualism and People of Honour', *History of
       Political Thought*, vol. 16, 1995, p. 191.

faults of Oakeshott's historical analysis, his emphasis on the continuity between the medieval and the modern eras at least allowed
him to avoid this crude view of medieval people.

Oakeshott's belief that European politics could be seen as the
product of a tension between two opposed types of character is not
as unusual as it might appear at first. Berlin, for example, suggested
that the history of political ideas in the twentieth century reflects two
conflicting notions of human nature, namely a belief in natural
human goodness and a belief in human imperfection.[3] Nevertheless,
it is difficult to regard this proposition as unambiguously historical.
It has a poetic quality and it may not be coincidental that Oakeshott's
opposition of the characters of the 'individual' and the 'anti-individual' resembles William Blake's idea that 'two classes of men are
always upon the earth, and they should be enemies: whoever tries to
reconcile them seeks to destroy existence'.[4]

We saw in chapter five that historians in the twentieth century
have paid considerable attention to moral phenomena such as 'individualism', but that they have not usually done so in terms of 'character'. In approaching the history of morals in this fashion,
Oakeshott regarded himself as reviving an approach more familiar
to preceding centuries. For example, he claimed that his idea of
'character' was simply a (somewhat historicised) version of what
Montesquieu had called *ésprit*.[5] Whether or not Oakeshott's concept
of 'character' was indeed faithful to the earlier idea of *ésprit*, it was
certainly an elastic notion. In our chapters on the philosophy of history we saw that any object of historical study, be it a person, an institution or an event, could be described as having a certain 'character'.

With regard to contemporary debates, perhaps the most important aspect of 'character' is the assumption of agency which it carried
when predicated of historical actors. It has been argued that thanks
to disciplines such as psychology and sociology, and more generally, the continuing belief that historical understanding must emulate scientific understanding, 'the will has been effectively
disenfranchised . . . and habit dissolved into . . . the language of com-
plexes and conditioning'.[6] Moral change is thereby reduced to a
function of social, psychological or economic 'forces'. To Oakeshott,
this represented a confusion of categories — to explain intelligent

---

[3]   Berlin, *Four Essays*, p. 6.

[4]   W. Blake, 'The Marriage of Heaven and Hell', *Complete Poems*, p. 189.

[5]   *MP*, p. 36.

[6]   Collini, 'The Idea of Character', p. 49.

practices and procedures distinguished by reflectivity and self-consciousness in terms of non-intelligent processes led only to error.

In other words, Oakeshott's use of 'character' in his accounts of the historical past postulated an understanding of actions and events in terms of 'human conduct', and 'human conduct', as we saw in chapter four, was one of the postulates around which he organised his later writings on the nature of historical knowledge. But, as we also saw, that formal connection has no bearing on the content of his writings on historical events. Nor did the author intend it to. Oakeshott always distinguished firmly between theorising about historical knowledge with the aim of improving historical practice (a concern with 'method') and doing so in order to understand the nature of historical knowledge itself, concerning himself almost exclusively with the latter aim. It must be emphasised, however, that Oakeshott's view of historical enquiry allowed historians to employ any ancillary sciences they considered appropriate.

It is a misunderstanding, therefore, to say that 'No serious historian can accept [Oakeshott's] constructionism'.[7] Oakeshott was not asking historians to accept or reject his philosophical writings on historical enquiry. He did not even expect that his philosophical 'ideal model' of historical understanding would be reflected perfectly in particular historical works. Furthermore, he explicitly stated that his work on this subject would be useless to historians, precisely because it was philosophical in character.

The second major theme of Oakeshott's work on the historical past was, of course, the history of liberal political thought and practice. For well over a century, from Blakey's *History of Political Literature* (1855) to Berlin's *Four Essays on Liberty* (1969) and beyond, the history of liberalism has been regarded as a defining feature of modern political thought and practice. Again, there is a connection between Oakeshott's work and later debates, for it seems that historians continue to wish to employ 'liberalism' in this fashion. Of course, as is also widely acknowledged, there is considerable uncertainty as to the meaning of 'liberalism' itself.[8] A few examples of the way in which 'liberalism' has been used may help pave the way for discussion.

Blakey presented the story of modern European politics as a struggle between the (English, Lockean) forces of 'liberty' and 'progress' and the upholders of monarchical and ecclesiastical absolutism.[9]

[7]   M. Stanford, *A Companion to the Study of History*, Blackwell, Oxford, 1994, p. 130.

[8]   G.J. Schochet, 'Why Should History Matter ?', in J.G.A. Pocock (ed.), *The Varieties of British Political Thought, 1500–1800*, p. 322 and n. 1.

[9]   R. Blakey, *The History of Political Literature*, vol. 2, Kennikat Press, Port Washington, 1970, pp. 4, 166, 414.

F.W. Maitland believed that 'liberty' and 'equality' had been the opposed 'ideals of English political philosophy' since the seventeenth century.[10] Berlin believed that European political history had been a contest between the defenders of an individualistic, 'negative' liberty and a 'positive', egalitarian attempt to impose 'one prescribed form of life'. On the one side, he saw a line of descent from Erasmus, via Locke, Jefferson, Burke and Paine to J.S. Mill — on the other, a rationalistic tradition stemming from the Greeks and becoming ever more pronounced in Spinoza, Rousseau, Hegel and Marx, ultimately producing modern totalitarianism.[11]

Thus, Oakeshott was not original either in making the history of liberalism a central theme of the history of modern political thought or in contrasting it with another, opposing doctrine. In certain respects, however, his account of this history appears somewhat novel, an impression that is strengthened when we recall the part Hobbes played in it. *Leviathan*, Rawls has said, 'raises special problems'[12] for liberalism. These problems are clearly discernible in Berlin's account of the history of liberalism, in which Hobbes occupies an uncomfortable position.

Hobbes, Berlin argued, was no believer in 'positive' liberty and human perfectibility. He 'must', therefore, be a defender of 'negative' liberty. But Berlin interpreted Hobbes's ascription of 'sovereign' authority to the Leviathan as a desire to 'increase the area of centralised control' — a desire, that is, to increase the power rather than the authority of the sovereign. This desire does not appear compatible with liberty of any sort. Because Berlin conceived the history of modern European political thought as a choice between submission to an 'infallible' authority and a 'utilitarian' view of authority which regards it as a 'necessary expedient',[13] he was unable to reconcile Hobbes's support for sovereign authority with a wish to preserve the liberty of the individual. By contrast, Oakeshott and his Hobbes did not regard liberty and authority as inimical to one another or identify 'sovereign' authority with 'absolute' power.

Berlin's view of the history of political thought 'owes more than a little to scholarship (mainly German) of the period before World

---

[10] F.W. Maitland, 'A Historical Sketch of Liberty and Equality as Ideals of English Political Philosophy from the Time of Hobbes to the Time of Coleridge', *Collected Papers*, vol. 1, pp. 1–161.

[11] Berlin, *op. cit.*, pp. 125, 144.

[12] J. Rawls, *A Theory of Justice*, Oxford, Oxford UP, 1972, p. 11.

[13] I. Berlin, *op. cit.*, p. 40.

War One'.[14] His view of Hobbes was almost identical with Gierke's, to whom, as we saw in chapter five, the Leviathan was simply a 'man-devouring monster'. In the later nineteenth and early twentieth centuries, Gierke and other agents of 'Wilhelmine cultural imperialism' such as Troeltsch, desirous of 'inventing a peculiarly German contribution to European culture', came up with the view of modernity as divided between German 'philosophical idealism, literary romanticism and cultural historicism' and 'an empiristic, rationalistic, scientistic and ahistorical "West"'.[15] 'Liberalism', on Gierke's view, had its origins in the seventeenth century and belonged to the rationalistic 'West'.

This, of course, was a view which Oakeshott set out to challenge. He insisted on the equivocal nature of the liberal tradition itself, arguing that authors commonly regarded as 'liberal' (such as Locke and Mill) wavered between two quite different conceptions of government. On the one hand, governing was thought of as the management of the pursuit of an end beyond itself, and the governed as united in promoting this end; on the other hand, governing was conceived as a non-instrumental activity of ruling which left the governed free to unite in collective endeavour but did not require them to do so. As we saw in chapter three, Oakeshott eventually decided that even Hobbes's writings could be seen as containing both these conceptions of the task of government.

While Oakeshott's opposition of 'civil' and 'enterprise' association may offer a novel perspective on past political ideas and events, one may suspect that his account of the history of liberalism rested on the application of two different philosophical ideal models of modes of governing to past events. As such, it could hardly avoid over-simplification. One may feel in the end that Oakeshott did not treat his own belief that detail was the essence of historical understanding with due respect. Had he done so, he might have altogether abandoned the dualistic arrangement of the history of political thought which he shared with Blakey, Maitland, Gierke and Berlin. Indeed, the subsequent generation of historians of political thought such as Pocock and Skinner appear to have done just this, preferring to concentrate on particular themes (such as the fortunes of 'republicanism') rather than construct schematic oppositions like that between 'civil' and 'enterprise' association.

----

[14] K. Haakonssen, 'Natural Law, Natural Rights and the Enlightenment Science of Morals', p. 21.
[15] *op. cit.*, p. 21.

So far, we have concentrated on the content of Oakeshott's accounts of the historical past. We must now say something of his views on the nature of historical enquiry. In chapter two, we saw that modern 'critical' philosophy of history was an intellectual enterprise begun by German neo-Kantian thinkers and developed by Italian and British Hegelian Idealists, notably Croce, Bradley and Collingwood. Oakeshott's philosophy of history was a continuation of their efforts, for he was concerned, as they were, with the conditions of the possibility of specifically historical experience. In other words, all his writings on the philosophy of history can be understood as asking the question 'What are the conditions in terms of which this object, person or event may be recognised as being of an historical kind?'

This, as we also saw in chapter two, is not the only conception of the philosophy of history. In some quarters, 'the philosophy of history' is still understood to mean 'an attempt to find a meaningful pattern in the overall development of human societies'.[16] Perhaps the best-known example of the 1990s was Fukuyama's dramatic declaration of *The End of History*.[17] As Fukuyama was well aware, the word 'history' in his title referred to 'History' in the sense of 'a single, coherent, evolutionary process', not to historical enquiry. His neo-Hegelian belief that liberal democracy constituted the 'end point of mankind's ideological evolution', 'the final form of human government',[18] provoked much debate, but the issue was whether Fukuyama was correct about the present and future development of our modern Western societies. The 'critical' philosophy of history scarcely entered the picture.

From Oakeshott's point of view, such 'speculative' philosophies of history were usually bound up with debates over the 'practical' past in which rival (future) courses of action are at stake. His own lack of interest in using the past to illuminate the present with an eye on the future has never been widely shared. It remains easy to find writers who defend the view that historical enquiry 'can inspire and aid the creation of a more intelligent future . . . serve those who would make sound public policy, and [provide] an antidote to the

---

[16] F. Fukuyama, *The End of History and the Last Man*, MacMillan Inc., New York, 1992, p. 55.

[17] As L. Niethammer's *Posthistoire* makes clear, however, it is by no means the only one. In a history of the idea of the end of history, he shows that it has had considerable influence on French and German intellectuals in the latter half of the twentieth century, more perhaps than on the Anglophone world.

[18] Fukuyama, *op. cit.*, pp. xi–xii.

misuses of the past by policymakers'.[19] Conversely, a denial of the
utility of historical study has often been treated as identical with a
denial of the worth of historical study, a view usually dependent on
the (frequently suppressed) premise that what is not 'useful' is val-
ueless. The belief that historical enquiry 'has lost all faith in itself as a
guide to the actions of men' and as a means 'to control the future'
was the main reason for J.H. Plumb's belief that the discipline was
experiencing a 'crisis' in the 1960s.[20]

Oakeshott's 'impractical' conception of historical enquiry lends
further support to the argument that the view of him as a Tory political propagandist from which we set out was misguided. It is often
taken to be a defining characteristic of 'Conservatives' that they
believe 'history is authoritative'.[21] If this is so, then Oakeshott was at
best an atypical 'Conservative' for he did not believe that history
was a store of wisdom and value. He did, of course, allow that a
'practical' past which could furnish sustaining myths was important
in a civilised society, but he made no sustained attempt to provide
such a past himself.

In chapters three and five we repeatedly encountered instances in
which Oakeshott wrote about the past in a manner which by his own
lights did not seem very 'historical'. Yet his departures from history
tended to be in an aesthetic rather than a practical direction. His own
philosophy made the hallmark of the practical an inevitable tension
between the world as it is and the world as it ought to be, but he was
usually very reluctant to commit any views he might have had on
that subject to print. Therefore, it is to all intents and purposes
impossible to extract any 'normative' policy proposals from
Oakeshott's writings on historical events.

Turning from 'speculative' to 'critical' philosophy of history, we
may identify three main twentieth-century approaches to the subject, none of which are quite in agreement with Oakeshott's position.
First, there are 'realist' thinkers who seek a 'scientific methodology'
for history and emphasise 'the objective and the tangible'.[22]
Mandelbaum and Hempel both belong in this class. They may also
be described as 'assimilationists'[23] because of their wish to assimilate
history as closely as possible to the kind of explanation they believed

---

[19] S. Vaughan, *The Vital Past*, Georgia UP, Athens, 1985, p. 5.

[20] Plumb, 'The Historian's Dilemma', in *Crisis in the Humanities*, p. 9.

[21] K. Haakonssen, 'Introduction' to *Traditions of Liberalism*, p. xi.

[22] H. Gilliam, 'The Dialectics of Realism and Idealism in Contemporary
      Historiographic Theory', *History and Theory*, vol. 15, 1976, pp. 232–3.

[23] Breisach, *Historiography*, p. 327.

the natural sciences offered, namely, explanation in terms of covering laws. This approach to the philosophy of history remained popular, if not dominant, throughout Oakeshott's career. This explains his repeated efforts to overturn the belief that either historical events were causally connected exemplars of a scientific law or laws or they were meaningless, a belief which chapters two and four showed was accepted by historians such as Postan and Cobban. As chapter six demonstrated, this 'scientism' prevailed into the 1980s and beyond.

Against the 'realist' theory, Oakeshott argued that historical and scientific enquiry were mutually exclusive forms of knowledge. As chapters two, four and six made clear, in *Experience and its Modes* and ever after, he maintained that historical enquiry was distinguished by certain presuppositions. 'Human conduct' was such a presupposition or postulate. If one does not assume that the past survivals to be investigated are evidence of intelligent agency, then historical enquiry cannot even begin, just as natural science cannot begin without presupposing that events may be described quantitatively in terms of forces interacting.

Oakeshott's argument that a relationship of dependence or contingency between historical events was a further postulate of historical enquiry allowed him to distinguish historical relations from the law-governed relations between scientific events. We saw in chapters four and six that by detaching the connotations of chance and accident from contingency, he was able to argue that there were intelligible relations between historical events, the irrelevance of natural laws or teleological purposes notwithstanding. These were relations of contingency which were themselves historical events. Oakeshott always stressed that an understanding in terms of contingent relations imparted no finality. No absolute, unconditional certainty was to be found in historical knowledge. But he did not go on to infer that historical knowledge was therefore mere nescience. The contingent had to be distinguished from the random and the accidental. That meaning in the historical past was conditioned by such postulates as human conduct and contingently related events did not render it insignificant.

Similarly, Oakeshott argued that the kind of 'objectivity' found in historical writing was not to be equated with the 'objectivity' of the physicist. Historical knowledge was not merely 'subjective' or personal, but equally, it did not explain events in terms of laws of motion, energy and the like. Instead, it assumed that it dealt with evidence for events understood as contingent outcomes of the interplay of human conduct. Here, an 'objective' explanation was one that succeeded in understanding past events as outcomes of other antecedent events and in avoiding approaching such events as if they were part of one's own present — demanding a practical response.

The realist theory also assumed that the stories historians relate are about or refer to an independently existing past. By contrast, Oakeshott saw the historical past as a construction of inferential reasoning based on present evidence aiming at the narration or relation of a passage of change. By rejecting the belief that there was a past with which historical narratives must correspond, he was able to avoid the scepticism which arises from the belief that we can never know whether or not historical writing accurately represents the past.

The second class of theory may be given the label of 'narrativist'. The narrativist view arose in the post-World War Two period. It is illustrated in the work of Gallie and Danto. 'Narrativism' was not necessarily hostile to the 'assimilationist' or 'realist' view. According to Danto, his aim was 'to demonstrate an equivalence between explanation as construed by Hempel, and narratives, thus vindicating the so-called "covering-law model" against the claim that narrational models were deeply alternative to it'.[24] Gallie took a somewhat different view, proposing 'that explanations in history subserved the general purpose of narratives, rather than vice versa'.[25] As we saw in chapters two and four, there are some similarities between Oakeshott's work and that of Gallie and Danto. For example, all three share the view that the past is constructed by historians. Nevertheless, there are also some important differences.

At the extreme, the narrativist identification of 'history' with 'story' elides the differences between history and fiction. Although Gallie and Danto themselves did not intend this consequence, it would appear to follow from their view that historical and fictional events acquire meaning in exactly the same way, being understood in the light of subsequent events. In chapter two, we watched Oakeshott's struggle in the 1920s to emancipate himself from his own youthful pessimism about the possibility of historical knowledge and the lack of a difference between history and fiction. Thereafter, however, he remained unmoved by any such doubts.

In chapter four we observed that after World War Two Oakeshott adopted a distinction between historical and poetic or artistic modes

---

[24] A.C. Danto, 'The Decline and Fall of the Analytical Philosophy of History', in *A New Philosophy of History*, ed. F. Ankersmit and H. Kellner, Chicago UP, Chicago, 1995, p. 71.

[25] R.T. Vann 'Turning Linguistic', in *A New Philosophy of History*, p. 46.

of experience and specified the different structures of historical and fictional narratives. Historical narratives, he argued, were distinguished by relating events in such a way as to make them intelligible exclusively in terms of the events that preceded them. In contrast, events in fictions (and in practical experience) are quite eligible to acquire new meanings in the light of subsequent events. This seems to provide a decisive reason for rejecting the elision of history and fiction and the pessimism about historical knowledge consequent upon it.

The third and final class of theories of history includes those 'constructionist' writers closest to Oakeshott's own position such as Croce and Collingwood. Despite their common roots in Hegelian Idealism, however, it is unwise to associate Oakeshott too closely with either. In the interest of brevity, we shall concentrate on the differences between Collingwood's position and Oakeshott's.

First, Collingwood believed in the practical utility of history. He hankered for a fusion of philosophy and history into 'a new discipline . . . History',[26] in the belief that historical 'knowledge of the past' was essential to the 'creation of the future', of 'something better'.[27] History was to show how the past led up to the present and how it can be used to shape the future.[28] Collingwood, although he distinguished historical and practical activity,[29] did not distinguish historical and practical kinds of past. Hence, he took the past of memory to be simply identical with the past of history — in either case it is a past that leads up to us.[30] Oakeshott, as chapters two, four and six demonstrated, was far more concerned to separate the practical and the historical past.

Second, Oakeshott did not separate history from other forms of experience such as practical life only to identify it with philosophy, as Collingwood did. Collingwood's identification of history and philosophy is clearly visible in his claim that Kant's philosophical presentation of his transcendental analytic was in fact an historical essay.[31] What he meant was that the results of earlier scientific and philosophical research were visible in Kant's philosophy, but while this is doubtless true, it does not render the *Critique of Pure Reason* an 'historical' work in either of the senses discussed by Oakeshott.

[26]   T.M. Knox, 'Introduction' to R.G. Collingwood, *The Idea of History*, p. xix.

[27]   Collingwood, *The Idea of History*, p. 334.

[28]   *op. cit.*, pp 169, 334.

[29]   *op. cit.*, p 311.

[30]   *op. cit.*, p 293.

[31]   Collingwood, *An Essay on Metaphysics*, p. 243.

Third, Collingwood believed that historians construct the past by thinking thoughts which are actually those of the past actors they study.[32] For Oakeshott, by contrast, the historical past was nobody's experience — attending to the thoughts and intentions of past actors was at best a step on the way to the construction of a kind of past necessarily unavailable to the actors in the events related, and hence in nobody's mind at the time in question.

With these qualifications, the label of 'constructionism' remains an appropriate one for describing Oakeshott's philosophy of history. In his later work, his efforts to be precise about the implications of his constructionism sometimes involved him in a daunting degree of philosophical abstraction. Nardin remarks with justification that 'The entities of history, on this difficult theory, have become as elusive as the particles of the nuclear physicist. A historical identity, properly understood, is nothing other than its own circumstantial coherence understood as a contiguity of discernible differences'.[33] Abstract or not, his work on this subject over a period of half a century demonstrates that historical knowledge is by no means impossible, and that history does not require replacement, reduction or assimilation to or by art, philosophy or any other of the human or natural sciences. Any doubts about the value of historical enquiry are seen to spring from inflated hopes for it rather than from any defect in the nature of the enquiry itself.

Oakeshott himself accurately summarised the history of the philosophy of history when he wrote that 'the logic of historical understanding is . . . a theme which first emerged in the writings of philosophers (particularly German) in the nineteenth century and has since acquired a settled place in the reflections of German, Italian, French, English and American philosophers'.[34] As we saw, the attempt to do for history what Kant's *Critique of Pure Reason* had done for the natural sciences was launched in 1843 by Droysen's *Historik*. In the latter half of the nineteenth century, Dilthey had taken this project upon himself, but his work remained fragmentary.

Oakeshott commented that Dilthey 'spent a long life stumbling around in the semi-darkness; he was unavoidably an explorer rather than a settler or a planter', but 'what he opened up to us — the idea of an autonomous "human" world, a world of expressions of human thoughts, to be understood in its own terms and not those of the natural sciences — was, perhaps, the most important of all the "redis-

---

[32] Collingwood, *The Idea of History*, pp. 293, 301.

[33] Nardin, *op. cit.*, p. 159.

[34] Oakeshott, Letter to Basil Blackwell, LSE 11/6.

coveries" of the nineteenth century'.[35] In 1947, Oakeshott had lamented Collingwood's death not least because he might have completed Droysen's and Dilthey's project. Yet it is perhaps not too great an exaggeration, after half a century, to reaffirm Collingwood's verdict that Oakeshott himself had provided a decisive vindication of the autonomy of historical knowledge. Undoubtedly, his efforts to provide that missing 'Critique of Historical Reason' will prove of lasting value.

Yet Oakeshott's view of history as the construction from evidence of a unique kind of past is important not merely because it identifies the postulates which distinguish historical thought from all other forms of understanding, but also because it explains why historical thinking and writing are valuable to human beings. Oakeshott's final view of the human condition was stark: 'We are, in the first place, doers and sufferers and as such we are only squatters in the world', was in effect his final position.[36] In the face of the 'long littleness of life',[37] history provides us with a kind of understanding of pastness of which we could otherwise know nothing, upon which both our reason and our imagination can be exercised in a deeply rewarding way. His rhetorical question 'Is there anything more pleasurable than the history of the Popes when one does not wish them to be different from what they were?' clearly required the answer 'no'.[38] Oakeshott thought that without the historical past, we would be severely impoverished as people, and this was reason enough to do history. Had he thought historical enquiry impossible, or despaired of the possibility of it, as his critics alleged, his defence of history as an autonomous form of knowledge would be unintelligible.

---

[35] Oakeshott, 'The Emergence of the History of Thought', p. 21.

[36] *op. cit.*, p. 4.

[37] Oakeshott, untitled address to LSE History Society, p. 6.

[38] *op. cit.*

Bibliography

J. Liddington's comprehensive bibliography (1992) of Oakeshott's published works and the secondary literature may be found in *The Achievement of Michael Oakeshott*, ed. J. Norman. A. Towlson's catalogue of the Oakeshott collection in the LSE archive can be obtained from http://library-2.lse.ac.uk/archives/handlists/Oakeshott/Oakeshott.html, or from the librarian. Therefore, I have generally listed only those of Oakeshott's writings and those secondary sources quoted or cited in the text. However, pieces by Oakeshott *not* included in Liddington's bibliography are marked with an asterisk, in the interests of maintaining an up-to-date bibliography of Oakeshott's writings.

Oakeshott: Unpublished Writings

'Thomas Wentworth, First Lord Strafford', 1921, LSE 1/1/1.
'History is a Fable', 1923, LSE 1/1/50.
'The Cambridge School of Political Science', c. 1924, LSE 1/1/2.
'A Discussion of Some Matters Preliminary to the Study of Political Philosophy', 1925, LSE 1/1/3.
'An Essay on the Relations of Philosophy, Poetry, and Reality', c.1927, LSE 1/1/33.
'The Philosophy of History', 1927, LSE 1/1/5.
Letter from W.W. Buckland, 24 April 1927, LSE 1/1/5.
'What do we Look for in an Historian?', 1927, LSE /1/47.
'A Declaration of War', 1933, LSE 1/1/8.
'Experience and its Modes', 1933, LSE 1/1/9.
'National Socialism (i)', c. 1936, private collection.
'National Socialism (ii)', c. 1936, private collection.
'The Structure and Idea of the National Socialist Society', 1936, private collection.
'Italian Fascism', 1939, private collection.

'The Social and Political Doctrines of Contemporary Europe', c.1939–40, LSE 1/1/10.
'On Peace with Germany', 1943, LSE 1/1/11.
Letter to K. Popper, 28 January 1948, Hoover Institution, Stanford, California.
'The Englishman and his Freedom', early 1950s?, LSE 1/1/32.
'The Interpretation of Human Character in History', early 1950s?, LSE 3/10.
'Fortuna', c.1950s?, LSE 1/1/34.
'The Idea of "Character" in the Interpretation of Modern Politics', later 1950s?, LSE 1/1/35.
'Work and Play', later 1950s?, LSE 1/1/48.
Address to Downing College Maitland Society, later 1950s?, LSE 1/3.
Address to LSE History Society, c. 1960, LSE 1/3.
Letter to N.K. O'Sullivan, 29 June 1964, private collection.
Letter to F.A. Hayek, 5 January 1965, pp. 2, Hoover Institution, Stanford, California.
'The History of Political Thought from the Ancient Greeks to the Present Day', LSE 1/1/21.

1.   'Introduction: The History of Political Thought'.
2.   'The Political Experience of the Ancient Greeks'.
3.   'The Greek Image of the World'.
4.   'The Political Thought of the Ancient Greeks'.
5.   'The Political Thought of the Ancient Greeks'. (ii)
6.   'Aristotle'.
7.   'Aristotle (ii)'.
8.   'Plato'.
9.   'Plato (ii)'.
10. 'Stoics and Epicureans'.
11. 'The Political Experience of the Ancient Romans'.
12. 'The Political Experience of the Ancient Romans (ii)'.
13. 'Roman Political Thought'.
14. 'Roman Political Thought (ii)'.
15. 'Roman Political Thought (iii)'.
16. 'Medieval Political Experience'.
17. 'Medieval Kingship'.
18. 'Medieval Law'.
19. 'Parliaments'.
20. 'Medieval Political Philosophy'.
21. 'The Character of the Modern European State'.
22. 'The Generation of the Modern European State'.
23. 'Modern European Political Thought'.

24. 'Interpretations of the Modern European State (i)'.
25. 'Interpretations of the Modern European State (ii)'.
26. 'The Authority of Governments and the Obligations of Subjects (i)'.
27. 'The Authority of Governments and the Obligations of Subjects (ii)'.
28. 'The Authority of Governments and the Obligations of Subjects (iii)'.
29. 'The Office of Government (i)'.
30. 'The Office of Government (ii)'.

MSc degree reading lists, bibliography, etc., 1960s, LSE 8/3.

'The Emergence of the History of Thought', 1966–7, LSE 1/1/23.

Festschrift Speech, c.1968, LSE 1/3.

Retirement Speech, c.1968, LSE 1/3.

Letter to F.A. Hayek, 19 January 1968, Hoover Institution, Stanford, California.

Letter to F.A. Hayek, 30 April 1968, Hoover Institution, Stanford, California.

'Present and Past', c.1971–3, private collection and LSE 1/1/26.

Notes on Heidegger, 1970s?, LSE 3/5.

Notes on Dilthey, 1970s?, LSE 3/3.

'Events: The Fortuitous, the Necessary and the Contingent', 1971–3, private collection and LSE 1/1/26.

'Change: Identity and Continuity', 1971–3, private collection and LSE 1/1/26.

Letter to N.K. O'Sullivan, 28 June 1977, private collection.

'Law', c.1980, private collection.

'Political Thought as a Subject of Historical Enquiry', 1979–80, private collection .

Letter to D. Martin, 30 December 1981, LSE 11/6.

Letter to Craddock, 13 August 1982, LSE 11/6.

Letter to N.K. O'Sullivan, 8 February 1986, pp. 4, private collection.

Letter to N.K. O'Sullivan, 9 February 1987, pp. 2, private collection.

Transcript of Conversation with K. Minogue, May 1988, LSE 8/4 .

Oakeshott: Published Writings

(with H. Howe) 'An Experiment in the Teaching of History', *Georgian* (the magazine of St. George's school), vol. 14, 1919, pp. 5–6*.

'Socialism as it Is!', *Georgian*, vol. 14, 1919, pp. 39–44*.

'Shylock the Jew', *Caian*, vol. 30, 1921, pp. 61–7*.

'Lord Acton', *Caian*, vol. 31, 1922, pp. 14–23*.

Review of J.S. Mackenzie, *Fundamental Problems of Life*, *Journal of Philosophical Studies*, vol. 4, 1929, p. 265.

Review of J.C. Powys, *The Meaning of Culture*, *Cambridge Review*, vol. 51, 1930, pp. 367–8.

Review of K. Feiling, *What is Conservatism?*, *Cambridge Review*, vol. 51, 1930, p. 512.

Review of L. Britton, *Love and Hunger*, *Cambridge Review*, vol. 52, 1931, p. 351.

'John Locke', *Cambridge Review*, vol. 54, 1932, pp. 72–3.

Experience and its Modes, Cambridge UP, Cambridge, (1933) 1991.

Review of L. Chestov, *In Job's Balance*, *Scrutiny*, vol. 2, 1933, pp. 101–4.

Review of L. Curtis, *Civitas Dei*, *Cambridge Review*, vol. 55, 1934, p. 450.

Review of O. Gierke, *Natural Law and the Theory of Society*, tr. E. Barker, *Cambridge Review*, vol. 56, 1934, pp. 11–12.

Review of H. Levy and others, *Aspects of Dialectical Materialism*, *Cambridge Review*, vol. 56, 1934, pp. 108–9.

'Thomas Hobbes', *Scrutiny*, vol. 4, 1935, pp. 263–77.

Review of H.G. Wood, *Christianity and the Nature of History*, *Journal of Theological Studies*, vol. 36, 1935, pp. 323–4.

(with G. Griffith) *A Guide to the Classics or How to Pick the Derby Winner*, Faber and Faber, London, 1936 .

'History and the Social Sciences', in *The Social Sciences*, Le Play House Press, London, 1936, pp. 71–81.

Review of F.H. Bradley, *Collected Essays*, *Philosophy*, vol. 12, 1936, pp. 114–6.

Review of N. Berdyaev, *The Meaning of History*, *Cambridge Review*, vol. 57, 1936, p. 453.

Review of W. Brock, *An Introduction to Contemporary German Philosophy*, *Cambridge Review*, vol. 57, 1936, p. 195 .

Review of L. Strauss, *The Political Philosophy of Hobbes*, *Cambridge Review*, vol. 58, 1936, p. 150.

Review of K. Mannheim, *Ideology and Utopia*, *Cambridge Review*, vol. 58, 1937, p. 257.

'The Concept of a Philosophical Jurisprudence', *Politica*, vol. 3, 1938, pp. 203–22, 345–60.

The Social and Political Doctrines of Contemporary Europe, ed. and intro. Oakeshott, Cambridge UP, New York, (1939) 1950.

Hobbes, *Leviathan*, ed. and intro. Oakeshott, Blackwell, Oxford, (1946) 1960.

'Cecil Grant', *Supplement* to *Georgian*, c.1946, pp. 12–13 (LSE 5/3)*.

Review of R.G. Collingwood, *The Idea of History*, *English Historical Review*, vol. 62, 1947, pp. 84–6.

Review of J. Bowle, *Western Political Thought*, *Spectator*, vol. 179, 1947, p. 626.

'Scientific Politics', *Cambridge Journal*, vol. 1, 1947–8, pp. 347–58.

'Contemporary British Politics', *Cambridge Journal*, vol. 1, 1947–8, pp. 474–90.

Review of K.B. Smellie, *Why We Read History*, *Cambridge Journal*, vol. 1, 1947–8, pp. 766–7.

Review of W.T. Jones (ed.), *Masters of Political Thought*, vol. 2, *Cambridge Journal*, 1, 1947–8, pp. 636–7.

Review of J.W. Watmough, *Cambridge Conversations*, *Cambridge Journal*, vol. 3, 1949–50, pp. 252–4.

'Stalin's Four Weak Points', *Evening Standard*, 20 November 1950, p. 9.

'Mr Carr's First Volume', *Cambridge Journal*, vol. 4, 1950–1, pp. 344–52.

Review of E.H. Carr, 'The New Society', c. 1951, LSE 1/2/1.

Reviews of H. Butterfield, 'The Whig Interpretation of History', c. 1951, LSE 1/2/1.

Correspondence, *New Statesman and Nation*, 28 July 1951, p. 100.

Review of G.J. Renier, *History, its Purpose and Method*, *Philosophical Quarterly*, vol. 1, 1951, pp. 284–5 .

Review of W.H. Walsh, *An Introduction to Philosophy of History*, *Philosophical Quarterly*, vol. 2, 1952, pp. 276–7.

Review of D. Forbes, *The Liberal Anglican Idea of History*, *Cambridge Journal*, vol. 4, 1952–3, pp. 248–51.

Review of H. Marcuse, *Reason and Revolution*, *Spectator*, vol. 194, 1955, pp. 404–5.

Review of H. Butterfield, *Man on his Past*, *Spectator*, vol. 195, 1955, pp. 595–6.

Review of G. Barraclough, *History in a Changing World*, *Spectator*, vol. 196, 1956, pp. 220–1.

Review of M. Cole, *The Story of Fabian Socialism*, *Sunday Telegraph*, 5 November 1961.

Rationalism in Politics and Other Essays, 2nd edn., ed. T. Fuller, Liberty Press, Indianopolis, (1962) 1991.

'Rationalism in Politics: A Reply to Professor Raphael', *Political Studies*, vol. 13, 1965, pp. 89–92.

Review of K. Marx, *Critique of Hegel's Philosophy of Right*, ed. J. O'Malley, *Spectator*, vol. 226, 1971, pp. 192–3.

Review of S. Avinieri, *Hegel's Theory of the Modern State*, *European Studies Review*, vol. 5, 1975, pp. 217–20.

Hobbes on Civil Association, Blackwell, Oxford, 1975.

On Human Conduct, Oxford UP, Oxford, 1975.

'The Vocabulary of a Modern European State', *Political Studies*, vol. 23, 1975, pp. 197–219, 409–14.

'On Misunderstanding Human Conduct: A Reply to My Critics', *Political Theory*, vol. 4, 1976, pp. 353–67.

On History and Other Essays, Blackwell, Oxford, 1983.

The Voice of Liberal Learning: Michael Oakeshott on Education, ed. T. Fuller, Yale UP, New Haven, 1989.

Morality and Politics in Modern Europe, ed. S. Letwin, Yale UP, New Haven, 1993.

Religion, Politics and the Moral Life, ed. T. Fuller, Yale UP, New Haven, 1993.

The Politics of Faith and the Politics of Scepticism, ed. T. Fuller, Yale UP, New Haven, 1996.

Other Authors

Anderson, P., 'The Intransigent Right at the End of the Century', *London Review of Books*, 24 September 1992, pp. 7–11.

Ankersmit, F. and Kellner, H. (eds.), *A New Philosophy of History*, Chicago UP, Chicago, 1995.

Archer, R., 'Oakeshott on Politics', *Journal of Politics*, vol. 41, 1979, pp. 150–68.

Auspitz, J.L., Review of *On Human Conduct*, *Commentary*, vol. 61, 1976, pp. 89–94.

Ayer, A.J., *Language, Truth and Logic*, 2nd edn., Victor Gollancz, London, 1948.

Barker, E., *Political Thought in England, 1848–1914*, Thornton Butterworth, London, 1915.

Berlin, I., *Four Essays on Liberty*, OUP, Oxford, 1969.

Black, A., 'Society and the Individual from the Middle Ages to Rousseau', *History of Political Thought*, vol. 1, 1980, pp. 145–66.

Black, A., *Guilds and Civil Society in European Political Thought from the Twelfth Century to the Present*, Methuen and Co., London, 1984.

Blake, W., *The Complete Poems*, ed. A. Ostriker, Penguin, London, 1977.

Blakey, R., *The History of Political Literature From the Earliest Times*, vol. 2, Kennikat Press, Port Washington, 1970.

Bodin, J., *Six Books of the Commonwealth*, tr. and intro. M. J. Tooley, Blackwell, Oxford, 1953.

Bolingbroke, *Historical Writings*, ed. I. Kramnick, Chicago UP, Chicago, 1972.

Bosanquet, B., *The Essentials of Logic*, MacMillan, London, 1928.

Bosanquet, B., *The Philosophical Theory of the State*, 2nd edn., MacMillan, London, 1910, .

Boucher, D., Review of *On History*, *History of Political Thought*, vol. 5, 1984, pp. 163–7.

Boucher, D., 'The Creation of the Past: British Idealism and Michael Oakeshott's Philosophy of History', *History and Theory*, vol. 23, 1984, pp. 193–214.

Boucher, D., *Texts in Context: Revisionist Methods for Studying the History of Ideas*, Martinus Nijhoff, Dordrecht, 1985, pp.280.

Boucher, D., 'Overlap and Autonomy: The Different Worlds of Collingwood and Oakeshott', *Storia, Antropologia e Scienze del Linguaggio*, vol. 4, 1989, pp. 69–89.

Boucher, D., *The Social and Political Thought of R. G. Collingwood*, CUP, Cambridge, 1989.

Boucher, D., 'Politics in a Different Mode: An Appreciation of Michael Oakeshott, 1901–90', *History of Political Thought*, vol. 12, 1991, pp. 717–728.

Bradley, F.H., *Collected Essays*, vol. 1, OUP, Oxford, 1935.

Breisach, E., *Historiography*, 2nd edn., Chicago UP, Chicago, 1994.

Brooke, C.N.L., *A History of Gonville and Caius College*, Boydell Press, Woodbridge, 1985.

Brooke, C.N.L., *The History of Cambridge University*, vol. 4, CUP, Cambridge, 1993.

Burckhardt, J., *The Civilisation of the Renaissance in Italy*, Penguin, London, 1990.

Burckhardt, J., Force and Freedom, Liberty Press, Indianopolis, 1979.

Burrow, J.W., *A Liberal Descent: Victorian Historians and the English Past*, Cambridge, Cambridge UP, 1981.

Butterfield, H., *The Whig Interpretation of History*, W.W. Norton, London, 1965.

Butterfield, H., *Christianity and History*, G. Bell and sons, London, 1949.

Bynum, C., 'Did the Twelfth Century Discover the Individual?', *Journal of Ecclesiastical History*, vol. 31, 1980, pp. 1–17.

Caine, S., *The History of the Foundation of the London School of Economics and Political Science*, G. Bell and Sons, London, 1963.

The Cambridge History of Medieval Political Thought, c. 350–c. 1450, ed. J.H. Burns, CUP, Cambridge, 1988.

Carrit, E. F., *The Theory of Beauty*, 5th edn., rev., Methuen, London, 1962.

Casey, J., *Pagan Virtue: An Essay in Ethics*, Clarendon Press, Oxford, 1990.

Coats, W., 'Michael Oakeshott as Liberal Theorist', *Canadian Journal of Political Science*, vol. 18, 1985, pp. 773–87.

Coats, W., *Oakeshott and his Contemporaries*, Susquehanna University Press, Pennslyvania, 2000. .

Cobban, A., 'History and Sociology', *Historical Studies*, vol. 3, 1961, pp. 1–8.

Cohn, N., *Europe's Inner Demons*, Paladin, St, Alban's, 1976.

Cohn, N., *The Pursuit of the Millennium: Revolutionary Millenarians and Mystical Anarchists of the Middle Ages*, Paladin, London, 1984.

Coleman, J. (ed.), *The Individual in Political Theory and Practice*, Clarendon Press, Oxford, 1996..

Collingwood, R.G., 'Oakeshott and the Modes of Experience', *Cambridge Review*, vol. 55, 1934, pp. 249–50.

Collingwood, R.G., *An Essay on Metaphysics*, OUP, Oxford, 1940.

Collingwood, R.G., An Autobiography, OUP, Oxford, 1967.

Collingwood, R.G., *The Idea of History*, ed. T.M. Knox, OUP, Oxford, 1989.

Collini, S., 'Sociology and Idealism in Britain 1880–1920', *Archives Européenes de Sociologie*, vol. 19, 1978, pp. 3–50.

Collini, S.,'The Idea of "Character" in Victorian Political Thought', *Transactions of the Royal Historical Society*, 5th ser., vol. 35, 1985, pp. 28–50.

Collini, S., Winch, D. and Burrow, J., *That Noble Science of Politics: A Study in Nineteenth Century Intellectual History*, CUP, Cambridge, 1983.

Condren, C., *The Status and Appraisal of Classic Texts*, Princeton UP, Princeton, 1985.

Condren, C., *The Language of Politics in Seventeenth Century England*, Macmillan, London, 1994.

Covell, C., *The Redefinition of Conservatism: Politics and Doctrine*, Macmillan, London, 1985.

Covell, C., *The Defence of Natural Law*, St. Martin's Press, New York, 1992.

Cowling, M., *Religion and Public Doctrine in Modern England*, vol. 1, CUP, Cambridge, 1980.

Crick, B., 'The World of Michael Oakeshott or the Lonely Nihilist', *Encounter*, vol. 20, 1963, pp. 65–7.

Croce, B., *History: Theory and Practice*, tr. D. Ainslie, Russell and Russell, New York, 1960 .

Crossman, R.H.S., Review of 'Political Education', *New Statesman and Nation*, vol. 42, 1951, pp. 60–1.

Davidson, W.L., *Political Thought in England from Bentham to J. S. Mill*, Thornton Butterworth, London, 1915.

Danto, A.C., *Analytical Philosophy of History*, CUP, Cambridge, 1965.

Devigne, R., *Recasting Conservatism: Oakeshott, Strauss and the Response to Postmodernism*, Yale UP, New Haven, 1994.

Dilthey, W., *Introduction to the Human Sciences*, ed. R.A. Makkreel and F. Rodi, Princeton UP, Princeton, 1989.

Droysen, J.G., *Outline of the Principles of History*, tr. E.B. Andrews, Ginn and Co., Boston, 1875.

Elton, G., *Political History*, Penguin, London, 1970.

Elton, G., *Reformation Europe, 1517–59*, Collins, London, 1963.

Falck, C., 'Romanticism in Politics', *New Left Review*, vol. 18, 1963, pp. 60–71.

Feaver, G., 'Michael Oakeshott and Political Education', *Studies in Comparative Communism*, vol. 2, 1969, pp. 156–175 .

Flathman, R., *Thomas Hobbes: Skepticism, Individuality and Chastened Politics*, Sage Publications, Newbury Park, 1993, pp. 184.

Forbes, D., *The Liberal Anglican Idea of History*, CUP, Cambridge, 1952.

Franco, P., *The Political Philosophy of Michael Oakeshott*, Yale UP, New Haven, 1990.

Franco, P., 'Michael Oakeshott as Liberal Theorist', *Political Studies*, vol. 18, 1990, pp. 411–36.

Franco, P., 'Oakeshott's Critique of Rationalism Revisited', *Political Science Reviewer*, vol. 21, 1992, pp. 15–43.

Frohnen, B., 'Oakeshott's Hobbesian Myth: Pride, Character and the Limits of Reason', *Western Political Quarterly*, vol. 43, 1990, pp. 789–809.

Fuller, T., Correspondence, *Times Literary Supplement*, 6 May 1994.

Fukuyama, F., *The End of History and the Last Man*, MacMillan Inc., New York, 1992.

Gallie, W. B., *Philosophy and the Historical Understanding*, Chatto and Windus, London, 1964.

Gellner, E., Review of R. Dahrendorf, *LSE: A History of the London School of Economics and Political Science*, *Times Literary Supplement*, 9 June 1995, p. 3.

Gellner, E., Review of C. Taylor, *Hegel*, *Encounter*, vol. 46, 1976, pp. 33–49.

Gerencser, S.A., *The Skeptic's Oakeshott*, St Martin's Press, New York, 2000.

Germino, D., *Modern Western Political Thought: Machiavelli to Marx*, Rand McNally, Chicago, 1979.

Gierke O., *Political Theories of the Middle Age*, ed. and intro. F.W. Maitland, Cambridge UP, Cambridge, 1951.

Gierke O., *Natural Law and the Theory of Society*, trans., ed., and intro. E. Barker, Cambridge UP, Cambridge, 1950.

Gierke O., *Community in Historical Perspective, A Translation of Selections from Das deutsche Genossenschaftsrecht (the German law of Fellowship)*, ed. A. Black, Cambridge UP, 1990.

Gilliam, H., 'The Dialectics of Realism and Idealism in Modern Historiographic Theory', *History and Theory*, vol. 15, 1976, pp. 231–56.

Gilmore, M. P., *Argument from Roman Law in Political Thought, 1200–1600*, Harvard UP, Cambridge Mass., 1941.

Goldstein, L. J., *Historical Knowing*, Texas UP, Austin, 1976.

Grainger, J. H., *Character and Style in English Politics*, CUP, Cambridge, 1969.

Grant, C., Letter dated 17 July 1924, LSE 5/1.

Grant, R., *Oakeshott*, Claridge Press, London, 1990.

Grant, R., 'Inside the Hedge: Oakeshott's Early Life and Work', *Cambridge Review*, vol. 112, 1991, pp. 106–9.

Grant, R., Review of *Religion, Politics and the Moral Life* and *Morality and Politics in Modern Europe*, *Times Literary Supplement*, 15 April 1994, p. 31.

Grant, R., 'Michael Oakeshott', in *Cambridge Minds*, ed. R. Mason, CUP, Cambridge, 1994.

Gray, J., Review of *On History*, *Political Theory*, vol. 12, 1984, pp. 449–53.

Green, T.H., *Lectures on the Principles of Political Obligation*, intro. A. D. Lindsay, Longmans, London, 1960.

Greenleaf, W.H., *Oakeshott's Philosophical Politics*, Longmans, London, 1966.

Greenleaf, W.H., 'Hobbes: The Problem of Interpretation', in *Hobbes-Forschungen*, ed. R. Koselleck and R. Schnur, Duncker and Humblot, Berlin, 1965.

Gunnell, J.G., *Political Theory: Tradition and Interpretation*, Winthrop Publishers, Cambridge Mass., 1979.

Haakonssen, K. (ed.), *Traditions of Liberalism*, Centre for Independent Studies, St. Leonard's, 1988.

Haakonssen, K. 'Natural Law, Natural Rights and the Enlightenment Science of Morals', unpublished lecture, 1995, pp. 22.

Harris, J., 'Political Thought and the Welfare State 1870–1940: An Intellectual Framework for British Social Policy', *Past and Present*, vol. 135, 1992, pp. 116–141.

Hayek, F., *The Road to Serfdom*, Routledge, London, 1946.

Hegel, G., *The Philosophy of History*, tr. J. Sibree, Dover, New York, 1956.

Hegel, G., *The Philosophy of Right*, 2nd edn., tr. T.M. Knox, Clarendon Press, Oxford, 1949.

Heidegger, M., *Being and Time*, tr. J. Macquarrie and E. Robinson, Blackwell, Oxford, 1992.

Hempel, C., 'The Function of General Laws in History', *Journal of Philosophy*, vol. 39, 1942, pp. 35–48.

Hernon, J., 'The Last Whig Historian and Consensus History: George Macaulay Trevelyan', *American Historical Review*, 81, 1976, pp. 66–97.

Hexter, J., *On Historians*, Harvard UP, Cambridge Mass., 1979.

Himmelfarb, G., *The New History and the Old*, Harvard UP, Cambridge Mass., 1987, pp. 209.

Hoffer, E., *The True Believer: Thoughts on the Nature of Mass Movements*, Harper and Bros., New York, 1951.

Howarth, T.E.B., *Cambridge Between Two Wars*, Collins, London, 1978.

Hume, D., *Enquiries Concerning Human Understanding and Concerning the Principles of Morals*, 2nd edn., ed. L.A. Selby-Brigge, Clarendon, Oxford, 1936.

Iggers, G. G., 'The Image of Ranke in American and German Historical Thought', *History and Theory*, vol. 2, 1962, pp. 17–40.

Joachim, H.H., *The Nature of Truth*, 2nd edn., ed. R. G. Collingwood, OUP, Oxford, 1939.

Johnson, N., 'Michael Joseph Oakeshott 1901–1990', *Proceedings of the British Academy*, 80, 1993, pp. 403–23.

Kant, I., *The Critique of Pure Reason*, tr. N.K. Smith, MacMillan, London, 1983.

Kant, I., *Political Writings*, 2nd edn., ed. H. Reiss, tr. H.B. Nisbet, CUP, Cambridge, 1991.

Kennedy, E., Letter to Oakeshott, 5 January 1980, LSE 1/6/3.

Kenyon, J., *The History Men*, 2nd edn., Wiedenfeld and Nicholson, London, 1993.

King, P.T. (ed.), *The History of Ideas*, Barnes and Noble, London, 1983.

King, P.T. (ed.), *Thomas Hobbes: Critical Assessments*, vol. 1, Routledge, London, 1993 .

Knowles, D., 'The Historian and Character', CUP, Cambridge, 1955.

Kristol, I., Letters dated 26 April and 14 September 1960, LSE 11/4.

Laski, H., *Faith, Reason and Civilisation*, Victor Gollancz, London, 1944.

Laslett, P. (ed.), *Philosophy, Politics and Society*, 1st ser., Blackwell, Oxford, 1956 .

Lecky, W.E.H., *History of European Morals from Augustus to Charlemagne*, 2 vols., Longmans, London, 1910.

Leff, G., Review of *On History*, *English Historical Review*, vol. 100, 1985, pp. 953–4 .

Liddington, J., *The Philosophy of Michael Oakeshott and its Relation to Politics*, unpublished PhD thesis, Balliol, 1986 .

Locke, J., *Two Treatises of Government*, ed. P. Laslett, Cambridge UP, Cambridge, 1990.

Lukes, S., *Individualism*, Blackwell, Oxford, 1973.

MacFarlane, A., *The Origin of English Individualism: The Family, Property and Social Transition*, Blackwell, Oxford, 1978.

MacPherson, C., *The Political Theory of Possessive Individualism: Hobbes to Locke*, Oxford UP, Oxford, 1962.

Maitland, F.W., *Collected Papers*, vol. 1, ed. H.A.L. Fisher, CUP, Cambridge, 1911.

Mandelbaum, M., *The Anatomy of Historical Knowledge*, Johns Hopkins UP, Baltimore, 1977.

Martin, D., Letter to Oakeshott, 27 October 1981, LSE 11/6.

Mazower, M., *Dark Continent: Europe's Twentieth Century*, Penguin, London, 1998.

McBriar, A.M., *Fabian Socialism and English Politics, 1884–1918*, CUP, Cambridge, 1966.

McCloskey, D., 'History, Differential Equations and the Problem of Narration', *History and Theory*, vol. 30, 1991, pp. 1–36.

McIlwain, C.H., *The Growth of Political Thought in the West*, Macmillan, London, 1932.

McIlwain, C.H., *Constitutionalism, Ancient and Modern*, rev. edn., Cornell UP, New York, 1947.

McTaggart, J. McT. E., *Philosophical Studies*, ed. and intro. S. V. Keeling, Edward Arnold, London, 1934.

Meiland, J.W., *Scepticism and Historical Knowledge*, Random House, New York, 1965.

Meyerhoff, H. (ed.), *The Philosophy of History in Our Time: An Anthology*, Doubleday, New York, 1959.

Michaud–Quantin, P., *Universitas: Expressions du Mouvement Communitaire dans le Moyen-Age Latin*, Librairie J. Vrin, Paris, 1970.

Mill, J.S., *A System of Logic*, 8th edn., Longmans, London, 1884.

Mill, J.S. *Utilitarianism, Liberty and Representative Government*, Dent and sons, London, 1948.

Miller, W.I., 'Deep Inner Lives, Individualism and People of Honour', *History of Political Thought*, vol. 16, 1995, pp. 190–207.

Minogue, K., 'Oakeshott and the Idea of Freedom', *Quadrant*, vol. 19, 1975, pp. 77–83.

Minogue, K., 'Michael Oakeshott and the History of Political Thought Seminar', *Cambridge Review*, vol. 112, 1991, pp. 114–17.

Minogue, K., and de Crespigny, A. (eds), *Contemporary Political Philosophers*, Methuen, New York, 1976.

Modood, T., 'Oakeshott's Conceptions of Philosophy', *History of Political Thought*, vol. 1, 1980, pp. 314–22.

Mouffe, C., *The Return of the Political*, Verso, London, 1993.

Morris, C., *The Discovery of the Individual, 1050–1200*, Society for the Promotion of Christian Knowledge, London, 1972.

Munro, D., 'Oakeshott, Godwin and Mrs Bloomer', *Journal of the History of Ideas*, vol. 35, 1974, pp. 611–24.

Murphy, M., 'Explanation, Causes and Covering Laws', *History and Theory (Beiheft)*, vol. 25, 1986, pp. 43–57.

Nardin, T., *The Philosophy of Michael Oakeshott*, Pennsylvania State UP, Pennsylvania, 2001.

Needham, J. (ed.), *Science, Religion and Reality*, Sheldon Press, London, 1925.

Nicholls, D., *The Pluralist State: The Political Ideas of J. N. Figgis and his Contemporaries*, 2nd edn., MacMillan, London, 1994.

Niethammer, L., *Posthistoire: Has History Come to an End?*, Verso, London, 1992.

Norman, J. (ed.), *The Achievement of Michael Oakeshott*, with a bibliography to 1992 by J. Liddington, Duckworth, London, 1993.

Oakes, W. J. (ed.), *The Stoic and Epicurean Philosophers*, Random House, New York, 1940.

O'Sullivan, N.K., Obituary, *The Independent*, 22 December 1990.

Owensby, J., *Dilthey and the Narrative of History*, Cornell UP, New York, 1994.

Passmore, J, 'The Objectivity of History' in P. Gardiner (ed.), *The Philosophy of History*, Oxford UP, Oxford, 1974.

Pitkin, H.F., 'Inhuman Conduct and Unpolitical Theory', *Political Theory*, 4, 1976 .

Pitkin, H.F., *Wittgenstein and Justice: On the Significance of Ludwig Wittgenstein for Social and Political Thought*, California UP, Berkeley, 1972.

Plamenatz, J. (ed.), *Readings from Liberal Writers*, Allen and Unwin, London, 1965.

Plato, *Republic*, tr. F. M. Cornford, Penguin, London, 1987.

Plumb, J.H., *Crisis in the Humanities*, Penguin, London, 1964.

Pocock, J.G.A., *The Ancient Constitution and the Feudal Law*, rev. edn, Cambridge UP, Cambridge, 1990 .

Pocock, J.G.A., Review of *On History*, *Times Literary Supplement*, 21 October 1983, p. 1155.

Pocock, J.G.A., (ed.), *The Varieties of British Political Thought, 1500–1800*, Cambridge UP, Cambridge, 1993.

Popper, K., *The Open Society and its Enemies*, 2 vols., 5th edn., Routledge, London, 1966.

Popper, K., *The Poverty of Historicism*, 2nd edn., Routledge, London, 1966 .

Popper, K., *Conjectures and Refutations*, Routledge, London, 1963.

Postan, M.M., 'The Revulsion From Thought', *Cambridge Journal*, vol. 1, 1947, pp. 395–408.

Postan, M.M., 'History and the Social Sciences', in *The Social Sciences*, Le Play House Press, London, 1936 .

Quinton, A.M., 'Absolute Idealism', *Proceedings of the British Academy*, vol. 58, 1971, pp. 303–29.

Raphael, D.D., Review of *Rationalism in Politics*, *Political Studies*, vol. 12, 1964, pp. 202–15.

Rawls, J., *A Theory of Justice*, Oxford, Oxford UP, 1972..

Reisch, G., 'Chaos, History and Narrative', *History and Theory*, vol. 30, 1991, pp. 1–20.

Rickert, H., *The Limits of Concept Formation in Natural Science*, tr. G. Oakes, Cambridge UP, Cambridge, 1986.

Robertson, J.M. (ed.), *Buckle and his Critics*, Swan Sonnenschein, London, 1895.

Sabine, G., *A History of Political Theory*, Henry Holt, New York, 1944.

Sandars, T.C. (ed.), *The Institutes of Justinian*, Longmans, London, 1922.

Santayana, G., *Five Essays*, CUP, Cambridge, 1933.

Schapiro, J. S. (ed.), *Liberalism: Its Meaning and History*, van Nostrand, Princeton, 1958.

Schmitt, C., Letter to Ellen Kennedy, 11 June 1980, LSE 1/6/3.

Schopenhauer, A., *The World as Will and Representation*, 2 vols., tr. E. F. J. Payne, Dover Publications, New York, 1966.

Schweitzer, A., *The Quest of the Historical Jesus*, tr. W. Montgomery, Adam and Charles Black, London, 1910.

Skinner, Q., 'Hobbes's Leviathan', *Historical Journal*, vol. 7, 1964, pp. 321–33.

Skinner, Q., 'Meaning and Understanding in the History of Ideas', *History and Theory*, vol. 8, 1968, pp. 1–53.

Skinner, Q., *The Foundations of Modern Political Thought*, vol. 1, Cambridge UP, Cambridge, 1978, pp. 305.

Skinner, Q., Rorty, R. and Schneewind, J. B. (eds.), *Philosophy in History: Essays on the Historiography of Philosophy*, CUP, Cambridge, 1984.

Skinner, Q., (ed.), *The Return of Grand Theory in the Human Sciences*, Cambridge UP, Cambridge, 1985.

Soffer, R.N., *Discipline and Power: The University, History and the Making of an English Elite, 1870–1930*, Stanford UP, California, 1994.

Sorman, G., 'C'est le maitre a penser des conservateurs britanniques', *Le Figaro*, 27 October 1984, pp. 110–112..

Stanford, M., *A Companion to the Study of History*, Blackwell, Oxford, 1994.

Stapleton, J., *Englishness and the Study of Politics: The Social and Political Thought of Ernest Barker*, CUP, Cambridge, 1994.

Stebbing, L.S., Review of *Experience and its Modes*, *Mind*, 43, 1934, pp.403–5.

Stevenson, J., *British Society, 1914–45*, Penguin, London, 1984.

Stone, L., 'The Revival of Narrative', *Past and Present*, 85, 1979, pp. 1–24.

Strauss, L., *The Political Philosophy of Hobbes*, Chicago UP, Chicago, 1963.

Strauss, L., *What is Political Philosophy?*, Free Press, Glencoe, 1959.

Strayer, J.R., *On the Medieval Origins of the Modern State*, Princeton UP, Princeton, 1970.

Taylor, A.E., *Thomas Hobbes*, Constable, London, 1908.

Taylor, A.E., 'The Ethical Doctrine of Hobbes's Philosophy', *Philosophy*, 13, 1938, pp. 406–24 .

Taylor, C., *Hegel*, Cambridge UP, 1975.

Thompson, M., 'Michael Oakeshott: Notes on "Political Thought" and "Political Theory" in the History of Political Thought, 1966–9', *Politisches Denken Jahrbuch*, vol. 2, 1991, pp. 103–19.

The Times, 'Obituary', 22 December 1990, p. 10.

Tönnies, F., *On Sociology: Pure, Applied and Empirical*, ed. J. Cahnman and R. Heberle, Chicago UP, Chicago, 1971.

Tully, J. (ed.), *Meaning and Context: Quentin Skinner and his Critics*, Polity Press, Cambridge, 1988.

Ullman, W., *The Individual and Society in the Middle Ages*, Johns Hopkins, Baltimore, 1966.

Vaughan, S. (ed.), *The Vital Past: Writings on the Uses of History*, Georgia UP, Athens, 1985.

Vincent, A. and Plant, R., *Philosophy, Politics and Citizenship: The Life and Thought of the British Idealists*, Blackwell, Oxford, 1984.

Vincent, A., 'Can Groups be Persons?', *Review of Metaphysics*, vol. 42, 1989, pp. 687–715.

Vinogradoff, P., *Roman Law in Medieval Europe*, Oxford UP, Oxford, 1929.

D. Walker, 'A Traditionalist with the Eye', *Times Higher Educational Supplement*, 18 January 2002, pp. 20–21.

Warrender, H., *The Political Philosophy of Hobbes*, Oxford UP, Oxford, 1957.

Wells, H., 'The Philosophical Michael Oakeshott', *Journal of the History of Ideas*, vol. 55, 1994, pp. 129–45.

Willey, T., *Back to Kant: The Revival of Kantianism in German Social and Historical Thought, 1860–1914*, Wayne State UP, Detroit, 1978.

Willis, K., 'The Introduction and Critical Reception of Hegelian Thought in Britain, 1830–1900', *Victorian Studies*, vol. 31, 1988, pp. 85–111.

Wood, N., 'A Guide to the Classics; the Scepticism of Professor Oakeshott', *Journal of Politics*, vol. 21, 1959, pp. 647–62.

Index

action, 13, 38-39, 91, 98, 144, 156, 162, 165, 172-4, 177, 212, 225, 231, 270

Acton, Lord, 14, 31, 35-38, 54, 80, 98, 175, 184, 187, 209

aesthetics, 17

agency, 13, 80, 163, 172, 178, 261

D'Alembert, J., 57

Althusius, J., 255

Anderson, P., 204, 210-11

Annales school, 75

anarchism, 30

Angst, 231

anthropology, 108, 161

Apollo, 139

Arendt, H., 10, 184

Aristotle, 4, 10, 27, 34, 46, 53, 73, 165, 173, 179, 184, 230, 244-6, 248-9

St. Aquinas, 10, 64, 112, 202

Attlee, C., 183

St. Augustine, 5, 10, 127-8, 207, 239, 244

Aurelius, M., 77

Austin, J., 113, 170

authority, 11, 21, 64, 131, 194, 203, 209, 263

Ayer, A.J., 12, 19, 32, 93-4, 168

Bacon, F., 119, 137-8, 214-5, 249-51

Balfour, Lord, 46

Barbarism, 60, 116

Barker, Sir E., 33, 50, 58-60, 156, 184

Baur, F.C., 50

Bennet, E.K., 39

Bentham, J., 15, 36, 50, 57-8, 64, 76, 85, 138-9, 209, 227

Berdyaev, N., 127

Bergson, H., 41

Berkeley, G., 44

Berlin, I., 216, 262-4

Bevan, A., 116

Beveridge, W., 118

Black, A., 25, 33 n., 142, 190-1, 200 n.

Blakey, R., 262, 264

body, 53

Bodin, J., 187, 209

Boethius, 125, 165

Bosanquet, B., 15, 34, 48, 88, 168, 170

Boucher, D., 7, 11

Boys Smith J.S., 50

Bradley, A.C., 39

Bradley, F.H., 11, 15, 17, 51, 53, 69-71, 74-6, 82-4, 87, 99-100, 143, 264

Braudel, F., 27, 235

Brooke, Z., 31, 32

Browning, R., 38

Bryce, J.B., 36

Buckland, W.W., 73

Buckle, H.T., 17, 68-9, 71, 80, 157, 237
Burckhardt, J., 39, 197-8, 205, 208, 235
Burke, E., 2, 48, 133, 138, 208
Burrow, J., 171
Bury, J.B., 22, 31, 102, 165
Butterfield, H., 55, 98, 122, 170

Calvin, J., 53, 214-6
Cambridge, University of, 6, 12, 14, 23, 45, 54, 62, 73, 134, 142, 169
capitalism, 30, 66, 135
Carlyle, T., 35
Carr, E.H., 15, 83, 155
causality, 17, 95, 100-105, 165, 238-41, 266
Chadwick, O., 55
change, 27, 42, 45-6, 52, 100-7, 235, 243-7, 253
character, 9, 13-14, 19-21, 23, 37, 38-39, 41, 51, 53, 58, 77, 81-2, 98-100, 103-4, 116-7, 130, 139, 141-9, 164, 178-80, 197-200, 205-8, 259-61
Charles I, 37
choice, 193-4
civil association, 24, 185, 204, 207, 209, 212-3, 219, 233, 264
Clapham, J.H., 55
Coats, W., 3, 4, 5, 11
Cobban, A., 7, 22-3, 158, 166, 175, 267
coherence, 77, 86-8, 233, 270
Cohn, N., 160, 206, 257
Coleridge, S., 49, 69
collectivism, 20, 24
Collingwood, R., 7, 17, 70-1, 82, 90, 112, 143, 154-5, 170-1, 173, 225, 234, 264, 269-70
Collini, S., 171

colonialism, 203-4
Comte, A., 157
communism, 2, 15, 57, 61, 64, 66, 119-20, 155, 216
Condorcet, M.J., 250
conservatism, 1-4, 56, 64-5, 266
Conservative party, 2-3
Constant, B., 209
constructionism , 77, 172, 233-4, 247, 249, 252, 262, 269-71
contextualism, 12, 46, 171, 234
contingency, 22, 73, 102, 152, 158, 163-7, 178, 182, 241-2, 247, 267
contract, 190, 193, 209
conversation, 12, 22, 79, 134, 152, 163, 177
Coulton, G., 31-2
Cranston, M., 170
Creighton, M., 38
Crick, B., 1
Croce, B., 17, 71, 74, 155, 264, 269
Cromwell, O., 138
Crossman, R., 2, 29

Dante, 165, 202
Danto, A.C., 22, 180-1, 268
deconstructionism, 99
definition, 41, 45, 46, 73
democracy, 26, 56, 60-1, 64, 66, 115, 199, 209
Descartes, R., 119, 125
Dewey, J., 92, 181
Dicey, A., 31
Diderot, D., 36, 57
Dietze, G., 256
Dilthey, W., 17, 69-71, 83 n., 230, 255, 270
Dionysius, 139
Dray, W., 7
Droysen, J.G., 68, 270
Duguit, L., 48, 140
Durkheim, E., 14, 25, 48, 161

economics, 108, 160
education, 46, 199, 253
Eliot, G., 69
Elton, G., 7, 55, 100, 187
Engels, F., 120
Encyclopédie, 36
England, 49, 120-22, 137-8, 189, 196, 262
Enlightenment, 36, 57, 215-6, 250-1
epicureanism, 8
Erasmus, 263
Evans, Sir A., 228
events, 12, 22, 27, 52, 72, 77, 79, 87, 102-3, 106, 143, 163-5, 180-1, 233-43, 252, 267
evidence, 16, 27, 75, 88, 98-9, 158, 167, 225, 227, 231, 234, 252, 267, 271
experience, 57, 83, 85-6, 132, 153, 158, 223-4, 242, 269

Fabian Society, 29-30
fact, 19, 23, 76, 87, 96, 99, 139
fascism, 15, 57, 61, 66, 119
Fichte, J., 60, 209-10
fiction, 80, 103, 105, 164, 178-80, 182, 253
Forbes, D., 7, 168
fortuna, 22, 165
Foucault, M., 8
Franco, P., 5
Frazer, Sir J., 5 n., 108
freedom, 194, 197
Freeman, E., 37
Froude, J., 79
Fuller, T., 53
Fukuyama, F., 265
Furet, F.,

Geneva, 214
St. George's School, 30, 125

Gerencser, S., 5
Germany, 9, 15, 19, 33, 59-62, 67-8, 115-6, 140-1, 205, 216, 259, 263-4
Germino, D., 210
Gewirth, A., 256
Gibbon, E., 79-82
Von Gierke, O., 25, 33, 34, 58-9, 61, 63, 124, 131, 184, 186, 192-4, 199, 212, 255-6, 263-4
Godolphin, S., 129
Goldstein, L., 158, 182
Gonville and Caius College, 6, 31, 32, 34, 39
Grainger, J.H., 142
Grant, Rev. C., 30, 125
Grant, R., 5, 83
Gray, J., 233
Greece, 24, 184-5
Green, T.H., 49-50, 124
Greenleaf, W.H., 5
Griffith, G., 55
groups, 25, 33, 59-61, 192-3

Haakonssen, K., 12
Habbakuk, H.H., 62
Hallam, H., 170
Harrington, J., 234
Harvard, University of, 8, 24, 146
Hayek, F., 4, 10, 21
Hegel, G., 3, 5, 13, 17, 25, 33, 39, 40, 46-8, 50, 56, 67-8, 72, 84, 90, 99, 111-12, 117, 170, 189, 191, 197, 209-13, 230, 244-5, 251, 264-5
Heidegger, M., 8, 27, 39, 41, 83 n., 228-31
Helvetius, 57
Hempel, C., 22, 27, 157-8, 238-41, 266
hermeneutics, 230
Himmelfarb, G., 7, 83

historical writing, 6, 78-9, 123, 163
historiography, 74, 248-52
Hitler, A., 60-2, 64, 66, 115, 205
history of political thought, 4, 10-11, 16, 20, 137, 143, 145, 209, 252-7
Hobbes, T., 3, 4, 9, 10, 11, 20, 46, 58-9, 112, 121-2, 124-34, 137-8, 141, 147-8, 162, 174, 178-9, 185, 189, 192, 199, 206-7, 209-11, 213, 226, 256, 259, 263-4
Hobhouse, L., 48
Hobsbawm, E., 62
Hoffer, E., 205
Hölderlin, F., 39
Huizinga, J., 140, 162
human conduct, 13, 139, 159, 163, 165, 167, 172-3, 199, 219-20, 225, 261, 267
humanism, 249-51
human sciences, 6, 23, 70
Hume, D., 138, 141, 157-8, 208-10
Von Humboldt, W., 68
Husserl, E., 83 n.

Idealism, 11, 15, 20, 35, 47, 49, 55, 69, 124, 142, 209-10, 264
identity, 27, 52, 100, 107, 252-4, 270
ideology, 248
imagination, 81-2, 124, 271
imperialism, 203
individualism, 4, 11, 14, 16, 20, 24-25, 33, 53, 60, 64, 100, 106-7, 131-2, 141, 147, 179, 199, 205-6, 259
induction, 44
intention, 12, 171-4
interpretation, 86, 99, 166, 171, 225-7
intuition, 40, 43, 85, 109

Italy, 15, 62, 115

Jaspers, K., 83 n.
Jefferson, T., 263
Jesus, 50, 69, 78, 117
Joachim, H.H., 86-8
Jones, Sir H., 41-42
Von Justi, J.H., 216

Kant, I., 9, 17, 40, 57, 67-8, 70, 84, 92, 96, 109, 155, 173, 179, 188, 209, 244, 250, 264, 269-70
Kedourie, E., 170
Kierkegaard, S., 83, 199
kingship, 195-6
Kitson Clark, G., 62
knowledge, 12, 18, 40, 76, 85-6, 88, 109, 134
Knowles, D., 142
Kristol, I., 2 and n.

Labour party, 2, 156
Langlois, C.-V., 74-5
Language, 46, 147, 167-70, 177, 179, 234, 242
Lapsley, G., 62
Laski, H., 1, 2, 14, 48, 168
Laslett, P., 168
Laud, W., 37
law, 11, 20, 25, 48, 57, 60, 122, 130, 137, 141, 177, 185, 189-91, 194, 196, 212, 251
Lawrence, D.H., 39
Leavis, F.R., 5 n.
Lecky, W.E.H., 104, 142, 170
Leibniz, G., 241
Lenin, V.I., 64, 155
Lenz, M., 201
Le Roy Ladurie, E., 237
Lessing, G., 250-1
Letwin, S., 170, 257

liberalism, 3, 11, 15, 16, 20, 25, 26, 48, 56, 64-6, 112, 119, 131, 135, 190, 199, 209, 259-60, 263

Locke, J., 4, 10, 15, 56-7, 59, 64, 85, 93, 120, 139, 189, 209, 225, 263-4

London School of Economics, 1, 9, 24, 26, 29-30, 48, 54, 119, 142-3, 162, 169-70, 177, 186, 220, 247, 253, 259
   Oakeshott Archive at, 8, 55, 115, 165, 230

Lovejoy, A.O., 191, 244

Luther, M., 117

Macaulay, T., 78-82, 198, 235

MacFarlane, A., 198-9

Machiavelli, 10, 22, 46, 137, 165, 189, 208, 227

MacIntyre, A., 170

Macpherson, C., 11, 170, 199, 210

Maitland, F.W., 14, 31, 33-4, 45, 57, 170, 184, 186, 192-3, 235, 262, 264

De Maistre, J., 250

Mandelbaum, M., 7, 19, 101, 166, 266

Mannheim, K., 109

Marburg, 39

Marsilius, 203

Marx, K., 10, 13, 17, 56, 61-2, 64, 109, 120, 189, 198, 209, 216, 248, 250

Marxism, 1, 11, 62-3, 140

McIlwain, C.H., 185-6

McTaggart, J., 32

meaning, 68, 70, 72-3, 76, 85-7, 106, 158-60, 170-1, 180-1, 227, 243, 267

medieval era, 10, 20-1, 24-5, 31, 33 and n., 121, 124-6, 136,

147-8, 184, 186-8, 192-3, 195-6, 198-9, 202-3, 260

Meiland, J., 83

method, 16, 108, 222, 262

Mill, J., 76, 85, 139

Mill, J.S., 4, 50, 57, 85, 94, 142-4, 157, 173 n., 209, 214, 264

Milton, J., 126

Mink, L., 242

Minogue, K., 170

Della Mirandola, P., 199

modes of experience, 18, 32, 40, 72, 79, 83-4, 88, 111, 135, 151-4, 159, 166, 176, 220-21, 268, 270
   practical mode, 18, 52, 90-2, 155, 224, 229
   scientific mode, 18, 19, 92-6
   poetic mode, 24, 38, 43, 152, 178-80, 268

Mommsen, T., 223

Montaigne, M., 5, 56, 141, 199, 207

Montesquieu, 146, 148, 209, 261

Moore, G.E., 32

morality, 20-21, 23, 39, 51, 77, 90, 98, 128-30, 142-3, 173-7, 198-200, 259-60

Morris, C., 198

motives, 173-4

Murphy, M., 238

mysticism, 40, 43, 91, 112, 266

Namier, L., 27, 235

Napoleon, 73

Nardin, T., 5-6, 70, 81 n., 88, 159, 176, 233, 242, 270

narrative, 22, 105, 166, 181-2, 243, 268

nationalism, 15, 60, 65

national socialism, 15, 19, 57, 59-61, 64, 66, 116, 118-20, 140, 205, 216

natural law, 58-9, 64, 67, 139, 185
necessity, 52, 58, 68, 81, 241
Needham, J., 50, 62
Nelson, H., 143
Newman, W.L., 34
Niethammer, L. 265 n.
Nietzsche, F., 8, 39, 60, 83 n., 109, 189, 199, 227, 229
nomocracy, 24, 135

Oakeshott, J., 29
Oakeshott, M.,
  Experience and its Modes, 9, 11, 18, 19, 22, 38, 40, 42, 45-6, 51-2, 55, 57, 62, 74, 77-8, 80, 82-4, 90, 92, 100, 102-3, 106-7, 110, 123, 151-4, 157, 159-61, 165-7, 176, 179, 211, 214, 221, 224-5, 233, 238, 267
  A Guide to the Classics, 55
  Hobbes On Civil Association, 31
  Morality and Politics in Modern Europe, 7
  On History, 26, 27, 41, 84, 151, 154, 164-5, 170, 182, 219-25, 228-9, 231-3, 238, 241-6, 252
  On Human Conduct, 3, 22, 24, 26, 27, 131, 135, 144, 149, 151-4, 156, 159-60, 163-5, 170, 172, 174, 176, 178-80, 182-3, 188-9, 197, 201, 207, 210, 212, 219-22, 224-5, 232, 241, 246, 257
  The Politics of Faith and the Politics of Scepticism, 8, 135-41, 188, 215
  Rationalism in Politics, 2, 7, 112, 152, 156, 169, 176, 214, 219
  Religion, Politics, and the Moral Life, 7

The Social and Political Doctrines of Contemporary Europe, 15, 60, 64, 111, 115
The Voice of Liberal Learning, 7
objectivity, 86, 175, 267
obligation, 11, 88, 130-1, 190
Oxford, University of, 1

parliament, 56-7, 121
Pascal, B., 199
past, 18, 26, 73, 77, 110, 164, 221-32, 268, 271
  practical attitude to, 18, 77, 92, 123, 132, 155, 181
Paine, T., 139, 208
St. Paul, 44, 127
persona, 15, 24-25, 41, 130, 205, 259
pessimism, 65, 141, 183, 256, 268
philosophy, 14, 32, 40, 42, 45, 47, 62, 72, 83, 88, 153, 162, 222, 266
  critical, of history 6, 10, 11, 17, 45, 67-72, 95-107, 162-82, 219-57
  speculative, of history, 13, 17, 33, 37, 63, 67, 75, 99, 214, 244, 265
philosophisme, 58, 64, 138
Pitkin, H., 169
Plamenatz, J., 209
planning, 16, 21, 25, 66, 119
Plato, 4, 15, 34, 41, 47, 127, 153, 184, 227
play, 162-3
Plumb, J.H., 23, 55, 266
Plutarch, 249
pluralism, 34, 124, 140, 142
Pocock, J.G.A, 7, 170, 231-2, 234, 257, 264
poetry, 40, 43, 51, 74
politics, 36, 44, 51, 54, 97, 134-5, 184, 254

Popper, K., 10, 20, 119, 134, 211, 239, 245

Postan, M.M., 19, 20, 55, 109-10, 267

positivism, 12, 32, 85, 93, 99, 109, 113, 151

practice(s), 156, 176-7

pragmatism, 27, 53, 64, 71, 90

progress, 56

psychology, 76, 89, 108, 144, 160, 261

Pound, R. , 48

Puritanism, 57, 138, 215

racialism, 60, 116

Von Ranke, O., 31, 38, 201, 208

Raphael, D.D., 2 n.

rationalism, 5, 18, 20, 21, 47, 58, 60, 78, 118-20, 123, 125, 132-4, 136, 206, 260

reality, 14, 19, 40, 99

reason, 41, 61, 109, 125, 134, 153, 271

re-enactment, 71, 171-2

Reformation, 25, 215

relativism, 60-1

religion, 14, 15, 32, 41, 43, 49, 50-54, 64-5, 75, 116-7, 133, 136, 214-5

Renaissance, 46, 60, 63, 119, 126, 132, 135-6, 183, 197-8, 249

republicanism, 139, 185, 188

Rickert, H., 69, 94, 228

rights, 60

Romanticism, 35, 47, 56, 65, 122, 135, 163, 211, 264

Rome, 24, 184-6, 196

Roosevelt, T., 116

Rousseau, J.J., 10, 40, 44, 46, 48, 58, 189, 209

Russell, B., 5 n., 32, 168

Russia, 155, 205

Ryle, G., 168

scepticism, 17-8, 23, 61, 85, 99, 119, 124, 137, 139, 141, 178, 256-7

De Saint-Simon, C., 216

Von Savigny, F., 251

Sabine, G., 254-5

Schiller, F., 163

Schlegel, W., 75, 99, 244

Schmitt, C., 5, 126

Schopenhauer, A., 17, 69, 71, 96

Schweitzer, A., 18, 51, 78, 170

science, 12, 19, 23, 32, 41, 44, 45, 68, 74-5, 92-6, 157, 162, 239, 266

secularisation, 15, 60, 65

Seeley, Sir J., 32, 45

Seignobos, C., 74-5

Shaw, G.B., 29

Shylock, 14, 35, 38

Simmel, G., 69, 228

Simpson, F., 62

self, 15, 47, 53, 91, 125, 162, 178, 199, 205

Shakespeare, W., 35, 207

Shapiro, L., 257

Sinclair, T.A., 253

Snow, C.P., 250

Spencer, H., 34

Skinner, Q., 23, 170, 173, 210, 255, 264

Smith, A., 138, 212

socialism, 1, 30-31, 61, 121, 135

societas, 24-6, 135, 189-200, 208-12

society, 14, 16, 53, 59, 190

sociology, 48, 78, 108, 161, 177, 261

Socrates, 46

sovereignty, 185, 189, 203, 209, 263

Spengler, O., 17, 75, 244

Spinoza, B., 14, 40, 42, 43, 44, 46, 127, 141, 209-10
De Stael, G., 48
Stalin, J., 66
Stapleton, J., 34, 59
state, 4, 11, 14-6, 20-21, 24-6, 33, 45, 47-50, 53, 58-9, 193-4, 197, 201, 203, 212-3, 216-7
Stebbing, S., 83
Stone, L., 235
Strauss, D., 50, 69, 97
Strauss, L., 4, 10, 20, 24, 130, 184, 189, 226-7
Strayer, J.R., 187
Stubbs, W., 31, 37
style, 78-9
syndicalism, 61

Tacitus, 117
Taff Vale, 34
Tawney, R.H., 121, 198
Taylor, A.E., 124
Taylor, C., 211
telocracy, 24, 135
Temperly, H., 62
texts, 10, 12, 171
Thatcher, M., 2-3
Thompson, M.P., 220, 248
Thucydides, 102, 179
De Tocqueville, A., 208
Tonnies, F., 25
Toynbee, A., 244
tradition, 3, 19, 52, 112, 133, 156, 176
Trevelyan, G.M, 62, 156
Tribalism, 61
Trinity College, Cambridge, 56
Troeltsch, E., 51, 263
Trotsky, L., 239
truth, 12, 19, 61, 86-7, 97, 99, 139, 167, 225, 233, 249
Tübingen, 39

Turgot, A., 250

Ullman, W., 199
understanding, 57
universitas, 24-26, 135, 189, 200-7
utilitarianism, 50, 56, 124, 144, 173
utopianism, 1

value, 53, 98
Victoria, 29, 57
Vico, G., 251
Vinogradoff, P., 186
Voegelin, E., 10, 184
Voltaire, 57, 250

Walsh, W.H., 7, 171, 242
war, 204
Webb, S. and B., 1, 29
Weber, M., 83 n., 109, 198
Wells, H.G., 118
Wentworth, T., 14, 37-8
Whiggism, 56, 122, 155
White, H., 81
Windelband, W., 69, 94
Wittgenstein, L., 5 n., 32, 56, 168-70
will, 60, 66-8, 73, 91, 98, 124, 131, 173, 193, 199, 261
Wolin, S., 210
work, 54, 161-3, 174, 215
World War One, 15, 49, 122, 263
World War Two, 2, 6, 9, 19, 21, 65-6, 107, 111, 113, 115, 122, 134, 168, 195, 259, 268